SOCIAL RELATIONS
AND
HUMAN ATTRIBUTES

SOCIAL RELATIONS
AND
HUMAN ATTRIBUTES

———

PAUL HIRST
AND
PENNY WOOLLEY

TAVISTOCK PUBLICATIONS
LONDON AND NEW YORK

First published in 1982 by
Tavistock Publications Ltd
11 New Fetter Lane, London EC4P 4EE
Published in the USA by
Tavistock Publications
in association with Methuen, Inc.
733 Third Avenue, New York, NY 10017

Printed in Great Britain by
Richard Clay (The Chaucer Press) Ltd,
Bungay, Suffolk

British Library Cataloguing in Publication Data

Hirst, Paul
Social relations and human attributes.
(Social science paperbacks; 229)
1. Social interaction
I. Title   II. Woolley, Penny   III. Series
302   HM291

ISBN 0-422-77220-8
ISBN 0-422-77230-5 Pbk

Library of Congress Cataloging in Publication Data
Hirst, Paul Q.
Social relations and human attributes.

Bibliography: p.
1. Sociology. 2. Social interaction.
3. Personality. 4. Reasoning (Psychology)
I. Woolley, Penny. II. Title.
HM51.H584   301   81-11308
ISBN 0-422-77220-8   AACR2
ISBN 0-422-77230-5 (pbk.)

CONTENTS

ACKNOWLEDGEMENTS

A good many people have read large parts of the manuscript and made useful critical comments. We are particularly indebted to Parveen Adams, Diana Adlam, Mark Cousins, Stephan Feuchtwang, Barry Hindess, Steve Horrigan, Tim Megarry, Jeffrey Minson, and Nikolas Rose. Special thanks are due to Beverley Brown and Geoff Wood who greatly helped with both criticism and preparing the manuscript, and also to Rosemary Allen and Audrey Coppard who typed a good deal of it. Mike Donnelly played an important role in helping to assemble the course materials on which the book was based. Sami Zubaida has taught the course at Birkbeck College jointly with Paul Hirst and had a large part in devising the original approach to teaching introductory sociology from which the book developed. Penny Woolley's colleagues at Hatfield Polytechnic helped greatly, both with encouragement and by standing in when she was on study leave; in particular, thanks are due to Derrick Dale. The illustration on page 1 is taken from *The London Sketch Book* (1874) and is reproduced by kind permission of the Mary Evans Picture Library.

PREFACE

This book has grown out of our experience in teaching introductory sociology to students of many different subjects and backgrounds. We must emphasize that it is not conceived as a 'textbook' in the conventional sense and it is certainly not introductory. We doubt that a genuine 'textbook' can be written in sociology, and for a very positive reason, that the subject is characterized by fierce and open debate about intractable and important questions. It would be a sad day if it came to be taught in the way that economics and experimental psychology often are. Instead of a textbook what we offer is an approach to certain key problems which may provide the teacher with ideas and may provide the relatively advanced student with a positive justification for the subject in its relation to others like psychology, philosophy, or biology.

Sociology *does* need justifying. Because of its openness and the politically explosive nature of many of the questions it deals with, it is an open target for conservatives and for people who expect knowledge to come in neat packages of guaranteed and useful 'science'. Introducing students, particularly non-specialists, to sociology brings home these problems in an acute way, which the teaching of specialized options to specialists often allows one to avoid. Sociology is a discipline fragmented into many different approaches and schools of thought, and there is little consensus between them as to concepts or subject matter. Marxism, ethnomethodology or structural-functionalism, for example, for all their own internal divisions and incoherencies, all presuppose a quite distinct set of objects and methods of study. Introducing students to this diversity merely produces confusion and a sort of intellectual vertigo. It is difficult, therefore, to introduce sociology as a substantive body of concepts and subject areas. Yet this is just what most textbooks and introductory courses set out to do. They achieve this either by the selection of one school of thought or by an eclecticism which brings together all concepts and problems, from 'alienation' to '*Zeitgeist*'. Where the one is misleading the other is bland and confusing.

Having said this, it might be thought we are writing off sociology as a mass of intellectual confusions. Indeed, one of the authors has in his previous works strongly criticized many kinds of sociology. But this is far from being our aim here. The value of sociology can, paradoxically, be seen with the greatest clarity when introducing it to people hitherto unacquainted with it. Its value is revealed in the resistances and difficulties offered by deep-seated social prejudices which tend to reduce social life to individual psychology and biology. It might be said that this is nothing new and that all sociologists, at least since Durkheim, stress the importance of the 'social' factor as against the individual. That is true but they tend to do so in an imperialistic and one-sided way, stressing the 'social' *against* the psychological or the biological. This subject exclusivism is of little use when confronted by intelligent psychology or biology students, for example, for it both fails to convince and promotes resistance. In the chapters below we have attempted to illustrate the influence of social relations on human activities, abilities, and attributes in a way which challenges established 'common sense' prejudices and which does not reject, but makes use of, biological and psychological knowledges.

It will be argued that many important mental and physical capacities of human beings and also their very forms of existence as persons are constructed through social categories. These categories are something far more than just names for phenomena or mere 'ideas': they are a crucial component of the social doctrines and practical activities which organize and even create the entities and attributes to which they refer. In Parts Two and Three we concentrate on such categories as 'the person' and 'rationality', arguing that they always involve a definite metaphysic, a complex and ultimately undemonstrable set of assumptions about the world and the entities in it. We therefore deny views which hold that 'rationality' is a basic human constant, that we cannot do without it because of the adaptational consequences of irrationality, and also views which hold that personal existence, the experience of 'self', is a human constant. We argue, on the contrary, that conceptions of what entities exist, of proper conduct, and of the form of the person are socially variable. Further, we argue that modern conceptions of rational conduct, of what is possible and impossible, of the person, and so on, though necessary accompaniments of modern social relations, are not in some sense more 'right', more truly correspondent to the nature of things than those different conceptions held by primitive peoples or the inhabitants of early modern Europe. This emphasis is an important part of our challenge to assumptions about the biological derivation and biological necessity of human institutions, or the individualistic tendency to identify modern social conceptions of the person with 'man' *per se*.

At the same time we are concerned to avoid the forms of moral relativism into which radical sociologists commonly fall when they argue that social categories such as 'crime' or 'madness' are variable and 'normative'. Although such categories and those such as 'person' vary in their character *between* societies, this does not make them any the less necessary or militate against their organizing role *within* the societies in question. It does not follow that simply because standards and expectations differ in different circumstances they are any the less compelling in those circumstances. We consider such problems of relativism in some detail, particularly in Part Two. We also spend some considerable time considering another trait which arises from the recognition of the social and cultural variability of beliefs and standards, the postulation of the autonomy of 'values' or the uniqueness of the realm of 'culture'. We argue that those ways in which sociologists and anthropologists commonly defend the autonomy of the social sciences have grave theoretical defects and they tend to lead to a devaluation of biology and psychology. We are therefore particularly concerned in Part One with arguments which draw a rigid demarcation between nature and culture, human and animal.

We have called the book *Social Relations and Human Attributes*, which may seem pedantic and clumsy, but we have done so with good reason. A title like 'Man and Society' is so bland as to be meaningless. But, more specifically, we are concerned to avoid the word 'society' for reasons which will become clear below; 'social relations' does not give the bogus impression of consistency and totality which 'society' does. A few words about 'human attributes': the book is concerned with the relationship between cultures or social institutions and general human biological and mental capacities and attributes. It is particularly concerned with the area of intersection between anthropological, psychological, and psychoanalytic theories. It is equally opposed to concepts of a fixed 'human nature' and to extreme sociologistic views of humans as infinitely malleable social products.

Certain limitations of our approach should be made plain from the start. We do not pretend to offer a comprehensive account of the biological basis of human behaviour or the determination of differences between individuals. There is little said here on topics such as heredity, intelligence, or instinct. Anyone interested in these topics should consult a good introductory book on the behavioural aspects of human biology. We recommend Vernon Reynolds' *The Biology of Human Action* (1980) or J.Z. Young's *An Introduction to the Study of Man* (1971). Likewise we do not attempt to deal with philosophical issues like the 'mind-body' problem. Such questions are beyond the scope of this work.

Our approach has been to avoid merely summarizing the standard 'literature' on a range of standard debates and questions. We have chosen the books, issues, and topics which seemed to us most original, interesting, or apposite. Thus we have drawn our sources broadly, from ethnology, psychology, psychoanalysis, philosophy, biology, linguistics, the history of art, and the history of ideas, as much as from sociology. We have tackled subjects as diverse as the intellectual consequences of printing, different cultural concepts of personality, and the development of the mental hospital. The reasons for this broad interdisciplinary approach are twofold. First, it offers non-specialists direct connections with their own concerns as students of, for example, psychology or the humanities. Second, it takes specialist students out of set debates and established theoretical antagonisms, it encourages them to think outside their 'ism', and to see that many of the best contributions to 'sociology' have been made by workers in other disciplines. The contents list of this book looks very different from many textbooks which contain a list of 'institutions' and 'sociologies of'.

We should also point out that while we have striven hard to be clear and straightforward we think the best way to do this is to argue on our own account rather than merely to repeat the arguments of others. Where we do summarize such arguments we have tried to do so as fully as possible. Sometimes, as with Freud or Foucault, or with certain concepts of linguistics, there are intrinsic difficulties of subject matter and conceptual terminology which no amount of simplification can eliminate – indeed it usually makes matters worse. In these cases we hope the non-specialist reader will bear with us.

We have said that this is not a 'textbook' in the strict sense, although it is concerned to offer an approach to teaching and a justification of the subject. But in order to present and justify the subject we have had to construct our own distinctive view of it, to adopt a particular conception of social relations. This view is not presented in the form of an explicit and internally consistent 'theory'. The book does, however, attempt to define and to resolve various theoretical problems, and it should therefore be of interest to the participants in a number of theoretical tendencies in modern sociology. We must stress that it is not an attempt to 'bring together' or to 'synthesize' a number of distinct schools; rather, it sets out to show how certain antimonies and theoretical dilemmas can be avoided. It may, therefore, be helpful to explain the book in the language of the theories to which it is relevant. The book is concerned with the ways in which beliefs and norms organize both social relations and forms of social personality. It thus engages with the domains of both the structural-functionalist and the culture and personality schools. It is strongly opposed to functionalist conceptions of society and forms of explanation, but it does take seriously the functionalist's concern with the organizing role social relations perform, even though it does not identify this with 'social order'. Likewise, it attempts to avoid some of the problems associated with cultural relativism whilst accepting the need to recognize and to take account of cultural *difference*. The book considers problems which Marxists have dealt with in terms of the theory of 'ideology', for example, the question of the formation of social agents as 'subjects'. It attempts to avoid the pitfalls associated with the concept of 'ideology', whilst examining in its own terms the relationships between social relations, belief systems, and what are called forms of 'conscious-ness'. It is not a specifically Marxist book, but it is in no way anti-Marxist either. Certain questions cannot be dealt with seriously if one is over-concerned with one's theoretical allegiances and with 'orthodoxy'.

Lastly, two sources of regret. This is a more limited book than the one we planned. Our method of treatment does mean that topics cannot be dealt with in the compass of a normal textbook chapter, and so we have had to omit several chapters to keep the book to one reasonably sized volume. Discussions of childhood, motherhood, and the family were cut out at a fairly late stage, and discussions of the evolution and social functions of punishment eliminated at a fairly early stage.

Regrettable as this may be, the central themes of the book remain largely unaffected by these omissions. We chose to retain and concentrate on the discussions of mental illness and witchcraft because they are central to our theses. Mental illness is used to illustrate the variation in social conceptions of the 'person', and to demonstrate that personality is a social category and an aspect of social relations rather than a given psychological datum. Similarly, witchcraft is used as a means of considering the concept of 'rationality' and its supposed status as a necessary and definitive human attribute. Personal identity and rational thought are widely taken as the distinctive attributes which mark off man from all other creatures. We have tried to show that the categories of person and of rationality involved here are both products of and means of organizing quite specific social relations. Categories of person and forms of what is to count as valid explanation vary so radically in their character between cultures and between the different periods in our own civilization as to undercut any idea of a basic cultural 'humanness'. Inevitably, in using these topics to make these points, we have also had to give due regard to the controversies about and explanations of mental illness and witchcraft beliefs and practices in their own right. As a result the reader must keep the general themes in mind when, as we sometimes do, we launch into a discussion of specific points which emerge from the literature on those questions.

Our second source of regret is that we had intended the book to be more extensively illustrated than it is. The economics of publishing have ruled out plates and limited us to a small number of line drawings.

Parts One, Two, and Three begin with short introductions, so we will avoid the repetition of summarizing our discussions here. The themes and theses which run through the book will emerge as it is read and require the support and qualifications which the discussion as a whole offers to them.

I
BIOLOGY AND CULTURE

'The leading forces of human evolution are intelligence, ability to use
linguistic symbols and the culture which man has developed. These exclusively, or nearly exclusively, human phenomena affect the biological
evolution of man so profoundly that it cannot be understood without
taking them into account. Conversely, human society and culture are
products of the biological evolution of our species. Human evolution is
wholly intelligible only as an outcome of the interaction of biological
and social facts.'

(Dobzhansky 1955: 320)

INTRODUCTION

This first part of the book covers what may appear to be a very diverse range of material, from man's physical evolution to the intellectual consequences of the invention of printing. Each of these varied topics is in fact chosen because of its bearing on a number of linked central themes. The first theme is to show the influence of social relations on the physical and mental attributes of man: thus palaeoanthropology and printing, apparently unrelated, are included because both illustrate an aspect of the social determination of human capacities, in the former case bipedal walking and in the latter faculties such as memory. The second theme is in a way the obverse, to question the ways in which social scientists have attempted to establish the uniqueness of the 'human', to demarcate between nature and culture. The argument here is that these attempts to specify the 'human' as the object of a distinct body of knowledge are problematic, not so much because of the difficulties they create in relation to biology and psychology but because of the conception of social relations they entail. This relates directly to the third theme, the dangers of a rigid demarcation between men and animals. Our extended discussions of the controversy surrounding 'feral' children and the nature of human language relate directly to the themes of both nature/culture and animal/human. The question of the possibility of 'feral' children has been a recurring flashpoint in the debates surrounding the relative importance of nature and nurture, and, therefore, the distinctiveness of human culture. We stress the continuity of concern and theories between the late eighteenth century and the middle of the twentieth century, the two peaks of active interest in this question. Similarly, our discussion of the nature and origin of human language is closely connected with these two themes, as well as the first. Indeed, questions concerning language recur in all three chapters in Part One. Language is conceived by many palaeontologists and anthropologists as important in the *physical* evolution of man. It plays a significant part in our discussion of printing when we consider the implications of writing. The possibility of 'feral' children learning to speak is *the* crucial aspect of the debates surrounding them and relates directly to conceptions of the nature of language and its distinctiveness to man. Finally, the attempt to find a rigid demarcation between human and animal societies, in particular between man and the other primates, has centred on the supposed uniqueness of language proper to man. In Chapter Three we consider these conceptions of the uniqueness of human language in detail and contrast them with the theories of the 'founding father' of modern structural linguistics, Ferdinand de Saussure.

Thus Part One is an integrated whole despite the apparent diversity of subject matter. What is more, certain of the issues raised here further set the scene for some of the discussions in Part Two — the eighteenth-century theories of language and learning introduced in Part One are central to the development of the asylum discussed in Part Two. The philosopher Condillac and the 'psychiatrist' Pinel, two leading eighteenth-century figures, play a major part in Chapters Two, Three, and Nine. Like-wise the discussion of the development of the asylum in Chapter Nine acts as a preamble to the discussion of the bearing of the 'social policy' of Absolutist states on the decline of witchcraft persecutions in Chapter Fourteen of Part Three.

Of all the themes, theories and topics which recur throughout the book, two in particular warrant mention here. Discussions of psychoanalysis and the nature of sexuality recur and inter-relate in all three parts and not merely in Chapter Eight. For example, in Part Three we return to these issues when we discuss the place of psychoanalytic concepts in the expla-nation of witchcraft (in Chapter Thirteen). Second, Michel Foucault has an important place in our discussion, and not merely when his book *Madness and Civilization* is considered in Chapter Nine. Foucault's views play an important part in our discussions of Victor, the wild boy of Aveyron, in Chapter Two and in the discussion of the decline of witch-craft persecutions in Chapter Fourteen.

Obviously the thematic and sequential integration of this book is less evident than in a more conventional textbook in which each expected and 'obvious' topic in the established curriculum follows 'naturally' into the next. We have had to forgo this easy, apparent consistency and coherence in the interests of doing something different. We hope the reader will work at recognizing and appreciating the other connections we have not highlighted. Part One thus leads directly on into the other two parts, and it is for this reason that these considerations are inserted here rather than in the Preface.

I
EVOLUTION AND CULTURE

We begin with Darwin's theory of natural selection as the appropriate theoretical framework in which to consider the fossil evidence for human evolution. Thus our interest in the fossil record is far from being a purely palaeontological one. Emphasis on the making and using of tools is necessary in order to illustrate the part which human culture and social relations have played in man's *physical* evolution. Our objective is to show the influence of social factors on human biology and physiology without, at the same time, attributing any necessary primacy to social relations. Rather we emphasize the complex interaction between cultural, ecological, and biological factors. What will be suggested is that 'culture' and specifically the use and making of tools, formed a significant part of the environmental pressures in the natural selection of man. It must be made clear at the outset that we are stressing here what are conventionally regarded as the 'material' rather than those 'symbolic' aspects of culture so often privileged by cultural anthropologists seeking to show that 'culture' is unique to man. (We shall return to the concept of the 'symbol' in Chapter Three.) The two aims of this chapter are, first, to show the evolutionary biological foundations of human culture, that human attributes are directly conditional upon man's animal past, and, second, that distinctively human physical attributes — particularly bipedalism, a truly opposable thumb, and a brain of a certain size and structure — have developed as a result of the selection pressures of a tool-making way of social life. It will be clear to any specialist reader that this discussion is entirely derivative and deeply indebted to the work of S.L. Washburn and T. Dobzhansky.

By the time Charles Darwin published *The Origin of Species* in 1859, the idea of evolution was by no means new. 'Evolution', in the sense that the modern forms of animals were the result of the change and modification of ancestral forms, was a well-established concept in the eighteenth century. What Darwin inherited was the complex intellectual history of the gradual abandonment of the notion of fixity of species. Before Darwin, however, evolution was still viewed predominantly as a *purposive* process, a completing and perfecting of the hierarchy of organic nature. For Darwin, on the contrary, evolution was not 'going' anywhere, not tending toward a definite 'end'. It was merely what *had happened* as the result of the action of natural causes. What was new in Darwin, and profoundly disturbing to the nineteenth-century intellectual and religious establishment, was the idea of *natural selection*.[1]

The Origin of Species is concerned to explain how, by 'natural' and non-purposive means, by the kind of processes we can observe acting today, species are subject to transformation and change in their physical characteristics, and how this process could lead to the development of new species. In this conception of a natural process of transformation Darwin was greatly influenced by the new theories in geology propounded by Sir Charles Lyell and others. The 'new' geology stressed that the successive strata of rocks forming the long and complex history of the earth were formed and laid down by the same kind of processes as were acting on the earth's surface today. Among animals the analogue of such causes acting to produce change was the 'survival of the fittest'. Darwin, with characteristic modesty, always credited the English political economist T.R. Malthus with the notion of the 'struggle for survival'. In his *Essay on the Principle of Population* (1798) Malthus had argued that if nature were allowed to take its course then human populations would breed up to and beyond the limits of available resources; an equilibrium between population and food supplies would be re-established with the extermination of a portion of the population by famine, disease, and war. And it was the weak and least industrious who perished and the fittest who survived, a thesis which was used as an argument against the system of poor relief which, it was claimed, enabled the poor to exist and breed in idleness. Malthus' view is still widely considered the most important influence on Darwin's theory of natural selection. Were this true, it would be an unusual example of social science influencing explanations in the natural sciences rather than the other way round. But Darwin was far too modest. A significant difference from Malthus is that Darwin's idea of the fittest carries no moral overtones of 'best', as Malthus' theory tended to do when applied to the justification of the social order. The fittest merely suggests that, among the population of varied individuals which make up a species, those best adapted to definite environmental conditions will tend to survive. Darwin's theory is an account of a contingent process since it is environmental change that defines the pressures which select who is or is not 'fit'. Second, though fitness *is* related to the idea that there are checks on the indefinite increase in the numbers of a given species, it is no mere matter of a 'law of population': predators, the climate, and disease, as well as a limited food supply, are aspects of the environment which threaten the individuals making up a species. Though this notion of checks on the indefinite increase of a population is Malthusian, there is in Malthus' law of population no idea either of selection between variant individuals or of the consequent differentiation of species which is crucial for the theory of natural selection. Adaptation is alien to Malthus; rather, his object is to preach submission to the laws of nature and private property.

For Darwin the physical characteristics of members of a species-population vary in certain generally small, but potentially significant, ways and these differences are transmitted by heredity and acquired by offspring. Selection between the variant individuals in a species-population is produced by the pressures of a changing environment: those individuals which have characteristics better adapted to the new features of the environment have a better chance of surviving and therefore leaving offspring (thus the knowledge that physical conditions *had* changed, derived from geology, was crucial to Darwin's conception of the mechanism of evolutionary change and made it appear credible). The characteristics of these better-adapted individuals are then transmitted by heredity to their offspring who, because of them, will stand a better chance of surviving to form part of the next generation of the particular species. So change in species takes place gradually over many generations as a result of the selection pressures of the changing environment favouring those animals best suited to it. This then produces the notion of a process of *natural* selection, in which characteristics are accentuated as in selective breeding, but without the intervention of a 'breeder'. The raw material of this process is the inherited variation of characteristics within species, and the active selective force of this process is environmental change. The relation of raw material and active selective force is contingent; therefore there could be no overall necessary direction or purpose to evolution. The changes in environment and the variation of individuals have different causes, and these causes always interact in a particular conjuncture. Successive conjunctures determine what *has* happened, but in no way determine the pattern of future development.

It will be obvious from what has been already said that Darwin was not an advocate of the notion of the fixity of species. For him the definitive characteristic of species was a population of interbreeding but varying individuals. He says, 'From these remarks it will be seen that I look at the term species, as one given for the sake of convenience to a set of individuals closely resembling each other, and that it does not essentially differ from the term variety, which is given to less distinct and more fluctuating forms' (Darwin 1970: 108).

Thus natural selection operates through the advantages conferred by particular variant characteristics in the struggle for existence and therefore the differential survival of individuals to reproduce. Since fitness in the theory of natural selection *means* success in leaving surviving offspring, those surviving offspring inherit the advantageous characteristics which enabled their genitors to survive to the age of reproduction and indeed reproduce more effectively than other individuals who were less well adapted. Differential reproduction is the key feature of natural selection. The accumulation of members exhibiting a certain definite variation over time would eventually result in their dominating the population and eventually the emergence of a new species. Natural selection must therefore conform to the known mechanisms of reproduction and inheritance.

Darwin recognized that there was a 'missing link' in this theory, a flaw in his argument: he was unable to explain either the nature and mechanism of inheritance and the hereditary transmission of characteristics from generation to generation or the source of variation between individual members of a particular species, which as we have already said provides the raw material of natural selection. Originally he followed the view that inheritance was a form of 'blending' of the characteristics of genitors but he recognized that a sufficient degree of 'blending' would eradicate species variation.

Mutations or 'sports', such as one finds in any animal population, could not on their own account for variation, since not only were such large-scale mutations relatively infrequent but, more important, they were generally deleterious. It is interesting that Darwin eventually adopted a form of modified Lamarckianism, or 'pangenesis', in order to resolve this intractable problem. Darwin thereby radically modified the nature of the theory of natural selection. In this revision, as with Lamarck, the environment *directly* influenced physical characteristics and these acquired characteristics were then transmitted to offspring. Darwin held that blood particles changed with changes in the environment and as a consequence sent changed messages to the organs of reproduction. Pangenesis rests on the thesis that all organs produce tiny vestiges of themselves, or pangens, which find their way through the blood stream to the sex cells. The organ modified by changes in the environment will produce modified pangens which, influencing the sex cells, will produce corresponding modifications in the next generation.[2]

Environmental factors could thus directly affect inherited characteristics. The way would be open for a 'manipulable' evolution, in which the capacity to control the environment would make possible the production of appropriate physical changes in the organisms. This environmentalist or neo-Lamarckian view was adopted in the 1930s in the Soviet Union against 'bourgeois' naturalism and was championed as a distinctively 'Marxist' outlook by the agricultural scientist, T.D. Lysenko. However, this is *not* the kind of influence of social relations on biological attributes we are concerned with here. Rather we are concerned with how 'selection pressures' are themselves set up by social relations in favour of certain inherited characteristics; these characteristics cannot be directly influenced by the environment in the way they are transferred to offspring (contrary to the claims of neo-Lamarckianism and pangenesis). Modern evolutionary theory has resolved Darwin's dilemma by providing a mechanism of inheritance which produces forms of variation broadly compatible with his view in *The Origin of Species*.

It is ironic, and a bitter twist of intellectual history, that the beginnings of an answer to Darwin's puzzle was in fact already available in the work of a then-obscure Czech monk named Gregor Mendel. However, Mendel's work on the genetic mechanism of inheritance was to remain in obscurity effectively until the 1920s when its addition to the theory of natural selection led to the production of what has come to be called the 'synthetic theory of evolution'. The importance of 'Mendelian' population genetics was that the generation of variety ceased to be tied either to mutations or to some form of pangenesis. This is because the creation of variety occurs as a normal part of sexual reproduction, the important point being the splitting of chromosomes from each parent and their recombination, which produces variation. The geneticist T. Dobzhansky succinctly explains how this mechanism affects evolution:

> 'The sexual process brought with it the evolutionary advantage of ever-new gene combinations. Sexual reproduction, however, requires mechanisms that would alternatively place together gene sets derived from different parents and recombine and sort out gene complements. This requirement became satisfied with the appearance and perfection of the mechanisms of fertilization and reproductive division or meiosis.'
>
> (Dobzhansky 1955: 70)

What Mendel discovered in the course of his now-legendary experiments with peas was that the factors transmitting hereditary information are discrete units transmitted by each parent to the offspring and preserved uncontaminated but reassorted in each generation.

We are interested in *human* evolution and so an (exceedingly simplified) account of human genetics is necessary here. Each human body cell contains forty-six chromosomes, or chains of genes; more precisely, these chains are paired alleles, twenty-three pairs altogether, one of each pair being from each parent. If the pairs of alleles are identical then the genes at this point are referred to as *homozygous*, if different then they are referred to as *heterozygous*; in this latter case the instructions carried by one of the alleles, the dominant, will over-ride the other, or recessive, allele. This has considerable importance for inheritance, and for evolution, since the phenotype, or individual characteristics, of the organism will be affected by the dominant gene(s) but the recessive gene(s) will still be carried in the genetic structure of the organism or genotype, and could therefore be transmitted to subsequent offspring — depending on the genetic combinations in reproduction. Genetic recombination, through the happenstance of sexual reproduction, could produce in the next generation an individual who is now homozygous for that recessive gene, that is, if two recessive genes combine. Inheritance is thus generative of variation. Dobzhansky remarks, 'Since new genotypes are constantly produced by the sexual process, selection always has new materials to work with' (1955: 125). He goes on to say, 'Mutation and recombination yield a supply of genetic variability which is then organized by the demands of the environment' (1955: 130). In the new 'synthetic' theory, therefore, the causes of variation and the causes of the selective pressures of the environment are once more separated, as they were for Darwin's pre-pangenesist formulation.

We are today so apparently familiar with the ideas of evolution, natural selection, and man's descent from the ancestors of modern apes that it is difficult for us to appreciate the furore Darwin's ideas created at the time of their publication. The key event in this scandal was the meeting of the British Association in Oxford the year after the publication of *The Origin of Species*, at which the Bishop of Oxford, Samuel Wilberforce, was fool enough or angry enough to ask of Thomas Huxley, who represented Darwin's party, whether it was through his grandmother or his grandfather that he was descended from the apes. Huxley replied crushingly:

> 'If ... the question is put to me would I rather have a miserable ape for a grandfather or a man highly endowed by nature and possessed of great means of influence and yet employs those faculties and that influence for the mere purpose of introducing ridicule into a grave scientific discussion — I unhesitatingly affirm my preference for the ape.'
>
> (cited by Durant 1980)

There will be cause to remember these words in later chapters when we encounter latter-day defenders of human 'uniqueness' (defenders, it must be added, far removed in their attitude from the fatuity of the Bishop). 'Uniqueness' no longer masquerades as a special favour from the Creator but as a natural attribute.

Darwin's hypothesis regarding man's descent from the apes, which he elaborated further in *The Descent of Man* (1871), is particularly remarkable when we realize the paucity of the fossil record available to him. In fact this was limited to Neanderthal man and the remains of a fossil ape, Dryopithecus. It was from the fossil remains of this hominoid that Darwin correctly inferred that by this time, at least 25 million years ago at the beginning of the Miocene age, the hominoid stock ancestral to both man and apes had already diverged from the creatures ancestral to modern monkeys.[3] We know now that during these ages there were other hominoid genera in addition to Dryopithecus; namely Sivapithecus, Proconsul and Ramapithecus.

Before going on to consider in more detail what the fossil record reveals, and specifically the hypothesis which relates the evolution of 'human' characteristics to tool use, it is important to clarify some of the taxonomic terms and to issue a word of warning. In the past many non-evolutionary biologists,[4] whilst recognizing man as a mammal, separated him in a distinct category from all other mammals. Today, however, the similarities between man and apes and monkeys are recognized by their sharing the order of Primates which includes modern man and the extinct species ancestral to modern man, Hominidae, the anthropoid apes, Pongidae, and the Catarrhine monkeys, Cercopithidae. Many zoologists suggest that man and the apes should be placed in one great super-family called Hominoidae in order to stress the similarities with each other and differences from the Catarrhine monkeys. Indeed, the similarities between man and ape are such that, on the basis of comparison of human and chimpanzee protein chains, it is calculated that as much as 99 per cent of our genetic material is shared with them.[5] But even though we now recognize our zoological and genetic resemblances to the family Pongidae this does not mean to say that we are descended from some creature like the gorilla or chimpanzee, orangutan, or gibbon which we can see in our zoos. The resemblances which connect the Hominidae and Pongidae stem from some common ancestor which both families shared many millions of years ago, during the Pliocene or Miocene age. The crucial question is when and how the split occurred among the ancient hominoids ancestral to both man and apes, and what produced the evolutionary divergence of hominids and pongids. It is now generally agreed that the crucial development was bipedalism, i.e., a capacity for upright posture and two-legged walking. This capacity has been associated with the gradual change from a tree-dwelling to a ground-dwelling way of life, a change which is in turn associated with the savannah grasslands of the Miocene age.[6] The question then is: 'how it was that a tree-dwelling ancestor became a ground-dwelling upright walker' (Washburn 1978: 153). Recent interest has centred on Ramapithecus, a Pliocene/Miocene hominoid with the characteristically reduced canines and incisors of all hominids; this feature justifies its modern classification as a hominid.[7] Fragmentary remains of Ramapithecus have been found in India, Pakistan, and across the near East and Balkans through to Africa. Whilst the evidence suggests that the early hominid has successfully adapted to a grassland environment, unlike Dryopithecus which died out with deforestation, it is still unknown whether Ramapithecus had adopted even a limited form of bipedalism.

As so often in the discussion of human evolution there is a minimum of 'hard' evidence in the form of fossils and a maximum of conjecture and hypothesis to supply behavioural and environmental circumstances. There are various hypotheses about the origins of bipedalism but it is agreed among human palaeontologists that this was the adaptation which accounted for the evolutionary divergence of the original hominoids into hominids and pongids. Generally the development of bipedalism is associated with deforestation and the environment typical of the southern African Miocene age, wooded valleys separated by tracts of open savannah grassland. W.E. Le Gros Clark has suggested that:

> 'the evolution of ground-living forms in the ancestry of the Hominidae was the result of adaptations primarily concerned, not with the abandonment of arboreal life, but (paradoxically) with an attempt to retain it. For in regions undergoing gradual deforestation they would make it possible to cross intervening grasslands in order to pass from one restricted and shrinking wooded area to another.'
>
> (1964: 187)

In the absence of any firm fossil evidence S.L. Washburn has suggested that bipedalism, albeit in a limited form, may have developed more than 4 million years ago and that this earliest (hypothetical, needless to say)

hominid would have had a small brain and would have walked, like recent
gorillas and chimpanzees, on its knuckles and would have been a ground
dweller.[8] The significance of this suggestion, as Washburn (1978) makes
clear, is that such a knuckle-walking, ground-dwelling creature would have
been able to carry sticks and even stones as it walked along, just as chimpanzees have been observed to do today.[9] The relationship between tools
and human evolution was suggested even earlier by Darwin, who conjec-
tured, in the light of an even scantier fossil record, that tool use was both
the cause and the effect of bipedal locomotion.

As we have already said, in Darwin's time the human palaeontological
record was virtually non-existent so there was little or no evidence to
support his hypothesis regarding the effects of tool use. However, even
when more hominid fossil remains came to light during the early years
of this century the established view was that only man, only large-brained
Homo Sapiens, used tools. Tool use was seen as part of man's unique
cultural heritage. Man was unique because he had culture, and tool use
and tool making were part of that culture. The predominant response
to the then fairly recently discovered hominid fossils — for example, the
discovery of Homo Erectus (Pithecanthropus) in Java in 1891 and of
further remains of Homo Erectus in China in 1927 — was extreme scepticism as to their 'humanness'. And scepticism was evident with the
discovery of the small-brained Australopithecus, the name (southern ape)
given by Dart to the well-known Taung skull in 1925. The response was
the same: culture was the monopoly of man and only some form directly
ancestral to historical man could have made tools, certainly not creatures
like Australopithecus with a brain no larger than a chimpanzee's.[10] The
basis for this incredulity was undermined when in 1959 Louis and Mary
Leakey discovered Australopithecine remains at Olduvai Gorge in
Tanzania alongside simple stone 'tools'. These tools were so simple that
they could be taken for ordinary unworked pebbles, except for the fact
that no such stones normally appear in the volcanic layer in which they
were found. This suggested that the stones had been transported to the
living site from elsewhere.

Similar discoveries had been made in other parts of Africa. In Sterk-
fontein in South Africa the tools were unworked river pebbles not
normally to be found in the limestone caves where they were discovered.
Sceptics of course could and did argue that such 'tools' could have been
brought to the site by bigger-brained creatures and not the Australopithecines whose remains were found alongside the artefacts. What made
the Leakeys' discovery so significant is that at Olduvai the fossil remains
were found alongside not only stone 'tools' but also waste flakes and a
hammerstone which must have been used in the manufacture of the tools.
Also of interest were the remains of various small animals such as juvenile
pig and antelope, and rats, mice, etc., which tend to contradict the supposition that man's early ancestors were aggressive hunters of large animals.
In fact the evidence suggests that Australopithecines were still largely

vegetarian. This view is supported by the pelvic remains which indicate that although Australopithecus was bipedal this capacity was still not fully developed. Australopithecus would not have been capable of the long-distance walking which is a prerequisite for specialized hunting in savannah conditions and is a feature of subsequent hominids like Homo Erectus.[11] What is significant about the pelvic remains of Australopithecus is that they exhibit the wide, short upper pelvis characteristic of man and directly related to bipedal locomotion, providing a cradle-like support for the spine and torso when held in an upright position. It is important to point out that today there is evidence of Australopithecus well into the Pliocene, which makes them even older than the Ice Age creature that they were originally thought to be. Their limited bipedalism fits in well with what we know to have been the increasing aridity and deforestation of this era.

Further evidence of the use of tools by hominid ancestors of man had been provided by the discovery of more advanced tools, cores and flakes, as well as animal bones showing signs of modification for use as implements, in the same deposits as Homo Erectus (Peking Man) at Choukoutien. The site also revealed evidence of the use of fire and even ritual cannibalism, all indicators of a 'very active communal life' (Le Gros Clark 1978: 111). For many years this evidence was treated with the same doubt which greeted the suggestion that Australopithecines could have used and 'manufactured' tools and it was maintained that the tools and the other indications of culture were the products of a more advanced type of hominid and not of Homo Erectus. Today, however, such scepticism is not widespread and there would be general acceptance of Bernard Campbell's statement in his addition to Le Gros Clark's *The Fossil Evidence for Human Evolution*: 'There is little reason to suppose that Pekin man was not culturally advanced, and he certainly demonstrates many behavioural traits characteristic of modern man' (1978: 111). If further evidence is needed that culture and particularly tool use is neither unique to Homo Sapiens nor dependent on a large brain then we can turn to the recent field studies of chimpanzees. Observations have been made of these animals' use of sticks and leaves: sticks to aid the chimpanzees' search for their much-prized delicacy, termites and ants, and leaves used as sponges to collect water and sometimes to clean themselves.

The argument advanced here will be that the limited bipedalism of Australopithecus made tool use possible and that the use of tools consequently altered the terms of natural selection by establishing pressures in favour of tool use and tool making which eventually resulted in the physical structure of modern man. The influence of these pressures can be seen at work in the fossil record with respect to changes which took place not only in the pelvis but the facial skeleton, teeth, and the surrounding musculature, hands and feet, as well as the enormous increase in brain size. Washburn has even suggested that distinctly human patterns of maternal responsibility and infant care can be attributed to bipedalism and tool use. Many writers have argued that the progressive adaptation and specialization of the hominid pelvis and other skeletal changes are related to the use of tools. It is suggested that once a way of life is established in which survival is increasingly dependent on the use of implements — as tools, as weapons, and so on — then selection pressures will operate in favour of those physical and mental features which are an advantage in tool use, such as coordination, stereoscopic vision, hands free from locomotion, and so on. Tools can give an enormous advantage to the user(s), in preparing food, in getting food — whether this involves hunting or digging roots, etc. This extends the range of available foods and increases the variety and protein content of the diet. Tools such as hard flints can be used to make specialized tools, knives, choppers, etc. As regards human evolution, the use of the hands for the holding of implements creates pressures not only in favour of modifications in the structure of the hand to allow more effective manual movements, greater precision and dexterity, but also in favour of a more erect posture and a greater facility for bipedal movement on the ground. This is because an upright posture and bipedal locomotion leave the hands free to hold and use implements whilst on the move. Efficient bipedalism makes possible specialized hunting and extends the possible range of hominids who are able to carry worked tools with them.

Such changes are apparent if we look at the various hominid fossils which have been found in company with tools of an increasingly sophisticated nature. We have said that the Australopithecine pelvis shows many characteristically hominid features but indicates that it fell short of full bipedalism. The evidence suggests that Homo Erectus, on the other hand, was fully bipedal and, what is more important, adapted to sustained walking. In hunting the ability to cover long distances at a steady pace is more important than running ability, and this is also true for gathering activities.[12] Most modern hunters and gatherers are semi-nomadic. Such staying power in locomotion is a compensation for the possible loss of speed due to bipedal rather than quadrupedal locomotion.[13] Judging from the fossils of deer and seeds found at the living sites of Homo Erectus, this hominid was already an efficient hunter and gatherer and, therefore, an efficient walker.

The structure of the hand has obvious significance in the making and using of tools; equally significant for the development of tool use is a structure which allows for the general manipulation of objects found in the external environment. This is an activity which, Bernard Campbell (1974) suggests, is largely confined to monkeys, apes, and man.[14] This manual dexterity is related to a feature especially developed in man, namely an opposable thumb, a combination of bone structure and corresponding musculature which allows the thumb to be rotated through an angle of 45 degrees and opposed to the other digits, giving what Napier has called both a power grip and, perhaps more important for tool use and tool making, a precision grip.[15] Evidence from Olduvai suggests that the hand of Australopithecus allowed for the former but not the latter, the fossil remains indicating evidence of opposability although the thumb was not long enough to allow for the precision grip. No remains of the hands of Homo Erectus were available when Campbell revised his first edition of *Human Evolution* but in his revision of Le Gros Clark's book he includes a comment on the fossil hand bones of the controversial Homo Habilis.[16] He makes it clear that this example of early man was endowed with 'a thumb capable of a wide range of movement including rotation out of the plane of the palm to give a precision grip' (Le Gros Clark 1978: 125). This degree of opposability would allow more efficient carrying of food as well as tools. Campbell comments:

'In early man the survival value of being able to carry objects without any disadvantageous effect on locomotion is of the greatest importance. Not only is it most advantageous to be able to carry food when surprised by a predator, but it can lead eventually to food sharing, food gathering and in particular, to hunting. A weapon at the ready is also of great survival value. The survival value of carrying also serves in turn to promote a physical structure adapted to bipedal locomotion.'

(Le Gros Clark 1978: 199)

Quite remarkable changes in facial skeleton and dentition can be observed in the fossil record for human evolution and a strong case can be made for associating these changes with tool use. In the case of the structure of the hand and the pelvis associated with bipedal locomotion we saw that certain modifications would have allowed for some limited tool use which then would have exerted selection pressures in favour of more efficient bipedalism and corresponding changes in the hand and the pelvis. In other words, a certain physical structure makes a certain activity possible, this activity then influences further the selection of individuals with the most developed features of that physical structure. However, the influence of tool use on the facial skeleton and dentition operated in a different manner. Hominid fossils exhibit a systematic reduction in the facial skeletal mass. Homo Erectus for example does not have the prognathism (protruding jaw) of Australopithecus nor the pronounced sagittal crest, that is, the bony protuberance on the top of the skull which was the anchorage point for the massive muscles associated with the Australopithecine's large jaw. Now it is important to point out that any maintenance of large size requires positive selection, it has to be selected *for* because 'the concept of biological efficiency suggests that if an organ is larger than necessary it will be reduced by genetic adjustment in the course of evolution' (Campbell 1974: 216). Once the functions of defence and attack, tearing and grinding food were increasingly transferred from the head and jaws to tools then selection pressures would cease to operate in favour of large-sized jaws and, on the contrary, would shift toward reduction. This reduction is suggested by the evidence of hominid fossils.

Reduction is observable not only in the facial skeleton but in the size of the teeth, particularly in the canines and incisors, the fighting and tearing 'implements' of other mammals. The canines and incisors of Australopithecus are already considerably reduced, the incisors in particular being little different in size from human incisors. It is only the molars of Australopithecus which are big relative to its other teeth, and which are also much larger than the molars of either man or modern apes. Washburn (1978) suggests that this could be related to the abrasive quality of the food dug from the ground with tools. As for the reduction in the canines and incisors of hominids, Washburn relates this to the transfer of functions to tools.[17] This association has been challenged by V. Reynolds (1976) who suggests (following Jolly) that even early hominid forms ancestral to man such as Ramapithecus had small canines and incisors associated with a diet of seeds. This might well be the case but it does not entirely refute Washburn's general thesis of the significance of tools for modifying human dentition. We simply do not know if Ramapithecus was a tool user or not because no tools have been found in association with fossil remains. What is interesting is that chimpanzees, which of all other primates show the most systematic evidence of the use of sticks, etc., also have small canines and incisors. The absence of any evidence of tool use in association with the fossil remains of Ramapithecus does not definitely prove that he did not use tools. After all, sticks would not remain in the fossil record and even Reynolds admits that Ramapithecus may have been a tool user, at least to the limited extent that chimpanzees are. If Ramapithecus was no more than 'a sporadic tool user' this, combined with seed eating, would account to some extent for its reduced canines and incisors.

Since large canines and incisors when associated with defence and attack require a large jaw and the motive power of extensive musculature, a reduction in dental armoury will have effects on these aspects of the facial skeleton. We have already observed evidence of this in Australopithecus. Homo Erectus shows as well a reduction of the pronounced bony eye ridges which remain a distinctive feature of Australopithecus, sure signs of a move away from close-in fighting and biting. This too can be related to a reduction of the masticatory apparatus associated with tool use. A smaller jaw also helps to resolve the problem of balancing the head upon the spinal column; thus the reduction in the mass of the jaw is further evidence of and an assistance to bipedalism. Washburn (1960) has made a further novel suggestion regarding the reduction of facial skeletal mass associated with tool use. He argues that as tool use made the hunting of large game possible it thereby produced a way of life based on learning and active cooperation among the hunters. This he suggests could have led to selection pressures in favour of more 'cooperative' individuals. His case rests in part on the selective breeding of domestic animals, chosen for their relatively 'peaceful' natures, a characteristic which has been found to be associated with smaller facial skeletons and brow ridges.[18] Washburn emphasizes the significance of the relation between cooperation and lack of rage. 'Rage' can be considered as a physiological mechanism adapting the animal's behaviour to the use of biting and tearing as a form of predation and defence. Tools for hunting and war require some degree of calculation and concentration (traps and the like), something not aided by rage. The shift from physical attributes to behaviour as a way of meeting certain functions implies both physical *and* physiological changes, a reduction in the degree of 'triggering' of behaviour by stimuli and physiological mechanisms.

So far we have been talking largely of the *reduction* in size of certain features in hominids, particularly the facial skeleton. There is one area of human evolution which has been associated with tool use but which is an exception to this tendency toward reduction – the brain. In the course of a relatively short time span in evolutionary terms the brain underwent a phenomenal expansion, doubling in size from Australopithecus to Homo Sapiens.[19] What is of importance is not mere size as such, but size relative to body weight,[20] as well as the growth of the different functionally specific areas – as Washburn points out, brains of similar size may vary considerably in the distribution of functional areas.[21] It is generally agreed that it is the cerebral cortex which has expanded most in Homo Sapiens relative to the brains of the other primates. Of the cerebral cortex it is the frontal, parietal, and temporal lobes which have expanded the most. This is exactly what one would expect if selection pressures operate in favour of the physical structures supporting and making possible motor skills, the integration of sensory information, and memory. It is also interesting that the extent of the increase in brain size in Homo Sapiens is to some extent disguised by the extent of folding in the human brain so that some 64 per cent of the surface of the cortex is hidden in the fissures compared with 25 to 30 per cent in the apes.

Washburn relates the increase in brain size to tool use, arguing that one of the areas of the brain which has expanded most during human evolution is the area associated with manual dexterity. This would have developed under the same selection pressures which favoured the distinctively large thumb of Homo Sapiens. He says, 'In man it is the areas adjacent to the primary centres that are most expanded. These areas are concerned with motor skills, memory, foresight and language; that is, with the mental faculties that make human social life possible' (1960: 13). Reynolds (1976) is sceptical of the association between tool use and the expansion of the human brain, particularly as the frontal lobes which have expanded so much relative to other parts are not much involved in the kind of activity required for making tools such as Australopithecus used. People with damage to this area of the brain are less capable of conceptual and abstract thought but are still capable of the sensory-motor coordination which would be involved in the making and using of tools. But then Reynolds is concerned with the human capacity for speech and symbolizing and how to explain the expansion of the related area of the human brain. The fact remains that the systematic use and making of tools could have set up selection pressures for larger, more complex brains. Livingstone (1969) suggests that imitative learning alone, of the kind that would be involved in the making and using of simple tools, could have increased selection pressures for bigger brains and that it is not necessary to attribute the enlargement of the human brain, as Reynolds and others have done, specifically to the adoption of language during the Palaeolithic era.[22]

Nonetheless, the greatly increased area of the human brain concerned with memory, foresight, and language has encouraged many writers to speculate about the origins of human language in an attempt to explain the expansion of these particular areas of the cerebral cortex. A.L. Kroeber, for example, associates tool use and language in so far as both are cultural manifestations: 'it would appear that the first rudiments of what deserves to be called language are about as ancient as the first cultural manifestations, mainly because of the theoretically close association of the two' (cited by Livingstone (1969) — 'cultural manifestations' here means tools and artefacts). Kroeber quite justifiably sees tools as indicative of culture but, since for him culture is a uniquely human activity dependent on 'symboling', then the existence of one aspect of culture, i.e. tools, presupposes another, in this case language. Livingstone seems to uphold the connection of culture and language but, at the same time, excludes stone tools, or at least the handaxes of the early Pleistocene, from cultural status. He says, 'I would argue that the answer to the dilemma is that handaxes are not culture — that the hand-axe sequence was the product of an animal with only imitative learning and no language' (1969: 47). But this is to throw out the baby with the bath water. It is quite possible to suggest that Australopithecus did have 'culture', as evidenced by tool use and tool making, in so far as they had a 'whole way of life' that was a product of learning and acquired rather than innate. Both Kroeber and Livingstone seem to be working with the same too narrow definition of culture from which Kroeber paradoxically draws unwarranted conclusions regarding Australopithecus' linguistic abilities, while Livingstone rejects the idea that Australopithecus can be said to have had any culture at all. But he himself admits:

'Hominids such as Sinanthropus [Homo Erectus] possessed fire and presumably were able to control it. If language did not appear before the Upper Palaeolithic, this would imply that an enormous amount of rational behaviour could exist without symboling; but this possibility seems to me no more unlikely than the alternative of a very early evolution of language.'

(Livingstone 1969:47)

Indeed, but presumably for Livingstone only a creature close to man, like Homo Neanderthalensis, has culture and therefore language. The implication is that 'culture' remains a uniquely 'human' attribute, a position which we would question here, arguing instead for the view expressed by Dobzhansky (1955), that culture is the whole way of life, including both material and non-material aspects, and not solely the latter. Certain other writers have deduced the origin of human language from the cooperative requirements of hunting activities of Australopithecus. But this is probably to exaggerate the extent of hunting by Australopithecus who we know to have been still largely vegetarian. Recent reconstructions of the vocal tracts of Australopithecus and Homo Erectus suggest that they were incapable of producing anything resembling human vocal sounds. Australopithecus apparently had a short ape-like pharynx which would have limited the variety of vowel sounds and consonants. The long bent human pharynx first appears in the Steinheim skull, regarded by B. Campbell (1974) as early Homo Sapiens. Such evidence must be inconclusive if only because this characteristically human pharynx is not present in human babies and only develops in the second year.[23] It is anyway unjustified to assume that cooperation in hunting depends on language. Cooperative hunting may depend on some form of communication but language as such cannot be seen as a prerequisite. We need look only as far as the cases of chimpanzees apparently cooperating in their occasional hunting forays. Other capacities may be brought into play to sustain cooperation, for instance, animals like Cape Hunting dogs without language hunt and cooperate in hunting over a wide area because of their speed and their specialized scent-following abilities.

It is possible to argue the evolutionary advantages of some form of communication:

'for a diurnal hunter or scavenger, operating away from the main group containing the females and their young, guided mostly by sight rather than scent, in rough wooded or savanna country, and under heavy pressures to return regularly to a base camp, exchange of environmental information would be a behaviour possessing enormous selective advantages.'

(Hewes 1973: 7)

J.B. Lancaster (1968) also agrees that the ability to make environmental reference and name objects would confer evolutionary advantage where hunting and foraging led to some division of labour. The problem is how this could have developed. Although non-human primates make sounds, only vervet monkeys are known to make sounds with environmental reference. For Lancaster the crucial factor in the development of language was the structure of the brain rather than the mechanism for making sounds — which would have involved no radical evolutionary changes and evolved with the selection pressures associated with the development of language.[24] But this leaves us none the wiser as to how such selection pressures were set up.

Richard Leakey and Roger Lewin argue that social structure 'demanded the facility of a sophisticated language' (1979: 174). Kinship and cooperation, the key features of a hunting and gathering economy, 'would be impossible without a series of *social rules* that could be elaborated only through the medium of the spoken word' (1979: 161). They claim that it is the symbolic demands of the new hominid mode of social life, and not tool use, which are the key factors promoting the development of intelligence. Indeed tool making beyond the simplest levels of technical organization is regarded by them as a *consequence* of social/symbolic organization. Whilst this view may appear attractive to social scientists it does little more than state what we know to be obvious — that social life as we know it involves linguistically formulated rules — and then extrapolates from it to the unknowns of our hominid past. Again the selection pressures leading to the development of spoken language as such are not explained and it is assumed rather than argued that 'a sophisticated language' is an adaptive advantage. This itself can be questioned as we shall see later in Chapter Three. We have in this chapter tried to stay within the more conservative estimates of the antiquity of hominids and of the development of genuine bipedalism rather than accept the claims of Richard Leakey and other modern palaeoanthropologists which push hominid development considerably further back in time. However, even accepting their views would not affect the basic structure of our argument, that human physical attributes are modified in the course of evolution by the selection pressures set up by social relations.

Some consider the search for the origins of *spoken* language to have been a red herring. Hewes (1973) suggests that hominid communication originated in gestural rather than vocal language, pointing out that the transmission of tool use and tool making need not have depended on vocal language but rather on the imitation of the gestures involved, much as we learn some aspects of manual skills today. The recent limited successes in teaching chimpanzees to use gestural signs makes this hypothesis credible to some degree. But still it is not easy to see how a 'language' of gestures could have formed the basis of *spoken* language or what pressures promoted the shift from one to the other. All we know about modern gesture usage leaves us none the wiser about this supposed shift from gestures to speech. Modern sign languages for the deaf are, after all, developed by users of spoken languages as a means of communicating with the deaf. They 'translate' spoken languages in a 'telegraphic' style that resembles writing more than the elementary gestures normally used to supplement speech. The ethologists notwithstanding, supposedly 'basic' human gestures are neither strictly universal in their significance nor more than a limited supplement to spoken language today. Specific gesture *systems* like those today used by bookmakers, participants in specialized markets, or workers in noisy factories are minimal and in no way amount to gesture 'languages'. Whilst they assist cooperative activities, they hardly offer much prospect of development. By contrast the evolutionary analysis of the influence of social relations on physical structure is well developed. It would be fair to say that the analysis of the 'evolution' of language remains speculative and has hardly advanced beyond the eighteenth- and nineteenth-century views catalogued by James H. Stam in *Inquiries Into The Origin of Language* (1976). The problem is that there is no definite correlation between the sign systems and the physical structures which make them possible. The development of the brain and vocal cords are preconditions for spoken language but we cannot, on the basis of those developments, explain language as a system of signs in use. We return to questions of the nature of language and signs in Chapter Three.

The purpose of this chapter has been to show how learned and social activities like tool use and tool making influenced modern man's physical make-up by placing selection pressures on certain vital characteristics. This development was, however, part of a process of *natural selection*, and modern social life depends on certain biological factors which have developed in the course of human physical and social evolution.

Notes

1 Readers interested in Darwin's predecessors are referred to B. Glass, O. Temkin and W.L. Strauss (eds) *Forerunners of Darwin 1745-1859* (1968) and H. Wendt *Before the Deluge* (1970). For the 'new' geology and the religious controversies surrounding the notion that the earth had a longer history than that proposed in Genesis see C.C. Gillispie *Genesis and Geology* (1959).
2 See Dobzhansky (1955); Lerner (1968).
3 See Simpson (1968: 4).
4 See Le Gros Clark (1964: 3).
5 See Washburn (1978: 152).
6 See Le Gros Clark (1964: 187).
7 See Le Gros Clark (1978: 153).
8 See Washburn (1978: 153).
9 See Goodall (1965).
10 The cranial capacity of chimpanzees ranges from 300-480 cubic centimetres, that of Australopithecus from 428-760 cubic centimetres; see Reynolds (1980: 74).
11 See Washburn (1960: 7-9).
12 See de Vore (1965: 33).
13 See Washburn (1960: 7).
14 Campbell (1974: 196-97).
15 See Napier (1962).
16 Homo Habilis — the status of these remains has been in dispute for some time. The term was first given by Louis Leakey to some of the remains found at Olduvai. Le Gros Clark (1964) maintained that this lighter framed hominid was in fact a sub-species of Australopithecus, Australopithecus Africanus. This view has since been revised, see Le Gros Clark (1978: 124, 172-78), and it is now suggested that Homo Habilis was an intermediate hominid between Australopithecus and Homo Erectus.
17 Washburn (1978).
18 Washburn (1960: 11).

19

Australopithecus Africanus	435-815 cubic centimetres
Homo Erectus	775-1225 cubic centimetres
Homo Sapiens	1000-2000 cubic centimetres

This table (from Campbell 1974: 272) differs slightly from the dimensions given by Reynolds (1980: 74) for Australopithecus; see above, n10.

20 See Reynolds (1980: 76).
21 See Washburn (1960: 11).
22 Livingstone (1969).
23 Campbell (1974: 355).
24 See Lancaster (1968).

2

THE SOCIAL FORMATION
AND MAINTENANCE
OF HUMAN ATTRIBUTES

This chapter is concerned to examine the ways in which social relations, in the sense of particular beliefs, practices and institutions, both organize and constitute human beings' bodily and mental capacities. But before we proceed, it is necessary to offer some words of caution.

Sociologists have, on the whole, energetically denied the importance of genetic, physical, and individual psychological factors in human social life. In so doing they have reinforced and theorized a traditional Western cultural opposition between nature and culture. Social relations can even be conceived as a *denial* of nature. Thus, in an example we shall have cause to return to again, the French anthropologist Claude Lévi-Strauss regards the incest taboo as a proscription of possible natural relationships and for that reason an *institution* par excellence, a denial of nature which is the foundation of all social rules.[1] Now in querying this we are not arguing that it is illegitimate to challenge forms of biological and psychological reductionism which make social relations and beliefs no more than a manifestation of the naturally given physical and mental attributes and capabilities of human beings. Instead, we wish to argue something quite different: that there is no hard and fast divide between nature and culture. Our analysis of the role of cultural factors in human biological evolution was designed to emphasize this point. Biological and psychological capacities clearly do organize and limit social relations. Without the *capacity* for tool use made possible by the opposable thumb and freeing forelimbs from the task of locomotion our social organizations would be very different and very limited. If our average intelligence level were what is measured by an IQ of 80, then again social relations between humans would encounter severe limits. In both cases these biological and psychological capabilities are not independent of and have been shaped by the consequences of humans associating in social organizations. They impose limits nonetheless and cannot be legislated away.

However, the primary danger in the rigid opposition between nature and culture does not lie in the denial of the importance of biological and psychological phenomena. Biologists and psychologists will always press these claims. They will do so *against* sociology, against a sociological imperialism and exclusivism. They will be right to do so, although the intellectual consequences are highly unsatisfactory. A rigidly environmentalist and anti-hereditarian sociology provokes its mirror opposite in biology and psychology. The primary danger, however, lies in *the conception of social relations* which arises from this rigid opposition between nature and culture. 'Society' is converted into an entity, and the 'social' is rigidly delimited from other realms of phenomena. It becomes a self-enclosed realm of causes and effects. At the same time as social relations are rigidly differentiated from biological and psychological conditions they are homogenized and unified, converted into a single interconnected whole, 'society'. We shall argue throughout this work that it is not necessary in order to analyse the effectiveness of social relations to maintain that they form one interconnected whole, nor that they be rigidly differentiated from biological or psychological phenomena.

The sociologist who most clearly did conceive the 'social' as rigidly distinct from biology and individual psychology and who conceived 'society' as a single unified entity is Emile Durkheim. Durkheim, although extreme in his emphasis on these points, is neither exceptional nor eccentric, as is testified by the number of introductory sociology courses which use his analysis of suicide to demonstrate the determination of apparently individual acts by social conditions, and hence the specific nature and effectiveness of the 'social'. We will thus start our analysis with a set of problems to which the Durkheim School made a notable contribution.

Death and belief systems

Durkheim's pupil, Robert Hertz, who tragically fell in the First World War before he had time to do more than complete a series of preliminary studies, wrote in 1907 an interesting essay entitled 'A Contribution to the Study of the Collective Representation of Death'.[2] Death, Hertz rightly argued, is a 'collective representation', or – in the usage we will adopt – a 'social category'. Death, while inescapable for humans, is not the simple self-evident phenomenon it might seem to the unreflective. This is not merely because modern medical knowledge has taught us the difficulties of defining 'death' physiologically and of devising tests to determine whether or not someone is 'really' dead. The problem for medical knowledge in this case is not merely a theoretical or technical one: it is a cultural one. Our Western Christian culture tends to define 'death' in opposition to a state of 'life' and to conceive the transition between the two as an instantaneous change of state. Physiologically, matters are by no means so simple.

Hertz argues that death is a 'collective representation' in that its nature, significance, and consequences depend upon social beliefs and categorizations. Many societies do not consider death as we do, as an instantaneous event, rather it is a slow change of condition, as evidenced by the phenomenon of secondary burial where an initial interment is followed by another final and symbolic disposition of the deceased. In secondary burial practices, Hertz argues, we see an analogue of other 'rites of passage': from childhood to adulthood, marriage, etc. The dead person passes from familiar social life to life in another realm; to a society spiritually integrated with and parallel to the familiar one. The period of bodily decomposition marks the interval of the two and secondary burial solemnizes the final change of state.

Hertz explains these rites by arguing that death, for 'primitives' like the Dyaks of Borneo, is not a natural event. It is a disruption of the socially constructed natural order of things. The collective consciousness, the 'social', is shaken by death because, in removing the individual from its grasp, it threatens its very existence. 'Society' must conceive itself as immortal, and thus conceives the deceased individual as merely temporarily excluded from human society. After an interval and rites of passage the individual is reintegrated in a parallel social existence linked symbolically and by real ties with the familiar social world. The collective representation of death is society's way of managing the trauma which threatens it by revealing its own transience.

Hertz's essay presents a curious paradox. On the one hand, he shows with great brilliance that death is a social category, that its nature, significance, and social consequences depend on how it is constructed and represented in belief systems and mortuary practices. On the other hand, his specific *explanation* of these beliefs and practices depends on conceiving society as already an entity represented to its members as superior and immortal, which is effective as an entity in and on the minds of its members. Now there is no reason to suppose that beliefs and practices do form a unity, or that they are co-present as a 'mentality' in the human psyche. Indeed, there is good reason to challenge this view precisely because it leads to conceptions like the 'collective consciousness' whereby social relations are conceived primarily as a set of beliefs and ideas seen as forming one consistent mentality equivalent to the philosophical idea of a human 'consciousness' (of thoughts as present to a recognizing subject which thinks them).[3] It is not merely the 'mentalistic' aspect of this type of theorizing which is at fault. The problem is more than this: in making social relations coherent as sets of collective representations it leads to the idea of a 'typical' individual who is a reflection of the collective, with automatic typical reactions to social circumstances. Thus death becomes a psychic trauma for the survivors because of its nature as a *class* of event, and as a result of the logic of belief systems. The survivors became mere receptacles of culture. This tendency is by no means confined to Durkheimians or to their concept of the 'collective consciousness'. It is widespread in sociology and social anthropology, as we shall see. (Various modern studies have continued the analysis of death as a social category, delineating its changing forms. Perhaps the best and most suggestive of these is Philippe Ariès' *Western Attitudes Towards Death* (1974).[4])

For all the defects of Hertz's analysis we have no intention of arguing that belief systems do not have consequences for conduct nor of arguing that the response to death is determined solely by some supposedly purely 'individual' psychological reaction. There is another way of approaching the relation between the physiological phenomenon of death and social categories and this is to consider how beliefs may play a part in instigating the physiological processes which lead to death. Readers of Durkheim's *Suicide* will be familiar with his concept of 'altruistic suicide' in which an individual kills himself or places himself in circumstances which lead to death in conformity with social norms, or, because social norms set a low value on the individual human life, in response to frustration or failure. Captain Oates' sacrifice in the hope of saving his fellows or a captain's going down with his ship are examples which illustrate one aspect of Durkheim's conception. In these cases death is the direct and obvious result of conduct. One man acts so that death from exposure will be the consequence and the other death by drowning. Beliefs provide the apparent ground for actions, but it is the *actions* which kill in these cases. The *death* itself presents no great mystery.

Consider the following case, however:

> 'I have seen more than one hardened old Hausa soldier dying steadily and by inches because he believed himself to be bewitched; no nourishment or medicines that were given to him had the slightest effect either to check the mischief or to improve his condition in any way, and nothing was able to divert him from fate which he considered inevitable.'
> (A.G. Leonard 1906, cited by Cannon 1942: 169)[5]

W.B. Cannon, a physiologist rather than a sociologist, investigated in his paper ' "Voodoo Death" ' (1942) the possibility that death could occur as a consequence of beliefs. What Cannon argues is that belief in a certain class of entities — evil spirits, maleficent magics, tabooed objects, which can do harm to persons by what we regard as 'occult' means — leads to the possibility of a state of fear on the part of the believer following from circumstances which bring these entities into action, such as giving offence to a spirit, being bewitched or cursed, or violating a taboo. The affected person considers himself doomed. An unutterably horrible fate awaits him. The resulting state of fear and terror in anticipation of this fate, if deep enough and prolonged enough, leads to physiological changes which are equivalent to severe wound shock. The ultimate effect of this condition is an irreversible decline in the capacity of the circulatory system and death as a result of denial of a sufficient supply of oxygen to vital organs. Here social beliefs and physiological processes closely interact.

The deaths in question stem from a state of terror induced by the conviction that nothing can be done to arrest or remove the spell or curse, or to compensate for the violation of the taboo, and that the entities which threaten the individual are awful and inescapable. The deaths which stem from deeply held beliefs about certain entities serve to reinforce in other individuals the conviction that these very entities do indeed exist.

They confirm through experience the action of occult powers. But, according to Cannon, there is nothing occult about the actual *mechanics* of 'voodoo death'. Beliefs working through the action of the higher brain centres excite the sympathico-adrenal system. The prolonged excitation of this system produces a gradual fall in blood pressure 'from the high levels of the early stages to the low level seen in fatal wound shock' (Cannon 1942: 177). The victim eventually falls into a coma and the whole process is then placed beyond cerebral control or reversal. Beliefs are thus effective through processes which render inoperative the higher brain centres on which they depend. Both the effectivity of social relations *and* the determining role of biological processes are confirmed by this example.

As Cannon points out this is the *physiological* logic behind a state of terror produced by certain beliefs. There is no corresponding logic *in the beliefs themselves* that automatically leads to certain physical results. And, as Cannon is aware, death is not inevitable in every case of bewitchment or violation of taboo where the victim subscribes to the beliefs in question. Counter-magic, attempts to induce the originator of the curse or spell to remove it, or gestures of propitiation in the case of a taboo are all practices which can remove or mitigate the source of the fear in certain circumstances. Cannon cites the example of a doctor in Queensland who threatened a witch-doctor with expulsion from a mission station and cutting off his rations if he did not convince his victim that a case of bone-pointing was a mere joke and that the victim's life was in no danger as the magical event had not actually come to pass. The doctor succeeded and the victim recovered.

Conditions other than a formal belief in the entities in question clearly intervene in determining the outcome in cases of 'voodo death'. Counter-magic may be of no avail, a shaman or witch-doctor may prove powerless to assist, or propitiation may fail to achieve its ends. The victim may shun the assistance of kin and comrades. In such circumstances we may well suspect guilt or some other such unconscious motivation or conflict. The individual feels at some level that a curse stems from a justified grievance, or that the violation of a taboo reflects a real fault and hence the punishment is deserved. Fear of occult powers would then be coupled with a psychic submission to them which has sources quite distinct from the belief systems themselves. We are by no means faced with a 'typical' individual who is no more than a reflection of the collective. The entities specified in beliefs provide the grounds for fear, but the fear itself is produced and reinforced by the complex and particular psychic dynamics of the individual. *Both* the effectivity of social relations *and* the importance of individual psychic states which are not simply derived from them are confirmed by this point.

Belief systems are by no means consistent in themselves or in their consequences. The threatening entities are paralleled by others, for example, the curse by counter-magic. Beliefs always exist in combination with practices and these practices may in large measure limit or counter the apparent consequences of the beliefs in question. Magical practices are combined with counter-magic: the witch doctor or shaman will practise both and while both activities confirm the beliefs in question, counter-magic may go a long way to reducing fear in witchcraft or evil spirits. Casting a spell or uttering a curse is a social action. It may be countered on the institutional or judicial plane as well as on the occult. Such actions can lead to accusations of witchcraft using judicial procedures to forestall or punish magical consequences. The victim of a spell or his kin are by no means helpless. We will return to these issues in our discussion of witchcraft in Part Three. The point to be made here is that belief systems are not 'representations' with a logic of ideas which is revealed in 'consciousness', nor is that 'consciousness' itself a mere reflection of social beliefs.

We have used the example of 'voodoo death' here, but an equally good one is the phenomenon of ecstatic trance and spirit possession. Trance and possession phenomena occur in definite social relations, as I.M. Lewis ably demonstrates in *Ecstatic Religion* (1971). Trance states are induced as a consequence of definite beliefs and practices. They serve objectives such as healing, divination, revelation, and communion with gods and spirits. *But* the trance state itself is not a mere behaviour, a register of beliefs. It is a definite mental/physiological condition. This is well demonstrated in William Sargant's *The Mind Possessed* (1976) — and one need not wholly subscribe to his particular variant of psychological explanation to agree with him. All the same, it would be curious if Pavlov's *Lectures on Conditioned Reflexes* were to be wholly irrelevant to the explanation of human actions. Possession or trance states consist in a radical reduction in the directive role and influence of the higher brain centres. There are a number of features of trance states and possession which illustrate this: subjects exhibit compulsive and uncharacteristic behaviour, in certain cases they are extremely open to external suggestion (similar to that in cases of hypnotism) and, whether the trance is controlled by the subject or by another person, withdrawal from it often depends on a 'key', a phrase or set signal. The role of the nervous system and the lower parts of the brain, just like the influence of the 'unconscious' elements of the psyche, as we shall see later, shows that we must be careful not to reduce conduct to an extension of belief systems and socially sanctioned requirements of action.

Techniques of the body

These cautionary remarks are essential in a chapter whose main purpose is to illustrate that humans' bodily and mental capacities are not 'naturally' given, that they depend in great measure on and vary with social beliefs, practices, and techniques. Again, in order to consider how social beliefs and techniques control, direct, shape, and distribute bodily powers and functions, we will resort to the work of the Durkheimian School.

We begin again with Robert Hertz, with his essay 'The Pre-Eminence of the Right Hand: A Study in Religious Polarity'.[6] Hertz asks why it is that there is such a striking inequality in our use of and attitudes to our two hands. The right hand enjoys privilege and primacy. To it go the most important and honoured tasks, and it is the symbol of nobility and favour. The left hand, on the contrary, is despised and subordinated. It is on the 'sinister' side. To it go the polluting and secondary tasks and it is the symbol of the common people and of opposition, of the 'left'. This is not a mere matter of symbolism but of use. It is the left hand that is used among the Arabs — and Muslims in general — to clean the anus while the right is reserved for food. Left-handed people have been discriminated against and bullied into using their right hands, and so on. Hertz raises the question as to whether this dysymmetry is organic in origin. Does it not reflect the predominant asymmetry of the two cerebral hemispheres? Hertz replies that such an answer is insufficient. Do we not see many instances of apparently natural conditions or abilities being denied or countered by social beliefs and training? For example, as we shall see, the Trobriand Islanders deny the role of the father in procreation. In the case of left-handedness, such a physical asymmetry could well be countered by social pressure, a deliberate training of the left hand, or a cultivation of ambidexterity:

> 'The fact is that right-handedness is not simply accepted, submitted to, like a natural necessity: it is an ideal to which everybody must conform and which society forces us to respect by positive sanctions .... Organic asymmetry in man is at once a fact and an ideal. Anatomy accounts for the fact to the extent that it results from the structure of the organism; but however strong a determinant one may suppose it to be, it is incapable of explaining the origin of the ideal or the reason for its existence.'
>
> (Hertz 1960: 93)

Again, Hertz's questions are better than the answers he gives, for he goes on to argue, following Durkheim, that the essential feature of religion is the division into the *sacred* and the *profane*. This opposition is at the foundation of almost all other social valuations and polarities. He argues that there is 'a natural affinity' (1960: 95) between the profane and the impure. Throughout the life of primitive man, and even into the modern period, religion or its transformed analogues have remained the primary source of social valuations. The polarity between right and left is a reflection of a general tendency of social beliefs to oppositional valuation. Man's body, he argues, is no more than a reflection of the macrocosm; right and left are given values like light and dark, and these values extend to man because he is at the centre of creation and reflects in his body its spiritual order.

Now one can see in terms of Hertz's argument why a significant physical difference should attract a symbolic polarity, but why should it be the *right* that is favoured? Hertz ultimately concludes that it is the *organic difference* 'which directs the beneficent flow of supernatural favours toward the right side' (1960: 111). Given that cranial asymmetry is no more privileged than *any other* biological circumstance this argument appears less than compelling.[7] Social valuations far from confirm a necessary physically based dominance — among the Zuni Indians, for example, the *left* side is favoured. This is something Hertz is forced to shrug off as a 'secondary development' (1960: 109).

Why is Hertz forced to assert the *universality* of the symbolism of the right and to relate this social preference to a universal biological predominance? It is due to his concept of 'society' as a single and unified class of phenomena defined in opposition to others, such as the psychological. Durkheim constantly uses the universality or consistency of a social phenomenon as a proof of its independent existence. The Durkheimians define the 'social' as a unitary entity in opposition to others and as being characterized by a single nature and course of evolution. All societies have the same origins and basic elementary characteristics.[8] While this does enable them to highlight the specific effectiveness of social relations, arguing against biological or psychological reductionism, it also lumbers them with a concept of 'society' as a single consistent entity. 'Collective representations' cannot vary radically in character among themselves if this conception of the social as having a basic general nature and being 'independent of individual manifestations' is to be upheld. Hence the need to justify the *universality* of the predominance of the right. Hence the reliance, despite the Durkheimians' eagerness to differentiate sociology as an independent science, on a *biological* polarity to prop up this supposed universality.

Marcel Mauss was Durkheim's principal disciple. He showed, however, an engaging lack of the tendencies towards theoretical dogmatism which characterized the master. His essay 'Techniques of the Body'[9] is a catalogue of the way social conventions, physical techniques and their forms of training organize activities and abilities we tend to regard as 'natural', such as walking, sitting, squatting, and so on. He cites the amusing example of the English troops he was attached to in the First World War who did not know how to use French spades and found French digging techniques difficult to learn. If digging or styles of walking appear a triviality, this is because we tend to rely increasingly on external apparatuses and mechanical aids to do the work or perform the functions previous civilizations and contemporary 'primitive' peoples have used and developed their own bodies to do. Numerous examples could be cited; a couple will suffice here: culturally acquired techniques of resistance to pain — which have led peoples such as the Chinese and Vietnamese to be regarded as 'backward' or less than fully human because they bear injuries with a stoicism Westerners generally do not; endurance — the explorer

Laurens van der Post (1963) reports how the bushmen of the Kalahari desert can run long distances in the searing heat of day in pursuit of game, a performance which would tax the strongest and most skilful modern athletes, but is accomplished by stockily built men no more than about five feet high.[10] Hearing, seeing, smelling, resistance to heat and cold all bear out this radical divergence of bodily skills and the role of socially constructed and transmitted techniques in producing them. Mauss's essay serves as a valuable corrective to the tendency to regard a given range of skills and capacities as 'natural', as the inherent limits or resources of the body itself; 'something we think of as normal, like giving birth lying on one's back, is no more normal than doing so in other positions, e.g. on all fours' (Mauss 1973: 79).

Psychological techniques

Social beliefs, practices, and techniques affect not only bodily capacities but also forms of mental functioning. We refer here not to the *content* of psychological processes, ideas and the like, but the *form* of those processes themselves.[11] Faculties like memory are dependent on techniques and training. These techniques relate directly to forms of social organization, types of technology, and conceptions of the role of knowledge. Here we will confine ourselves to the consequences of certain media and techniques for faculties like memory, language use, etc. We will consider the role played by written language and its mechanical reproduction in printing.

The consequences of writing for social relations tend either to be ignored or to be excessively emphasized and over-rated.[12] Two related but different scholarly attitudes to writing are responsible for this simultaneous neglect and overestimation. The first demotes writing to the status of a mere cultural 'technique', a medium for representing ideas and symbols. This fits in well with one of the modern anthropological concepts of 'culture', as the sum total of a people's beliefs, skills, and institutionalized ways of acting and which includes along with 'culture' in the narrow sense things like cookery and its associated beliefs, burial practices and rites, etc.[13] It also fits in well with a traditional scholarly humanist tendency to prioritize the expressing subject and the symbolic content of a work over the graphical or other means in which it is actually presented. The second attitude promotes writing as the definitive hallmark of 'civilization'. It makes possible written records, the preservation of culture and its transmission in a stable form, and the formation of literate dominant elites. Illiterate peoples have traditionally been regarded in Graeco-Roman culture and its derivatives as 'barbarians'. Without sharing this sort of prejudice, the great archaeologist V. Gordon Childe still regards writing as representing:

'an epoch in human progress . . . the true significance of writing is that it was destined to revolutionize the transmission of human knowledge. By its means a man can immortalize his experience and transmit it directly to contemporaries living far off and to generations yet unborn. It is the first step to raising science above the limits of space and time.'

(Childe 1956: 186)

Likewise the author of a standard modern history of the evolution of writing, I.J. Gelb, remarks 'Writing exists only in a civilization and a civilization cannot exist without writing' (1963: 222). Gelb's statement is either circular or evidently false. The Inca civilization of Peru lacked 'writing' in Gelb's sense but, on any account, had every other attribute of civilization.

The first attitude reduces writing to 'technique' in the pejorative sense, as a mere medium for reproducing something whose significance lies beyond it, the living words of the language. What this ignores is the effect of the supposed 'medium' on what is 'expressed' through it. One need not echo the excesses of Marshall McLuhan — 'the medium is the message' — to stress this point (see *Understanding Media* 1964). Writing does permit, at a minimum, certain genres and certain forms of grammatical construction, certain forms of display which depend on simultaneous visual presentation of words rather than sequential oral delivery (as in scientific diagrams or forms of poetry). The capacity to signify in writing affects what can be said. Symbols, the concepts they present, and their resulting performance capacities are closely related — thus algebra permits mathematical theories and forms of mathesis otherwise impossible. A language which relied on signalling in code using lights or flags would be most limited: we can tolerate waiting for and retain 'England expects . . .' but not *Bleak House*.

The second attitude may seem opposed to the first but it can all too easily go along with it. Writing is an 'obvious' skill and so basic to advanced culture that no 'civilized' people can be without it. But, curiously, the problem here is a marked indifference to what writing *is* and, therefore, to the question of why 'civilized' culture is confined to it. What are the effects of writing? Why are these effects confined to 'literate' peoples?

To answer these questions it is necessary to give a more or less rigorous definition of 'writing'. I.J. Gelb in *A Study of Writing* (1963) draws the dividing line between writing proper and various systems of representational signs, such as pictograms, in terms of the principle of phonetization. Writing proper uses visual signs to represent sounds or sound groups in spoken language. This is not a literal mirroring for the relation between the written and spoken languages is always inexact and conventional, even in alphabetic systems. Egyptian hieroglyphic writing was a form of representation of spoken language. Even modern Chinese takes some account of spoken elements. Gelb is thus arguing that a pure logography, in which signs represent individual 'ideas' independent of spoken sounds, has never existed. The burden of memorizing the thousands of signs needed to represent idea units or words would radically restrict its communicative or even mnemonic value.

Now this enables us both to define *and* to limit the effects of writing proper. As a means of record and information storage, writing based on the principle of phonetization has its rivals. The records of bureaucracies and techniques of complex administration can make do with other simpler systems, which do not attempt to represent or 'stand for' spoken language at all. Sophisticated literatures and high cultures do not necessarily depend on writing or physical mnemonic devices. Oral poetry, based on techniques of composition in recitation (which we shall return to in more detail), can create grammatically and thematically complex genres. Thus, while writing systems do affect what can be said in important ways, they by no means define the preconditions of 'civilization'. Large-scale administrations and 'literate' elites can exist without writing in any proper sense or at all.

Writing is not the dramatic innovation it seems to be, the enabling condition of an entirely different level of culture — or, rather, it is not so until its mechanical reproduction and stabilization in printing. Large literate populations and scribal-based public literatures are to be found perhaps only in the heyday of the Roman empire and in the cities of the later Middle Ages immediately prior to print. The former came to ruin, preserved in patches and almost by chance. The latter civilization was transformed and immeasurably aided in its work of recovering the literature and culture of Antiquity by the invention of printing. Scribal culture prior to print was fragile and far from independent of the spoken language.

We shall now consider how 'illiterate', unlettered peoples have been able to deal with the following tasks: to practice elaborate 'literary' composition and storytelling; to carry on a complex large-scale administration of a state or empire. This is not to decry writing as a technique but, on the contrary, to stress that the techniques by which complex mental operations are made possible and furthered are various. We will therefore be examining *other* techniques which affect the form and capacities of human thinking, devices which have some of the effects commonly imputed to writing alone.

A work like Homer's *Iliad* is indisputably 'literary', having an elaborate story and complex stylistic devices. How could such a work be composed before writing? Even if Homer's epic *had* been composed in writing by a single author, how could it be preserved from destruction in the process of its dissemination in a non-literate culture by the numerous bards and storytellers who would have been essential to its widespread public reception? Such a process of memorization and re-telling invariably involves forms of 'drift', a process of garbling, changes and substitutions which both break up the integrity of and proliferate versions of the 'original' text. This difficulty arises when one supposes an 'author' (or even several authors) and asks how was this original work preserved. Albert Lord, in *A Singer of Tales* (1960) attempts to answer these questions by radically changing their terms,[14] and moving away from the idea of an origin-text which is preserved-distorted. 'Homer' was unquestionably an oral poet. He 'composed' not a set text, but a tale capable of oral transmission by bards. It would be impossible for the bard to memorize and repeat a set text. To show *how* Homer was relayed by bards Lord turns away from Antiquity to contemporary Yugoslavia, to the methods of the folk poets, who compose and perform oral epic poetry in a largely non-literate culture. The text is 'preserved' by its being composed and recomposed in recitation. Tales are constructed as a storyline delivered according to a set of formulaic elements which are learned, repeated, and recombined. The bard learns a repertoire of devices and phrases appropriate to certain themes and situations. He draws on these to produce a text *in recitation* rather than remembering a given text. The notion of 'drift' is alien here. The text exists only in performance and necessarily varies. 'Homer' is thus the property of a collectivity of specialist reciter-composers.

In like manner we can challenge the need for 'written' records in the accounting and control of resources necessary for large-scale administration. Karl Polanyi argues persuasively that non-literate peoples may possess 'administrative devices which served operationally as substitutes for written records' (Polanyi 1966: 41). Such techniques are, for certain purposes, *operationally* equivalent to writing. As Polanyi shows in *Dahomey and the Slave Trade* (1966), the warlike African kingdom of Dahomey which rose to power in the eighteenth century depended on a system of tight controls on the available military population and livestock. Censuses were taken, with military quotas and tax levels worked out from the returns provided. The king's administration kept a careful check of the figures and was able to prevent local frauds. The means used was an 'accounting' system based on tallies of pebbles kept in boxes, and 'returns' in the form of pebbles in sacks sent in by local notables.[15]

A similar technique serving a complex administration is to be found in the Inca empire of pre-Columbian South America.[16] The Inca ruled an elaborate and extensive state system in which there was detailed administrative control of production and distribution. State magazines provided clothes, supplies for war and to relieve local disasters. Records and stock control for this complicated system were based on an instrument called the *quipu*. The *quipu* was a cord about two feet long from which cords were suspended like a fringe and knotted. These devices could be used both to enumerate resources and to signify their nature. Colours signified different objects, white threads standing for silver, yellow threads for gold, etc. Specialist officials, called *quipucamayus* (keepers of the *quipus*), were assigned particular tasks: population census, recording production by artisans, recording resources in the magazines. They reported annually to the capital by means of a system of runners and good paved roads. In addition the *quipus* could be used to represent abstract ideas, for instance, white cords signified peace and red war; they could thereby be used to send 'messages'. The *quipu* were also used to keep the national annals. The specialist annalists, *amantas*, used the *quipu* as mnemonics to record the history of the empire and recall it in oral delivery. The historian William Prescott concludes perceptively in his *History of the Conquest of Peru*:

> 'Yet we must be careful not to underrate the real value of the Peruvian system, nor to suppose that the *quipus* were as awkward an instrument in the hand of a practised native as they would be in ours. We know the effect of habit in all mechanical operations, and the Spaniards bear constant testimony to the adroitness and accuracy of the Peruvians in this. Their skill is not more surprising than the facility with which habit enables us to master the contents of a printed page, comprehending thousands of separate characters, by a single glance, as it were, though each character must require a distinct recognition by the eye, and that, too, without breaking the chain of thought in the reader's mind.'
>
> (Prescott 1959: 59)

And so, to printing.[17] Printing may be defined as the mechanical reproduction and duplication of writing by means of movable type. The consequences of this technology are by no means so limited as the definition might imply. The medium transforms reading, writing, and learning in their techniques and character as well as what is read, written, and learnt. Before we proceed it is important to note both how *recent* the invention of printing is in relation to the previous millenia of literacy — from experiments in the middle of the fifteenth century, it was in general use by its end — and how *rapid* was its rise to dominance, which is illustrated by the fact that by the end of the sixteenth century culture and instruction throughout Europe were based on the printed word. The output of the early presses was huge, even in modern terms. Febvre and Martin (1976) estimate that 20 million copies of books were printed *before 1500* and between 150 and 200 million copies were published in the sixteenth century.[18]

Preceding 'literate' civilizations differed from our own in that, firstly, *oral language dominated written language* and, secondly, literacy and illiteracy had implications different from those associated with our own print-dominated civilization. The key work in the investigation of this difference between scribal culture and a printed culture is H.J. Chaytor's *From Script to Print* (1945), a short but suggestive essay by a leading student of medieval literature. We will sum up the effects of print in a series of themes.

Dominance of the spoken word

We forget the labour needed to make a manuscript book. Scribal texts and records cannot last if they are frequently used by many hands. The wastage of printed books does not concern us because of the reproductive powers of the press. In the production of books by hand, however, copying is not only laborious and time-consuming, it also introduces numerous copyists' errors and variants into the text. Scribal culture was always a struggle to prevent or keep up with wastage and demands for new copies, and to preserve the integrity of the text against the dispersion imposed by copying. Paradoxically, the whole tendency of scribal culture was towards locking the book away. Texts and books in a scribal culture must therefore be relatively rare items of restricted use.

Mass schooling in a literate culture is thus almost impossible without printing. Literacy in a pre-print civilization cannot therefore define 'culturedness' in the way it does for us. Whilst this limitation on education meant that the literate person in a non-print civilization possessed a valuable specialized skill, it was a skill exercised in the service of a *spoken* culture. As a member of the mainstream culture the literate person's learning and language was dominated by orality. Literacy was not the everyday means of cultured communication, but a skill ancillary to it.

Because manuscript books were limited in number, personal possession of them was limited to the relatively wealthy and in the case of scholars or lawyers to little more than a few texts essential to work. Books therefore tended to take the form of compendia, either a single work serving all aspects of a subject, like natural history, or a single book serving many functions, as in books of hours. Manuscript books often served as a store of materials for *oral* reproduction. Textbooks would be read from by teachers at the universities (*lecturer* meant literally 'reader of books') and students would produce their own copies by listening and taking notes. Tales and poems were often *composed* in a written form in the European Middle Ages but delivered in an oral form. Spoken performance therefore sets its demands on composition, dictating a good deal of the preference for romances consisting of a series of episodes sufficient in themselves and not too long to tax listeners, and in style emphasizing enunciated literary effects such as alliteration and rhyme. The literate man or woman preserved spoken language and enunciated written language: writing was a practice conducted in direct relation to the mass of non-literate language-users. The person who could not read was not cut off from literature. Thus in the 'courtly' civilizations of Provence and Burgundy the members of a highly cultivated nobility were often illiterate and yet steeped in literature composed in writing.[19]

This dominance of the spoken word affected the nature and usage of written language. The written text was always subjected to patterns of spoken usage, condemned to follow patterns of language drift and to suffer the mutilations of scribal drift. Written language lagged behind, rather than imposing its forms on, spoken language. Given what has been shown about the forms governing recitation, this is of course not to posit spoken language as a natural and spontaneous expression.

Memory

'Our memories have been impaired by print; we know we need not "burden our memories" with matter which we can find merely by taking a book from a shelf. When a large proportion of a population is illiterate and books are scarce, memories are often tenacious to a degree outside modern European experience.'

(Chaytor 1945: 116)

This tenacious memory was not something that 'just growed'. It was the product of definite techniques and had psychological and intellectual consequences. We have seen that in a scribal culture books were rare and precious commodities. Most students would not have access to them for private study and most people would not have easy access to them once away from court, town, or monastery. Culture could not be left in books. One was all too easily sundered from them.

High Antiquity and the later Middle Ages presented the combination of complex bodies of learning and knowledge (law, medicine, philosophy, and theology) conducted through writing but by practitioners who had only limited and intermittent access to the written word. The contradiction was resolved by forms of systematization of knowledge and training of memory. In *The Art of Memory* (1969) Frances A. Yates describes how the classical 'art of memory' was revitalized and developed in the Middle Ages, and she reconstructs these memory techniques and their intellectual consequences. These techniques included straightforward mnemonic devices such as imagining a street or a cathedral, a series of shops or niches, which provided ordered receptacles to 'place' information. Retention and recall were thus aided: to retrieve some item of knowledge one conducted an imaginary walk past the 'places' in question until one found it. These imaginary spaces served both as systematic stores for information and 'keys' to the retrieval of any given unit. It is interesting to note that the Soviet psychologist A.R. Luria (1975) found just such devices in use by a music hall memory artiste he studied in the 1920s.

But the necessities of memory also affected the forms of order and the content of knowledge itself. Thus the Middle Ages are marked in analytic and observational knowledges by the dominance of 'systems' − ordered hierarchies of categories exemplified by Aquinas' *Summa Theologica*. The importance of the forms of order needed to *retain* knowledge limited the ability to re-cast it or to eliminate material from the corpus of the known. Yet it would be absurd to regard medieval philosophy as inherently *uncritical*. No period which could produce

'Ockham's razor' could be accused of that. Nor was observational knowledge indifferent to new materials: A.C. Crombie (1961) has rehabilitated
the 'empiricism' of medieval science. Rather, the problem consists in
certain powerful conservative and syncretistic tendencies imposed by the
basis of storing, presenting, and recalling knowledge itself. The tendency
was to add the new to the known, rather than re-ordering the known to
accommodate the new. One's memory theatre could not easily be re-cast,
but it could easily be added to. Texts that were alluded to in compendia
could seldom be seen, compared, or cross-referenced. Accounts could
seldom be placed alongside others and discrepancies noted. The means
to systematize the body of the known tended to eliminate or suspend
the contradictions in it. By contrast, a so-called 'critical attitude' tends
to accompany the accumulation of material on a massive scale and the
co-presence of different accounts both made possible by print. *Selection
and rejection* became necessary skills to the scholarly reader as against
retention as the primary faculty of a trained memory. A non-print literate
culture will tend to reinforce forms of order which are conservative of
material rather than techniques of analysis interpretative of material.

Stability and order in language use

Printing has effects on the forms of language use which are the opposite of
its effects on the content of knowledge: definite tendencies towards
stabilization and conservation. However, the ramifications of these
tendencies have been revolutionary rather than conservative. The printed
page makes possible the uniform and standardized presentation of
language. Rationalized typefaces and page layout, stylized punctuation,
the organization of a book by a contents page, index, and so on, all
impose new forms of order on language. We should note the immense
effort that went into this process in the first century of print. It was
anything but 'automatic'.

Chaytor (1945) contends that medieval readers, even highly 'literate'
ones, read aloud or inwardly *recited* the text. Because the written was
dominated by the spoken word, forms of recognition and retention were
auditory; language was fixed and operative through *acoustic images*.
Modern readers, once proficient, visually scan the text, absorbing 'blocks'
of print and recognizing only key features of the letters on the page. For
reading print, language is fixed in *visual images* and these correspond
with forms fixed by print.

Thus the dominant means of reproduction of language before print
was speech, governed by acoustic images. Copying was a difficult task
in an unfamiliar medium, made more difficult by the absence of stabilized
spelling and presentational conventions. Language was subject to an
unstoppable modification resulting from the drift in sound, patterns
of speech, and the accumulating non-standardized errors and variations
of scribes. To illustrate this we have only to turn to a work written in a

pre-print culture. Chaucer's *Canterbury Tales*, written in middle English, is intelligible only with difficulty to a modern native English speaker. The King James Bible, written in a language stabilized by print, *is* readily intelligible and continued until very recently to exert a powerful influence on contemporary language use. Drift in sound patterns has not stopped since the early seventeenth century, but then and now written English has come under the hegemony of the printed text, a process radically hastened by the English Bible itself.

Print's capacities for standardization were rapidly accelerated by two powerful social forces in the period of its emergence. First was the Reformation which generated a demand for mass literacy in order that the people might read the Bible — a demand printing could meet by multiplying both Bibles themselves and grammars and first readers to educate the populace. The success of Protestantism is difficult to imagine without the power of the press. Second, the centralizing tendencies of new 'national' states and Absolutist monarchies generated a demand to constrain and subordinate local powers and cultures. Printing reinforced the tendency towards the scholarly, literary, and administrative use of the 'vernacular' languages, not least by contributing to their standardization and definition, stabilizing one form from amidst a variety of dialects.

Standardization of language accompanied political and reinforced cultural centralization. Printing aided this political process, which had begun before its invention. This is well-evidenced by the policies of successive French monarchs.[20] Regional dialects were suppressed from printed culture as a matter of state policy. High literary languages like the troubadors' Langue d'Oc were thereby converted into the speech of the unlettered common people. The French Academy served as a kind of cultural 'police', defining the forms and usages proper to the national language. The stabilization and uniformity imposed by print made possible the very idea of a proper or 'official' language use. The mass production of educational materials made possible the placing of models of this 'proper' language before everyone who learned to read and write. Language was thereby taken out of the hands of the unlettered common people — although one should be careful not to be too romantic here, for maybe as many as half of the people in urban centres in Protestant countries could read.[21] Slang, illiterate and common speech were disvalued against cultural and official printed language. Such a process would have been much more difficult before print when the written culture was necessarily dominated by oral culture. Education and linguistic homogenization could, after printing, be based on stable models and these made available on a large scale.

The standardizing *tendencies* of print undoubtedly favoured centralization, and large-scale book production was directly connected with religious and state power. Battles over 'official' languages and struggles to get subordinate national languages taught through books in schools, continue to the present day, as the struggle over the teaching of Welsh testifies. *Other* tendencies made possible by print, however, challenged religious and political authority and conformity. Print might stabilize and homogenize the language, but it also made possible the preservation and dissemination of heterodox and novel ideas. Books could be easily smuggled and silently read. Protestant heterodoxy was greatly aided by print, carried silently beyond the centres of official state-supported worship.

Books might promote conformity in linguistic use, but they made possible forms of selectivity and discrimination in respect of ideas and beliefs. The mass production of the stock of *existing* ideologies, beliefs, and knowledges made the contradictions between them and within them — at least potentially — apparent. In the scribal era it was seldom possible to consult more than a fraction of the written culture, generally in the form of the most widely copied compendia of established views. In the era of print, personal libraries and the quantities of works read expanded enormously. As Elizabeth Eisenstein (1979) points out, this increased the possibilities of criticism, the *public* recognition and preservation of differences.[22] In this way a cultural technique, apparently a mere medium of presentation, could radically affect attitudes to beliefs and knowledges by changing the form of their presentation and the patterns of their distribution. By making possible new levels of selectivity, discrimination, and criticism, print contributed to the development in the seventeenth century of the conception of the person as an autonomous and self-possessed entity, a theme we shall discuss in Part Two. It thus affected not merely certain mental operations or capacities but the very conceptions of mentality and personality themselves.

Authorship and property in the word

If the Middle Ages are popularly held to be dominated by 'authorities' — Aristotle, Saint Thomas, Galen, Ptolemy — we encounter a paradox. The scholars of the period and the copyists took liberties with the texts of these 'authors' that would be unthinkable today. Professors would be sacked for plagiarism and incompetence, publishers sued for breach of copyright or malpractice. The 'authorities' were not considered as authorial property, a set text belonging to a particular person. Prevailing attitudes are well illustrated by these remarks of Saint Bonaventura writing in the thirteenth century:

> 'A man might write the works of others, adding and changing nothing, in which case he is simply called a "scribe" [*scriptor*]. Another writes the work of others with additions which are not his own; and he is called a "compiler" [*compilator*]. Another writes both others' work and his own, but with others' work in principal place, adding his own for purposes of explanation; and he is called a "commentator" [*commentator*] .... Another writes both his own work and others'

but with his own work in principal place adding others' for the purpose of confirmation; and such a man should be called an "author" [*auctor*].'

(cited by Eisenstein 1979 Vol.1: 121-22)

Apart from entirely ignoring the dominant modern sense of 'author' — the originator of completely new work — this defines the dominant scribal and scholarly practices very well. Everyone from 'scribe' to 'author' is a 'maker of books'. But books, once 'made', enter a public domain in which they are copied, cannibalized, and commented on. Knowledge is conceived as an impersonal domain, presided over by the great masters (now dead), and open to public appropriation, subject to modification and addition in the body of the texts themselves.

The absence of a stable set text, the need to copy, incorporate, and interpolate in order to 'make' books of general service, makes irrelevant modern concepts of the integrity of the work. We can afford to regard modification and addition by unauthorized others as illegitimate, but the scholar who had limited access to a book and copied portions of it into his own, that new work in turn to be passed on and copied from, was doing a public service.

Print, in stabilizing the text, permits the assignation of *limits* to it. Those limits in turn permit us to mark off the domain of an author, who can then advance a proprietorial claim to it. Medieval conditions of 'book making' could hardly stabilize and limit the text even when they wanted and tried to do so. Medieval manuscript 'copies' vary notoriously and even the *scriptoria* (attempts by the universities to organize supervised copyists' workshops producing required standard texts) could hardly be said to prevent scribal drift. Printing was seized upon by Renaissance humanists and Protestant bibliophiles alike because it offered the prospect of exact reduplication and multiplication of certain texts held to be of cardinal value and authority, the works of the Ancients and the Bible.

The typical medieval 'book' was in fact the binding for a number of manuscripts. It was by no means common to have one text separate from others. Many 'books', as we have seen, were collections of extracts and passages from various other manuscripts, rather like a student's notebook today. Collections of tales and tidbits of information were popular and were re-compiled and re-cycled until their provenance became a matter of convention, conjecture, or indifference. In this context, and in an oral-dominated culture in which tales were recounted in public, the conception of plagiarism could hardly take root. The notion of copyright is an absurdity in a predominantly oral civilization where every book copied is a minor victory over ignorance and wastage. Intellectual property becomes a significant conception only with mechanical reduplication and commercial sale.

The author in the era of print had to wait a considerable time before the recognition of his personal connection with the work became owner-

ship of it in commercial law. The author was differentiated by the characteristics of the printed product, typically a single volume bearing his
name. Printers encouraged this identification as a selling device and
actively promoted recognition of the author by the new device of a title
page at the front of the book. Febvre and Martin comment in *The Coming
of the Book*:

> 'while in the Middle Ages authors had had little interest in attaching
> their name to a work, printers were led to seek out . . . the true identity
> of the author of the works they printed . . . . Contemporary writers who
> had their names attached to hundreds and thousands of copies of their
> works became conscious of their individual reputations. This new kind
> of stimulus was also the sign of a new age when artists began to sign
> their works, and authorship takes on an altogether new significance.'
>
> (Febvre and Martin 1976: 261)

Again we see print contributing a practical basis to the development of
new conceptions of personal identity and of the status of person-as-
proprietor. This change is connected with a myriad of significant changes
in practices related to reading and writing introduced by print.

But we must be careful here. There are no automatic and general effects
of printing or any other technology, no effects independent of social
relations and organized systems of beliefs. Print is a medium which *does*
have significant effects, but not as a medium in and of itself. This is the
primary error of Marshall McLuhan's *The Gutenberg Galaxy* (1962)
— an error, we might add, not shared by the more important of his sources
like Chaytor or Febvre and Martin. McLuhan argues that there are standardized typical psychological effects which result from reading the
printed page and that these effects are virtually irrespective of context,
social relations, and practices, or attributions of significance on the part of
the reader. This can be summed up as the dominance of eye over ear, the
separation of thought and action, head and heart — the formation of a
detached 'typographic man'. This creature can best be sent to join *homo
economicus* and other such 'typical' individuals. As Elizabeth Eisenstein
(1979) suggests, it is foolish to argue that print separated heart and head
— not least because of the mass of suggestive, bawdy, and pornographic
material produced in the first two centuries of print — or, thought and
action — printing actually drove intellectuals into commerce and workshops (the humanist, Aldus Manutius, became a publisher and the astronomer Kepler was kept busy directly supervising the production of his
work in the print shops).[23] What is wrong with such automatic effects
and 'typical' individuals is *not* that they run counter to ideas of individual
free will, creativity, and uniqueness. The human being as a free subject and
author of its own acts is no less of an intellectual construction than 'typographic man'. The fault with conceptions such as McLuhan's is rather that
they ignore the conditions of production of the effects to which they lay
claim. For McLuhan, printing has certain necessary consequences and,

in order that these *necessarily* follow, what they are effective on — the human mentality — must be both constant and directly receptive to these effects. The result is that McLuhan and others like him must construct a human subject with *given* attributes and capacities, even if these attributes amount only to being a blank sheet or *tabula rasa* on which certain media technologies write their effects. It is to counter this notion that human attributes are given, and given independently of definite social relations, that this book has been written. McLuhan, far from confirming our analysis of the specific effects of certain techniques and practices on bodily and psychological skills and capacities, leads to a rigid technological determinism founded upon a fixed conception of human nature.

Isolation and its consequences

Human attributes are the product of training and practice, and they depend for their maintenance on use. Language is a case in point. We all know the disasters involved in trying to put rusty schoolboy French to useful employment. Alexander Selkirk, the model for Defoe's *Robinson Crusoe*, after four years of isolation 'had so much forgot his language, for want of use, that we could scarce understand him, for he seemd to speak his words by halves' (cited in Shattuck 1980: 193). Forms of personal reference and identity are no less dependent on practical application in social relations. Personality and social agency are intimately connected. The 'person' is an effect and support of the repertoires of conduct employed in definite sets of social relations. Social personality depends on being specified in forms of address, in activities like signing one's name, or tending the graves of one's ancestors. Personality is a social and practical construct, dependent on use, and by no means the immediate product of some essentially 'human' experience of consciousness. The social construct — 'person' — is by no means a unity in the way 'consciousness' is held to be in Cartesian philosophy, for example. It is constructed out of the warp and weft of social relations, with all their inconsistencies and just plain contradictions.

Isolation, severance from established repertoires of conduct, can have a marked effect on human attributes and capabilities. We are all familiar with the dramatic rigours of 'brainwashing' and the staged ordeals of 'sensory deprivation' experiments: people can thus be reduced to gibbering idiots or cooperative zombies. *Sensation* as such is not at issue here. Dogs can be made suggestible and cats disorientated. *Any* animal whose mental functions depend on sensory inputs for orientation will suffer more or less radically from their denial — the sole exception would probably be a telepathic sponge. Rather we are concerned with the consequences of reductions in the scope for conduct and the opportunities to practise beliefs and employ skills. Such deprivations may be accompanied by adequate levels of sensory input and still produce marked effects on the capacities and attributes of the individual.

Cohen and Taylor in their book *Psychological Survival* (1972) are concerned with the consequences of long-term imprisonment. Detention under high security conditions for many years leads to a marked deterioration in the capacities and competencies of the individuals involved, unless serious efforts are made to compensate for these deprivations. Cohen and Taylor compare such imprisonment with the isolation of explorers in the polar winter or the severance from normal social relations of the survivors of a natural disaster. What these cases have in common is a reduction in the forms of conduct and practice associated with the 'normal' relations of the persons in question. The beliefs, forms of personal reference and identity, and the mental skills associated with these forms of conduct and practice are thereby threatened with disuse and atrophy.

Isolation in itself does not lead to degeneration. Selkirk fashioned as near a normal and regular life for himself as he could on his desert island. Notwithstanding his difficulties with spoken language he appears to have remained alert and competent. An even more remarkable case is that of Ishi, 'the last wild Indian in North America'.[24] Ishi's tribe, the Yahi, were exterminated by the whites. His small band was finally reduced to fragments and he was alone for several years until he was found exhausted and starving in 1911. During those years of isolation he kept alive the customs and activities of his tribe: he acted like a human museum until he found his last home in the University of California's Museum of Anthropology.

An even more interesting instance of isolation is the cases of 'feral' or abandoned children. In recent years an enormous interest has developed in this issue, sustained by a steady flow of books.[25] This enthusiasm recalls an earlier period of attention at the end of the eighteenth century. In both cases a scientific or philosophical debate and a popular craze fasten on to the same object. The savants discuss the respective roles of nature and nurture, the debts to experience, and the possibility of a genuinely 'feral' existence. The people come to gaze or attend theatrical shows – today they read books or see films.[26] But the common interest and concern, one independent of intellectual fashions or popular tastes, stems from the way these children straddle the boundary between nature and culture. A genuinely feral existence on the part of a *human* child threatens this central opposition in Western beliefs. It threatens both the divide between man and nature and the place of culture as definitive of the human as against the animal.

In considering 'feral' children we cannot, therefore, plunge straightforwardly into questions of nature and nurture, heredity and environment, asking what these cases tell us about the debt we owe to social training. The reason is that these questions are not independent of beliefs in our own civilization which border on the mythological. The furious denials of the very *possibility* of these children having something more to them than the mere diagnosis of a case of idiocy or autism are

A family of 'wild men'

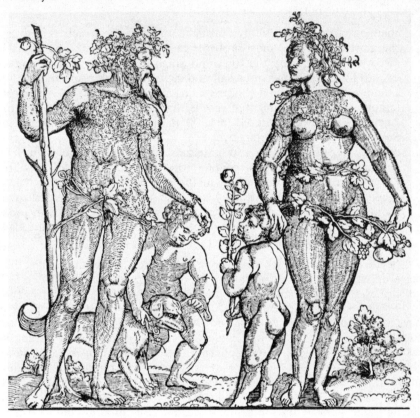

Source: woodcut by Hans Schäufflein from a broadsheet printed in Nuremberg *c.* 1570. Warburg Institute.

denials that a normal child can exist outside of human culture. We find sociologists, anthropologists, and environmentalists just as concerned to deny the 'normality' of these children as were and are believers in heredity and degeneration as explanations of human differences and abnormalities. Two tasks will be interwoven in this discussion: the first, to assess how these debates reflect on the question of the opposition between nature and culture in our culture. This is not merely a matter of attitudes to 'wildness', but also of ideas of human perfectibility, of the opposition between heredity and environment, and so on. And second, thus sobered by the recognition of our continuing investments in mythology, we may be able to realize why such cases of 'feral' children can never function as a 'crucial experiment' in questions of child development, language learning, the acquisition of sexual identities, and so on.

Before we begin these tasks, it may be as well to define what we will consider under the heading of 'feral' children and cite some of the notable cases.[27] Three main types are distinguishable:

i.   abandoned or stolen children brought up by animals such as wolves: the most famous and most probable case is that of Amala and Kamala discovered in 1920 by the Reverend Singh in a wolves' den in north-eastern India, aged one and a half and eight and a half respectively;
ii.   abandoned or absconded children living alone in a wild state: the most famous and best documented case is that of Victor, 'the wild boy of Aveyron', who was captured in 1800 at the village of Saint-Sernin in Southern France aged about twelve;
iii. children kept in isolation and materially supported by adults but left without significant human contact: the two most notable cases are Kaspar Hauser who was found in the streets of Nuremburg in 1828 aged about seventeen, having been kept in isolation in a darkened room since early infancy and fed from behind by a man who took care not to be seen, and Genie, kept in similar isolation in a suburban house in California till 1970 when she was aged about thirteen.

The theme of 'wildness' is no invention of the eighteenth century, no mere derivation from the notion of the 'noble savage'. Indeed, *l'homme sauvage* is a mutation and philosophization of the old folk belief in the 'wild man' common throughout Europe since pre-Christian times. We have not wholly dispensed with him, the wild man and life outside of social relations remain popular, indeed compulsive themes, as instanced by Tarzan and Mowgli. Richard Bernheimer in *Wild Men in the Middle Ages* (1952) points out that there are two prominent and opposed strands in the mythology surrounding the 'wild man'. The first concerns wildness in opposition to culture — the wild man is extravagantly strong, bestial (being large, hairy and unkempt), capable of malice, and sexually predatory. He has all the extravagance and power of nature untamed. He is a threat to be hunted and fought. The second concerns wildness as freedom — the wild man's unrestrained life in the woods is a transgression of the limits of culture; the wild man partakes of the purity of nature and, although free and unrestrained, is capable of unpremeditated good. The savage and the noble savage are combined in one unstable complex of images which present both the fear of and the desire for a transgression of the limits of culture.[28]

The wild child has never been seen as a physical threat — this aspect of our mythologies has passed to the 'savage' proper. But the ambivalence remains. Victor's dirtiness and uncomprehending indifference repelled philosophical observers and environmentalists like Philippe Pinel. Victor was marked down to the animal extravagance of 'idiocy', which reveals the brute in man.

Yet it would be idle to maintain that the *philosophes* of the Enlightenment merely continued and amplified folk beliefs. In the eighteenth century savages and wild children cease to be marvels and become one more means to the investigation of man's nature, phenomena to be observed and analysed. This transformation begins with natural history. The object of this discipline — the exhaustive description and classification of all living creatures — eliminates the space of the marvellous and the monstrous. All living beings could be placed in one systematic table, classified as part of a great hierarchy and continuum of organic nature. Linnaeus, in his treatise *Systema Naturae* (1758), delineated the wild man as a distinct variety of the human species, *homo ferus*, along with the different races of man. 'Monsters' (*homo monstrosus*) were also a natural phenomenon, distinct from wild and normal men in possessing gross physical abnormalities. Linnaeus attempted to summarize the characteristics of reported cases and observations, putting mythology into the language of science and reducing the monstrous powers of wildness to the mere attributes of an animal. *Homo ferus* was *mutus*, *hirsutus*, and *tetrapus*, a hairy being without language who ran on all fours and yet had a 'human' shape. Man properly speaking is, however, a speaking, hairless animal of erect posture. Classification and exhaustive description thus served to establish the observable attributes definitive of the species.

It is philosophy which makes the question of wild children or 'natural man' an important one, and which endows such cases with the status of a 'crucial experiment'. Radical empiricism or sensationalism, the dominant philosophical theory in the eighteenth century, maintained that men acquire their knowledge, ideas, and attributes through sensory experience. John Locke, in challenging the thesis of innate ideas, argued that all knowledge of the external world, all complex ideas, consists in generalizations from simple ideas which are the mental images of sense perceptions. Locke's philosophical position was most systematically developed and amplified by the French philosopher Étienne de Condillac whose most important work in this regard was the *Essai sur l'origine des connaissances humaines* (1746). Condillac carried empiricism or sensationalism to its logical conclusion: for him there is no essential difference between animate and inanimate matter. The differences between classes of being are acquired properties which depend on their capacity to receive, store, and utilize experiences. Men are superior to other animals because they possess reason, but they do so *only because they have developed the use of complex signs*. Condillac thereby attempts to get over a notorious philosophical difficulty in radical empiricism: how to move from individual images of sense perception — which must be unique, discrete, and fleeting — to complex ideas which group such perceptions into classes and recognize them as being the same. Signs, and language in particular, enable us to develop ways of representing complexes of perceptions, a means of calling them to mind again, and the formation of links between them. Language thus provides the basis for reasoning in providing connections between, and generalizations from, sense perceptions. Language is an acquired ability of the human species and each individual has to be trained in its use, recapitulating the natural development of man.

Ideas and signs are linked; so likewise are knowledge and needs. Capacities to know depend on the keenness with which different senses are developed and sense impressions differentiated. This differentiation depends on the demands placed on our senses, and those demands on our needs. Extend the range of human needs and one extends the range of sensations and, therefore, of human abilities. Environment, language, and social development are thus essential to the formation of the capacities conceived of as distinctly 'human', to reason and to speak. Isolation will thus reveal purely 'natural' endowment, what sense experience, unassisted by training and civilized needs, can produce in the individual. Condillac mentions feral children as such a form of demonstration.

So did Jean-Jacques Rousseau. Rousseau has been labelled as the father of the 'noble savage', but Rousseau's 'man in the state of nature' is anything but noble. In his *Discourse on the Origin of Inequality Among Men* (1755) Rousseau argues that man's current attributes are the product of a long history of association and that postulating the 'state of nature' is a kind of exercise in abstraction, a stripping away of all that man owes to social relations. Natural man is a creature of instinct and appetite, a virtual zombie — without language or self-consciousness, morality or guilt, without the need to labour or to claim property. Such a man is solitary and wild, living in an eternal present, without ideas and subject to his immediate needs.

Such would be a fair description of the being caught by a tanner digging vegetables from his garden in the cold winter in January 1800. He had been living wild for several years since about the age of five or six. Nearly two years before he had been caught but had managed to run away. Victor, as he came to be called, was the first 'feral' child to be more than a marvel and to come into contact with the new human sciences.[29] The difference between Victor's case and earlier ones, like Peter of Hanover, is remarkable. It reflects a transformation in knowledges and institutions in the preceding half century.

The local government commissioner notified the central authorities and suggested Victor be passed on to the Institute for Deaf Mutes in Paris. This happened after some months during which time he stayed at the orphanage in Saint-Affrique. What is of interest about the Institute is that it had come into existence barely ten years before, when the Revolutionary government gave support to the efforts of the Abbé Sicard to educate the deaf. It was the one type of place then existing which had the educational programme capable of dealing with a child like Victor. The education of the deaf was a direct descendant of empiricism. Its pioneer, the Abbé de l'Epée, agreed with Locke's position that there was no *natural* relation between sounds and ideas, language was just one system of conventional signs which could be replaced by another. Hence the prospect of a systematic language of gestures corresponding to the words of the French language and translatable into it. Condillac endorsed and commended Epée's programme in 1775, and the ambitions of this programme indicate that the attention devoted to Victor was only in part philosophical. Empiricist philosophy had created the possibility of a scientific investigation of man but also, through the role it assigned to signs, sensations, and experience, the possibility of his transformation. It therefore gave rise both to practices of observation and measurement of man, and practices of reform, education, and control. These latter practices, for all their philosophical sponsorship, are not philosophy, but a new and independent domain. The new institutions and techniques of reform, education, and control would have a whole independent history. We shall turn later, in Part Two, to the birth of the asylum and 'moral methods' in the treatment of the insane. What marks these institutions − special schools, asylums, penitentiaries − is their organization around the object of training or reforming the individual through the systematic control of his experience, the influences reaching him, and his needs.

When Victor came to Paris he was lodged at the Institute and became the special charge of a body called the Society of Observers of Man. This society, which included Sicard and Pinel among its members, was strongly influenced by Condillac and the philosophers following him who called themselves the Ideologues. The Ideologues were committed to the rigorous measurement of man and to a naturalistic analysis of the origin and contents of thought. The members of the Society who examined Victor found him wanting: Pinel, chief among them, diagnosed him as an 'idiot'. Victor would probably have been sent to the chronic wards of the asylum of Bicêtre had it not been for the intervention of Jean Itard, surgeon at the Institute.

We have here a dispute between the disciples of Condillac. Pinel, committed to 'moral methods' in the treatment of insanity, was dependent on linguistic communication in his methods of therapy. Since idiocy was held to be the result of organic lesion or inherited deficiency, the 'idiot' was incapable of education and normal language use and therefore beyond such therapy. Pinel's report is a good example of bad and tendentious diagnosis. Confronted with a mute, filthy, and distracted boy he notes only those signs which fit the clinical picture of idiocy. Particularly damning were Victor's lack of attention and weak faculty for imitation, deficiencies which meant there was no prospect of education. Pinel concludes that, far from being a 'savage', he is just a common idiot abandoned by his parents. Itard, Pinel's diagnosis notwithstanding, was permitted to attempt to educate Victor.

Itard began a programme of education especially designed for Victor. He sought to develop his faculties by diversifying his experiences and multiplying his needs, using techniques based on Condillac's conception of the development of human knowledge. With the goal of developing a capacity for language use, Itard's techniques were designed to show Victor the relation between signs and their referents. Curiously, he did not try to use sign language or to encourage and respond to the limited sounds the boy produced as one would with an ordinary baby, or to put Victor in a position where the boy had to communicate with other children. His techniques, although constantly inventive and without precedent, were crippled by a philosophical theory of the nature of the sign and the conviction that language use is based on an explicit recognition of the relation between words and things.[30]

In his Reports of 1801 and 1806 Itard showed that Victor was far from being an 'idiot' in Pinel's sense, that is, wholly ineducable and incapable of forming lasting human associations. Victor had shown an ability to learn, a definite independence of mind, and formed a genuine and lasting attachment to Itard and Madame Guerin. He was in many respects indistinguishable from a normal child, though admittedly one who could not speak and therefore had no access to the higher mental functions and more complex activities conducted through language. Itard considered this deficiency to be a result of his own failure to teach the boy the use of language. For all that, Itard's 'failure' with Victor laid the foundation for his work in the education of the deaf and his successors' work in the education of supposedly ineducable 'idiots'. As Harlan Lane (1977) points out, the techniques he developed to teach Victor have become part and parcel of what we now call 'special education' and of nursery school education.[31]

The issues at stake in the case of Victor were twofold, and they have continued to be relevant in analogous cases of isolated, deprived, and deficient children to the present day. The first is the question of what human beings owe to nature and what to experience: such children are seen as offering a test of the existence of innate ideas and a crucial experiment which would reveal what imprint society had upon man. This debate has always been inconclusive. Indeed the experiment could never be 'crucial'. It could never decide the issues at stake because in large measure they are undecidable in the terms which they are posed. How does one resolve the poles of a rigid opposition between 'nature' and 'culture'? The result of the 'test' must always await the future because the abilities and capacities such children acquire depend largely on the skills, techniques, and theories of their trainers. This is the crux of the second issue. Can such children be trained and humanized? In eighteenth-century terms this meant, can we move from simple ideas, sensations, to complex ideas and human sentiments through patterns of the gradual and cumulative association of ideas alone? In modern terms the question centres on whether or not there is a 'critical period' for the acquisition of language and when this period occurs. The two sets of issues have always been complexly related. The limits of available techniques set the limits of the attainments of 'idiots' or children like Victor. The second issue has, however, a definite independence from the first, for it raises questions which are not merely philosophical: questions of special education, pedagogic technique, and diagnosis.

The complex relation between these two issues means that there is no *simple* opposition between environmentalists and hereditarians. Thus we see Pinel — committed to Condillac's sensationalism and to 'moral methods' in the treatment of the insane — place Victor as an idiot in a category beyond reach of these methods. We will see the child psychiatrist Bruno Bettelheim 150 years later make exactly the opposite claim, considering 'feral' children as actually treatable cases of infantile autism. Yet the tactics of the two show some striking similarities, as do their objectives. Bettelheim uses a similarly impressionistic diagnostic technique to resolve these children into a category of commonplace pathological individual, and thereby remove the problems for a *social* science that genuinely 'feral' children would present. We see in the grounds Pinel advances for his judgement the form of the denial of the genuineness of cases of 'feral' children which has predominated up to the present day.

Empiricism had begun its battles with certain forms of philosophical essentialism, with ultimately religious ideas of a fixed nature or spirit innate in man and given by God. Empiricism came to be widely accepted as a methodological doctrine in the sciences, but the thoroughgoing environmentalist implications of thinkers like Condillac were by no means so popular. The poles of the debate shifted from religious essentialism versus empiricism to environmentalism versus naturalism or biologism. Man's nature was not given by God, but by his biological endowments. Children like Victor could thus be placed in a class of biological deficients. They were idiots who happened to stray. Their characteristics were the simple products of organic degeneracy or hereditary defect. Pinel washes his hands because biology has placed the child beyond his environmentalist methods of therapy. This view of 'feral' children was echoed by those who had no place in the environmentalist camp, by the founder of phrenology Franz Joseph Gall (phrenology was not considered an absurdity in the early nineteenth century, a matter of feeling bumps on the cranium, equivalent in its methods to astrology, but as an empirical natural science of the physical determination of human characteristics), and by Johannes Blumenbach, one of the founders of physical anthropology. The systematic study of man faced two ways. Observation and measurement could be conducted in the interests of practices of modification and reform (not all of them radical by any means — in Part Two we shall see a *conservative* environmentalist at work when we come to discuss the birth of the asylum; Condorcet and Godwin never had a monopoly on human 'improvement' and were dilettantes in its practice compared with Pinel and Bentham). Observation and measurement could also sustain a 'natural history' of man, an account of his biologically given nature, and the way in which this fixed and determined his attributes. The Society of Observers of Man, which considered Victor its special charge, faced both of these ways at once.

As the nineteenth century progressed the relations between these two forms of 'scientific' study of man became more complex and antagonistic. Naturalism and biologism received an immense fillip from Darwin*ism*

— idiots, lower races, almost any form of abnormality, could be considered as regressions to lower stages of human development and atavisms.[32] Environmentalism received an immense fillip from socialism and Marxism — man is infinitely perfectible and capable of making his own nature through collective practice. The ideological opposition between varieties of biologism and environmentalism continues to the present day. The hysteria of some of the opponents of sociobiology indicates that more is at stake in such controversies than the relative merits of one scheme of explanation over another. At the same time we see complex 'crossings' of the terrain of the debate — sociologists who rely on biological explanations to exclude certain phenomena from sociological consideration and to defend the integrity of their own institutionalist or culturalist explanations. We saw a variant of this earlier with Robert Hertz's explanation of the universality of right-handedness. We will see another in Lévi-Strauss's contention that 'feral' children are defectives.

From the debates surrounding Victor we turn to those occasioned by the case of Amala and Kamala. The controversy developed following the publication in 1942 of the Reverend Singh's memoir by the good offices of the American anthropologist R.M. Zingg some twenty years after the capture of the two children and more than ten years after the death of the surviving child, Kamala. Singh claimed that the children had been found in a wolves' den by a hunting party (in which he was involved, although on certain occasions he tried to hide his own part in the capture). His account of their behaviour and progress presupposes them to have been raised by wolves and to have acquired from the wolves habits such as running on all fours, nocturnality, eating raw offal, etc.

Bruno Bettelheim sensed the substance of myth in this account — although it had been given relatively wide credence among social scientists.[33] Bettelheim says, quite correctly, that the idea of children being raised by animals, particularly wolves, is an ancient and widespread myth. He argues that it reflects basic human needs to wish away or rationalize certain uncomfortable phenomena. First, the myth that animals did suckle and care for children served to assuage the guilt of parents who exposed their unwanted offspring. It felt a little less like murder to suppose that a friendly wolf might care for the child. Second, the idea that certain children have an 'animal' nature, are no better than beasts, serves to explain away the savage and disgusting behaviour often exhibited by children suffering from infantile autism. Autism is the product of emotional neglect. To conceive of the child as biologically defective assuages the parents' ambivalence and guilt while providing a socially acceptable explanation for inhuman behaviour.

Bettelheim's case for the myth and its origins appears convincing, but there are a number of objections to it. First, his conception of myth is that it is the functional servant of needs. It serves to wish away the unpleasant or rationalize life's contradictions. Now there is no reason to suppose myths arise from 'needs'. This mode of explaining ideas arises because we find their content wholly wrong, absurd, or impossible: there has to be some other reason why someone thought *that* or said *that*. To qualify as 'myth' ideas must be considered incapable of standing on their own merits. Such explanations in terms of 'needs' seldom trouble us in the case, say, of pure mathematics or the twelve-tone scale. Moreover, what 'myths' say is frequently far from comforting and often *creates* contradictions. Consider myths that the world may end through its being devoured by a huge animal. To the extent that what we call 'myths' are complex sets of ideas and categories, it is evidently dangerous to extract one element and assign it, independently of the others, to an origin in a general human need. It can just as easily be considered as being there *because* of its relation to the other elements, as part of a structure of signification, as having the same relation to the complex as a theme in a symphony.[34] Bettelheim's mode of analysing 'myths' is an old one, somewhat discredited in modern anthropology.

Second, the 'needs' myths are supposed to serve in Bettelheim's analysis show that he relies on the idea of generalized and typical human emotions or motivations. As a psychoanalyst, Bettelheim is correct to assert the autonomy of the psychic domain, to insist that human beings are not the mere receptacles for whatever is poured into them by specific sets of social relations — a point we shall return to in our discussion of Freud in Chapter Eight. But that psychic domain does not work like a 'psychology', producing a typical human consciousness. Rather it interacts with and parallels socially specified patterns of conduct, expressions of affect, and expectations as to events. In a society in which children are *regularly* exposed as part of the normal course of events, it is idle to expect the same responses and emotional investments as in the United States where it is assumed that parents will be loving and caring. In discussing why Amala and Kamala were abandoned Bettelheim is reduced to simple, speculative reconstruction because he had no knowledge of the customs and practices of the people in question, the Santals. He refers constantly to a 'culture of poverty' in explaining the behaviour of primitive peoples. The Santals, although a backward minority people in Indian terms, were not 'poverty-stricken' nor did they have a custom of abandoning children in the forest.[35] Mothers would, however, take their children to the fields and leave them close by when working. They could thus be snatched by an animal like the Indian wolf whose habits do include scavenging around human settlements when hungry.

Third, myths about 'wildness' are in no sense confined to the themes mentioned by Bettelheim, as our account of Bernheimer's book shows. There are positive and negative sides to the belief in 'wild' men. The animal is not merely a negative pole in contrast to human nature. Animals can serve as projections of and models for man; their conduct becomes a kind of moral theatre, as in Grandville or the *Fables* of Aesop. Many American Indian peoples, unlike the Europeans, esteemed the wolf as a noble animal.[36] Animality, wildness, and wolves have no general and stable significance across human cultures. These diverse significances cannot easily be accommodated to the notion of a general human 'need', to a common rationalization. Bettelheim puts the reasons for the scholarly and scientific investments in the existence of 'wolf children' rather well:

> 'Embodied in certain theories of behaviourism and social anthropology is the wish ... to see man as wholly created by society. If infants raised by wolves were to become, to all intents, wolves, then we would have to accept that man is nothing but the product of his surroundings and associations. It would seem that there are no inborn functions, no potentials that can either be developed or not by the circumstances of life, but never altered entirely.'

(Bettelheim 1967: 347)

He challenges this view, appealing to psychoanalysis and saying that it has shown that 'no known society has ever done more than to modify *innate* characteristics' (1967: 347, our emphasis). His rejection of this extreme environmentalist view is reasonable but the grounds on which it is made are questionable. Freudian psychoanalysis certainly does regard the human psyche as more than is contained in manifest social codes and institutions but it does not regard the psychic as *innate*. Biological drives are operative and biological capabilities activated by 'psychic representations', through symbols and mental processes. These symbols and processes are not contained 'in' the individual but have a collective dimension. Bettelheim thus supports the existence of innate characteristics against acquired characteristics. He gravitates to one pole of the nature-nurture opposition in a way Freud never did.

Bettelheim is deeply committed to the view that 'I tend to believe from our experience with autistic children, that these wild children could not have survived for very long by themselves, even allowing for the clemency of the Indian weather' (1967: 354). He contends that 'no infant deprived of emotional closeness can live, or not at least as a human being' (1967: 382). The odds on an isolated infant past the weaning stage surviving unaided are remote, for many practical reasons. But are they impossible? Bettelheim seems to think so because of his view of human socialization in general. Central for Bettelheim here is the notion of 'human' — to grow up 'human' depends on emotional care by adults. Without any wish to praise harsh or unfeeling child-rearing practices, we must point out that many children in different times and places have grown into adulthood having survived isolation and neglect. For example, this was the fate of many children put out to wet nurses for their mothers' convenience. The problem here is the notion of the 'human', as if human and non-human, man and animal, were rigidly differentiated. Victor lived for perhaps six years in the wild, from about the age of five or six — he survived severe winters. Until driven distracted by the journey to Paris, and the mixture of neglect and exposure as a public spectacle that followed his arrival there, he welcomed the human contact he received. He inspired affection in the old man, Clair, who first looked after him, and he was tolerated by the peasants whose potatoes and roots he stole whilst still 'wild'. They evidently were not so fussy about the distinction between human and non-human and were content to leave him be. He did not respond to these first human contacts like an autistic child, nor later with Itard or Madame Guerin.

Bettelheim eliminates such ambiguities that threaten the notion of a distinctly 'human' nature by reducing all cases of 'feral' children to autistic children who have been recently abandoned when found. Autism is a phenomenon which arises in culture. It is an evil men do to themselves (in the shape of their children). It can be explained in terms of strictly human motives — of unwanted children neglected and mistreated. We should say here that we have no intention of denying the validity of the category of 'autism' or denying Bettelheim's valuable accounts of therapeutic work with such children — our criticisms start precisely at the point where he strays beyond that specialism into questions of nature and culture. We should add, however, that 'autism' is a syndrome specifying a functional disorder. It is a clinical-observational category like 'schizophrenia' and has similar problems of application in diagnosis.[37] A diagnosis of 'autism' is therefore hardly an unproblematic matter, even for a clinician able to observe a child in some depth.

To diagnose from reports prepared by people ignorant of the category 'autism' is thus highly dangerous. Bettelheim compares the Reverend Singh's memoir point by point with instances from his own case histories to show Amala and Kamala were 'like' autistic children — just as the clergyman did to show that their behaviour was 'like' that of wolves. Neither practice, Singh's or Bettelheim's, can be very conclusive. 'Autism' is a syndrome based on observed behaviours, but not all behaviours like those so classified need proceed from causes similar to those postulated for the syndrome. Now what makes this attempt to 'account for' the behaviours mentioned in Singh's memoir appear both plausible and necessary is the supposition that the children could not have lived with wolves. It does appear absurd to have real-life equivalents of Romulus and Remus in the twentieth century. Bettelheim draws support for his denial of the wolf aspect of the clergyman's tale from the experiences of the American sociologist, W.F. Ogburn in trying to verify cases of 'feral' children when in India.

Now Ogburn convincingly debunked the story of the 'wolf boy' of Agra.[38] He also tried to get to the bottom of the story of Amala and Kamala, but could find neither the village near where they were said to have been captured nor any witnesses.[39] Bettelheim says, 'When Ogburn's report rekindled my interest in the whole subject, a rereading of Singh's account made it altogether likely that out of similar needs he wove [a] fantastic myth and came to take it for the truth' (1967: 351). Which is the nicest possible way of saying that the Reverend Singh was a liar.

Charles Maclean in his book *The Wolf Children* (1979) goes a long way to upset Ogburn's testimony. Worried by the blank drawn by the American sociologist's investigation, the British journalist started to look into how his predecessor had gone about it. He discovered that Ogburn, not unreasonably considering his age and the climate, had done little of the legwork himself and had left matters to his Indian collaborator N.K. Bose, who appears not to have pursued the matter too energetically. Maclean claims that he *did* find the village in question, Godamuri, now renamed Ghorabandha, and in the nearby Santal village of Denganalia met an old man, Lasa Marandi, who had taken part in the hunt which found the girls. This testimony, he assures us, was produced under critical close questioning and revealed incidental details which only a participant or one well-versed in the literature on the case would have known. Which goes to show that almost any event, from the fantastic to the everyday, like a traffic accident or a case of fraud, leaves the neutral observer to choose between contradictory accounts. Bettelheim's grounds for scepticism are thereby undercut but, we very much doubt, finally eliminated. Sceptics will doubt and believers believe. It is useless in issues like this to try to rescue them by going to the 'facts' of the case. Far from being a solid ground for argument, they generally turn out to be a marsh. What is more revealing is to look for the doctrines and beliefs that lead the protagonists to adopt different attitudes to the 'facts' in the first place.

Claude Lévi-Strauss is clear on this point: 'No empirical analysis ... can determine the point of transition between natural and cultural facts, nor how they are connected' (1969: 8). He shows a healthy scepticism about the possibility of an *empirical* differentiation between nature and culture on the grounds that we can find no pre-social state in the evolution of the human species and because there is no clear way of assigning attributes exclusively to natural causes or to social conditions. But, for all that, he retains the distinction between nature and culture as a means to characterize the specificity of the social. Nature and culture are thus opposed as distinct domains. What is specific to culture are rules which do not reflect natural necessities and even deny natural possibilities of human action. Instituted rules offer 'the surest criterion for distinguishing a natural from a cultural process' (1969: 8). We will return to these points in our discussion of the universality of Freud's concept of the 'Oedipus complex' in Chapter Eight. The point to be made here is that Lévi-Strauss continues to use the notion of 'society' or 'culture' as a homogenous entity of a single class and which can be opposed *theoretically* to (if not differentiated empirically from) 'nature'. He remains more of a Durkheimian than he might think.

Lévi-Strauss dismisses the significance of 'wolf children': 'it seems clear enough from past accounts that most of these children were congenital defectives, and that their imbecility was the cause of their initial abandonment, and not, as might sometimes be insisted, the result' (1969: 5). We have seen how dubious was Pinel's judgement in the case of Victor. 'Past accounts' are by no means 'clear enough' to allow Lévi-Strauss to make this claim. Lévi-Strauss supports a point made by Blumenbach against the idea of 'feral' children, which is that since man is a social animal he has no inbuilt natural behaviour to which he could regress, unlike a domesticated dog or cat. Wild children 'may be cultural monstrosities, but under no circumstances can they provide reliable evidence of an earlier state' (1969: 5). Yet this seems hardly to have been the main point at issue in the disputes surrounding 'feral' children. Even Rousseau's 'man in the state of nature' was a theoretical device which served to reveal human malleability and the vicious influence on man's character of depraved and servile social customs. The protagonists of environmentalism were looking for just such evidence of malleability, educability, and the absence of a fixed nature, and not for evidence of some actual pre-social state. Lucien Malson continues this environmentalist investment into the twentieth century in his book *Wolf Children* (1972). He rebuts Lévi-Strauss's point and draws the conclusion that 'human nature' is a myth. The evidence presented by cases of wild children confirms the view that man's nature is social and depends on education.

This is a suitably socialist conclusion (one that no doubt justified its anomalous translation in a left-wing series). But, one's own political sympathies apart, 'feral' children neither confirm nor deny such a view. If children *can* survive from early infancy unaided by parents or complex learned social skills then human existence as such in no sense depends on social relations. Such an existence may be 'nasty, brutish and short', but it is not impossible. It is for this reason that those who, like Bettelheim, are committed believers in the crucial role of affection and education in human development deny the existence of genuinely 'feral' children. Lévi-Strauss is right that there is no *empirical* resolution to the opposition between nature and culture, nor is there, we might add, to the other oppositions related to it — nature and nurture, human and animal, and so on — certainly not one that could be offered by the, deeply disputed, existence of 'feral' children.

We have tried to show that the sources of definite mental and physical attributes can be sought in forms of technique, training, and practice dependent on social relations. At the same time we have seen that these forms intersect with and are made effective by definite physiological processes and bodily aptitudes. To move beyond particular attributes, beyond physical skills and mental processes, into questions of 'human nature' seems to us dubious in the extreme. Both the proponents of a fixed human nature *and* the believers in the infinite malleability and educability of man are committed to rival and sterile essentialisms. We have tried to show that there can be no resolution of such theoretical and ideological antinomies, only ways of effecting their dissolution by asking other questions.

One question has been absent from this discussion. Whilst language has occupied the primary place in our discussion of the educative efforts of Itard and Singh, sexuality has been virtually ignored. In Itard's and Singh's reports sexuality is relegated to the margins, it is an ominous silence, and it sneaks in only when matters of 'decency' are at issue. Itard admits he had to curtail hot baths and massages because they excited the boy too much. Further Victor was clearly disturbed by the onset of puberty. He was attracted to girls, but had no idea of what to 'do' with them. This caused Itard some embarrassment in his excursions with Victor. We cannot expect Itard, the pioneer of 'special' education, to have been a pioneer of sex education too. We know no more about the boy's sexuality, and about that of Amala and Kamala virtually nothing. Genie, it is reported, masturbated incessantly.

One could use such cases as evidence of the thesis that human sexual practices and identities must be learned and are not 'naturally' given. But one must be careful in doing so. Psychoanalysis demonstrates that children acquire sexual beliefs and practices remarkably early. None of these 'feral' children can be viewed as a sexual *tabula rasa*.

Notes

1 Lévi-Strauss, 'The Family' (1971) and *The Elementary Structures of Kinship* (1969: Chs. 1 and 11).
2 First published in *Année Sociologique* **X** (1907: 48-137) and reprinted in Hertz *Death and the Right Hand* (1960). Hertz's essay has also been reprinted together with a number of valuable essays on the right-left polarity in particular cultures in R. Needham (ed.) *Right and Left* (1973).
3 This conception of society is examined and criticized in P.Q. Hirst *Durkheim, Bernard and Epistemology* (1975).
4 Ariès has also published a longer study than the short volume of lectures published in English, *L'homme devant la mort* (1979).
5 Cannon's account of the *physiological mechanism* of 'voodoo death' can be supplemented by reading Marcel Mauss' interesting essay 'The Physical Effect of the Idea of Death Suggested by the Collectivity' which refers to ethnographers' and travellers' accounts of such deaths in Australia and New Zealand (Mauss 1979: Part II). Mauss contends that these facts confirm Durkheim's theory of anomic suicide (1979: 54). The problem with this is that, apart from seeming more aptly to be a case of altruistic suicide, Durkheim defines a suicide as 'a positive or negative act of the victim himself, which he knows will produce this result' (Durkheim 1951: 44). In a case of bewitchment, however, the individual believes he is subject to an inescapable process, not engaging in an *act*. The result is known with certainty but precisely because it is believed that no act on the part of the victim can avert it. It is difficult to call such cases of death 'suicides' unless we ignore the beliefs in question considering the individual 'really' responsible for his own death, but if one does so set them aside we would be at a loss to explain the state of fear which causes death.
6 First published in *Revue Philosophique*, **LXVIII** (1909: 553-80) and reprinted in Hertz (1960).
7 See the footnote by R. Needham to Hertz (1960: 90). Ted Polhemus *Social Aspects of the Human Body* (1978) argues that Hertz satisfactorily unites biologi-

cal and sociological explanations, allowing workers in the two fields to cooperate. We have tried to show that Hertz does nothing of the sort, that he uses a biological grounding for an explanation and a conception of sociology that is exclusively sociological.

8   See Hirst (1975: 122-35).

9   First published in English in *Economy and Society*, 2 1 (1973: 70-88) and reprinted in Mauss (1979: Part IV). Mauss' essay is discussed in Mary Douglas *Natural Symbols* (1970a: Ch. 5) and in Polhemus (1978).

10   Laurens Van der Post (1963). Marshall Sahlins (1974: Ch. 1) points out how dangerous it is to assume the life of hunting and gathering peoples is 'nasty, brutish and short'. Western travellers and ethnographers have done so because they have put themselves in their position, ignoring their special bodily and economic skills and capacities.

11   We are well aware how dubious the distinction between 'form' and 'content' is, as is the notion of 'idea': they are used here merely for expositional purposes and imply no theoretical commitment.

12   A notable exception to these tendencies is the work of Jack Goody. In *The Domestication of the Savage Mind* (1977) he tries to examine the problem of fundamental differences in 'forms of thought' with reference to the consequences of literacy. In terms of our analysis he places too much emphasis on writing as such as against printing, he differs in his use of the work of A.B. Lord and Milman Parry, and he tends to treat as consequences of *literacy* forms of thinking and practices which, arguably, were by no means well established in the mid-seventeenth century – after almost two centuries of printing. His treatment of list making and tabular presentation are most interesting. See also Goody and Watt (1963).

13   See Kroeber and Parsons (1958).

14   Lord owed a great debt to Milman Parry and continued his work.

15   See Polanyi (1966: 40-9). In a similar way Alexander Thom has shown that megalithic stone circles in Britain are laid out in ways that suppose surveying methods and which imply certain geometrical capabilities. These capabilities were, however, probably not obtained by means of geometrical theories like those of the Greeks, rather through techniques which have similar – though unreflected – operational effects; see Thom *Megalithic Sites in Britain* (1967).

16   See W. Prescott *History of the Conquest of Peru* (1959) for the classic account of Inca institutions; for the *quipus* see Ch. IV. For a modern account of the Inca civilization see Victor Wolfgang von Hagen *The Ancient Sun Kingdoms of the Americas* (1973: Chs. 13-18) and especially (1973: 314-17) for the *quipus*.

17   The account given below is largely dependent on the following works: H.J. Chaytor *From Script to Print* (1945); E.L. Eisenstein *The Printing Press as an Agent of Change* (1979); L. Febvre and H.-J. Martin *The Coming of the Book* (1976).

18   Febvre and Martin (1976: 248, 262).

19   We must avoid the danger of assuming that spoken language prior to *writing* is like colloquial language in the modern era. To do so is to deny that it can possess 'writerly' qualities in eloquence, syntax, etc. The dominance of printing has led to a tendency to privilege the *spoken* word as more real and more personal, as the true evocation of the speaking subject. And in consequence to treat writing as a mere record – although a distorting and reductive one – of the spoken. Jean-Jacques Rousseau is a notable example of these philosophical tendencies which

are still influential today. Jacques Derrida in his book *Of Grammatology* (1976) has tried to argue against this philosophical and popular prejudice by contending that *writing* is not reducible to marks on paper, that *all* language is *like writing* in that it is not the pure presence of the voice, of the person. Rather, it is a *trace* — a construction which always leaves something unsaid, whose 'meaning', to be completed, must always be doubled by the 'next line' and so on *ad infinitum*. Although immensely difficult for the philosophically or philologically unprepared reader his works repay close study.

20 For the politics surrounding the development of the French language during the Revolution but also with some account of the Ancien Regime see Renée Balibar and Dominique Laporte *Le Français national* (1974).

21 See C.M. Cipolla *Literacy and Economic Development in the West* (1969: Ch. 2 — particularly p.60).

22 Eisenstein (1979: Vol.I, Ch.2).

23 See Eisenstein (1979: Vol.I, 150-53).

24 See Kroeber (1961) for an account of his tribe and a touching memoir of his life.

25 Of special value are: Lucien Malson *Wolf-Children* (1972); Harlan Lane, *The Wild Boy of Aveyron* (1977); R.M. Zingg 'Feral Man and Extreme Cases of Isolation' (1940). All of these offer general surveys of cases and/or an extensive discussion of the philosophical issues at stake. E. Dudley and M.E. Novak (eds) *The Wild Man Within* (1972) is a useful survey of the relation of conceptions of 'wildness' to western intellectual debates.

26 Two notable films are François Truffaut's *L'Enfant Sauvage* and Werner Herzog's *The Enigma of Kaspar Hauser*.

27 Both Malson (1972) and Zingg (1940) attempt to list the known cases at the time of their writing.

28 For a further discussion of Western cultural responses to the themes of 'wildness' and 'primitivism' see Boas and Lovejoy (1935) for Antiquity and Boas (1948) for the Middle Ages. Wittkower (1976) discusses the medieval depiction of monsters and marvels; see also Hayden White 'The Forms of Wildness: Archaeology of an Idea' in Dudley and Novak (1972).

29 Peter the 'wild boy' of Hanover was brought to London in 1726 and given to the famous Dr. Arbuthnot, who had been physician to Queen Anne, to train. However, he had no system and Peter made little progress, being boarded out in the country until his death. The case generated none of the mass of materials we associate with Victor because the institutional and intellectual conditions for the later forms of attention were not then in existence (Shattuck 1980: 194-95); see also M.E. Novak 'The Wild Man Comes to Tea' in Dudley and Novak (1972: 183-221).

30 For Itard's techniques and their relation to problems of language development see Lane (1977: Ch.7).

31 Lane (1977: Chs.8-10).

32 Darwin*ism* is by no means the same thing as Darwin's theory of natural selection, see Hirst (1976a: Ch.2). Moreover, believers in the hereditary transmission of qualities like intelligence, genius etc. need not deny the possibility of 'feral' children — Francis Galton believed in them. Marx and Engels took up Darwin's views enthusiastically *because* they believed in the malleability of human nature — Darwin's view established the *changeability* of species characteristics, as against the more conservative palaeontologists who held to the fixity of species.

33 A good example of sociological treatment of 'wolf children' as a mere variant of cases of extreme isolation is Kingsley Davis' famous textbook *Human Society* (1961: 204).

34 See for example Lévi-Strauss 'The Structural Study of Myth' (1968: Vol.1).

35 For Bettelheim's remarks about 'poverty-stricken' peoples see *The Empty Fortress* (1967: 355-56). On the Santals and the habits of the Indian wolf see Maclean (1979: Ch.2).

36 For an account of humans' attitudes to wolves see Lopez *Of Wolves and Men* (1978).

37 See Chapter Ten for a discussion of the problems associated with the category of 'schizophrenia'. Lane and Pillard point out that infantile autism is now held to include at least two different varieties, that it can be difficult to distinguish autism from schizophrenia and other disorders, that there is 'no specific test for autism' and that: 'Further studies analysed the families of autistic children ... and found nothing to link the home environment with autism. Currently ... [the] ... psychogenic explanation of autism is out of vogue' (1978: 113).

38 Ogburn (1959); for an even more vigorous example of debunking of a reported case of a 'feral' child in Burundi in 1974 see Lane and Pillard (1978).

39 Ogburn and Bose (1959).

3

THE SIMILARITIES AND DIFFERENCES BETWEEN HUMAN AND ANIMAL SOCIETIES

'while the human world depends on the senses, and the whole panoply of organic characteristics supplied by biological evolution, its freedom from biology consists in just the capacity to give these their sense.'

(Sahlins 1977: 12)

'There is clearly some sense in which human action and society are related to animals, for we have a long animal social past, our bodies and minds are the outcome of evolution and we *are* in fact animals, not vegetables or gods.'

(Reynolds 1980: 45)

In the last chapter we considered a number of themes of importance for the debates we will consider in this chapter: the opposition between nature and culture, the various lines of differentiation between the human and the animal, and attitudes to 'wildness'. In this chapter we will develop and explore these themes, concentrating on the debates surrounding primate societies and attempts to interpret human social relations in terms of ethology and sociobiology. We saw that the question of language occupied a central place in the debates about 'wolf children', and that of sexuality an equally important place as an ominous silence. The questions of language and sexuality are similarly central in the analysis of the similarities and differences between human and animal societies.

The issue at stake in the debates about the methods of analysis of human and animal societies is the autonomy of 'culture'. Sociologists and cultural anthropologists are concerned to defend their claim to a distinct object of study against methods which assert its fundamental continuity with the biological realm. The boundary dispute is hardly a new one: Durkheim staked an exclusive claim to the social on behalf of sociology at the turn of the century. The modern descendants of Durkheim are still fighting for the notion of the 'social' (or 'culture') as a distinct and autonomous realm which exclusively defines the human. In querying this conception, we have no intention of arguing *in favour* of an ethological or sociobiological account of human social relations. These theories suffer from evident and incapacitating weaknesses if they purport to give anything resembling a comprehensive account of human practices and social institutions. Sociobiology is far from being in a position to fulfill the fond hopes of its creators and form the key discipline of a 'new synthesis'. Indeed, the leading representative of sociobiology, E.O. Wilson, has at least formally conceded the need for a specific non-biological account of human social relations in his most recent work *On Human Nature* (1978). However, we shall argue that the characteristic forms of defence of the autonomy of the social sciences lead to a conception of social relations and culture which is extremely unsatisfactory. Autonomy from biological imperialism is won at the price of social or cultural essentialism. In arguing this we are developing the points made in our discussion of Robert Hertz's work in the last chapter.

It is easy to discount attempts to stress parallels between human and animal societies where the creatures used for comparison are bees or geese.[1] A.L. Kroeber scored an easy victory in showing the enormous differences between the human child and a puppy: 'dog speech, and all that is vaguely called the language of animals, is in a class with men's noses, the proportions of their bones, the colour of their skin ... and not in a class with any human idiom' (1957: 28). He would have felt less comfortable had he encountered a young chimpanzee demanding to be tickled in the sign language of the human deaf.[2] It is the primate order, including all monkeys, apes, *and* man, which is the relevant domain of comparison in any attempt to draw a rigid distinction between the categories of 'human' and 'animal'. Modern apes and men have evolved in distinct ways from a common primate stock, a separation which took place at least some 14 to 15 million years ago.[3] Apes, monkeys, and men all live in the close company of their fellows, as Irven de Vore says, 'Essentially, primate life is group life' (1965: 26). But these circumstances make possible both comparison *and* differentiation. First, as we have seen in Chapter One, the interaction of biological and cultural evolution led to important changes in both the size and the make-up of the human brain, in human sexual characteristics, and in child-bearing. Evolution whilst giving us a biological continuity with our nearest contemporary 'relatives' has also led to important physical differences from them. Second, the close observation in recent years of primate groups 'in the wild' now makes it possible to compare the patterns of social life among monkeys, apes, and man.

The characteristics of primate social life

Irven de Vore argued some years ago that it was possible from recent field studies of monkeys and apes to describe a 'fundamental primate way of life' (1965: 26), common to monkeys, apes, and man, but excluding prosimians like lemurs and lorises. Primates live in relatively large, organized groups of 20 to 200 with a stable membership. The group includes both sexes and all ages and is differentiated into roles and statuses based on age, sex, and position in a dominance hierarchy. Childbearing is a group activity; this differentiates primates from other mammals which also form herds or groups, for these are either mere aggregates, from which females separate to bear and rear their young, or a 'harem' of females and juveniles attached to a dominant male.

This generalization has important and evident exceptions. Primate social organizations vary considerably. The orangutan appears to live a more or less solitary existence. Chimpanzee groups are much less structured and inclusive than de Vore's account, based on baboon groups, would allow. Some New World monkeys pair like gibbons, and live separately from others in 'family' units.[4] Further, non-primate social groups are by no means as rudimentary as de Vore claims. Wolves, for example, form stable, organized groups which cooperate in hunting.[5]

De Vore's generalization applies most accurately to baboon groups. Baboons form the most structured of the primate societies and they are savanna dwellers like early man, feeding on open semi-arid plainlands. For this reason baboons and gibbons have been taken as the 'model' of early human society by popular writers like Robert Ardrey who wish to stress the continuity between man and the primates. Ardrey in *African Genesis* (1961) and *The Territorial Imperative* (1971) takes the 'typical' features of baboon society, a male dominance hierarchy maintained by aggression and a rigid territoriality with respect to other groups and argues these are characteristic of early proto-human hunters. Men are likewise territorial, hierarchical, and aggressive by nature. These features, which reflect human origins, are also the most important factors in explaining human social life.

The dominance hierarchy and the resultant social relationships can be seen when the baboon group is on the move. The dominant males occupy a place at the centre of the group whence they can move to shield the females with infants, who are close by them, from predators coming from any direction. The less dominant males form a rearguard and an advance guard which serves to give warning, while other females and juveniles march on the edges of the central group. Baboon social organization is structured around the rearing and protection of the young, who enjoy a prolonged period of infancy and social learning. Adults of both sexes take an active interest in the infants of the group. But allowing all this, it is important to add that baboon social behaviour is hardly as Ardrey imagined it. De Vore (1965) and Washburn and de Vore (1961) point out that baboons are much *less* aggressive and territorial in the wild than was supposed, earlier studies having been based on groups of captive animals in relatively confined circumstances. Different troops in the wild will share a common waterhole, mingling without direct social contact but also without fighting. The dominance hierarchy actually serves to reduce fighting and competition within the group; when it works baboon groups show little evidence of aggression.

But, aggressive and territorial or not, baboons are ill-chosen for comparison with early hominid and human groups. The first reason is that early hominids, far from being aggressive hunters in their adaptation to ground dwelling, as Ardrey supposes, may have been specialized seed eaters. Evidence of this is the reduced canines in the fossil remains of Ramapithecus.[6] The social organization of these seed eaters was in all probability quite unlike that of baboons. Had they followed the baboon model of closed groups with a dominance hierarchy whose members all move together, then it would have been difficult to change and to adapt social organizations to a sex-based division of labour in which the males hunt and the females remain at a fixed location and engage in gathering. The baboon group is constantly on the move, does not have a 'base' and the sick or injured must keep pace or perish.

The second reason follows from the first and is based on archaeological evidence of prehistoric human hunters and gatherers and on contemporary observations of what appear to be very similar hunting groups. Human hunters and gatherers do not behave like baboons. Hunting societies are characteristically organized around a division of labour based on age and sex. In this division active males go on hunting and foraging expeditions, working cooperatively, whilst the women, old people, and juveniles either engage in gathering, or handicrafts, or tasks like education in relatively close proximity to the base camp. A charming and sympathetic picture of such a division of labour is to be found in Laurens van der Post's book, *The Lost World of the Kalahari* (1963).[7] The baboon group does not split up in this way, and protection depends on the members of the troop remaining in close proximity. Nor do human hunters rely on 'dominant males' for protection, but on the predators' fear of their weapons, fire, and cooperation. Baboons do not cooperate in foraging nor do they share food with one another; human hunters do. Finally, human hunters occupy and range over an area comparable in size to that of other cooperative hunting animals such as wolves (some eighty square kilometres) whereas 'an entire baboon troop can live in an area which is too small to support a single human hunter' (de Vore 1965: 33). This pattern of life marks off human hunters not merely from baboons but from forest- or semi-woodland-dwelling apes as well. Chimpanzees in a forest environment seldom stray as much as a kilometre from their usual haunts, generally remaining well within sound of their companions.

The baboon troop is small and inbred. There is no lasting pair bonding and so no basis for the formation of 'families'. Indeed, among the primates one can speak of 'families', even in this figurative sense, only among gibbons which divide into groups composed of male, female, and offspring. But these groups are rigidly separated by strong antagonism among males and form isolated units which could be said to have more in common with breeding pairs of birds than with human family groups. Human family groups are part of a larger unit; in hunters and gatherers a 'band' of some twenty to fifty members is characteristic.

This larger unit is subject to exogamous marriage rules which mean that members must find partners from other groups. Thus again humans differ from baboons in that their groups of immediate association are not closed and inbred. Whilst hunters do occupy definite 'territories', they do not do so exclusively, but meet and collaborate with members of other bands for certain kinds of seasonal hunting or gathering or for ritual purposes.

Other primate societies are more 'open' than that of baboons, but even here the patterns are quite different from human hunters. Chimpanzees belong to loosely structured groups: young males and females will move between groups, periodically forming temporary adolescent groups, females will attract a retinue of males when in oestrus, and so on. But this primate equivalent of Engels' pre-familial 'promiscuity' is quite unlike the patterns of kinship in human hunting societies, since movement between human groups is organized and marriage leads to the formation of more or less stable pairs.[8] To the extent that we have considered sexuality here, it has been within a general context of social relations. In the final section of this chapter we shall return to the question of the relation between human and primate sexuality, having dealt with the issues sociobiology raises about the connection of genetic considerations, kinship, and evolution.

As De Vore (1965) argues, the differences between baboons and human societies outweigh the similarities, and the differences between human and other primate groups are no less marked. But this does not mean that the evolutionary status of man as a primate is discounted. One must be careful in arguing about human evolution on the basis of accounts of contemporary hunters and gatherers, for these groups are themselves the products of as long a process of development as Western societies. The same caution applies to those prehistoric peoples who left a rich enough archaeological record for us to recognize them as the ancestors of the contemporary hunting way of life. At some point in the evolutionary process, there must have been no more than a hair's breadth of difference in capacities and skills between the hominid ancestors of man and the other primates. The difference between man and the primates is not an essential difference, like the religious differentiation of man and beast, but a difference produced in evolutionary development and contributed to by the behaviour of the human animal. That the differences between man and primates *have* become massive, however, undercuts any attempt to treat *contemporary* man as merely a 'naked ape' or a territorial and aggressive baboon in clothes.

Naturalism and biologism

This point is by no means uncontroversial. If anything, attempts to explain human society in terms of animal societies or in terms of biological needs and instincts have become more widespread and influential in recent years. Writers like Desmond Morris and Robert Ardrey have become popular best-sellers. Ardrey's message is clear: he wants to claim that territoriality, aggression, competitiveness, and a male dominance hierarchy are all part of the inescapable biological endowment of man.

Human sentiments and activities are merely precipitates of evolution and instinct and beyond human control. Man must use what knowledge he has in order to *conform* with his nature rather than futilely trying to change it. No wonder egalitarians, feminists, and socialists have rushed to close the breach against such biologistic ideologies.

It would be dangerous, however, to treat all such popular writing on the theme of man and animal as merely attempts to hide the cloven hoof of capitalism and sexism in the 'naturalness' of instincts. It would be erroneous, moreover, to suppose that drawing a rigid line between man and animal is a progressive thing to do. Jane van Lawick-Goodall's field studies of chimpanzees or, on a less serious plane, Joy Adamson's observations of lions, are all of great public interest. Part of the reason is anthropomorphism, a desire to see nature humanized and animal life made into drama. Such interest is also a sign of a changing attitude toward animals and nature in Western societies. Before Carpenter's studies there was very little field observation of primates by trained zoologists or anthropologists. In literature and films in the pre-war years the people who 'knew' about animals were typically professional white hunters and, indeed, scientists did often take them seriously. Now hunters have been largely discredited as a source of reliable information, while animals are increasingly recognized as something more than pets or an economic resource. Wild animals are of interest and value to us for what they are in themselves. Their abilities, skills, and behaviours are less and less measured negatively against man's own or in terms of human utility. This goes along with a changing attention to matters of ecology, to the contribution of other animals and vegetable species to our own well-being and conditions of life, and to the impact of our actions upon them. This attention has also promoted a scepticism about the rapid social changes which have accompanied industrialization, particularly in its post-war phase. Socialism and egalitarianism have come to be associated in many people's minds with a 'humanism' that regards man as infinitely perfectible and the world as merely the laboratory of man's self-realization. Appreciating other animals, recognizing our evolutionary continuity with them, and accepting our common need for air, water, and food is something quite different from using biology and evolution to make certain socially specific human attributes or institutions inevitable parts of the nature of things.

The most sophisticated attempt to explain human societies in biological terms is quite different from the work of Robert Ardrey or even intelligent ethological observers of animals like Konrad Lorenz. In these cruder works definite parallels are drawn between human and animal societies, and the argument is based on supposed similarities between humans and baboons, or between human states, private property, and the territorial behaviour of animals.[9] This is why, in our opening discussion of human and primate societies, we sought to undercut the observational status of these parallels. However, even if human and baboon societies did appear reasonably similar, this would by no means justify the conclusions drawn by Ardrey. As Vernon Reynolds (1980) points out, this supposes that similar results have similar causes, an evident non sequitur.[10] By contrast, sociobiology does not rely on such observational parallels, or the claim that human society is the same as some definite animal society. Rather it argues that they must each be studied by similar *methods* because both humans and animals are subject to similar evolutionary necessities and common biological processes *even though the resulting adaptations may be very different.*

We cannot hope to review the various theories of sociobiology and the debates surrounding them. The controversy has produced a whole literature and we will refer the reader merely to what seem the best critical contributions to the debate.[11] Sociobiology will be considered here as presented in E.O. Wilson's *Sociobiology, the New Synthesis* (1975). Sociobiology is concerned to relate, in a single mathematically formulated theory, evolutionary biology, population genetics and animal behaviour. It starts from a question which is considered to be puzzling for conventional Darwinian evolutionary theory: why are some animals programmed to act in ways that threaten their survival, warning others of the approach of predators and the like? This *reduces* the chances of survival for the individual animal in question. Such questions are pertinent because what sociobiology does is to extend considerations of cost-benefit analysis to animal populations, on the one hand and to make the object of that analysis the genes of the individual animal and its close relatives, on the other. In Darwin's theory of natural selection, it will be recalled, changes in the environment (leading to differential selection pressures) interact with processes of random genetic mutation (leading to variant characteristics) to produce changes in species characteristics that may ultimately lead to the development of a new species. As we have seen in Chapter One, the selection pressures of a changing environment act differentially on the members of a species to favour certain random mutations which produce variant characteristics. These pressures give some variant individuals in a population of interbreeding animals a higher probability of survival than others. These individuals will therefore tend to live and reproduce offspring, transmitting their characteristics to them and so on until these characteristics come to be definitive of the species-population. Thus 'altruistic' behaviour, acting so as to increase one's chances of getting killed, puts one in the category of 'also ran' in Darwin's terms, however much it may benefit other animals in a group or herd. Such animals as behaved in this way would appear to be selected *against*.

The object of natural selection in Darwin's theory is the group. Selection pressures act on the group of animals in a species-population as a whole, weeding out the unfit and favouring those with adaptationally advantageous characteristics. 'Group selection' cannot explain 'altruism', and hence the sociobiologists contrast the 'group selection' they hold to be characteristic of Darwinian theory with 'kin selection'.

In cost-benefit terms, considered in regard to the genes an animal shares with its close relatives and which will be reproduced in future generations, such 'altruistic' behaviour is *not* in the category of 'also ran' if it permits a number of close relatives to survive to breed and transmit common genes to future generations. The referent here is not the welfare of the individual animal but the reproductive success of the genes it shares with close kin. A number of close kin will actually carry *more* distinctive genes than any one individual. The issue which decides the evolutionary rationality of an 'altruistic' act is the 'coefficient of relationship', that is, the average degree of genetic material shared with a class of relative (sibling, cousin, etc.) *plus* the number of relatives so benefited. Genetically determined behaviours which operate so as to produce such mathematically favourable outcomes will be rewarded by (Darwinian) natural selection — sociobiology claims to be an extension of evolutionary theory and not a rival competitor. Behaviours and characteristics which confer reproductive advantage permit certain genes to be carried by larger numbers of future related animals. Differential reproduction of kin groups *within* a species is a new measure of evolutionary success. Thus to Darwin's *selection out* of animals less fitted to survive in a given environment is added a consideration of forms of *selection for* genetically determined behaviours which promote differential reproductive advantage. Genetically transmittable behaviours are assessed in terms of their functions in promoting or hindering the transmission of the genes animals share with relations; as Wilson says, any behavioural pattern 'that can insert a higher proportion of certain genes into subsequent generations will come to characterize the species' (1975: 3).

In mathematical and genetic terms, animals have definite 'interests' and patterns of behaviour which favour those 'interests'. A mammalian female has a higher 'investment' in reproductive activity since she must carry offspring to term and rear them. A male would appear to have a genetic 'interest' in promiscuity, in siring the maximum number of offspring from as many females as possible. Pair bonding is thus explained, for example, as a strategic behavioural path which maximizes the chance that offspring will survive till maturity (thus meeting the female 'interest') and at the same time assures the male of successors. The male is wedded to this path through female behaviours which are designed to allure and hold him after copulation. Pair bonding and its associated behaviours are selected for because the outcome is that more offspring survive through the effect of prolonged care by both partners and these offspring are then likely to carry on these behavioural genes.

The concepts of 'altruism', 'inclusive fitness', and 'kin selection' are all closely related and serve to define the same basic process. 'Altruism' is any potentially self-destructive act which, in permitting the survival and reproduction of close relatives, makes possible a greater chance of survival of the altruistic animal's genes. 'Reciprocal altruism' occurs when animals who are not closely related aid one another to attain reproductive advantage, for example, where dominant male baboons assist one another in warding off challenges of subordinate males. Here cooperation allows both animals to increase their chances of mating with females and maximizing their progeny. 'Inclusive fitness' defines a condition in which reproductive advantage is maximized for a group of related animals, in which the greatest chance of transmission of shared genes distinctive to the group is attained. This may involve some of the animals *not* reproducing and therefore not directly transferring genes to actual descendants. An example is specialized worker bees which forgo the capacity to reproduce in favour of queens who specialize in reproduction (and are their mothers or sisters); they serve to maintain the hive as a collective entity through their self-denying efforts. 'Kin selection' is thus the process whereby animals within a species-population struggle to attain reproductive advantage. It consists in the promotion of the greatest reproductive success by a group of animals related by descent and therefore sharing a common genetic inheritance.

Selection of this kind involves both competition against unrelated members of the same species and due regard in altruistic behaviour for the degree of relation of the sacrificing animal to the animals which benefit from this behaviour. An animal which is 'too altruistic' is an evolutionary loser. The theory thus works on probabilities and on a calculation of advantage for animals that behave in ways which pay due regard to the genealogical relation of others to them. It is concerned with outcomes, and is interested in genetically programmed behaviours which happen to lead to the promotion of inclusive fitness. Nevertheless these outcomes are simply unattainable if animals do not possess some means of unconscious or inbuilt knowledge of these blood ties. This is further confirmed by the use of concepts like 'selfishness' and 'spite', in which an animal acts directly to promote its own advantage over another individual. Again, if this is to work in cost-benefit terms, it must respect the coefficient of relationship involved and must include some behaviourally effective (if not deliberate) calculation of closeness of relations.

Any characteristic or behaviour is therefore potentially explicable by differential reproductive advantage. It confers adaptive value in the sense of enabling certain sets of related individuals to produce more surviving offspring with a common heredity than do sets of individuals either altogether without such behaviours or characteristics, or who possess them to a less effective degree. Adaptive value is considered here not with primary reference to the probability of an individual animal's physical survival in an environment (and therefore the probability of its reproducing) but relative to the *future*, to the reproductive success of a kin group in its competition to transmit its genes against others in the same species.

'A genetically based act of altruism, selfishness or spite will evolve if the average inclusive fitness of individuals within networks displaying it is greater than the inclusive fitness of individuals in otherwise comparable networks that do not display it.'

(Wilson 1975: 118)

This theory can be applied to human behaviour. Human kinship is explained by Wilson in sociobiological terms. Kinship is a 'universal feature' of the *biology* of the human species and human animals are behaviourally guided by genetic considerations in practising incest avoidance. This is because inbreeding reduces heterozygosity[12] and so reduces the available genetic material which contains possibilities for environmental change. Controlled outbreeding is a strategy which optimizes between genetic transmission of kin heredity while keeping adaptive options open. In consequence human social groups display 'behavioural mechanisms that avoid incest' (1975: 79). It follows that, both to avoid incest and to favour in one's altruistic behaviour kin with the highest coefficient of relationship, humans must possess an 'intuitive calculus of blood ties' (1975: 11). At some level human behaviour in kinship and marriage must take account of real genealogical relations, of 'blood'. It is on this question that we will concentrate in considering the applicability of sociobiological concepts to human social relations. In doing so our account will be almost entirely based on Marshall Sahlins' admirably clear, honest, and thorough critique of sociobiology, *The Use and Abuse of Biology* (1977).

Wilson's *Sociobiology* produced a furious debate, with sections of the left, inside and outside the biological sciences, accusing the sociobiologists of being 'racist, classist and sexist'.[13] Whilst holding no brief for the main substance of Wilson's theory, and being equally appalled by his notorious gaffes when it comes to discussing human social relations in what are virtually no more than casual asides, it is not clear in some of these ripostes how *any* attempt to account for significant human attributes or behaviours in terms of genetic transmission or in terms of natural selection could ever be other than a neo-fascist ideological onslaught. This type of criticism amounts to making the human a preserved domain which the natural sciences can enter only if they declare in advance that their results will loyally support egalitarianism and human perfectibility. This would do no more than make us hostages to our own ignorance. Genetics as a science is hardly out of its infancy. This type of response has more in common with Bishop Wilberforce and the defenders of *Genesis* than it has with Marx and Engels.

If significant human attributes and behaviours are genetically determined, it does not follow that they cannot be compensated for or counteracted.[14] Even if one did accept the sociobiologists' theories, it does not follow that either social policy or scientific enquiry need regard certain genetic traits as a fixed and unalterable 'nature'. Awesome and appalling as the prospect may be, genetics may possibly give rise to technologies and means of intervention in genetic coding and transmission, thereby modifying human characteristics, behaviours, and attributes. But this is hardly the point in the case of sociobiology, which has neither established the genetic tendencies it claims nor involved any specific advances in genetic theory but merely uses certain genetic concepts in a model of evolutionary change.

Sociobiology's conception of and explanation of human social relations is simply primitive. There is no need to refer to the supposed ideological motives behind it in order to show the weaknesses in Wilson's argument. At the same time, the conception of social relations used by Wilson's opponents, if less primitive, is hardly less problematic, erecting the 'human' as a distinct realm guaranteed to arouse the suspicions and hostility of biologists.

The first major strand of criticism of sociobiology concerns its use of genetics. The issues here are complex and beyond our competence and we will no no more than refer to accounts which seem convincing to us. J.C. King (1980) argues that sociobiology relies on a theory of transmission in which single genes carry particular characteristics and evolve on their own in the form of quantum mutational 'jumps'. He contrasts this 'uniformist' view with that of the 'variabilists' who emphasize forms of interaction between genes to transmit characters and produce changes.

'To the variabilists what selection appears to be doing, instead of picking out genes for their individual excellence, is preserving a variety of gene combinations in individual chromosomes such that, when these chromosomes are randomly combined to produce new individuals, the new combinations will have a high probability of producing individuals of the modal phenotype.'

(King 1980: 88)

He argues that phenotypes which differ from the species norm in certain exaggerated characteristics will tend to be less reproductively successful than those which tend to conform to the mean. Recent developments in genetics have confirmed the variabilist view, and this makes sociobiology's claims to explain incest avoidance behaviour extremely dubious:

'Since single-gene genetics fails to explain a very large part of metabolic pathology, it is very likely that its role in determining behaviour is even less substantial. Yet Wilson insists that human rules against incest have a genetic basis.'

(King 1980: 95)

If this tendency to favouring the modal phenotype is both the main tendency of genetic transmission and the most favourable evolutionary outcome, then all questions of 'kin selection' are idle and such behaviour in animals genetically futile.

This point is reinforced by the leading physical anthropologist and specialist on human evolution and primate behaviour, S.L. Washburn

(1980). Drawing on the estimate that man and chimpanzees share 99 per cent of their genetic material and that the races of man are fifty times closer than man and chimpanzees, he argues:

'Individuals whom sociobiologists consider unrelated share, in fact, more than 99 per cent of their genes. It would be easy to make a model in which the structure and physiology important in behaviour are based on the shared 99 per cent and in which behaviourally unimportant differences, such as hair form, are determined by the 1 per cent. The point is that genetics actually supports the beliefs of the social sciences, not the calculations of the sociobiologists. The genetic basis for the behaviourally important common biology of the species (in evolutionary order — bipedal walking, hand skills, intelligence) lies in the 99 per cent and is undoubtedly modified by genes in the 1 per cent.'

(Washburn 1980: 276)

Neither of these views denies that individual differences or general bio-social capacities are determined or conditioned by genetic transmission. What is opposed here is the view that kin-specific and hereditarily transmittable characteristics are of *evolutionary* importance in human beings, that 'kin selection' is a possible mechanism of modification of the human species. Arguing an important role for the genetic determination of the biological conditions of human capacities and of differences in humans' abilities does not mean arguing for sociobiology.

It is not only Wilson's theory of gene selection and transmission which has been questioned. Central in sociobiology are certain genetically programmed *behaviours*. Wilson is an entomologist and it is from the genetically coded behavioural instructions of insects that he draws his views on the evolutionary significance of behaviour in general. Even in insects the degree of 'programming' can hardly be 100 per cent since bees have been seen in experiments to change their behaviour and develop otherwise latent physical characteristics. As Vernon Reynolds says: 'The whole question of how genetic instructions are transformed into behavioural outcomes is largely unsolved' (1980: 28). Men exhibit wide differences and also radical changes in 'behavioural outcomes'. In the last 30,000 years, it appears that the basic genetic make-up of the human species has hardly changed, yet human life has been transformed from a hunting and gathering existence through a series of rapidly increasing institutional and technological changes. Vernon Reynolds concludes that:

'Man is still subject to natural selection, but as there are no genes for actions, it cannot select for or against actions as such, only for underlying physical structures (brain mechanisms, perceptual mechanisms, etc.).'

(Reynolds 1980: 29)

Rejecting sociobiology does not mean rejecting natural selection.

The second major strand of criticism comes from anthropologists like Sahlins and concerns the applicability of sociobiological analysis to human kinship institutions. Sociobiology is committed to an account of human kinship in terms of genetically based behaviours and ones which, if they are to be successful in terms of natural selection, must pay due regard to the actual biological ties of blood. Sahlins claims:

'there is not a single system of marriage, postmarital residence, family organization, interpersonal kinship, or common descent in human societies that does not set up a different calculus of relationship and social action than is indicated by the principles of kin relation.'

(Sahlins 1977: 26)

Kinship institutions define who is and is not of the same 'kind' by means of rules which, whilst relatively consistent, do not reflect biological co-efficients of relationship in the ties and obligations they establish. Sahlins says:

'Such human *conceptions* of kinship may be so far from biology as to exclude all but a small fraction of a person's genealogical connections from the category of "close kin"; while, at the same time, including in that category, as sharing common blood very distantly related people or even complete strangers. Among these strangers (genetically) may be one's own children (culturally).'

(Sahlins 1977: 75)

Many peoples, far from possessing an 'intuitive calculus of blood ties', seem determined to undermine its very possibility in their genealogical doctrines and inheritance practices. The Trobriand Islanders deny the role of the father in procreation and reckon descent through the female line. Yet they insist, as with the Code Napoléon, that the 'father of the child is the husband of the mother' and Trobriand fathers apparently accept as their own (in the sense of social obligation) children born in their absence during a sea voyage of more than two years. Adoption is, among Polynesians, a major form of entry into kin relations; Sahlins cites the example of Tahiti where 25 per cent of all children are adopted. In such circumstances, genealogical doctrines follow from social patterns of family membership and neighbourhood co-residence, often reckoning descent through a common fictive 'ancestor'. Descent reckoning and biological relationship may be far removed from each other. The same is the case for cooperation and altruistic associations, which follow social obligations rather than the kind of biological interests necessary for Wilson's 'altruism'. To show how strong social ties may be coupled with an utter confusion about biological relations of descent, Sahlins cites the following statement by a Hawaiian woman:

'Kealoha is my brother's child. Of course my brother isn't really my brother as both he and I are *hanai* [adoptive] children of my father. I

guess my father isn't really my father, is he? I know who my real
mother is, but I didn't like her and I never see her. My *hanai* brother is
half-Hawaiian and I am pure Hawaiian. We aren't really any blood
relations I guess, but I always think of him as my brother and I always
think of my [adoptive] father as my father. I think maybe Papa [her
adoptive father] is my grandfather's brother. I'm not sure as we never
asked such things. So I don't know what relation Kealoha really is,
though I call her my child.'

(Sahlins 1977: 52)

Finally, we must consider incest avoidance. The rule of *exogamy* is
crucial to the operation of structures of human kinship since it provides
the necessity and the pattern of the movement of persons between groups.
It would be dangerous to equate this practice of 'marrying out' with a
behavioural pattern aimed at the avoidance of incest in the biological
sense. The reason is all too obvious: as Sahlins (1977) points out, the
human groups which exchange members in marriage — and which are the
product not only of kinship ties but of many other circumstances — are
social rather than biological groupings and are *not* composed of members
'of the same blood'. Clientship, and slavery, adoption, and migration are
important routes to social group membership. Exogamy ensures circulation between social groups which are *already* diverse in the biological
sense. Here the defender of sociobiology might retort that this situation
is precisely the product of incest avoidance — kinship *does* prevent incest
and natural selection has favoured groups which have arrangements which
perform this function. Durkheim provided an answer to this sort of
reasoning in *The Rules of Sociological Method*: '*When, then, the explanation of a social phenomenon is undertaken, we must seek separately
the efficient cause which produces it and the function it fulfills*' (1966:
95, emphasis in the original). If we turn to 'efficient causes' and consider
the possible conditions of emergence of kinship systems we find ourselves
condemned to silence or to an inappropriate use of functional explanations. We have no adequate explanation of the 'origin' of human kinship, and little in the way of materials which could serve as 'evidence'. The
search for such an 'origin' has generally led to methodological disaster
— as we shall have cause to see in Chapter Eight when we discuss Freud.
We certainly cannot assume a beginning of the kind sociobiologists need
to postulate, groups 'of the same blood' who started (unconsciously and
intuitively) to exchange members 'for the good of their genes' and were
then favoured by natural selection.

And, what is more, whatever one says about the origins of kinship
systems their contemporary effects are unambiguous: *they 'avoid' incest
so well that they undermine any possibility of 'kin selection' working
among humans*. The human groups which exchange members are biologically diverse and they enforce patterns of cooperation and association
which bear no relation to genealogical closeness of 'blood'. If human

beings do have a 'largely unconscious and irrational' 'gut feeling' which 'promotes the ritual sanctions against incest', as Wilson contends in *On Human Nature* (1978: 38), then these feelings have led to an over-reaction of such a degree that any basis for an 'intuitive calculus of blood ties' and for a sociobiological explanation of human kinship has been undercut. If sociobiologists cannot explain kinship there is little else in human social relations that they have much prospect of explaining.

The symbol and the superorganic

The opponents of sociobiology are correct to challenge its method of explaining social relations. Sahlins is right to insist that human kinship institutions work through specific social rules and that the activity of following a rule is something quite different from genetically programmed or conditioned behaviour. But, in challenging sociobiology, critics like Sahlins and also Vernon Reynolds go on to make claims about human societies which are no less problematic. It should be said straight away that the defence of the specificity of kinship and other social institutions need not depend on such claims and actually does not do so in the sub-stance of Sahlins' or Reynolds' arguments against sociobiology. These claims are a kind of philosophical excess baggage – strictly unnecessary to the critique but revealing a pervasive sociological and anthropological attitude toward the human.

What is the substance of this 'excess baggage'? It consists in a rigid differentiation between man and animals, located in the uniquely and exclusively human capacity to bestow meaning on the world in the form of symbols. It is this capacity which is held to account for the radical autonomy of human culture from biological explanation. It is an independent realm whose significances can only be understood in its own terms. Thus Sahlins says: 'while the human world depends on the senses, and the whole panoply of organic characteristics supplied by biological evolution, its freedom from biology consists in just the capacity to give these their own sense' (1977: 12). The 'symbolic faculty' defines culture (1977: 65), this means that 'human beings are not socially defined by their organic qualities but in terms of symbolic attributes; and a symbol is precisely a meaningful value ... which cannot be determined by the physical properties to which it refers' (1977: 61).

Why should we challenge this view? Surely the thesis that it is 'symbolic attributes' rather than 'organic qualities' which define human beings is central to our book? Yes, insofar as the concern is to define and defend social relations as a distinct sphere of effectiveness which needs to be explained by specific concepts and methods. No, insofar as our concern is to oppose the rigid counter-position of 'nature' and 'culture', the tendency to make the organic and the symbolic opposed entities. We have tried both to show how social relations create and condition 'biological' attributes (as in the case of bodily techniques) *and* to show how social practices, relationships, and beliefs work through and are only effective because of physiological processes (as in the case of 'voodoo death').

We have three main reasons to be wary of Sahlins' conception of the 'symbolic' as definitive of culture. First, the concept of a rigid differentiation between humans and animals, a difference of *quality*, is a very old one in Western cultures and is religious in origin. Animals are seen as sentient beings without a soul, whereas humans are blessed with reason and immortality. As A.L. Kroeber remarked: 'A way of thought characteristic of our Western civilization has been the formulation of complementary antitheses, a balancing of exclusive opposites' (1957: 21). A way of thought or form of belief to be investigated, certainly, but hardly one to serve as an anthropological explanation or maintain anthropology as a distinct discipline. But that is just what Kroeber does in the paper − 'The Superorganic' − of which the quotation is the first sentence. We will try below to avoid treating of human and animal as 'exclusive opposites'. Second, as we saw in Chapter Two, this rigid opposition between 'nature' and 'culture' tends to lead to a view of culture as a unitary entity − a point we need not labour here. Third, and this is the main reason for our wariness, is the precise conception of the *sign* or of language involved in this notion of the symbolic as definitive of culture. We will argue that this leads to a simplistic view of language, and one which greatly overestimates its adaptive value in human evolution.

In this discussion we will concentrate on the role of the linguistic sign. This not merely for reasons of space or convenience, since language is absolutely central in views such as Sahlins' for establishing the difference between man and animal as being 'one of kind', not degree. Kroeber contends 'the difference between the so-called language of brutes and that of man is infinitely great' (1957: 27). Leslie A. White gives the clearest expression to this conception of language in his concept of the 'symbol' (White 1949). Sahlins (1960), in particular, depends very much on White. White says:

> 'It is the symbol which transforms an infant of Homo Sapiens into a human being; deaf mutes who grow up without the use of symbols are not human beings. All human behaviour consists of, or is dependent upon, the use of symbols. Human behaviour is symbolic behaviour; symbolic behaviour is human behaviour.'
>
> (White 1949: 32)

and

> 'The thesis that we shall advance and defend here is that there is a *fundamental* difference between the mind of man and the mind of non-man. Man uses symbols; no other creature does. An organism has the ability to symbol or it does not; there are no intermediate stages.'
>
> (White 1949: 34)

By the 'symbol' White means approximately what we, following modern linguistics, will call the 'sign'. But, in their theoretical implications concepts of symbol and sign are by no means similar. White defines the symbol as follows:

'as a thing the value or meaning of which is bestowed upon it by those who use it .... The meaning, or value, of a symbol is in no instance derived from or determined by properties intrinsic to its physical form.'

(White 1949:34)

The meaning of the symbol is conventional and is in no way determined by the physical properties of the objects or other means through which it is represented. Sahlins in a later work — *Culture and Practical Reason* (1976) — draws the conclusion from this that meaning patterns the material world in symbolic terms, that man lives in it according to these terms and the meanings therein, and that man follows symbolic purposes. No physicalist account, stating human needs in biological or environmental terms, is adequate because 'it is culture which constitutes utility' (Sahlins 1976: viii).[15]

The problem with this analysis is that language is conceived as the conventional attribution of 'meanings' to 'things': certain physical forms become the cultural signs or counters of 'meaning'. Language is equated with communication, the transmission of common and conventional meanings between individuals. Symbols are conceived as conventional and as the conditions for conceptual thought or 'reason'. This view closely corresponds to the theories of the sign and its function in human thought advanced by Locke and developed by Condillac. Indeed White cites with approval John Locke's phrase that signs 'have their signification from the arbitrary imposition of man'.

This conception of signification advanced by White et al. is tied to two key postulates:

i.   that the sign or symbol is *arbitrary*: its conventional character and its independence from its physical means of representation establish the *autonomy* of culture;

ii. that the sign or symbol denotes a common meaning or objective referent; that in making possible human communication about objects, states of affairs, and actions it confers on man adaptive advantage.

The symbol is thus both inexplicable in utilitarian or physicalist terms, since it is purely conventional, and yet it has a utility in evolutionary terms — of advancing man's adaptive potential. Both of these postulates are undermined by the leading trends in modern linguistics and the philosophy of language. The 'founding father' of modern structural linguistics, Ferdinand de Saussure, did indeed assert, in his *Course in General Linguistics* (1915), as a fundamental axiom of linguistics that there is an *arbitrary relation* between signifier and signified, between a sound image (*kæt*) and the concept it signifies (a 'cat' — an animal with certain characteristics, pointed ears but also craftiness). But as Emile Benveniste points out in *Problems in General Linguistics* (1971), Saussure has re-introduced the *thing referred to* back into the definition of the sign — something he had explicitly and rightly sought not to do. Benveniste says that the relation between signifier and signified is *not* arbitrary, except if we attempt to state its relation to 'reality'. There is indeed no reason why the 'thing' which is a cat should be referred to by the group of sounds *kæt*; it could be served equally well by *dǫg*. However, *within* the process of signification this relation of signifier and signified is *not* arbitrary. The two are related as a condition of sense. If *kæt* were merely arbitrary and conventional in its function as a signifier then language could not form a system since signs would then be singular and their relation one to another arbitrary. Sense would, therefore, be impossible. Indeed, White, does treat the 'symbol' as standing for a *thing*, rather than for a *signified* which is a *concept* and, therefore, part of a significatory system and of 'sense'.[16]

The sign for Saussure derives its 'value' from being part of a series; signs take on their significatory value from their relation with and difference from other terms. At the level of signifiers· (sound images), *kæt* is differentiated from *ræt* ('rat') and also, therefore, can be differentiated on the plane of the signifieds (concepts). Values are relative but *to each other* and from this emerges their inter-related necessity as parts of the structured whole which is language (*langue*).

Further, when we move from Saussure's concept of language as a series of structured values attributed to sounds and productive of sense (Saussure's *langue*) and turn to its deployment in speech (Saussure's concept of *parole*) we find that signs, far from being conventional and arbitrary, have definite functions. Language involves a series of 'empty' signs, whose sense and value is dependent on their place in discourse upon who speaks and upon what has gone before. These include pronouns which establish the positionality of the speaker or person referred to in discourse ('I' or 'you'), also words like 'today' or phrases like 'as you know' and performatives like 'I name this ship . . . .' The meaning of these terms is context-specific and in those contexts it is necessary rather than arbitrary.[17]

The point of these examples is to show that languages are *both* phonemic *and* semiotic systems. We are all compelled to follow (unconsciously) the rules of the *phonemic* system, that is, the series of sound relations, except on pain of producing unintelligible series of sounds (*ætk*, etc.). The semiotic *system*, that is, the series of signifiers/signifieds constitutive of sense, is no less compelling in its consequences. The concepts which are related to sound images to form 'signs' are by no means arbitrary, they form definite systems of beliefs and expectations about the world and the entities which exist in it.

We have moved quite quickly from regarding language as a conventional tool at man's disposal, bestowing 'meaning' on things, to regarding it as a controlling system of sounds and sign-concepts which together govern what can be said. Saussure, it is interesting to note, took his conception of the relation of the individual speaker to language as a system from Durkheim's view of the relation of the individual to the 'collective conscience', in which the individual's actions are governed by the patterns specified in collective 'representations'. Language in this view is no less a continuing and structured necessity than is any physical or biological circumstance. But this does not mean that it is timeless. Saussure was, for all his 'structuralist' concepts, aware that language changed. Change, however, is for him a gradual process of phonetic 'drift' at the level of sounds, and this is unconscious and unintended. Change in patterns of sense is, for him, outside the scope of linguistics proper, but it follows that such change cannot arbitrarily re-structure the language; rather the series of *signifiers* and their relative values one to another imposes patterns of order and stability on their corresponding *signifieds*.

To turn from the notion of the 'conventionality' or 'arbitrariness' of the symbol to the idea of 'meaning': we have seen that Saussure sought to analyse the sign as a purely internal relation of signifier and signified within language and to bracket off any reference to 'things' — *and* that he failed to do so in his definition of the 'arbitrariness' of the sign. The reason for this attempt at 'bracketing' is the view that signification, the production of 'sense', has no *necessary* relation to 'things'. Saussure, as a linguist, was content to let 'furious green dreams sleep peacefully'; unlike logical positivist philosophers, for example, who are concerned to analyse statements in order to determine whether or not they contain reference to empirically existing states of affairs. If such statements do, then they are 'meaningful' propositions; if they do not, then they are 'meaningless'. A paradigmatic example of such analysis is A.J. Ayer's *Language, Truth and Logic* (1948). Signs in Saussurean linguistics are not 'symbols' in the sense of words or other representations which denote things.

If we go beyond linguistics into the philosophy of language we find several trends opposed to the logical positivist theory of meaning. The later work of the Austrian philosopher Ludwig Wittgenstein (to which we will return in Chapter Fifteen when we discuss witchcraft) is a good example, as is the work of the contemporary French philosopher, Jacques Derrida. Both argue, persuasively, to our minds, that, to the extent that language is 'meaningful' it does not consist in a series of propositions about empirical states of affairs. For this to be true we would need to have an *independent access to reality* to measure the 'truth value' of such linguistically formulated propositions. But if language is a series of signified *concepts*, rather than of symbols or signs which stand for *things*, we have no guarantee of such access. Both Wittgenstein and Derrida agree that in order to define the 'meaning' of a word, its 'sense', we need to double it with other, different, words. One has only to open a dictionary to see their point. 'Meaning' is never at an end, never complete in itself, rather it is part of an infinite chain of the continuous use of language.[18]

If the philosophy of language proposed by Wittgenstein is not a mere absurdity then it is impossible to argue in an unqualified way that language confers adaptive advantage upon the human species. We have no doubt that this will appear to be an outrageous thesis, but we believe it to be more the salvation than the ruin of the independent explanation of social relations. Language is not 'meaning', in the sense of the conventional denotation of 'things'. Hence it cannot be merely a less cumbersome way of handling things. It involves ambiguity, dispersion, and dispute — the babble of tongues after the fall of the tower of Babel is as fitting a parable of what happens *within* languages as what happens between them. A statement is as likely to lead to a question, or a 'what do you mean?' as it is to anything else. This contradicts the view of 'communication' as a transfer of unambiguous conventional meanings about 'things' between human minds.

Further, insofar as language permits the 'autonomy' of culture Sahlins speaks of, it makes possible the construction of beliefs and the entities they refer to. But these are of dubious evolutionary 'advantage': consider religion, magic, myth, tribal customs and so on. Men walk in fear of witchcraft, starve and become celibates, or seek to murder one another to the last man. Sahlins is correct to argue that culture cannot be defined in terms of 'utility', in terms of beneficial evolutionary outcomes or of human success. He does this in spite of his support for a view of language and symbols which *is* committed to seeing these forms as constituting an evolutionary advantage for man. Sahlins has changed his views considerably in the better part of two decades which separates 'The Origin of Society' (1960) from *Culture and Practical Reason* (1976) but he still continues to endorse White's theory of the symbol, even though he has attempted to engage with and adopt the work of Saussure.

We have defined language in a way that makes it extremely complex. Surely, therefore, we must agree with the view that language is peculiarly and uniquely definitive of the 'human'? Just as we refused to align the human and the 'symbolic' against the organic, here too our answer is a resolute 'no!' We have already argued against the attempt to constitute language in terms of its special 'symboling' properties. Now we must consider the claim that it is available only to humans. This is part of our concern to avoid a rigid and exclusive differentiation between 'human' and 'animal'. The problem is that *we* observe animals and impute capacities to them and *they* become a mirror of *our* hubris and *our* ignorance. Vernon Reynolds, a careful and meticulous commentator, nevertheless feels sufficiently certain to make the following statement:

'It is that animals (by this I mean all species other than man) do not think conceptually; they respond to stimuli or configurations of stimuli coming from within their own bodies and from the surrounding environment, but do not conceptualise either themselves or others, or the external world and its parts or their social group. The reason is that animals other than man lack symbolic-language systems needed to produce the cognitive constructions that are necessary to concept formation.'

(Reynolds 1980: 45-6)

Now there are objections to this view. The first is that chimpanzees *have* been taught to use Ameslan, the sign language of deaf people in America, in limited ways, but sufficient to produce new sentences in that language.[19] The second is that dolphins and whales show evidence of co-operation and intelligence in their actions *and* produce complex patterns of noises that we cannot understand, perhaps for reasons no more or less than our ignorance of hieroglyphic writing before Champollion's break-through, that we lack the key to render them into our own tongue. The third is that linguistic theorists such as Noam Chomsky (1966 and 1968), have argued that *human* language cannot be understood in stimulus-response terms (as behaviourists like B.F. Skinner would have us do), because language has a distinct *biological* and not cultural basis. Chomsky (1959) argues that humans' *capacity* to learn languages and to produce new and grammatical sentences from the beginning stage is evidence of a neurological programming of a basic 'grammar' (one that underlies all languages, whether English or Chinese). The distinctive character of human language, therefore, has a *biological* rather than a cultural basis in this view. None of these objections is decisive and yet they all threaten the rigid divide between man and animal. In evolutionary terms a 'talking ape' is as possible as is a 'naked' ape: there is no *essential* difference between Homo Sapiens and any other animal.

Reynolds' view that language is necessary to conceptual thought repeats a proposition put forward in the eighteenth century by Condillac. Condillac could make conceptual thought the consequence of signs because of his view of man as a *tabula rasa*, as a being that derives its attributes from the imprint of the experience of the senses. Attributes are thus externally derived from the environment, as in Condillac's model of the statue that gradually acquires human faculties through the developing complexity of its sensations and needs. Condillac's conclusion is thus reached on the basis of very different assumptions from Reynolds. Modern biology and psychoanalysis challenge the notion of a *tabula rasa*. *No* animal could ever be a *tabula rasa*, certainly not one with a psyche as complex as man's. It is true to say that humans lack an elaborate 'biogrammar' which programmes their social actions, but is it true to say that 'conceptual thought' depends upon language? We may leave aside stories of 'wolf children' or slighting references to the deaf here. Tiny children are capable of elaborate organizations of 'experience' and, to our safely sanitized minds, fantastic constructions about where children come from, the sexual nature of faeces, etc. — all this long before they are able to speak. To believe the full extent of this we must place trust in the psychoanalytic *and* 'observational' work of Freud and Melanie Klein.[20] Whether this is 'conceptual thought' is a debatable question. 'Conceptual thought' can be defined in such ways as to depend upon linguistic concepts, QED, but this restrictive definition is hardly a helpful or an intellectually rigorous practice. It threatens to reduce the human psyche to what Freud, following the philosophers, called 'consciousness' and found to be merely the starting point in the understanding of human thought. Dreams reveal to us unconscious 'wishes' and celebrate constructions of events which, far from being linguistic, consist primarily of 'images'. Language is necessary to *interpret* the unconscious, but is not necessary to unconscious *thought*. In short, if the discoveries of psychoanalysis are accepted, we find elaborate pre-linguistic 'theories' about (children's sexual researches) and constructions of (unconscious thoughts as revealed through dreams) possible events. We may say that all this is not truly 'conceptual', but it is difficult to say that it is not *thought*, that it does not establish complex connections and relationships between entities, and that it plays no part in human actions. These halting beginnings of a knowledge of ourselves should at least make us wary of writing off animals because they do not speak. Anthropology is not the only 'human' science which can enlighten us on the question of thought and language, and psychoanalysis confronts us with awkward materials which make the view presented by White and others less tenable.

Our discussion has reviewed the three main propositions of Condillac's theory of signs and has found each of them wanting:

i.   the view that signs are conventional representations of things;
ii. the view that sensations and needs extend the range of experience and therefore of thought. Language is not adaptive in an evolutionary sense nor does it meet 'needs' in a utilitarian sense;
iii. the view that conceptual thought depends on signs.

We should not be surprised that we can draw parallels with the work of a man who has been dead for some two centuries. In matters which touch on the metaphysical we have made only the most tentative steps away from the oppositions and assumptions of our Christian culture. We cite Condillac not to humiliate contemporaries but to honour an exceptionally rigorous thinker whose thought remains of relevance to us. Each of these propositions is central to White's view of the symbol. Even the second had an important part in Sahlins' view before he wrote *Culture and Practical Reason* and, to fully sustain the theories of that later book, that culture cannot be explained in utilitarian terms, whether they be those of Marxism or those of Malinowski, he would both have to fully accept Saussure's theory of language and to reject his use of a rigid distinction between human and animal. Such a distinction is not necessary to a specifically 'human' social science.

Human and primate sexuality

Marshall Sahlins, in a widely influential paper, 'The Origin of Society' (1960), strongly contrasted human and primate sexuality. Early proto-human groups had to break from the primate pattern of sexual/social organization if they were to develop a viable hunting and gathering way of life:

> 'Sex is not an unmitigated social blessing for primates. Competition over partners, for example, can lead to vicious, even fatal, strife. It was this side of primate sexuality that forced early culture to curb and repress it. The emerging human primate, in a life and death econ-omic struggle with nature, could not afford the luxury of a social struggle. Cooperation, not competition, was essential. Culture thus brought primate sexuality under control.'

(Sahlins 1960: 6)

Sahlins contends that: 'Among subhuman primates sex had organized society' (1960: 6).

This contrast of primate society dominated by biological urges and characterized by competitive sexual strife, with primitive human society governed by cultural rules and the 'harmony and solidarity' (1960: 6) they bring appears strongly favourable to an autonomous social science. However, it is far too simplistic, as Sahlins himself would now probably agree. Primate sexuality is far from being a matter of simple biological instincts; primate sexual behaviour is influenced by learning and by social relationships of dominance. Primate societies are not organized by sex alone. Nor does primate sexuality necessarily involve vicious competition. De Vore (1965) while stressing the differences between primates and early human hunter-gatherers, at the same time insists that protection, not sex, dominates baboon social organization, and that the male dominance hierarchy, although it 'depends ultimately on force ... leads to peace, order and popularity' (1965: 29). This inverts Sahlins' 'nasty, brutish and short' conception of primate sexuality and attributes to baboon groups some of the valuations Sahlins attaches to human hunters and gatherers.

Again, as with primate society as a whole, it is hazardous to make generalizations about primate sexuality. At one time it was thought that primates differed from other mammals in that they have no definite 'breeding season' but are capable of year-round sexual activity, though it is closely tied to the female reproductive cycle, generally occurring when the females were in oestrus (on heat). This led some writers like Zuckerman (1932) to suggest that this year-round sexual activity was the basis of group life among primates.

Later studies have qualified this view. Let us take baboons again, as the most structured of primate societies. The female baboon is in oestrus for approximately one week out of every month and is sexually receptive at this time. When first in oestrus the female will present and mate with juvenile, subadult and less dominant males, only later presenting and finally mating with the dominant male/s and forming a consort pair for a few days or hours. Dominant males copulate with the receptive females exclusively at the time of the greatest swelling of the sexual tissue surrounding the posterior region. The period of maximum turgescence is also the time of ovulation and therefore the dominant males are most likely to be the effective breeders in the group. Washburn and De Vore comment, 'Estrus disrupts all other social relationships, and consort pairs move to the edge of the troop' (1961: 10). They contend that this is true of other species of monkey and that: 'Sexual behaviour appears to contribute little to the cohesion of the group' (1961: 10). Still sexual behaviour, though disruptive, is not a source of savage competition. To the extent that a dominance hierarchy is established, it prevents much competition. Moreover, even dominant males do not attempt to 'monopolize' females and no male is associated with more than one female in oestrus at any one time.[21]

Washburn and De Vore (1961) make the point that in a baboon troop, and the smaller it is the more this holds, there may be no female in oestrus for some months at a time. Yet members do not leave in search of sexual partners. This is not merely because the troop offers protection against predators. They stress that the baboon troop is an organization of child-rearing and learning, and that all adults play a part in this process. Washburn and Hamburg stress the evolutionary advantages of group life:

'It is in a social group that the primate learns to express its biology and adapt to its surroundings .... The group is a locus of knowledge and experience far exceeding that of the individual members. It is in the group that experience is pooled and generations linked. The adaptive function of prolonged biological youth is that it gives the animal time to learn.'

(Washburn and Hamburg 1965: 612-13)

These are exactly the terms in which the evolutionary advantage of a prolonged learning period in *humans* is normally discussed.

'To emphasize the importance of learned behaviour in no way minimizes the importance of biology. Indeed, learning can profitably be viewed in the adaptive context of evolutionary biology. The biology of the species expresses itself through behaviour, and limits what can be learned. Evolution, through selection, has built the biological base so that many behaviours are easily, almost inevitably, learned '

(Washburn and Hamburg 1965: 613)

Learned behaviour confers adaptive advantage because it enables the species to respond rapidly to changes in environment. As we have seen in discussing language, it is just this view, which seeks to unite biology and learned behaviour, which is problematic if we accept the thesis of the 'autonomy' of *human* culture. Such an account of primate societies in terms of the adaptive advantage of learning minimizes the difference between primate and human society Sahlins sought to emphasize in 'The Origin of Society'. To the degree that it stresses a common functional advantage for *all* primates — man included — in social learning, it weakens the thesis of a distinctive basis to human society. Perhaps it is for this reason that Sahlins in his later *Culture and Practical Reason* so strongly opposes any utilitarian account of human culture.

To return to baboon sexuality. These views which minimize the importance of sex as the cement in primate social life are reacting against stereotypes of the primate horde united by lust and riven by fratricidal competitive strife. But there is a degree of over-reaction which leads them to overlook the wider sense in which sexuality does prevail in primate group relations. The dominance hierarchy is centred on controlling access to sexual partners, however much it may control competition. By concentrating on coitus, and heterosexual copulation at that, they limit the scope of 'sexuality' — grooming and play are in a broad sense 'sexual' activities and are more or less continuous. They play an important part in 'learning' too.

Even if it is no longer possible on the basis of such recent studies to maintain the absence of a breeding and mating season as Zuckerman did in 1932 it still appears that year-round (if discontinous) sexual activity, mating, and births are a characteristic of primate species. It appears that the most common is what is called a 'birth peak' rather than a breeding season.[22] A further point in support of the importance of sexual activity among primates is that some primate juveniles, certainly baboons and chimpanzees — both males and females in the latter case — display an almost complete replica of adult sexual behaviour.[23] Adult chimpanzees too are known to engage in sexual activity at any time during the female's reproductive cycle and not only during oestrus.[24]

So even if it is true that among baboons in the wild long periods may elapse before a female is in oestrus, by virtue of the number of females in a troop as well as the fact that a female does not come on heat while she is lactating (with gaps of eighteen to twenty-four months between births), nonetheless sexual activity does play an important part in group life. Baboons, within the confines of the dominance hierarchy, are promiscuous, and the same is even more the case among chimpanzees.[25]

Human beings have the biological capacity to be just as 'promiscuous' as baboons and chimpanzees. Humans have no 'breeding season' or period of sexual receptivity. Indeed, in many societies, both 'primitive' and 'modern', the young are allowed considerable sexual licence before marriage. But such 'freedom' has definite limits. Among the Trobrianders, Malinowski (1937) reported a virtually indiscriminate sexual play among adolescents, *except* for a strict prohibition on such activity between brother and sister. Thus human societies' kinship institutions and the customs associated with them both limit and direct sexual conduct.

Patterns of prescribed and proscribed sexual conduct vary between cultures. Human sexual conduct, unlike that of primates, is subjected to the demands of beliefs and the constraints of social relations. In every human society such rules are both kept *and* broken, and this combination of licit and illicit sexuality is peculiar to human sexual organization. But, this is not because a 'naturally' promiscuous human sexuality is interdicted by social prohibitions. As we shall see when we come to discuss Freud in Chapter Eight, human sexuality is itself both psychically and socially constructed. Social rules are not therefore repressing a 'given' biological and natural pattern of conduct. Illicit and 'perverse' sexuality is a psychic and social product, no more natural than the rules it violates.

However, this psychic/social nature of human sexuality should not be counterposed to biology. On the contrary, it is made possible because it has a definite biological basis. Evolutionary development has made the cultural patterning and even repression of sexuality possible. The primate order is marked by the progressive emancipation of sexual behaviour from hormonal control. In insects sexual behaviour is centred in the abdomen and the role of the brain is purely inhibitory. In vertebrates, however, it is controlled by the brain. In sub-primate mammals sexual activity is tied to the sexual receptivity of the female, only occurring when the female is in heat. This depends very largely on the influence of the sex hormones, so that a female can be experimentally brought on heat and made sexually receptive as a result of hormone injections. So for these species sexual activity is firmly tied to a biologically triggered function of reproduction. In the case of both New and Old World monkeys, sexual activity is already less tied to hormonal control and the female reproductive cycle. Beach (1947) points out that a female rhesus monkey will sometimes permit copulation by the male when her ovaries are inactive and this indicates a certain degree of freedom of sexual activity from hormonal control.[26] In apes such as chimpanzees this freedom is much more marked and behaviour so much less controlled by hormonal secretions that male chimpanzees have to learn to copulate.[27] With Homo Sapiens the limited nature of hormonal control is even more marked and sexual activity is in no way dependent on the reproductive cycle — 'in our species the potential effects of ovarian hormones are so obscure as to be nearly if not entirely unrecognizable' (Beach 1947: 300).

Evolutionary development makes possible the cortical control of sexual behaviour and, therefore, the psychic/social construction of human sexuality. We share a degree of psychical control over, and the social learning of, sexual behaviour with our primate relatives. But we do not share either kinship institutions or the complex psychical construction of sexuality with the other primates. Much has been made by anthropological writers like Lévi-Strauss and Sahlins of the incest taboo as the basis of exogamy and therefore of kinship institutions. But it has been said that we share incest avoidance with the primates. This would upset such anthropological arguments about incest. Sade (1968) reports that son-mother mating is extremely uncommon among rhesus monkeys. Reynolds (1980) reports similar conclusions for chimpanzees, despite their promiscuity in all other respects. It is thus argued by Reynolds that it is wrong to assume that the incest taboo is a prohibition of behaviour which is 'natural' among primates.[28] Reynolds goes on to say: 'Here then ... we have a marvellous behavioural basis for the human institution of *exogamy*' (1980: 79). Sade draws the same conclusion, contending: 'We may now speculate that a pre-existing condition became invested with symbolic content during hominization' (1968: 37).

If this argument could be sustained it would point to a most definite continuity between human and animal societies. Such a continuity would by no means fill us with horror, but we have to say we find it implausible. The first reason for this is supplied by Sade himself. Sade shows that it is primarily the position of the male in the dominance hierarchy which conditions whether son-mother mating takes place: 'Males who remained subordinate to their mothers did not mate with them' (1968: 32). Yet nothing we can infer about hominid societies, and nothing we know about contemporary hunters and gatherers, leads one to suppose that a dominance hierarchy was a feature of early proto-human groups. If the primary cause of incest avoidance in rhesus monkeys is not evident in human evolution it is worse than mere speculation to try to base human institutions in the effects of such a cause. The second reason has been advanced in our criticisms of Wilson. Human kinship avoids incest 'too well'. One could argue that this is mere symbolic overkill. But if so, the supporter of continuity between man and the other primates would be hardly doing his own case a service. For in that case, human institutions would still have developed to the point where they work in ways radically different from behaviour patterns among rhesus monkeys or chimpanzees.

The danger with this view of the incest taboo is the same as that which threatens Sahlins' (1960) view of kinship − it exists to serve an adaptive function. Sahlins' view can be summed up as follows:

> 'The incest taboo is a guardian of harmony and solidarity within the family − a critical matter for hunters and gatherers, for among them the family is the fundamental economic as well as social group. At the same time the injunction on sexual relations and marriage among close relatives necessarily forces different families into alliance and thus extends kinship and mutual aid.'

(Sahlins 1960: 6)

The family is presented as a *cultural*-evolutionary adaptation just as Sade's incest-avoidance is a behavioural-evolutionary adaptation.

The very cultural specificity and diversity of kinship institutions Sahlins refers to in *The Use and Abuse of Biology* (1977) in order to criticize Wilson should lead us to wonder about these earlier claims on his part. Sahlins is by no means alone in analysing kinship in functional terms, as productive of social solidarity and as contributing to survival through mutual aid. Yet kinship institutions and relations can be both functional *and* dysfunctional – promoting certain forms of social solidarity *and* creating certain planes of conflict. It is likewise with the doctrines of sexuality and the prescribed patterns of sexual conduct which accompany kinship practices. Such doctrines and conducts both impose forms of order and generate forms of anxiety, psychopathology, and deviation. As we shall see in Chapters Five to Eight of Part Two, the doctrines and social relations concerned with sexuality, personality, and child-rearing are by no means productive of a healthy adaptation to the 'environment'. To the extent that human sexuality *does* differ radically from that of the primates, in terms of its socio-psychic constitution, it is less rather than more susceptible to functionalist analysis.

This is not to deny the value of an evolutionary perspective. Human beings *are* animals and are subject to natural selection. But it does not follow from this that our social institutions and beliefs are necessarily answers to urgent problems of physical survival and adaptation to environment. Man has no significant non-human predators. Even hunters and gatherers have a significant degree of control over the production of necessities so that their life is far from being constantly threatened by want, scarcity, and privation.[29] Even chimpanzees have plenty of time to sleep and play.[30] Human beliefs, institutions, and practices like art, kinship, and religion consume a great deal of time and energy, but they are neither necessarily adaptive to the environment nor productive of social order. Our discussion of witchcraft beliefs and accusations in Part Three illustrates the dangers of assessing social relations in terms of their contribution to adaptation or to the social order.

This chapter must necessarily be inconclusive. We have been concerned, on the one hand, to challenge the methodological claims of sociobiology to treat human social relations as the products of genetic and evolutionary forces and, on the other, to challenge the forms of rigid distinction between man and animals which are made in the interests of an 'autonomous' social science. Human and animal societies show marked differences, and these are demonstrable without an essentialization of the human.

Notes

1 See Emile Benveniste's discussion of von Frisch's studies of the communication of bees (1971: Ch.5).
2 This sign language is called Ameslan, for an account see Linden (1976).
3 See Reynolds (1976: 48-9 and 1980: 64-5).
4 See R.D. Martin's review of Leakey and Lewin 'People of the Lake', *New Society*, 11 October 1979. Not *all* baboons form structured groups, the Hamadryas baboons form 'harems'; see Reynolds (1976: 41).
5 For the hunting habits of wolves see Lopez (1978).
6 A view put forward by C.J. Jolly and discussed in Reynolds (1976: 51; 1980: 67).
7 We have selected this book in preference to many more substantial anthropo-

logical accounts because of its sympathy and literary merit. For a good introduction to the anthropology of hunting and gathering societies, see E.R. Service *The Hunters* (1966).

8 'Promiscuity' is the stage which precedes the formation of human kinship relations in Engels' *The Origin of the Family, Private Property and the State*. For chimp social patterns see Reynolds (1976: 52-6; 1980: 68-72).

9 We do not intend to deny that ethologists like Lorenz have produced interesting observational studies of animals. However in such parallels between human and animal behaviour the controls and disciplines which ethologists use in making deductions from animals' behaviours are of little use in making their analysis of human practices and institutions. As S.L. Washburn points out: 'Human ethology ... is based on a direct observation of behaviour, free of experimental intervention. Human ethology might be defined as the science which pretends humans cannot speak' (1980: 273). Given the impossibility of 'pure observation', human ethologists rely on various tacit knowledges and expectations about humans. Anthropologists have learned to their cost that they cannot suppose and rely on 'basic' repertoires of human gestures, conducts and responses.

10 Reynolds (1980: 13).

11 See Reynolds *The Biology of Human Action*, 2nd edition (1980), Sahlins *The Use and Abuse of Biology* (1977) and Montagu (ed.) *Sociobiology Examined* (1980).

12 For heterozygosity see Ch. One, p.9.

13 An example of the tone of such responses is the short article by the 'Science as Ideology' Group of the British Society for Social Responsibility in Science in *New Scientist* 13 May 1976: 'It is, of course, racist and sexist – and classist, imperialist and authoritarian too' (p.348).

14 Mary Midgley points out in her book *Beast and Man* (1978) and in her article 'Rival Fatalisms' (1980) that genetic or other biological causes acting on human characteristics does not mean, therefore, that human behaviour is largely or wholly predetermined and that there are no ethical, political, or practical choices to be made.

15 Sahlins' attack on attempts to limit the way culture patterns the physical world in biologistic or utilitarian terms may be compared with Max Weber's contention that 'The transcendental presupposition of every *cultural science* lies not in our finding a certain culture in every "culture" in general to be valuable but rather in the fact that we are *cultural beings* endowed with the capacity and the will to take a definite attitude toward the world and to lend it significance' *The Methodology of the Social Sciences* (1949: 81, emphasis in original).

16 Sahlins is well aware of the difference between White's concept of the 'symbol' and Saussure's concept of the 'sign' (1976: 59n, 105). He needs to continue to use White's concept because of his conception of 'culture' – the 'symbol' is an arbitrary representation of 'things' rather than a structured and conditioned part of a semiotic system.

17 For a discussion of these points see Benveniste *Problems in General Linguistics* (1971) especially Ch.4 but also Chs 18 and 20.

18 For Wittgenstein's view see *Philosophical Investigations* and for an introduction see Pole *The Later Philosophy of Wittgenstein* (1958). On the philosophy of language generally a clear and valuable book is Ian Hacking *Why Does Language Matter to Philosophy?* (1975).

19 The question of what progress chimpanzees have made is a vexed one. For an enthusiastic report of successes using Ameslan see Linden *Apes, Men and*

Language (1976). For a characteristically challenging and sceptical review of the debate see Martin Gardiner 'Monkey Business' in *The New York Review of Books*, **XXVII** 4, 20 March 1980.

20 Klein and her school have pushed the analysis of complex psychical processes further back into childhood; for an account of her work see Segal (1978).

21 See Washburn and de Vore (1961) and de Vore (ed.) *Primate Behaviour* (1965: Chs 2 and 3).

22 See Washburn, Jay and Lancaster (1965).

23 See Beach (1947: 299, 308).

24 See Beach (1947).

25 For chimpanzee behaviour see Reynolds and Reynolds (1965) and Goodall (1965).

26 Beach (1947: 299).

27 Beach (1947: 309).

28 To be strictly fair to Lévi-Strauss he does not say this, rather he argues that the 'nature' which is denied is a human *possibility* and not an animal actuality.

29 See 'The Original Affluent Society' in Sahlins *Stone Age Economics* (1974).

30 It is interesting how far field studies have changed our estimation of other animals' behaviours. For chimpanzees 'carnivals' see de Vore (1965: 409-15), for juvenile play de Vore (ed.) (1965: 421-22). It also used confidently to be said that 'only man uses tools'. Chimpanzees have been observed to make halting and limited use of 'tools', for example, using sticks to 'fish' for termites with a twig; see Goodall (1965: 440-43). As with language use, this proto-technology should make us cautious of 'only man can ...' type statements. They are anti-evolutionary in implication.

II
MENTAL ILLNESS AND PERSONALITY

'Berserk' bus driver left trail of destruction

A bus driver left a trail of death and destruction when he went berserk in April, killing one woman and seriously injuring five others.

Mr Eddie Brown, of Waldgrave Road, Broadgreen, Liverpool, was dragged from his cab screaming: 'We are all going to die. You are dead, I am taking you with me. I am God. I am the Devil,' Liverpool Crown Court was told yesterday.

Mr Brown pleaded not guilty to the murder of Mrs Kathleen Savage, aged 36, of Alness Drive, Rainhill.

His plea of guilty to manslaughter due to diminished responsibility was accepted by the court. He was ordered to be detained in a high-security hospital.

Mr Michael Maguire, QC, prosecuting, told the court that Mr Brown said in a statement to police: 'I had a terrible experience the night before. I rang my father and told him I was going mad. He said if I could ring him about it I was responsible enough and I was not mad.'

The Guardian 3 October 1980

'Exorcise the insane' — report
by William Thomson

Exorcism should be used to help cure some of Britain's most dangerous, criminally insane patients, a leading mental health campaigner urges in a report to Health Minister Patrick Jenkin.

The report by Peter Thompson, chairman of the Matthew Trust, a mental health reform group, says there should be a review of traditional methods of treatment. Exorcism should be considered as a method of cure.

The aim is to give 'last resort' treatment to the 150 incurable patients in Britain's top four mental hospitals — Broadmoor, Rampton, Moss Side and Park Lane.

The recommendations of the Matthew Trust will rekindle a fierce controversy. There have been deaths resulting from exorcism. The most recent involved two men who stamped a woman to death trying to 'drive evil spirits out' during a ritual. Both were sent to Broadmoor.

Mr Thompson, a former patient at Broadmoor, prepared the report after Mr Jenkin asked him to study possible treatment for gravely ill top security prisoners.

'My proposal is that exorcism is offered as a last resort to see if spiritual help can be given to patients who have committed inexplicably violent acts and those who are being thought fit for discharge,' he said.

The Observer 12 October 1980

4
INTRODUCTION AND THE
MEDICAL CONTEXT

To almost all of us in the modern West the application of the categories 'madness', or, more commonly today, 'mental illness', implies reference to a medical or therapeutic framework. Mental illnesses are conditions requiring specialist curative intervention or trained chronic management. The categories, in common usage, also imply pathology, a deficiency in mental functioning that needs to be remedied or compensated for if normal capacities are to be restored. Mental illness is thus assigned to medicine in the shape of psychiatry and attracts to itself the expectations of cure we attach to modern medical practice. Medical interventions have come to enjoy tremendous prestige in the last hundred years or so. Rising expectations of, and corresponding commitments of resources to, physical medicine have reached a point where demand for therapeutic results exceeds satisfaction. The 'crisis' of modern health systems, equally evident in the privately based US system as in the socialized NHS, is in large measure one created by medicine's past successes. It has created the dream of and the demand for effective therapeutics for all diseases and for all men.

Psychiatry has suffered more than most branches of medicine from this revolution of expectations, expectations so great that they will inevitably be thwarted. The mental hospital or insane asylum stands as a monument to failure, their chronic cases evidence of an inadequate therapeutics. One response to this 'failure' of scientific medicine to extend itself to problems of mental health and resolve them in the same way it has mastered bacterial infections are the various 'anti-psychiatries' — arguments and movements in favour of removing mental illness from the medical framework and, in many cases, for removing it from the sphere of pathology altogether. 'Anti-psychiatry' has enjoyed a considerable vogue partly because it has coincided with a general pressure among social service professionals and administrators to 'liberalize' the legal and institutional forms of psychiatric treatment. Thus the 1959 Mental Health Act made admission to psychiatric hospital treatment possible on the same voluntary basis as for general hospitals. Liberalization has in turn been fuelled by the revolution in medical expectations. Reforms in NHS practice in the 1970s resulted in an attempt to absorb acute psychiatric care as far as possible into the framework of the general hospital; long-term problems would be dealt with by out-patient treatment, by 'community' care and by social services departments' facilities. Psychiatric treatment was to be absorbed into the administration of general medicine and residual problems of care turned into a welfare problem. Mental illness thus remained, despite the anti-psychiatrists, firmly within the medical field, and public commitment to an effective therapeutic solution was strengthened against the (apparently more expensive) practices of specialist custodial management. To a considerable degree this liberalization has been predicated on the development in the last thirty years or so of effective psychotherapeutic drugs.

Mental illness has not always been thus medicalized. In the European Middle Ages 'madness' in certain of its forms was conceived as an inescapable affliction or, in the forms of melancholy or folly, as temporary states of mind which could afflict anybody. In neither case was there any effective medical remedy. The raving mad would be confined, the merely crazed or foolish licensed to beg. These conditions were afflictions different in kind from demoniacal possession. Moreover, possession *could* be remedied in certain circumstances by counselling and by exorcism. In other non-Western cultures conducts we would ascribe to mental illness are considered as cases of spirit possession. In some cultures the spirit is an affliction to be cast out but in others, like the *loa* of the Haitian voodoo cult, it is a visitation to be cultivated.

Until recently these other classifications of conducts and practices in respect of them were treated as evidences of backwardness and barbarousness from which scientific rationality has rescued us. A good example of this attitude is Gregory Zilboorg and P. Henry's *History of Medical Psychology* (1941), an attitude and a work to which we shall have cause to return in our discussion of witchcraft in Part Three. Sociologists have been prominent in challenging this notion that our categorizations of conduct are simple manifestations of medical reason. They have argued that medical institutions are social institutions which work by social rules, embody social pressures, and are subject to the processes and demands of the wider society. Labelling someone 'insane' is not a socially neutral act; it can lead to loss of income and social status, to degradation and incarceration. Diagnosis and categories of treatment are not socially neutral. Thus Hollingshead and Redlich (1958) attempted to show that chances of commitment to custodial care varied systematically with social class positions. Diagnosis depends on a repertoire of conducts, in which certain acts and statements appear as evidences of pathology. Rosenhan (1973) reports how several 'pseudopatients' gained admission to mental hospitals and were diagnosed as schizophrenic on the basis of reporting the simple symptom of claiming to hear voices. Erving Goffman, in his best-seller, *Asylums* (1961), treated mental hospitals as social institutions in which inmates were compelled to conform to pathological and dependent conducts. He contended that

'the society's official view is that inmates of mental hospitals are there primarily because they are suffering from mental illness. However, in the degree that the "mentally ill" outside hospitals numerically approach or surpass those inside hospitals, one could say that mental patients distinctively suffer not from mental illnesses but from contingencies.'

(Goffman 1961: 135)

Such studies have formed the dominant consensus among sociology teachers and students that mental illness is a normative category applied to conducts in definite social conditions.

Sociologists often take this relativity of definitions of conduct and categories applied to it, the fact that there is no given immediately observable datum of 'madness', as the starting point for a challenge to the medical conception of 'mental illness'. This sociological relativization has some value in promoting a critical assessment of psychiatric institutions and claims, challenging what has often been a simple-minded public acceptance of the medical framework. This is especially true in the United States where psychiatric conceptions of 'illness' and practices of diagnosis have been much more all-encompassing than in England.

But this relativistic criticism suffers from a major flaw. Even if there is no essential or given 'madness', there are substantial numbers of disorientated, depressed, suicidal, or irresponsibly dangerous persons who need more than tea and sympathy, and who also may be unwilling to accept the reality of their own impairment. This means accepting a role for medical psychiatry and involuntary options in forms of treatment. It is by no means self-evident that social services' departments or voluntary associations are the best means of dealing with the great mass of 'disturbed behaviour' that now tends to get referred to them, or that psychiatric therapies can operate on the basis of consent alone. Therapy and management of the 'mentally ill' remain necessary, and, *precisely because they are not part of some neutral realm of pure scientific techniques*, such means of treatment have definite social conditions of existence and functioning.

To say 'mental illness' is a normative category and, therefore socially relative, is to say nothing about the validity of its application. All such categories (possessed by a spirit, outcast, leper, Elect of God, etc.) are *always* normative and constraining of the conducts of social agents. 'Possession' was normative and stigmatizing. The Christians of the Middle Ages could no more dispense with it for that reason than they could tolerate heresy. Sociological relativism, in showing that certain categories or institutions are neither necessary nor inevitable, that they depend on certain conditions and that things are ordered differently elsewhere tends to neglect or to suspend the very effectivity of those (conditional) social relations. Relativism tends to avoid this paradox by refusing to situate itself *in* definite social relations, by refusing to take questions of policy, reform, and genuinely available alternatives seriously.

Many sociologists, because of this relativistic approach, have been sympathetic to 'anti-psychiatry'. But 'anti-psychiatry' is no less problematic in its response to the question 'what is to be done?' It tends both to dismiss the problem of limits to conduct expressed in terms of pathology and treated by medical practices, and to propose substitutes for psychiatric institutions which amount to a programme for 'social health'. Mental illness *is* recognized to the degree that the category, and the treatment meted out to those who fall under it, is presented as a symptom of the need for a total re-ordering of social relations. R.D. Laing and T.S. Szasz may be radically opposed in their ideologies and proposals for social change, but they have one thing in common, a thoroughgoing utopianism which makes their work equally irrelevant to any practice of development and reform of the psychiatric 'complex'.

Thus Part Two has two somewhat contradictory tasks to accomplish. The first is to explain that 'mental illness' as a category has social and institutional conditions of existence — that modern psychiatry is not a pure scientific discourse but is necessarily situated in institutions and practices which makes both its phenomena and its discourses on them possible; that psychiatry occupied a 'social space', of law, of the hospital, of the assessment of individual differences and competencies, long before its modern pretensions to scientificity came into existence, and that it still functions within that space; and that each of the successive nosographies[1] to which attach the claims of 'science', those of the periods of Pinel, Esquirol, Charcot, and of Kraepelin, reveal a succession of problematic categories — 'monomania', 'masturbatory insanity', 'hysteria', the 'psychotic' — which reveal changing concerns of social discipline and changing conceptions of normality. The essential guide to this task is Michel Foucault, whose path-breaking *Madness and Civilization* (1963) and *The Birth of the Clinic* (1973) will be the basis of our account. The second task is to combine with this situating of the psychiatric 'complex' an attention to practical problems of reform and alternative directions of development; to argue that whilst the categories of modern psychiatric[2] medicine are in no sense neutral or objective, the problem of 'mental illness' remains an inescapable one, and further that no single therapeutic 'solution' is possible.

It may be helpful to summarize the contents and organization of what must necessarily be a long, complex, and involved discussion. In the following section of this introductory chapter we examine the revolution in medicine in the past century and the place of psychiatry within medicine. It will be argued that *all* medicine, physical and psychic, involves the application of norms of functioning and complex socially conditioned choices as to the forms of therapy to be developed and emphasized. In Chapter Five we will consider the applicability of the categories of institutional psychiatry to non-Western civilizations. We ask whether there are mental disorders which are specific to the cultural and social context in which they occur. We will review certain culturally located syndromes, *Koro*, *Pibloktoq* and *Windigo* psychosis. It will then be argued in Chapter Six that concepts of person and conceptions of acceptable conduct vary considerably between cultures and between different eras of our own Graeco-Christian civilization. On this basis, the idea of a given 'human subject' centred in the experience of self or consciousness will be challenged in Chapter Seven. Some of the theories which criticize this idea of the subject and conceive of it rather as a complex of capacities constructed by various conditions and practices will then be considered. The views of thinkers like Louis Althusser on this question are complex and often inaccessible without philosophical preparation, but we will attempt to explain some of them as simply as possible. We will then turn in Chapter Eight to examine the debate between Sigmund Freud, Ernest Jones, and Bronislaw Malinowski about the applicability of the concept of the 'Oedipus complex' to different cultures and to family structures which differ from those of Europe. This discussion will be used as a vehicle to introduce certain of the major concepts of psychoanalysis. In Chapter Nine we will summarize and criticially assess Foucault's *Madness and Civilization*. In Chapter Ten, the final section of this discussion, we will evaluate the debate between psychiatry and 'anti-psychiatry'. Laing and Szasz are the main proponents of alternative theories of and therapies for mental illness to be considered. J.K. Wing's *Reasoning about Madness* (1978) will be examined as an attempt to defend the orthodox position against these criticisms.

The medical context

Considering the prestige which attaches to modern medicine it is easy to forget how recent is the appearance of *effective* professional interventions. By 'effective' we mean capable of lowering mortality rates and of raising the average period of life expectancy. Yet the dramatic transformation in population patterns which presaged and accompanied the industrial revolution in Europe and then elsewhere owes little to the curative activities of doctors or to specifically medical knowledges. The classic 'pre-industrial' population regime, in which a high birth rate countered the effects of a high death rate, subject to the periodic catastrophes of epidemics and famines, was a pattern in which population grew gradually through a cycle of demographic collapse and recovery. Its displacement was effected largely by changes in habits, by improved nutrition, and by public health measures.[3] Industrial production, and the forms of provision of urban facilities it made possible for a rapidly expanding population of town dwellers, served as multipliers for this process of declining death rates. Improvements in medical intervention were marginal to this process. The main factors involved in this revolution in the conditions of life and health of the masses were: better nutrition, made possible by the development of means of transportation; new sources of heating; improved shelter; the availability of changes of clothing and regular ablutions; effective sewage disposal and clean water; a shortening of the working day; and the conversion of the house into a specialized unit of consumption tended by a 'housewife' whose primary task was to feed, clean, and care for her family.[4] More people survived into adulthood because they were better cared for, better nourished, and less exposed to infection. The public health measures that stopped cities from consuming their indigenous populations and growing only by the ingestion of further supplies of migrant rural dwellers were effected largely by non-medical personnel and did not depend as such on modern theories of disease causation.[5]

Modern medicine is the product, not the creator, of industrial civilization. But when that is said, the transformation of medical capacities in the nineteenth century and their accelerated development in the twentieth does mark a qualitative advance. Medicine was transformed firstly in its institutions; the constitution of the hospital as a centre of investigation and teaching rather than a place of care made possible the systematization and dissemination of clinical-observational knowledges of diseases.[6] Medical knowledge was then revolutionized by the application of the new chemical and biological sciences to the experimental analysis of bodily processes and functions. There are four important elements in this advance which significantly affect mortality rates or improve the quality of individuals' lives. Probably the most significant in demographic terms is the development of a medically trained and supervised midwifery in which the importance of such factors as asepsis was recognized. The application of the new medical knowledges to public health measures made possible the systematic elimination of disease threats by determining the agents which are their cause and the means of transmission of those agents; diseases such as malaria and yellow fever can thereby be contained or eliminated. This has had an important demographic effect outside the developed temperate world. Curative medicine has changed out of all recognition since the mid-nineteenth century. Physiology provided a specification of 'diseases' in terms of the process whereby function is impaired, and thereby provided a new analytic diagnostics to complement and increasingly to supplant the observational diagnostics based on the isolation of symptoms into syndromes. Knowledge of disease physiology and of the bacterial, viral, and other pathogenic agents provides the basis for the application of the new synthetic pharmacopaeia produced by chemistry. It should be remembered that antibiotics, the drugs with the greatest impact on the lives of individuals, removing the fears associated with many infections, are extremely recent – some thirty or forty years old. Lastly, although most immediate in producing the public estimation of the 'marvels' of medicine, is the nineteenth-century revolution in surgical practice, the intervention in internal conditions made possible by antiseptics and anaesthetics.

These medical advances in the preventative and therapeutic capacity of medical knowledge and practice are probably of more relevance to the future than to the past. Increasing medical competence and means of intervention will in all likelihood serve to offset tendencies towards declining success of organizational and industrial means in lowering (or maintaining at existing levels) the death rates in advanced industrial countries. Industrial production may well be *worsening* health in the form of 'junk' food and pollution. Improved conditions of life for women (greater freedom, opportunities for waged work) may actually reduce the time and effort available for child care.

It has become fashionable to draw the conclusion from the marginal role of medicine in the revolution in population patterns that specialized medicine is an expensive and unnecessary conspiracy foisted on society, carrying with it the unwanted side-effects of iatrogenically induced illness. This is the view expressed by Ivan Illich in his *Limits to Medicine* (1977) where he argues the need to devolve medical care back onto 'society'. This is an analogue of the 'anti-psychiatry' argument in the field of physical medicine. It hovers on the verge of absurdity, even though it makes many telling criticisms of modern medical practice. The reason is that there *is* no way to 'devolve' the specialist knowledges on which the capacities of modern medicine depend. Moreover, those knowledges and capacities need to be deployed far more extensively and effectively than they are in the realms of preventative medicine and public health if the industrial, organizational, and medical advances of the last hundred years are to be consolidated and built on. We have become lax because of the achievements of the Victorians in the super-vision of urban and industrial life, and because we have been able increas-ingly to rely on curative medicine to pick up the consequences of any mess created by that laxness.

Problems of public health, medical supervision, and social organization are again becoming intractable and threaten powerful vested interests − just as they did in the era of the cholera epidemics. A list may make the point: air pollution from automobiles, noise, the potential dangers of nuclear power and synthetic substances, over-processed food, smoking, too little exercise or strenuous and useful work, increasing neglect of the old, and less thorough parental socialization and supervision of children. In many of these areas (effect of chemicals and foods, for example) only increased medically informed supervision can pinpoint damage to health and indicate effective ways of checking it, ways that stop short of a whole food, pure air, pre-industrial utopia and which involve specific technical interventions. In other of these areas social reforms or new patterns of social organization are needed. Neither medi-cine nor public health can be simply 'devolved', since they demand specific institutional agencies with the powers and resources sufficient to their task. The achievement of 'Victorian' social engineering involved coercion: Factory Acts, town planning, and Boards of Health constrained the wealthy and the poor; the factory inspectors' supervision of factory masters accompanied the compulsory medical inspection of prostitutes and the surveillance and delousing of tramps in workhouse casual wards.

Illich sounds fine until you stop to think that 'society' does not exist except as definite institutions, administrative bodies, and practices.

The purpose of this discussion is to situate the place of psychiatry within modern medicine. Radical sociologists often consider medicine the paradigm of all professions, as an organized conspiracy against the public. We have tried to make the point that while the achievements of medicine are comparatively recent, its current capacities for the alleviation of sickness and suffering are very great. The prestige and relatively high income of doctors in both socialized and private systems is in part a reflection of this fact. But doctors' salaries are only a portion of the resources committed to medical provision, and independent practitioners of curative medicine are only a part of the 'medical' apparatus of advanced states. We have stressed the importance of medical knowledges in informing public health measures (in which doctors are career officials) and in organizing practices carried out by much less well-paid, if highly regarded, personnel such as midwives and district nurses.

Psychiatry was created as a specialized branch of medical practice in the medical revolution of the nineteenth century.[7] It would be tempting to say it had remained there, marooned in relation to the developments in physical medicine at about the level of the mid-nineteenth century. This may seem an odd claim to make, but it applies most accurately to orthodox psychiatry which models itself on somatic medicine and seeks to reduce mental disorder to biological processes. Psychoanalysis is another matter entirely, less easy to place either theoretically or institutionally within the medical field. It is important to add, however, that Freud was trained as a medical doctor, studied under Charcot at the Salpêtriere, and that most of the early analysts were likewise medically trained.

A number of significant differences emerge between psychiatric and general medicine:

i.   that there is little in the way of actually locating psychiatric disorders in physiological mechanisms, despite much experiment and comparative studies with patients suffering from conditions such as schizophrenia;
ii. that psychiatry possesses few drugs or techniques whose mode of curative action is known or which function as specifics for definite disorders; rather drugs are most commonly used to produce certain effects on performance and conduct, such as sedation or relief of depression or anxiety;
iii. there is no equivalent of the rationalization of public health measures produced by medical knowledge in cases such as malaria: rather psychiatry operates as a curative practice on individual cases of mental disorder referred to it.

What psychiatry has had in common with general medicine is the *hospital*, the insane asylum. Pinel instituted practices of clinical classification and observation at the same time as his colleagues in the general hospital system. All the great classificatory systems of mental disorders from Pinel to Kraepelin and beyond have been hospital- and observationally-based. Psychiatric entities like 'schizophrenia' or 'chronic depression' are syndromes, identifiable complexes of symptoms exhibited by patients and isolated by clinical observation. The hospital, in Foucault's terms, is a *machine for observation*; its observations are not mere illusions or projections of ideology, but they do depend on definite conditions and circumstances, on what Foucault calls 'surfaces of emergence'.[8] J.K. Wing (1978), no disciple of Foucault's, confirms this concept elegantly, and in contradiction to his own view of the autonomy of psychiatric rationality when he denies the reality of 'hysteria', claiming it to be a product of 'suggestion' on the part of doctors such as Charcot.[9] The 'phenomena' of the hospital, differentially admitted, classified, and separated, are far from being a *brutum factum*. Not only that, but the machine for observation must confine itself to what is 'distinctive', to what forms a clear clinical picture. Hence the search for 'distinctive features', classic, stable symptoms which permit recognition and identification. Many cases which do not exhibit such features fall into a kind of clinical no-man's-land. Aetiologies are usually missing or weakly specified in psychiatric medicine, and diagnosis therefore lacks an analytical base in physiological mechanisms and tests for their presence independent of observation. The result is that outside of clear identifying symptoms (such as hearing voices, delusions of external direction, etc.), pathology is a matter of individual clinical judgements based on observation of and conversation with the patient. Thus it is all too easy for those with 'disorders' of conduct, and who are for various reasons unacceptable to relatives or public authorities and therefore referred to a psychiatrist, to be classed as 'mentally ill' − illness here being considered a direct analogue of a feared or loathed physical disease like cancer or syphilis.

All medicine implies the application of a norm. One is not pointing to the limitations of psychiatry on the grounds that it involves norms, but because the conditions of their application are weakly specified. The concept of 'disease' involves the notion of impairment of function, that vital capacities of the organism are destroyed or reduced in efficiency in ways that threaten the organism's existence or its capability in coping with its environment. This involves normativity in two senses:

i.   setting an acceptable level of performance or efficiency for organs and processes: this involves physiological or functional norms − the point beyond which interventions are necessary. This point is not a physiological given but depends on the available techniques, the level of resources committed to a condition and what levels of functioning patients, parents, and employers, etc. come to expect;

ii. in taking the standpoint of 'pathology', pathology is a concept which involves the observer in *making a choice* between elements of processes and types of organisms. The very notion of 'vital functions' involves a valorization of 'life' and of the life of complex organisms which are to be sustained. Processes like sclerosis of the arteries are 'normal', in the sense of being regular and expected in the life history of the human animal, but nonetheless are regarded as pathological to the extent that they endanger the vital function of circulation and require medical intervention to inhibit them. The destruction of vital processes such as respiration by the consequences of infection also involves 'life' (bacteria and viruses), but we prefer ourselves to these parasitic organisms. Disease and normality involve the same physiological laws, as the famous physiologist, Claude Bernard, argued in 1865.[10] Medicine involves a *choice*, based on the preference for human life, to prevent certain processes and organisms and foster others.

Further, all medical practice involves choices between possible interventions and degrees of intervention, just as the police make choices as to which laws they enforce and how vigorously. Modern Western health systems have tended to concentrate resources and effort on acute curative interventions in certain types of disease and conditions. This is because higher professionals have been given considerable organizational autonomy in both socialized and privately based systems. Doctors' preferences in research and forms of work significantly influence patterns of spending and set the conditions for administrative decisions. Preventative medicine has been significantly neglected, and 'advanced' areas like coronary surgery and cancer research have been favoured over much pain-relieving and mobility-enhancing basic health care.[11] The fact that doctors advise patients to take exercise, not to smoke, etc., is irrelevant. This 'fireside wisdom' is not reflected in hard cash and preventative practices. Such criticism of the norms informing current medical practice clearly is not equivalent to a denunciation of normative practices *per se*.

The problem in psychiatry is that the norms applied to establish pathology pertain to concepts of *mental* functioning and *conduct*. On the one hand, the physiological basis of attributions of pathology is weakly specified. On the other, the norm applied is that of a socially competent and acceptable subject. This involves notions of normal 'mental' processes; modes of reasoning, forms of statement, and resultant patterns of conduct. Yet, significant, unacceptable, and involuntary deviations from norms of this kind can take place even when there is no physiological disorder. This is the basis for the anti-psychiatric critiques which further argue that it is socially unacceptable conducts and behaviours which are stigmatized by the concept of 'illness'. What this critique refuses to recognize is that these conducts may be problematic for the subject himself and for others, *precisely because they differ from expected patterns of statement and behaviour*. The conditions of such conduct may not even be representable by the subject himself as 'voluntary', or recognized by others as such.

Psychiatrists judge cases according to clinical criteria which more or less explicitly incorporate prevailing conceptions of how the 'person', as a complex of capacities and social requirements, is to exist. These conceptions are variable: 'personality' is not a given, social expectations as to capacity and conduct differ, as do the forms of their existence in subjects' practice. To hear 'voices' or to have impressions of direction from without are, for example, classic distinctive features of schizophrenia in psychiatric diagnosis. But until recently masses of people in the West have striven to hear 'voices', of God or of the saints, and to be directed from without. Prayer as a personal practice has rested on the hope of direct communication with God. Such religious practices now appear, to a cynical and pragmatic public discourse, as excessive, absurd, or pointless. Religious belief and prayer may have, in the periods of mass commitment, produced distress, anguish, and pathology, but they also created a set of conditions of practice in which certain conducts and experiences could not be *decisively* identified as pathological. Religious mania and melancholy were recognized conditions probably since the sixteenth century, 'possession' since much earlier, but as pathologies they had complex (non-'distinctive') signs of recognition and were always subject to the interdiction of an interpretation which proclaimed the case to be a genuine religious experience of enthusiasm, ecstasy, or despair.

Psychiatry's norm of mental functioning involves a concept of the subject or person. The concept psychiatry uses is a relatively recent one, and it has enjoyed dominance and stability only since the seventeenth century. It is the conception of the person as centred in a unitary consciousness, a subject 'self-possessed' in its conducts, experience, and thoughts, all of which flow from a single and continuous origin. Consistency in conduct, self-originated action, and unity of memory and experience are all criteria of normality of this subject as conscious origin of itself. This conception has enjoyed such complete dominance that we forget it is a *construction* placed on a mass of conducts, and on their diverse conditions and circumstances. However, conceptions of subjects their capacities and competencies, can be other than this, and relate to definite practices which have effects on the form of subjects as social agents. In the next chapter we will consider this variability of the concept of the person. The point to be made here is that, however variant this concept of personality on which 'normality' is based, it is not *illusory* – it is a register of social expectations and necessities. Psychiatry cannot be other than a practice adjusted to what subjects need to be in their conducts and relations with others. This is no less true of psychoanalysis.

Notes

1 Nosographies – systematic classifications of disease entities and syndromes.
2 Psychoanalysis is sometimes included within the field of psychiatric medicine for the purposes of this discussion.

3 For a simple and readable account of changes in population patterns and population growth see C.M. Cipolla *The Economic History of World Population*
   (1965). Emanuel Le Roy Ladurie illustrates brilliantly this cyclical regime of
   population and economic growth for a particular region in his *Peasants of
   Languedoc* (1974).

4 It is important to stress the positive aspect of the creation of this specialist
   woman's occupation given the criticism directed by the Women's Movement at the
   devaluation of women's work. The socialist and labour movements in the nineteenth century fought for the emancipation of women *from* work, in order to care
   for their families. Donzelot (1980) — as discussed in Hirst (1981) — stresses the
   implication of the housewife in practices of socialization and medical supervision
   by public authorities. This implication did result in important changes in the
   standards of social supervision of childrearing.

5 Chapter Six of McNeill's *Plagues and Peoples* is a most accessible account of the
   role of medicine and science in the transformation of the balance between men
   and the micro-organisms which threaten them which accompanied the industrial
   revolution:

   'Long before Koch's microscope thus provided doctors with an empirical base
   for the modern view of how cholera spreads, the alarm it created in American
   and European cities provided essential leverage for those reformers who sought
   to improve urban sanitation, housing, health services, and water supply. Models
   of what to do and how to do it were readily at hand, for during the eighteenth
   century European governments discovered that soldiers' and sailors' lives were
   much too valuable to squander needlessly, when simple and not overly expensive measures could check the ravages of disease.'

   (McNeill, 1979: 246)

6 This process is brilliantly analysed in Michel Foucault's *The Birth of the Clinic*
   (1973).

7 The fact that it began as 'medical psychology' outside the *existing* medical profession and in specialist institutions, insane asylums, is an irrelevancy to its place
   within the medical field. Andrew Scull in his *Museums of Madness* (1979) makes
   much of the struggle for 'professionalization' on the part of asylum directors,
   etc. This emphasis is misplaced, for the asylum develops like the hospital — as a
   site of investigation, observation, and classifying the symptoms of its population.

8 Foucault (1972: 41).

9 Wing (1978: 70); see also Yap (1951: 313).

10 'Diseases at bottom are only physiological phenomena in new conditions still
   to be determined; toxic and medical action ... came back to simple physiological
   changes in properties of the histological units of our tissues' (Bernard 1957: 198).

11 Disease prevention is something many societies have unconsciously achieved
   through a stabilized customary cuisine and patterns of conduct, but which, in our
   case,' because of an industrialized diet and changing customs, needs the intervention of specialist agencies and knowledges. The preferences of Western medicine also correspond to lines of popular resistance; any system of medical 'police'
   which did try to eliminate smoking, excessive drinking, etc. would face real
   difficulties. Ordinary people appear on average to prefer medical practice to
   try and manage the mess created by conduct rather than adopt a new regime.

5
CULTURAL RELATIVITY AND PSYCHIATRIC PRACTICES

We have seen that psychiatry constructs its disease entities with reference to conceptions of 'normal' mental functioning and by means of clinical observation. Both the norms which define pathology and the space of its emergence – the psychiatric hospital – have specific discursive and institutional conditions of existence. Psychiatry is implicated in modern Western conceptions of rationality and personal conduct, and in institutions which depend on Western forms of social organization. The applicability of its 'observations' in other contexts may well, therefore, appear questionable. P.M. Yap puts the question succinctly:

'Modern psychiatry has developed in Western Europe, largely under French and German aegis, and latterly in the United States. It is pertinent to ask, since it deals with human behaviour in all its variety, if the concepts, working principles and empirically derived conclusions of psychiatry possess universal validity, wherever it might be practised.'

(Yap 1951: 313-27)

Often this question is taken to imply that what appears as vice or insanity on one side of the Pyrenees may, on the other, walk the streets as the utmost respectability or sanity. While stressing the cultural specificities of Western psychiatric conceptions of the 'norm', the personalist metaphysics implicated in those conceptions, and the dangers of applying them to other non-Western cultural practices and to other periods in the history of our own civilization, we shall also be concerned to challenge the extremes of nominalism often entailed in cultural relativist views. Victims of general paralysis of the insane (GPI) may exhibit elements of different culturally specific repertoires of symptoms, but they suffer a common affliction with the same physiological mechanisms. Mental illnesses are incapacitating even if they do take culturally specific forms; the victim of *Windigo* psychosis is a menace to his own family just as surely as the English sufferer from senile dementia who insists on smoking in bed. There are biologically based disorders which affect mental functioning and which appear to be virtually universal – GPI, senile dementia, and a portion of the cases diagnosed by means of the complex of symptoms we call 'schizophrenia'. There appear to be no cultures which lack categories and cases of involuntary mental pathology, whatever the conception of its forms and causes.[1]

The social distribution of definite 'syndromes' can in no sense settle the question whether 'mental illnesses' in general arise from biological causes or from social sanctions and patterns of conduct. The 'either/or' here is absurd. It arises, on the one side, from a professional desire to conceive psychiatric therapy as a socially neutral technique, rather than a complex and compromised practice constantly implicated in social norms and demands of social discipline. On the other side, it arises from sociological imperialism and utopian egalitarianism which are unwilling even to consider biological limits to social causality and human malleability. Yet the social and geographical *distribution* of different symptoms and disease entities tells us very little about their causation. There are a number of reasons for this:

i.   It is well known that there are substantial epidemiological differences in the incidence of physical diseases, such as cancer and bronchitis. Yet geographical variation is not taken to imply that the *disease mechanism* is social, although the circumstances affecting the rates of incidence may well be so;

ii. Social and cultural factors, diet, forms of activity, levels of stress, etc., may intervene to arrest or accentuate the incidence of physiologically based mental disorder;

iii. Physiologically based disease, if defined and identified through behavioural symptoms, may not be directly recognizable (it is expressed in a different repertoire of symptoms, in conducts which differ from those of Western 'mentally ill' sick roles) and may lack 'distinctive features'; or individuals may exhibit behaviours akin to the 'distinctive features' of mental illness but which actually stem from different sources (e.g., yogis and certain shamans enter a state of prolonged trance which resembles catatonia[2]).

The prevalent psychiatric assumption that mental disorders ultimately resolve themselves into biological processes does not help to resolve the question. Does this mean that patterns of conduct which do not resolve themselves into biological processes should cease to be considered part of the practice of psychiatry? This would be a view all too consistent with Szasz's sterile antinomy of physiologically based disease or voluntary conduct. It would also be refused most vigorously by the majority of psychiatrists. Because of the social demands placed upon it, psychiatry cannot escape the management of conditions with no organic basis or clear symptomatology. The opposition between physical illnesses with effects on mental functioning and voluntary conduct is an impossible one for psychiatry to sustain, because it is a social practice. Most psychiatric 'cases' in Western practice are neither sufferers from some physiologically determined disorder nor persons whose chosen conduct merely violates established social norms. Such persons are the victims of obsessions, fears, anxieties, states of depression, and so on which have a necessity and compulsion which remove them from the realm of chosen conduct, which are distressing to, and recognized as pathological by, the sufferers themselves, and which have no evident or plausible biological basis.[3] Yet established psychiatry prefers, even in this shady area which dominates its practices, a regime of treatment coincident with physical medicine. Drugs and ECT are still the dominant therapeutic techniques, with conditioning therapy as the least threatening alternative to the medical model of treatment. It is in this problematic area that psychiatry is confronted with a mass of conditions in other cultures, conditions which lack 'distinctive features' and which relate but tangentially to its own rhetorics of symptoms.

Certain conditions with marked effects on mental capacity, such as mongolism, senile dementia, and syphilis present no great problem because there are physiological diagnostics and non-observational tests. 'Schizophrenia' is far less clear both because the evidence of biochemical and other changes is still too slight to provide either a physiological disease mechanism, or a test for it, or a means of acting upon it, and because it remains an observational syndrome. Ari Kiev (1972) points out that other cultures exhibit symptoms which deviate from the established clinical pictures constructed through observation of Western patients.[4] As a syndrome, 'schizophrenia' can all too easily be stretched to cover a wide variety of symptoms and conditions; it then becomes no more definitive of a specific disease entity than the eighteenth-century concept of 'fever'.

The danger in such modification of the original disease entities to apply to 'local' conditions is that the basic classifications remain unaffected. It is assumed that there is simply a given realm of mental pathology which has to be recognized in different cultural registers. This assumption is an effect of medico-psychiatric discourses' tendency to suppress the role of the clinic as a specific 'surface of emergence', as an institution and a complex of practices which specifies and forms the objects it encounters and denotes. Medical education assures the clinical trainee that he or she confronts the brute fact of pathology itself. Other cultures, however, involve institutions, practices, and discourses which constitute *other* 'surfaces of emergence' and other modes of formation of objects.

No social organization is devoid of concepts of entity which have effects on mental capacity, of norms for conduct, and of concepts of pathology. The necessity of norms of conduct and capacity arises from the fact that all human repertoires of conduct and assemblages of personal capacities are *limited*, that is, they have definite conditions of formation and maintenance. These limits will be to a degree publicly recognized in, for example, the prescriptions and proscriptions of training and upbringing, and in the forms of avoidance and control of factors undermining capacities, so that the conditions for the effectiveness of a capacity or practice are not breached. Thus Ojibwa boys are trained to refuse food and suffer hunger in order to strengthen their capacity to endure the rigours of the hunt and also their capacity to sustain spirit visions. Likewise, respectable Victorian boys were exhorted to sexual continence and closely supervised to prevent masturbation. Capacities and practices are not independent of discourses or doctrines or the entities and objects constituted by them. Whilst Victorian boys were warned of the dangers of not preserving their 'vital fluids', of the dangers to their own strength and sanity and to their capacity to foster offspring, Trobriand boys were allowed an entirely different regime of sexual expression, a regime not unaffected by the circumstance that public knowledge refuses to recognize the role of the father in procreation. In both cases patterns of sexual education and control are governed by doctrines as to the nature of sexuality, doctrines which exceed the demands of 'social function' or 'social needs'.

An *unlimited* range of human attributes and abilities is as mistaken a notion as that of a fixed and pre-constituted 'human nature'. As we have seen in Chapter Two, human attributes depend on definite socially constructed techniques, practices, acquired competencies, and patterns of association which exclude others of the kind by their very existence. Prevailing repertoires of conduct imply, therefore, a *de facto* norm simply by their existence. On top of this, definite conceptions of conformity, deviation, and pathology are an explicit normative addition imposed on those repertoires by social institutions and discourses. Though such conceptions are related to the entities specified in various socially accepted doctrines, they may exceed the necessities of developing and maintaining the capacities and conducts they purport to sustain. Indeed, such conceptions of pathology and conformity may be as problematic for the social relations they police as they are supportive of them. For example, norms of conduct which do not permit failure, which ascribe it to individual weakness or incompetence or desertion by spiritual powers, can neither actually remove the circumstances which produce failure nor mitigate its consequences. The Ojibwa male who suffers what we would consider a run of 'bad luck' in hunting is placed in a desperate position not merely because his family is hungry but primarily because he thereby knows himself to be abandoned by the sustaining power of his spirit visions. Likewise the sexual mutilants and perverts Stephen Marcus chronicles in *The Other Victorians* (1967) are the other side of an enforced regime of sexual conformity and continence.[5]

Pathologies are both identified *and* produced by the complexes of discourses we call 'cultures' and the amalgams of institutions and practices we call 'societies'. We are thus faced with two things, other concepts of abnormality *and* other abnormalities. This circumstance can often be presented as relatively unproblematic; as the differential cultural means of expression, the different forms of the 'sick' role, into which individual sicknesses or disorders are channelled. Kiev takes this stance:

'To the extent that the emotionally ill are all expected to fit the behaviour patterns of the "insane" role, there will be a certain amount of similar behaviour on the part of patients in the same culture who may in fact be suffering from different disorders. Behavioural patterns and symptoms, having been learned in a particular culture, are then grafted on to the underlying disorder.'

(Kiev 1972: 31)

Van Loon (1927) treats the condition *Amok* in this manner. A violent state, it is the mode of expression peculiar to the Malay race for a variety of conditions, including delirium deriving from malarial infection.[6]

But the question of other abnormalities has more at stake in it than different conceptions of how to be pathological. Conceptions of entity, required capacities and performances, expectations and forms of discipline are themselves the sources of fears, anxieties, and failures which produce pathological reactions directly related to those sources. It is widely accepted that it is to court a mass of dangers to diagnose whole cultures psychiatrically, using categories derived from Western psychiatry such as 'paranoid'. Yet this is just what Ruth Benedict did in *Patterns of Culture* (1961). But she did so in the service of objectives which confound her critics,[7] to challenge the notion of a given 'human nature' and to stress the radical effects on thought and conduct of systems of beliefs. Whilst it may be mistaken to call Dobuan culture 'paranoid', since Dobuans are not like paranoid schizophrenics in our own culture, it does serve the purpose of emphasizing that they live in constant fear of witchcraft and consequently act in a suspicious and withdrawn manner towards others. The entities implicated in practices like witchcraft and counter-magic, spirit mediumship and possession, and so on are not *mere* 'beliefs' any more than categories like 'nation' and 'race' are mere beliefs in our own era. These entities and practices constitute the very objects of their reference.[8]

We will now consider certain 'disorders' viewed as pathological in the culture in which they occur and which bear no clear relation to Western institutional symptomatologies. What they do bear, however, is the clear mark of certain doctrines of entity peculiar to these cultures, and of the demands and pressures imposed by a particular pattern of social relations. Within this context of doctrines and cultures, they exhibit a definite symptomal consistency, but in relation to Western symptomatologies they appear displaced and confused — which is not to say Western forms of psychotherapeutic discourse cannot be brought to bear to analyse them. Psychoanalysis serves to point to features in these disorders which are not given in the forms of representation commonly adopted in their own cultural context. In this respect psychoanalysis has the definite advantage over medical psychiatry that it is not concerned with the clinical isolation of stable disease entities but, rather, with using certain general concepts to illuminate the dynamics of psychical development and possible forms of conflict.

Koro

Koro is a disorder encountered among male Chinese.[9] Its essence is an acute and incapacitating fear, producing a state of panic, that the penis is retracting into the abdomen. If this happens, it is believed, then death will result. Yap comments:

'That this is a psychogenic illness resting on superstition there can be no doubt. There is a wealth of folk-lore in connection with this disease, but it is probable that actual hysterical anaesthesia of the penis, or some disturbance of the body image occurs . . . . Nosologically, *Koro* is, I believe, an acute anxiety (panic) in persons with sexual conflicts and preoccupations.'

(Yap 1951: 318)

There are two points to note here. The first is that sexual conflicts and preoccupations are hardly unusual among the Chinese. Sexual frustration, anxiety, and guilt about intercourse with prostitutes and sexual excess generally are apparently common, these being related to traditional Chinese family patterns and child-rearing practices. The second is that the Chinese interpret *Koro* in Taoist terms as a humoral imbalance, using concepts of sexual economy and its relation to somatic health different from but, in their capacity to produce anxiety, analogous to Victorian doctrines about masturbation and spermatorrhea. The anxiety in question, therefore, is directly related to certain family practices and doctrines of sexuality. The acute fear involved depends on a conviction that the entities in question can really harm the individual.

Pibloktoq

Pibloktoq is a syndrome among the Polar Eskimo. It is a complex of symptoms which can vary from case to case but which are identified by the Eskimo as a specific disorder and attributed to a form of spirit possession. It tends to affect women more than men, and tends to take more florid forms among women. A 'typical' episode might be abstracted from the cases as follows: a sudden outburst of crying and 'speaking in tongues' followed by a berserk running about, often naked, over the ice, into the water, and so on, followed by collapse, sleep, and a failure to recollect the attack.[10]

Brill, the American psychoanalyst and translator of Freud, described *Pibloktoq* as a form of 'hysteria':

'And yet is there really so much difference between the hysterical mechanisms as evidenced in *Pibloktoq* and the *grande hysterie* or other modern hysterical manifestations? We may answer unhesitatingly that the difference is more apparent than real. The deeper determinants as we have seen are the same in both. With due apologies to Mr Kipling we may say that the modern lady and the Eskimo Julia O'Grady are the same under the skin.'

(Brill 1913: 520)

Indeed! Brill attributes *Pibloktoq* to 'sex in all its broad ramifications', to the repressed and subordinate position of the Eskimo wife as a chattel, servant, and sex object of her husband. But other accounts make it clear that Eskimo marriage is not without its affections, forms of interdependence, and commitments. Men and women clearly value one another, otherwise the husband in the Eskimo 'tale' Gussow (1960) reports would not have had a premonition that something was wrong and returned to assist his wife.[11]

The problem with Brill's account is that in fact *Pibloktoq* is a generalized response to a variety of circumstances involving stress, anxiety, and so on. Often it will occur when difficulties are largely overcome, or when the victim is sure that assistance is at hand. It thus may function as a response to anxiety and as a means of release or discharge from it. It affects both men and women. It is a temporary, if recurrent, state and not an incapacitating condition like hysteria — it would be absurd to equate this with a case like that of Dora.[12]

Moreover, as Gussow points out, *Pibloktoq* incorporates a number of elements common in Eskimo cultural practice. Nudity and running in the snow are not uncommon, Eskimo are often nude indoors and run naked after a sweat-bath. Glossolalia, 'speaking in tongues', is a part of Eskimo shamanism and religious rituals, whilst wailing, crying, and so on are a part of mourning rites. *Pibloktoq* can be considered as a 'culturally patterned panic reaction' (Gussow 1960: 233). The Eskimo regard *Pibloktoq* as an ordinary and common phenomenon which could happen to anyone; no stigma attaches to the sufferer of an attack. But it is still viewed as abnormal or pathological behaviour to be held in check, particularly because of the dangers of frostbite or drowning, rather than as sanctioned conduct. The 'cultural patterning' involved, therefore, does not amount to public recognition, sanction, or prescription. The variability of the symptoms may well be an effect of the fact that, although publicly recognized as a phonomenon, it does not derive from socially established doctrines of entity — an established course and set of consequences for the disease — in the way that a disorder such as *Koro* does.[13] It articulates a diverse set of tensions and stresses relating to the environment, to fears of loss of husbands whilst hunting, to disorientation when out of sight of land when at sea, and so on. This is also unlike *Koro* which centres on a single fear and an underlying related complex of frustration and anxieties concerning sexual capacity. Nevertheless, both the symptoms and the precipitating factors derive from a cultural context. Beyond very general notions like 'anxiety', 'panic', 'stress' it bears no definite relation to disorders identified in Western psychiatry textbooks.

Windigo psychosis

The *Windigo* or *wiitiko* psychosis affects the Cree and Ojibwa Indians who live between Lake Winnipeg and Labrador in Canada.[14] It takes the form of a disorder involving obsessive cannibalism. The sufferer becomes morbid and depressed, feels nauseous and rejects ordinary foods, and is subsequently obsessed with ideas of being bewitched and impelled to kill and devour those around him. He believes himself possessed by the spirit of the *wiitiko* monster, a huge being with a heart of ice who feeds on human beings. Apparently the disorder, it is said, can lead to homicidal cannibalistic attacks on those around him (often close family members), whom he regards as fat and desirable animals he wishes to devour.

Clinical psychologists and psychoanalysts will both readily interpret this psychosis. Kiev (1972), although reserving a commitment on aetiology, suggests it can be interpreted as a depressive form of schizophrenia. Psychoanalytic interpretations, based on cannibalistic fantasies among Western adults and children, are readily and easily applicable. Parker (1960), however, locates the *wiitiko* 'complex' in terms of certain specific Ojibwa child-rearing practices, familial roles, and expectations of competency. He argues that the harsh training for independence of the male child leads to a frustration of dependency, and to the development of 'magical' expectations of his parents' capacities for support and succour, expectations which give rise to unsatisfied and repressed dependency cravings. The Ojibwa believes that he owes his strength and success to the 'spirit visions' he is encouraged to seek through starvation and self-denial. The Ojibwa hunter lacks means of coping with failure or depression; success and strength are not conceived as the subject's own resource but as a 'gift' obtained by self-denial and supplication. Ojibwa culture endows food and eating with a special significance, the successful hunter is the provider of abundant food. Ego-esteem, gratification, and ambivalent feelings based on self-denial and suffering centre on hunting and eating.

Whilst cannibalistic fantasies are widespread, occurring in many different cultures with radically different regimes of child-rearing and familial relations, among the Ojibwa they form part of religious beliefs and ritual. The *wiitiko* is an entity publicly accepted and believed in by the Ojibwa. It is not therefore treated as a fantasy or a delusion of the cognitive faculties of the individual subject but as an actual form of possession and conversion of the subject into the possessed. The nearest equivalent in Western beliefs would be lycanthropy, 'werewolfism'. But the werewolf, although feared and sometimes even 'caught' and tried, has never been a central element in Western religious beliefs and practices (see Part Three, Chapter Thirteen below). The Ojibwa, moreover, in their social training and religious life actively seek forms of spirit possession. Thus *wiitiko* possession is a 'pathological' or monstrous variant of an approved social activity. Because of both the 'complex' of factors in Ojibwa social relations linking food, sexuality, and ego-esteem and the nature of the *wiitiko* as a publicly recognized and feared entity, it is insufficient to treat this particular disorder either as a mere local manifestation of universal psychic structures and Oedipal conflicts or as a form of 'going crazy' into which persons place their particular pathologies. Yap, no simple-minded protagonist of cultural 'uniqueness', remarks as follows in respect of the *wiitiko*:

'This mythological creature is greatly feared, but sometimes actual cannibalism takes place, as though the patient were impelled towards the very behaviour that is feared. The belief is so strongly held that sometimes alimentary symptoms like loss of appetite or nausea arising from quite ordinary reasons causes the patient to fall into great excitement for fear of being transformed.'

(Yap 1951: 320)

Wiitiko beliefs, combined with the pressures of social relations and circumstances of illness or failure, can be considered as *generative* of anxiety and depression and not merely as a form of expression of already given pathological traits.[15]

The purpose of this section is not to argue that clinical psychiatric or psychoanalytic categories and concepts are inapplicable to 'other' cultures. Psychiatric clinics have been built in non-Western areas since colonial days and practices of observation and diagnosis carried out. Psychoanalysis claims both that the 'primary process' is universal and extra-social, and that the institutions of repression and the formation of appropriately 'sexed' subjects are universal in their basic form and effects, underlying local and institutional diversities. Rather, our purpose here is to insist that the disease entities formed by clinical observation of symptom-complexes and the categories which derive from the results of analysis are not independent of certain institutions, practices, and dis-courses. The dangers of the indiscriminate application of those categories are the creation of the illusion of a universal and objective pathology, forms of a disorder which manifest themselves irrespective of other concepts of norm and entity and their effects, or of a universal symbolism in which complexes of discourse and conduct become the manifestations of a single psychic domain. We cannot dispense with the category of 'schizophrenia' — clinical observation is not an illusion. Nor can we dispense with analytic concepts, but we must be prepared to limit and modify them in conditions of application other than their own institutional and discursive sites. And, being prepared to do that, also to recognize their limitations and conditions of existence in those very originary sites, the psychiatric clinic and the analyst's couch.

Notes

1   Yap (1951) points out that it was often assumed that general paralysis of the insane did not exist in non-European cultures; the reason for this generalization was the limited facilities for regular observation of populations and the failure of patients to present themselves to such facilities as did exist. Likewise, he points out that the reason senile dementia was thought to be rare among Chinese was because families preferred to keep aged, and honoured, relatives at home rather than break their own codes of conduct by delivering them to asylums.

2   It is often claimed that what differentiates the yogi from the schizophrenic is that the former can alter his state at will, while the latter cannot do so nor control its manifestations; see, for example, Yap (1951: 315). This is too simplistic. Franz Alexander (1931) points to tendencies within Buddhistic doctrine and practice which reveal that more than a simple technique is at stake; prolonged trance is a state of self-obliteration which corresponds to the 'wishes' Freud considers to be at the heart of the Death Instinct. Repeated entry into trance could be viewed as a form of 'compulsion to repeat' − a phenomenon analogous to shell-shock victims of the Great War who returned to their experiences in dreams, a phenomenon generally regarded as pathological. Likewise, if the reports of writers like Goffman are to be believed, 'deteriorated schizophrenia' is not a given condition, but includes elements of a pattern of conduct, differential levels of communication, attention, and interest. The voluntary/involuntary opposition here may well not survive serious inspection.

3   Devereux points out that pharmacological 'efficacy', in sedation, inhibation of anxiety, etc., in no way justifies either the notion of a biological aetiology or the 'rationality' of medical interventions. 'Primitive' peoples use their pharmacopaeia to treat 'mental illness' but they often believe the agents in question act to harm or discomfort, and therefore to expel, a spirit or demon. He sensibly comments: 'It would be preposterous indeed to argue on this basis against chemotherapy in the treatment of psychosis, but it is equally preposterous to infer that their effective treatment by chemotherapy *proves* their organic causation' (1958: 370).

4   Kiev (1972: 58-65).

5   It may be useful here to offer a word of caution to the reader who believes *our* regime of sexual beliefs to be an enlightened one based on objective realities. Victorian 'repression' as normality produced its monstrosities, but the present notion of normality, of sexual gratification (in approved forms) also has its pathogenic aspect. Not only does it continue to isolate even more radically certain classes of pervert but it can create tensions and feelings of failure in those who fear they fall below the norm of gratification. Foucault's brilliant (and infuriating, for the reader committed to the value of psychoanalytic knowledges) *History of Sexuality* (1978) challenges this notion of the 'liberal' and healthy nature of our sexual regime, its motto is 'We, Other Victorians'. Any regime that claims to be adjusted to 'reality', defining itself in relation to previous sexual 'ignorance' should be treated with the greatest suspicion.

6   'Race psychology' offers a quite different account of the problem of the universality of psychiatric disorders. It may be formulated on ideological or cultural grounds, or some mixture of both. Van Loon refers to the 'oriental soul' and the 'Malay psyche' as distinct racial types of mentality. The paper can be read with profit for its intelligent psychiatric observations and for its rigidly colonial

mentality with its unquestioned assumption of white superiority. Clearly, in arguing for culturally specific pathologies we mean nothing of this kind.

7　For example, see Kiev (1972: 29).

8　Which is to say rather more than W.I. Thomas' banal: 'If the situation is defined as real, it is real'. We are not concerned here with 'definition'. A people may think the moon is made of lemon jelly, but this is a matter of supreme irrelevance, however 'real' they may believe it to be, unless as a doctrine it articulates definite practices and bears on conducts. These practices and conducts are not mere consequences of a logic of 'definition', they may have diverse non-definitional conditions of existence. Thus, as we shall see in Part Three, Chapter Fifteen, the 'poison oracle' among the Azande depended for its prestige on the supposed fact that, properly used, it could *not* be manipulated and on the supposed unimpeachability of the Prince's oracle as a court of last resort. The characteristics of *benge* (the poison) and of Zande governmental institutions are not mere matters of definition, nor do they exist merely for the convenience of certain beliefs about witchcraft.

On the other hand, apparently 'monstrous' and absurd objects *can* be made to appear if certain doctrines are combined with appropriate institutions and practices. Doctrines of race psychology, even widespread popular 'beliefs', can create the categorical basis for the practices which really do isolate and circumscribe 'races' as homogeneous entities, with required attributes and conducts. A complex and divided cultural category, the 'Jews', became a menaced unity after the Nuremburg laws. Divisions of origin, religious allegiance and social class were finally obliterated in a common isolation in the camps.

Nor is it to say as little as is offered by the purveyors of 'subjective meaning'. The entities in question are part of public knowledge and the practices in which they are implicated are often obligatory. Doctrines of sexuality, race purity, spirit mediumship, for example, require social subjects to take a definite form, they 'interpellate' their bearers as subjects of a certain range of attributes and capacities.

9　See Yap (1951: 317-18) and Kiev (1972).

10　See Gussow (1960), Brill (1930), and Wallace (1972).

11　Gussow (1960).

12　See Freud's 'Fragment of an Analysis of a Case of Hysteria' (*SE* VII).

13　Whilst the fantasy involved in *Koro*, of the retraction of the penis, is found in similar forms among Westerners it does not take the form of a publicly recognized and sanctioned knowledge, it is not an entity in the way Western beliefs about the dangers of masturbation have been.

14　See Parker (1960) and also the discussion from a contrary point of view in Kiev (1972: 98-100, 105-08). The *wiitiko* disorder predominantly appears to affect adult males.

15　It should be noted that none of the sources consulted on *wiitiko* mention a non-Ojibwa observer being present in a case of cannibalistic attack.

6
CONCEPTS OF PERSON
AND
REPERTOIRES OF CONDUCT

A central problem concerning the applicability of psychiatric categories becomes apparent when we ask the question *what is it* that they are applied to. Surely the answer is self-evident. It is the person, the individual mind of consciousness, revealed to us in speech, gesture, and conduct. However, a reference to the history of physical medicine will check any such over-confident response. The 'evident' locus of application of medicine, the 'body', a separate and internally determining unity ᴏf phenomena and processes enclosed by the skin is, as Foucault argues in *The Birth of the Clinic*, the product of a revolution in medical discourses and institutions at the end of the eighteenth century. The 'body' becomes an object of medical observation and practice only when separated from the complex space of humours and harmonies which linked health and disease inextricably with environment and regimen. In like manner we may say the 'person' is not a given entity, concepts of 'person' differ between cultures and between periods in our own Graeco-Christian civilization. And not only *concepts*, the practices, institutions, and forms of reference which constitute 'personalities' also differ, and with them speech, gesture, and conduct.

Marcel Mauss confronted this question in a brilliant essay, 'A Category of the Human Mind: The Notion of Person, the Notion of Self'.[1] Mauss challenges the idea that the conception of person or self is a natural concomitant of human experience, a datum of consciousness. Forms of specification of individuals exist in all societies but they are not necessarily specified *as* individual subjects, as unique entities coincident with a distinct consciousness and will. Individuals may be *named*, specified as places within the systems of persons and ritual entities of the clan or tribe. Names and statuses *specify*, but do not 'individualize' in our sense: they may repeat ancestors — successive generations occupying a particular named social place; or identities may change with status — with social maturity or on becoming an elder and so on. Developed conceptions of the subject as social agent may neither individualize nor identify agency with consciousness. Mauss remarks of traditional Chinese forms of specification:

'the individuality of the Chinese is his *ming*, his name .... But at the same time it has removed from individuality all the character of a perpetual, indivisible being. The name ... is a collective noun, it is something that has come from elsewhere: the corresponding ancestor has borne it and it will be inherited by a descendant of the bearer. And when the matter was considered philosophically, when in certain metaphysical systems the attempt was made to express the matter, it was said that the individual is a compound of *shen* and *kuei*, two more collective nouns, during his life.'

(Mauss 1979: 76-7)

He concludes that these notions 'which have made the person a complete entity independent of any other save God are few' (1979: 76-7).

The modern Western concept of the person developed within Graeco-Christian civilization. Antiquity developed the concept of *persona* from that of particular status or role, to which attach certain obligations, into that of a person as an independent moral entity, a being whose conduct is self-governed. Christianity invested this moral *persona*, responsible for its conduct, with additional metaphysical attributes. It became both an agent and an immortal soul, the well-being of the soul being influenced by the conduct of the agent. Christianity produces a conception of the individual as a unity in its conduct, as a unique entity independent of particular social statuses, and of a transcendent value irreducible to considerations of social utility. It was not until after the Reformation that this form of individuation clearly linked identity with *consciousness*, and made self-consciousness the ground of individual moral existence. This conception is closely connected with the individuation of the subject within Christian belief and practice, with an unmediated relation between the person and God — a relation based on prayer as a dialogue, on introspection and the searching of 'conscience'. Mauss contends:

'The importance of sectarian movements throughout the seventeenth and eighteenth centuries for the formation of political and philosophical thought cannot be exaggerated. It was they who posed the questions of individual freedom, of the individual conscience, of the right to communicate directly with God, to be one's own priest, to have an inner God. The notions of the Moravian Brothers, the Puritans, the Wesleyans, the Pietists are those that constitute the basis on which was established the notion that the person = the self, the self = the consciousness — and is a primordial category.'

(Mauss 1979: 88)

Foucault has recently given an interesting confirmation and modification of Mauss's view. In *The Will to Knowledge*[2] he has stressed the importance of practices of *confession* in defining and individuating the subject. The individuation of the subject in Christian practice is not confined to the Protestant sects; the post-Reformation development of Catholic practices of confession provides another route to the systematization of conduct and the differentiation of the individual 'soul'. We should not be surprised that these two writers so clearly link the development of the modern concept of the subject to Christian practice rather than, as sociological prejudices would lead us to expect, to the development of capitalism or the modern state. Religion was, until recently, the primary means of conceiving and directing *conduct in general*, not merely a set of 'ideas' about another world but an institution for organizing individuals in numerous activities and training them in numerous capacities in this world.[3]

We must be careful to avoid two deeply rooted responses in examining this development of the concept of the person. On the one hand, we must avoid reducing it to the process of *recognition* of what has always been present, the inherent and irreducible datum of 'consciousness'. In this view modern man differs merely in that he gives explicit self-conscious regard to consciousness. Now Mauss, it is true, treats of the development of the concept of person as the career of an 'idea', but this is primarily due to compression of argument rather than to any methodological commitments. Mauss is a loyal Durkheimian to the extent that he believes collective representations are always inscribed in and effective as social relations, practices, and rules. We may reinforce this by insisting that 'consciousness' is *not* a given datum. Humans' capacities for self-representation and self-reflection depend on definite forms of discourse and definite activities in which they are trained and implicated as agents. These capacities vary. The concept of 'person' is intelligible only with reference to a definite substratum of categories, practices, and activities which together give the agent its — complex and differentiated — form. Prayer, for example, does not have one universal form, nor are the attributes of the subjects who support forms of prayer universal. The mechanical repetition of the *Ave Maria* and the earnest dialogue with God imply and produce very different subjects. Thus it is important to stress that subjects or social agents are the differentiated terminals of the varied capacities and practices they engage in. The subject as social agent does not have a unitary form, even if it is *represented* as a unity in various discourses or before various institutions (confession, the courts, etc.). Thus the same person who serves as the mechanical subject of repeated penitential prayer may become in confession a subject interpellated as a responsible being who must account for and review the whole of its conducts.

On the other hand, we must avoid converting the development of conceptions of the person into an *evolution*, a necessary process of progress from lower to higher forms of existence. While this view accepts that forms of personality do differ, this is because it considers certain of them to be lower stages in the process of becoming of the 'higher' forms. Hegel saw the development of the subject (of consciousness) as the process of becoming of an immanent potentiality. He regarded the Chinese and other nations who lack the Western concept of subject as the partial moments of fulfilment of that process, frozen at a particular stage of development which is not that of the subjectivity it is Man's destiny to be.[4] This view must be rejected not only because of the weakness of the teleological explanations which ground evolutionary schemes but also because there is no objective and non-evaluative way of ranking different conceptions of personality. The metaphysics of 'consciousness' are no less metaphysical, no closer to the same original 'reality' of human experience, and no more necessary than are those of Taoism. The modern concept of the person is no less a *construction* placed on certain specific human capacities and attributes. This modern concept tends to obliterate this in its claims, making the 'person' an inherent, unitary, given, and constitutive reality. Mauss, following in the anti-evolutionary tradition of Durkheim, rejects any teleological conception of the development of personality:

'Who knows even if this "category", which all of us here today believe to be well founded, will always be recognized as such? It was formed only for us, among us. Even its moral power — the sacred character of the human person — is questioned, not only everywhere in the East, where they have not attained our sciences, but even in some of the countries where the principle was discovered. We have a great wealth to defend; with us the Idea may disappear. Let us not moralize.'

(Mauss 1979: 90)[5]

Hegel in *The Philosophy of Mind* considers insanity as a derangement of reason and approvingly mentions the 'founding father' of psychiatry, Philippe Pinel. Hegel can do so without embarrassment or contradiction because psychiatry (or 'medical psychology', as it was called at the time) is the *practical application of philosophical categories*. The notions of mind, its derangement, and the means of its repair are derived from philosophy. Pinel, as we have seen, was a disciple of the sensationalist philosopher, Condillac. Hegel defines the reference point or mental norm of philosophy in that period with considerable economy and clarity: 'the fully furnished self of intelligent consciousness is a conscious subject, which is consistent in itself according to an order and behaviour which follows from its individual position and its connection with the external world, which is no less a world of law' (Hegel 1971: 123). It is essential to add immediately that conceptions of both mentality and mental illness have developed and changed considerably since Pinel's day. But these modern conceptions still remain consistent with Hegel's definition of the 'fully-furnished self' — mentality remains defined in terms of the conscious and self-possessed self. The object of psychiatric practice is set by its reference-point conception of the 'normal' subject — as a unitary entity coincident with consciousness, an entity whose actions exhibit a pattern of consistency consequent upon its recognition of external states of affairs and the prevailing necessities of relating to others. Hence the importance, in psychiatric nosographies from Pinel to Kraepelin, of distortion in the unity of the subject — in identity and conceptions of self-direction — and of distortion in its cognitions — fantasies and delusions — and in any tendency toward dispersion in its pattern of conduct. To this 'intellectualist' account of the subject we may add the requirements of a certain regime of affect, a stable and non-violent disposition, and due concern for others. Behaviouralism and psychoanalysis have modified but not obliterated this conception of mentality encountered in psychiatric textbooks and in clinical practice.

Now if psychiatry were *merely* a continuation of philosophical discourse, such conceptions of mentality might well be candidates for consideration as pure projections applied to the behaviour of others, as a process of imposing norms or labels on others whose conducts differ. But psychiatry has always been more than a system of 'ideas'. We should not forget that the other conventional 'founding father' of 'moral treatment' in psychiatry is the Quaker, Samuel Tuke. Tuke also introduced the practice of 'moral treatment' but on an entirely different intellectual basis. Tuke was inspired by Quaker ideals of man's inherent reasonableness, his essential goodness, and his ability to be reached by and respond to kindness. Tuke proposed to treat the insane as his co-religionist Penn had treated the Red Indians, as men and brothers. But kindness, attention, and domestic society were to be used to restore the lost one to consciousness, consciousness of himself, his conduct, and his God. We are not concerned here only with theoretical 'categories', but with practices, and with the forms of mentality and individuation implicated in them. Psychiatry's conceptions of the subject correlate with widely held social beliefs and practices which produce the very forms of individualization which make the application of its norms possible. The modern conception of person is not an illusion or idea, it is specified by a mass of institutions and practices and individuals are designated in terms of it. Psychiatry seeks to adjust social agents to those forms of specification and designation.

Our last remark illustrates the point made at the end of the last section, that psychiatric discourse has both specific institutional and wider social conditions of application, and that its 'objects' are implicated in those conditions. It is possible to find examples of social relations in which conceptions of social agents and forms of specification of those agents radically impede the application of contemporary psychiatric norms. Likewise, there are other repertoires of conduct which violate current normal expectations as to bodily behaviour, patterns of affect, and relation to others. Before turning to consider theories of the subject or social agent which do not conceive it as necessarily located in a given and unitary consciousness, we will examine conditions which indicate why this alternative theoretical conception, which conflicts so violently with our 'obvious' experience, is necessary. Our examples will not range from China to Peru. They will be confined to previous eras in our own civilization. First, we will consider forms of reference to and representation of agents in the *Illiad* and the *Odyssey*, works of literature which until the last few decades were central in the education of the European intelligentsia. Second, we will examine the behaviour of nobles and people in the First Crusade, giving particular attention to that class on whose ideals of conduct the modern category of 'gentleman' was modelled.

The Homeric 'soul'

E.A. Dodds in *The Greeks and the Irrational* (1973) and Bruno Snell in *The Discovery of Mind* (1953) both investigate the forms of reference to persons in Homer's *Iliad* and *Odyssey*. In the period when the Homeric epics were composed (around the seventh century BC) the Greek language did not deploy the opposition, central to later Greek thought, between *psyche* and *soma* (spirit/mind and body). Snell remarks: 'We find it difficult to conceive of a mentality which made no provision for the body as such' (1953: 6). The early Greek texts present the human body not as a homogeneous unit but as an assemblage of distinct parts. The phrase 'his limbs' where we would refer to 'his body' conveys this usage well. The human figure is a series of distinct and articulated components. Thus in the conventions of representation in early Greek vase paintings and statues limbs are 'articulated' rather like those of an insect.

Figure 1 illustrates a typical Western child's conception of the human body as an integral unit centred on the trunk. Figure 2 illustrates the early Greek conception of the body as an 'articulated' combination of limbs; head and trunk are much less significant than in the first figure and relative to the second figure's legs and buttocks.

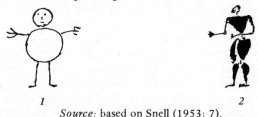

1   2

Source: based on Snell (1953: 7).

As with the body so with the mind. Dodds considers the Homeric subject through the medium of the various forms of psychic 'intervention' deployed in the texts, that is, the ways in which what appear to us as distinct supernatural beings or forces determine the conduct of the subject. The first of these forms is *ate*, an infatuation compelling a man to a rash or disadvantageous course of action. *Ate* is the product of the intervention of one of three forces. The first is the god Zeus, *moira* (the individual's fate, considered as a definite independent force), and the Erinys who walks in darkness (one of the Furies). The second is *menos*, a heightened force or power given to man by one of the gods, particularly in a situation of need. The third is the intervention of dreams and visions, which are considered to be objective, external, and able to enter into men. Thus the Greeks would speak not of *having* a dream but of *seeing* one.

The agent on whom these forces act is not presented as a unitary consciousness but as a complex of faculties or organs, neither purely mental nor physical. The *psyche* or 'soul' is not an active force, the vital principle of the mind; rather its only function is to leave man at death and serve as his representation in Hades. The *thumos* is the organ of will and feeling which is located in the chest and has an independent efficacy, able to compel or direct actions (it is referred to as if it were not part of the subject but an independent inner voice with its own volition). *Noos* is the organ of knowledge, and character or behaviour is presented as if it were an act of knowing: thus Achilles 'knows wild things', which means he is capable of wild actions. Dodds comments on this presentation of character as knowledge that 'If character is knowledge, what is not knowledge is not part of character, but comes to man from outside' (1973:17).

The total effect of this complex of entities is to define the 'individual' as a social status which is the terminal or point of action of the forces implicated in conduct. Thus 'Agamemnon' is a named social status, king, to which attach certain expectations and obligations as to conduct. 'Agamemnon' is *liable* for the consequences of but not necessarily responsible for his actions. The public person can make amends for actions which are due to infatuation, to actions caused 'without his knowledge'. His status and honour is not thereby touched by them. Conduct which deviates from expectations and norms may be required to be compensated for, but this cannot be construed as a demand for consistency in behaviour because the means to systematization of conduct are not at hand.

Dodds argues persuasively that we can infer that all those usages in the Homeric corpus are not merely due to poetic conventions but refer beyond them to prevailing social representations of the subject. Moreover, representation and practice are not to be separated. Men did not merely conceive dreams in a certain way but sought dreams and used them for purposes of divination or to reveal the nature of their sickness and its cure. And not merely the Homeric Greeks. Commitment to oracles and to the practice of medical incubation of dreams (as in the fifth century BC cult of Asclepius) grew in significance and spread throughout the Hellenistic world. *Menos* provides the expectation of and the model for going berserk, a valuable resource in personal combat where the result may well depend on summoning unexpected reserves of strength and motivation. The fact that any action may be, in Dodd's words, 'overdetermined' (he borrows the term from psychoanalysis), that is, due to more than one psychically effective force, and perhaps beyond the agent's knowledge and capacity for control, serves to limit the forms of feuding that would follow with the same institutions in combination with the presence of notions of complete personal responsibility. Revenge or a quarrel could thus be forestalled by restitution or penance and without loss of honour.

Now it should be clear that such agents and social relations disrupt forms of psychiatric diagnosis based on the assessment of individuals' statements and behaviours in terms of norms. What can be said of agents who do not consider themselves as unitary and self-possessed conscious-nesses, who consider many of their actions as the products of external forces or of organs not under their control, or who consider components of mental life, such as dreams, as objective and external realities? Distinc-tive features of schizophrenia, decomposition of personality, delusions of direction, etc. are threatened by such different public definitions of normality and competence. In the same way paranoiac traits, as under-stood by psychiatry, are disrupted in their identification by the lack of any firm boundary to the materiality of the agent and the acceptance of psychical intervention as commonplace. Again, considerable vari-ations in patterns of affect, the rapid attenuation of depression and exultation, are common; even if they are not prescribed or required behaviours, they are 'normal' in the sense of being not unexpected.

Other conducts

Modern psychiatry presupposes both a pattern of consistency in the conduct of agents and limits strictly the range of conducts which can fall within the norm. Exaggerated expressions of emotion or the ab-sence of emotion, the expression of or finding enjoyment in non-socially sanctioned violence, trance and exultation, self-exposure and naked-ness, and so on, are all sure means of being brought to some form of psychiatric attention, often through the medium of the courts. It does not follow, of course, that the result of this attention will be a judge-ment of pathology or psychiatric institutionalization, as the more extreme proponents of the thesis of psychiatric labelling or stigmatization would lead us to believe. The important point is that such conducts have become matters of psychiatric attention, issues upon which a judgement is re-quired. In other circumstances and social relations these limits have been set differently, and behaviours which for us are almost by definition pathological or psychopathic have been tolerated, encouraged, and even required.

Norbert Elias in *The Civilising Process* (1978) illustrated the develop-ment of a pattern of systematic control of bodily functions, exposure, and deportment.[6] 'Civilization' in this sense is not only a matter of morality, proscribing gross excesses like rape and murder, but primarily a mass of minor controls which pattern and constrain conduct and 'manners' to the smallest detail. This process begins with the Renaissance court; the nobility are the first persons to be subjected to this *secular*, as opposed to religious, systematization of conduct. The ideal of the 'gentleman' becomes invested in a mass of petty niceties, minor aesthetics of deportment, and taboos. Spitting in public, eating with one's fingers, defecating in public places, all became progressively outlawed in 'civilized' company from the Renaissance onwards. Bodily conduct is subjected to codes, disciplines, and regulatory practices which valorize certain ways of doing things and certain avoidances. Certain of these taboos on manners are no longer so earnestly observed — no one is really surprised by spitting in the street or eating with one's fingers in an Indian restaurant — but others remain and go well beyond the domain of an aesthetics of conduct. They are expectations of 'normality'. Try habitual exposure in public places (other than ritual sites like holiday beaches or nudist camps) or persist in defecating in the street and you will find it will probably lead to an appearance in a magistrate's court; show the slightest truculence there and you will probably be referred for a social worker's (psychiatrically informed) report.

Consider, therefore, the following figures from another universe of conduct. In 1095 Urban II proclaimed the First Crusade at Cleremont. His call was addressed to rich and poor alike, and it produced an unexpected response. Masses of peasants and common people abandoned their homes and set off for the Holy Land. The first 'People's Crusade' under Peter the Hermit ended in disaster. Many poor people continued to follow the later expeditions, and from them were recruited the 'Tafurs':

> 'Barefoot, shaggy, clad in ragged sackcloth, covered in sores and filth, living on roots and grass and also at times on the roasted corpses of their enemies, the Tafurs were such a ferocious band that any country they passed through was utterly devastated. Too poor to afford swords and lances, they wielded clubs weighted with lead, pointed sticks, knives, hatchets, shovels, hoes and catapults. When they charged into battle they gnashed their teeth as though they meant to eat their enemies alive as well as dead. The Moslems, though they faced the crusading barons fearlessly, were terrified of the Tafurs, whom they called "no Franks, but living devils". The Christian chroniclers themselves — clerics or knights whose main interest was in the doings of the princes — while admitting the effectiveness of the Tafurs in battle clearly regarded them with misgiving and embarrassment. Yet if one turns to a vernacular epic written from the standpoint of the poor one finds the Tafurs portrayed as a Holy People and "worth far more than the knights".'

(Cohn 1957: 46)

Conducts far removed, indeed, from the 'civilization' of napkins, forks, and hair oil. The description of the Tafurs reads like the very image of the medieval notion of the 'wild man' we considered before, a being outside normal human society and capable of savage excess.[7] Yet we can see that the Tafurs are not merely monstrous, they are also subjected to definite forms of valorization by those chroniclers among the educated classes who show sympathy toward the common people (Cohn cites the example of Raymond of Aguilers). They can appear as models of religious inspiration, incarnations of holy poverty, self-sacrifice, and zeal in crushing the infidel.

The Tafurs appear to have played a central and savage part in the capture of Jerusalem:

> 'The fall of Jerusalem was followed by a holocaust; except for the governor and his bodyguard, who managed to buy their lives and were escorted from the city, every Moslem — man, woman, and child — was killed. In and around the temple of Solomon "the horses waded in blood up to their knees, nay up to the bridle." .... As for the Jews of Jerusalem, when they took refuge in their chief synagogue the building was set on fire and they were all burnt alive. Weeping with joy and singing songs of praise the crusaders marched in procession to the Church of the Holy Sepulchure .... But a handful of the infidel still survived: they had taken refuge on the roof of the mosque of al-Aqsa. The celebrated crusader Tancred had promised them their lives in exchange for a heavy ransom and had given them his banner as a safe-conduct. But Tancred could only watch with helpless fury while common soldiers scaled the walls of the mosque and beheaded every man and woman save those who threw themselves off the roof to their death.'
>
> (Cohn 1957: 48-9)

Norman Cohn, a meticulous and sober historian of popular 'millenarian' movements in the Middle Ages is, rightly, appalled by such behaviour. The illusions and savageries of chiliastic populism recall those of the Nazis, a parallel which structures *The Pursuit of the Millenium*. His response to this behaviour, however, is to reach for the categories of mental pathology, and it is here he strays onto dangerous ground. The 'prophets' who encouraged the common people to join the Crusade Cohn labels as 'paranoid megalomaniacs' (1957: 71) and he refers to the 'paranoid fantasies' of the whole population (1957: 73). We shall have need to return to Cohn's notion of 'collective psychopathology' later, in our discussion of witchcraft in Part Three. Here we will merely note that it is social status alone which rescues Tancred or Urban from the charge of 'megalomania'. Urban's call was instantly moderated by the constraints of office and policy, his conduct directed by what was necessary to ensure that the expedition did not escape from the authority of the incumbent of the throne of Saint Peter. The *other* Peter, poor and without office, had no option but to rouse the people by preaching and to lead them in person. In terms of the prevailing ethic of the ruling classes, neither Urban nor Tancred had any objections to massacre *as such*, what mattered was who did it, why, and when. Tancred had an interest in his infidel captives and in the regular knightly forms of warfare which preserved valuable captives. The Tafurs, on the other hand, are presented as motivated by Christian religious ideals, to take Jerusalem and purge it of any other faiths so that it should become a pure Christian city.[8] Tancred's position appears to be 'reasonable', but only in the circumstances. In other circumstances men like him behaved like the Tafurs.

Members of Tancred's class had no objections to killing for the pure enjoyment of it or to massacres if it served their interests as, for example, during peasant uprisings. The following quotation reveals an open pleasure in killing, an aesthetics of battle, which belongs to a repertoire of conducts and their valorization even less intelligible to us than the religious fervour of the savage Tafurs:

> 'I tell you ... that neither eating, drinking nor sleep has as much savour for me as to hear the cry, "Forwards!" from both sides, and horses without riders shying and whinnying, and the cry "Help, Help", and to see the small and great fall to the grass at the ditches and the dead pierced by the wood of the lances decked with banners.'
>
> (cited in Elias 1978: 193)[9]

Virtually every social group in the European Middle Ages specifies in accepted public discourses or reveals as accepted and valorized public practice forms of conduct which would be considered as evidence of psychopathology by the public standards pertaining in the West today.

We face, and must judge in terms of, a different repertoire of conducts. This is not because we are in some abstract sense 'better'. It is because the prevailing forms of training, social commitment, and organization make us behave differently. Who would follow Peter the Hermit in London today? Mortgages, council tenancies, pension expectations, a steady job, or social security payments bind almost all of us to social locations. Policing, passports, and airlines constrain at the very same time as they make possible mass travel. Obligations and commitments existed in the Middle Ages too: oaths of loyalty, ties of villeinage, the membership of a guild, or articles of apprenticeship. But religious fervour provided an undeniable means to over-ride such obligations and legitimate such adventures. A mass of socially marginal persons — hermits, beggars, landless peasants, masterless men-at-arms — had little or nothing to lose, while the domain and administrative capacity of the various authorities was so strictly limited that they lacked the means to supervise or prevent such movements. Today we have to turn away from Europe to find analogues of the 'People's Crusade' in messianic movements of popular resistance.

Our own age abounds in savageries, massacres, and atrocities against which the doings of the Tafurs seem both inconsiderable and innocent. But official morality, in the West at least, persists in regarding such behaviours as abnormal, as criminal, or pathological. They are inconsistent with the view of the social and political order as emergent from the consent and cooperation of free and responsible human beings. The doctrines of democracy, human rights, legal responsibility, religious tolerance, and private property on which Western politics is based do not permit of treating men and women as mere means, of advocating violence except as a means to restore legal order and right, or of the elimination of whole groups by reason of their beliefs. The leading Nazis — who did valorize savagery to racial inferiors — were tried at Nuremburg for war crimes. The Allies were not merely hanging and gaoling their beaten enemies, they claimed to act as agents of humanity and justice. Public pressure forced the US Army to try Lieutenant Calley for his part in the massacre at Mai Lai, although the bureaucracy protected him from anything like the full rigours of military law. Western states both perpetrate atrocities *and* support the standards which condemn such acts. This should not lead us to abandon such standards on the grounds that they either cannot be enforced or are not absolute. They are all we have. But, at the same time, we cannot equate our forms of valorization of conduct with some objective and universal standard, with normality and health. We should therefore take care not to 'pathologize' others whose repertoires of conduct are radically different from our own. 'Pathology' can only be judged, and evaluatively even then, with reference to the universe of conduct in which individuals and associations are implicated. Recognizing different universes of conduct, recognizing the absence of absolute ethical precepts or universal norms of 'health' in conduct, does not mean, however, the abandonment of the standards current in Western civilization. These standards are more than mere 'values', matters of personal choice, they are implications of and means of conducting certain forms of social organization.

Notes

1 Originally given as the Huxley Memorial Lecture in 1938 and reprinted in Mauss (1979).
2 Vol.1 of *The History of Sexuality*.
3 We are not here concerned to take the part of Weber against Marx. It is true that accounting practices, forms of property law and contract, and so on, ideational prerequisites and concomitants of capitalism, all imply and produce subjects of a specific type. But forms of calculation, law, economic institutions are specific discursive and practical constructions and not the necessary and subsidiary effects of the logic of a 'mode of production'. Weber is no less committed than Marx to a certain necessary logic of effectivity, but in his case it is an effectivity of ideas or beliefs themselves. Although he is not ignorant of religion as a social institution he tends to treat religious *doctrines* as decisive. But most religious concepts, far from having a logic of necessity, have a multiplicity of interpretations and effects in practice and in their continuation in religious discourse. Further because of his personalist, essentialist concept of the human subject as a being free to endow the world with meanings, the problem of the differential form and capacities of subjects can hardly be registered in his analysis. Subjects are always potentially 'outside' the values they espouse. For a discussion of Weber's personalism, see Hirst (1976a). We shall have cause to consider and challenge again this notion of a 'logic' of ideas or beliefs in Part Three.

4 See, for example, his discussion of these points in *The Philosophy of History*.
5 We should note the date of this lecture, 1938. The victory of the Nazis dealt a shattering blow to lingering beliefs in progress or in any providential teleology. Mauss's oblique reference makes it quite clear who needs to defend what against whom.
6 Elias, however, tends to neglect other and different codifications of behaviour and conduct in the Middle Ages — both monastic and knightly life imposed patterns of regulation and strict training. These differ radically from those of 'civilized' man, but they are codifications of bodily conduct nevertheless.
7 See Bernheimer (1952) discussed in Chapter Two. The wild man served in the Middle Ages as a register of the difference represented by civilized human society, much as the savageries of everyday conduct in the Middle Ages serve Norbert Elias as the register of our own order.
8 Following the disaster that befell the 'people's Crusade' the Jews of Europe were subjected to bloody massacres. The Bishop of Spier placed the Jews of his city under his protection. It should be added that this was not unconnected with the Jews presenting him with a handsome sum of money. A similar attempt at payment did not produce the same results at Mainz. The Jews were massacred and the archbishop was forced to flee to Rudesheim. The refugees of the massacre escaped to Rudesheim and pleaded for asylum with the archbishop to whom they offered a large sum. Showing great tact and sensibility, he tried to convert the victims. The Rabbi, Kalonymous, attacked the archbishop in his despair. He and his fifty companions were in consequence killed on the spot. See Steven Runciman, *A History of the Crusades* (1978 Vol.1: 137-39). It is interesting to contrast Cohn's and Runciman's portrayal of events. On the one hand, Runciman ignores the Tafurs and their reported part in the seizure of Jerusalem. On the other hand, his account of the massacres paints a morally greyer picture of the whole affair than does Cohn: he fails to lay the blame for the massacres solely on the common people and he portrays the archbishop as a good deal less saintly.
9 A war hymn attributed to the minstrel Bertram de Born.

7
THEORIES OF PERSONALITY

The 'subject' has become the object of a great deal of fashionable theorizing in recent years, in work associated with a number of French authors
– Althusser, Barthes, Derrida, Foucault, and Lacan.[1] One consistent
theme in this otherwise highly disparate corpus is the challenge to the
metaphysics associated with the concept of the 'person'. Challenged is the
notion of the person as a given entity, the author of its acts and centred in
a unitary, reflexive, and directive consciousness. This challenge has
provoked cries of outrage from traditionalists in a number of disciplines,
the most recent and vociferous of whom is the historian Edward
Thompson in his broadside against Althusser, *The Poverty of Theory*
(1978). This outrage was inevitable. 'Anti-humanist' philosophy entered
the Anglo-Saxon intellectual arena at a time when personalist and existentialist ideas had become established as one of the main lines of defence
against the methodological presuppositions of behaviourism. It also
appeared to challenge the defence of human rights and civil liberties
to which large sections of the intelligentsia, left, right, and centre, had
committed their abilities in opposition to Nazi and Soviet authori-
tarianisms. The new challenge appeared to threaten a universal determinism, rendering human conduct a mere 'effect', and a consequent disregard
for human dignity and freedom.

   Politics and the metaphysical status of the 'person' are closely
entwined. The opponents of 'anti-humanism' were wrong to suppose that
it presages a descent into savagery. What is challenged is not the *status* of
person, free agent, or subject of right but rather the claimed ontological
foundations of that status. The notion that men are 'free agents', directed
by a sovereign and integral consciousness, is a metaphysical 'fiction'. It is
not an illusion, any more than the notion of God was an illusion to our
recently departed Christian civilization. It is implicated to a greater or
lesser degree in our legal system, in our conceptions of contract and the
wage labour relationship, in many of our assumptions about education,
and so on.[2] It cannot simply be 'written out' of social organization
because it does not comply with certain conditions of philosophical
argument. Yet the philosophical challenge has a serious purpose and
one which touches questions of social organization. Social organization
and conduct as such do not, and cannot, be made equivalent to the

suppositions of personalist metaphysics. In certain circumstances individuals are held to be 'free agents', in others they cannot be. Social organization and social relations cannot be reduced to the 'fiction' of a domain of interacting and consenting 'free agents'.[3] Problems of social policy, political organization, and so on compel us to think in other ways. The Christian idea of God gave rise to chiliastic fantasies of a purged and pure dominion in which right would prevail. The metaphysics of the 'person' give rise to fantasies in which social organization will be made consistent with the needs of the 'free agent'. Fantasies of this kind have abounded before and since Rousseau's *The Social Contract* (1762).[4] They consist in the idea of a libertarian social order in which no man is constrained or compelled to conducts save by his own consent. We shall have cause to return to these fantasies, both left and right, in Chapter Ten when we come to consider the various anti-psychiatries, in particular Laing and Szasz.

Savageries are no less possible in the service of a metaphysics of personal freedom. It was Rousseau who gave us the famous and chilling paradox of men being 'forced to be free', a 'forcing' which has been put into practice on countless occasions since 1762. Thus to challenge the metaphysical fiction that men are 'free agents' in the interests of a more complete account of the determinants of their conducts and capacities is in no way to be committed to a rival deterministic metaphysics. It certainly does not mean rejecting social categories which organize practices, categories like 'contract', 'obligation', 'responsibility', 'fault' and 'guilt'. These categories do not depend on individuals being in some inherent, ontological sense responsible or guilty, but they do require that conduct is attributable to individuals, not as its origin but as its locus. They may be held responsible for their acts, except in certain specified cases of incapacity, without us believing those acts arise from purely consciously determined purpose. We have seen that social relations *can* be organized in terms of categories of social agent other than those on which personalist metaphysics is based. We shall also see, in our discussion of witchcraft in Part Three, that there can be social relations — those of the Azande — organized in terms of conceptions of universal determinism, in which concepts of 'responsibility' like our own are not used, but which nevertheless do confront specific individuals with liability for consequences.

If the issue were merely one of 'ideas' then the question of which general conception of social agent prevailed would be no more important than the dispute between the Big-endians and Little-endians in *Gulliver's Travels*. But the psychology of Homer's heroes was not introduced as an exercise in esoteria. Early Greek thought registers certain forms of 'psychic intervention'. Psychology was confronted with the phenomenon of 'intervention' in the nineteenth century. 'Animal magnetism', first propounded by Mesmer in the 1770s, provided a new means of investigation of the mind and new therapeutic technique.[5] It was through hypnotism that Freud, studying under Charcot at the Salpêtriere, began his path to the discovery of the 'unconscious'. Freud soon rejected hypnotism as a means of investigation and therapy in favour of 'psychoanalysis'. He discovered phenomena which, from the standpoint of the philosophy of 'consciousness', could only be considered as 'psychic intervention' — thoughts, images, and wishes emanating from *another site* than the consciousness of the subject. This *other site* he called the 'unconscious'. Intervention takes many forms: some trivial, like 'slips' of the tongue, interventions in the order of statements, unmotivated by the consciousness of the speaker; some regular and everyday, like dreams — which Freud showed could be interpreted as expressing in an overdetermined and distorted form unconscious wishes and desires; others bizarre, like compulsions to perform certain acts or avoid objects and places, compulsions unintelligible in utilitarian terms; and others again which transform the equilibrium of the body, like hysterical paralysis. The unconscious is not to be understood as the unthought or the forgotten, it cannot be accommodated as a hidden resource of consciousness, potentially subject to its recall and dominion. Freud scandalized orthodox psychology and philosophy by insisting that the unconscious is a distinct *psychic* system or register, using what appear to be contradictions in terms like unconscious 'thoughts' or unconscious 'wishes'. Freud's work is not merely the construction of an intellectual system. Many others before him had come close to the concept of the unconscious mind, notably Nietzsche and Schopenhauer.[6] But Freud produced his theories on the basis of a new technique of production of psychic phenomena, psychoanalysis. Psychoanalysis is a practice of investigation and therapy guided, but unconstrained in its results, by psychoanalytic theory. Freud strove throughout his life to make the theoretical superstructure of psychoanalysis consistent with the constantly developing results of its practice.

The unconscious divides and fractures the subject of consciousness. Conduct must always be examined with reference to the complex and often incalculable effects of that *other site* of psychic determination. The human psyche is therefore inconceivable as an integral 'subject' coincident with consciousness. Consciousness and the ego are *formed* in the splitting consequent on the repression of wishes, desires, and fantasies prohibited by the social order.

Theories of the social agent cannot conceive individuals as necessarily unitary subjects centred in a determinative consciousness if the results of ethnography and cultural analysis, revealing other modes of conceiving and specifying social agents, and of psychoanalysis, challenging the view of the subject as self-possessed by consciousness, are to be taken into account. Perhaps the most serious attempt to theorize social agents as other than constitutive subjects of consciousness is that offered by the French Marxist philosopher Louis Althusser. Althusser tries to produce a concept of social agent which does not explain its actions as originating in some pre-given 'subject', in free-will, or as being determined by external causes. Althusser seeks to conceive of a *socially constituted* agent who is at the same time capable of being the 'bearer' of social relations, who is not a mere effect or cipher. He does so for reasons which are very different from our own. His objective is to explain how capitalism as a system is perpetuated, why it functions as a 'society'. He conceives social relations as *totalities*, as a whole governed by a single determinative principle. This whole must be consistent with itself and must subject all agents and relationships within its purview to its effects. We on the other hand consider social relations as aggregates of institutions, forms of organization, practices, and agents which do not answer to any single causal principle or logic of consistency, which can and do differ in form and which are not all essential one to another.

Althusser's theory will be briefly summarized insofar as it bears on our purposes in this discussion.[7] Althusser argues that 'ideology' is an inevitable component of any social totality because men's 'lived' relation to their social relationships can never be an adequate account of the conditions on which those relationships depend. The thesis that men are self-conscious subjects and that 'society' is nothing but the results of their inter-subjective relationships one with another is inadequate precisely because it ignores such conditions. It must convert society into the result of a pure act of will on the part of its various members, as in Rousseau's *The Social Contract*. Althusser argues that, on the contrary, far from assenting to society in a constitutive act of will, men live in an 'imaginary' relation to it, a relation which depends, in Marx's phrase, on conditions which are 'prior to and independent of their will'.

It is *because* men are not mere effects, mere causal traces that they cannot exist in social relations without having access to some means of generalizing and systematizing conducts. This is what the 'imaginary' relation is − it is a form of presentation of the agent's existence in such a manner that a definite pattern of conducts is implicated. For Althusser the imaginary relationship to the totality of the subject's social relations is both constitutive of the subject and the basis for its actions 'as if' it were a free, self-determining consciousness. The imaginary makes the metaphysical 'fiction' we referred to earlier appear to be a reality and, Althusser says, to the extent that subjects act 'as if' it were, then it is.

The means by which such subjects are constituted and given the capacity to act 'as if', Althusser (1971) calls 'Ideological State Apparatuses' (ISAs). ISAs create subjects with conceptions and capacities appropriate to their places as agents in the (exploitative) social division of labour. In the feudal mode of production the coupled institutions of Church and family conditioned individuals to accept their lot. In the capitalist mode of production the Church is superseded by educational institutions. The coupled institutions of school and family have a more complex task than to justify an exploitative and hierarchical, but relatively simple, class structure such as characterizes feudalism. They must distribute individuals in roughly the right proportions required by a much more complex division of labour based formally not on status but on ability and acquired skill. The educational system must produce so many people capable of functioning as managers, so many as technicians, skilled workers, unskilled workers, etc., and who accept and conform to their allotted role in this (exploitative) social division of labour. ISAs must make subjects both capable of being exploited and for whom at the same time this exploitation is invisible. They must 'live' their social relations in a specific 'imaginary' manner, one which makes work appear a chosen and necessary conduct.

The subject and its imaginary relation are constituted through the ideological mechanism of 'interpellation'. This mechanism involves what Althusser calls the 'dual-mirror' structure. This structure is composed of a master Subject (the Other who 'hails' the subject) and the subject (who is hailed, 'interpellated' – literally, interrupted by being spoken to). This is the structure which constitutes concrete individuals as social subjects, assigned the attributes of definite ideological formation. The subject is constituted through its recognition of an imaginary master Subject (God, conscience, etc.) which hails its recognizor. The Subject addresses the subject, recognizing it, speaking to it as a subject. In being interrupted by and recognizing this address the subject recognizes itself as subject, as spoken to as a subject. All ideology involves a form of master Subject as one pole of the dual-mirror relation. This structure of duality is called 'specutary', a reflection and counter-reflection of a single image. The being the subject becomes is a reflection of its Other the Subject, made by Its word in Its image. Subject and subject exist only in mutual recognition. The subject comes into existence as subject only through its recognition of itself in the Subject, only because it accepts being spoken to and the content of the spoken. Conversely the Subject exists only through its recognition by subjects, it has no being apart from its effects, apart from its activation in the recognition by subjects. There is no originary constitutive Subject or subject prior to this imaginary dual-mirror structure. Concrete individuals become social subjects of a definite form through this process. This process begins with the infant in the family (the being of the mother becomes whole through the imaginary, as an Other – it should be noted that Althusser draws on the concepts of the French psychoanalyst Jacques Lacan) and develops as the child encounters articulated ideological systems (religion, ethics, knowledge) and enters the social practice of the school. Through 'living' the commands of the Subject, the subject constitutes itself as the bearer of a pattern of conduct.

Constituted as a subject in the imaginary relation to the Subject, the subject recognizes itself as *constitutive*. It is spoken to, interrupted as if it were an already existing self-subsistent being-as-subject. The Subject speaks to it as if it were a constitutive subject and the subject responds by recognizing itself as such. The effect of interpellation is to constitute a subject which thinks of itself as free, which chooses to obey the commands directed at it by the Subject and which commits itself to patterned actions as the consequences of principles it itself has chosen. Subjects 'work by themselves', internalizing their subordination in and by ideology as choice and autonomous will: 'the individual is interpellated as a (free) subject in order that he shall submit freely to the commandments of the Subject, i.e. in order that he shall (freely) accept his subjection' (Althusser 1971: 169). It is in this way that the ISAs produce subjects capable of operating in the ways required by the relations of production and accepting the forms of imaginary representation of those relations as necessity. Ideological practice thus serves to provide agents appropriate to a certain form of totality and the 'society effect' is produced by articulating the subjects into the structure through the imaginary relation.

Althusser's theory is ingenious and suggestive. It explains the interrelation between a particular form of the subject and a pattern of conduct. It accepts the necessity of *constituting* agents, that the social agent is not given in the human individual, and at the same time that the result is an *agent*, whose conduct – although patterned – is not determined. But it has a number of important weaknesses. These generally derive from Althusser's attempt to link this concept of subject to the question of how a mode of production, as a totality, reproduces itself. The result of this linkage is to convert the agent into a mere means of continuing the system, a socially obedient cipher. The concrete individual and the subject of 'interpellation' tend to be identified. But, as a result, Althusser's subject becomes identical with the unitary self-possessed subject of 'consciousness'.

But the dual-mirror structure of interpellation is more specific than this since it characterizes only *certain* forms of social personality. It fits most clearly the modern Christian concept of the person as a subject before God. Now within Christian religious doctrine and practice the person is indeed treated as a patrimony or property given by God into the subject's own charge; the person is the steward of his own soul[8] and answerable for it before God. But there are other forms of specification of social agents, which do not make them unitary self-possessed entities whose whole conduct is under the surveillance of an all-seeing eye. In the Homeric example given above or in that of the Azande given below there is no single 'Other' who hails the subject. Rather there is a multiplicity of expectations and taboos related to context, and conduct is subject to no notion of a unitary locus of supervision. Again, the 'consciencization' of conduct is by no means inevitable. Conduct may be patterned but not necessarily by reference to a systematicity in the *will* of the agent. It may depend on the decisions of non-subjective and non-manipulable techniques like oracles. Systematicity in conduct, therefore, may not be located by the prevailing social discourses *in* the subject, but in a pattern of cultural obligations and techniques. Other 'mechanisms' of ideology would be needed to account for different social forms of construction of personality.

Further, Althusser tends to assume that the 'consciencization' of conduct leads to social *order*. This is because he conceives such doctrines as deriving, ultimately, from a coherent social whole whose needs they serve. Once this supposition that the social whole is a unity is removed the systematization of conduct by reference to a doctrine and its inter-pretation by 'conscience' are by no means conservative and preservative of social stability. It can equally serve as a means of deviation from patterns of conduct specified by authority. If the Reformation ushers in this conception of person and conscience, it also confirms this point, for it began with an act of unparalleled religious disobedience. Luther's 'Here I stand, I can do no other' exemplifies the socially explosive nature of this conception of the person as the steward of his own soul. If the 'Other' is a transcendental subject whose commands cannot be fixed in prescribed moralities, then prophecy, revelation, and judgement can serve to plead God's Will *against* social obligation or law. Doctrines systematiz-ing conduct can serve many different and often unexpected roles. This should make it clear that 'values' have no necessary social consequences, no inherent logic in social relations — a point worth insisting on when attention to such issues almost invariably conjures up the name of Weber. Confucianism is generally assumed to be the foundation of a stable, hierarchical, and patrician social order. But Liu Shao Chi's *How to be a Good Communist* is suffused with a Confucian ethic, a point which did not go unnoticed in the later stages of the Cultural Revolution. A great deal of revolutionary discourse transforms and utilizes religious models, substituting 'nation' or 'people' for God as the reference-point before which conduct is judged and justified.

'Consciencization' also has its limits, however, for the concrete individ-ual is *not* a 'subject'. The 'steward' does not confront a unitary entity. Discourse and statements cannot be confined to an origin in consciousness — as forms of 'interruption', slips of the tongue, dreams, etc. indicate. Conduct likewise owes part of its determination (and by no means the minor part) to that other site — as compulsions, obsessions, fears, and aversions indicate. We must never reduce individual social agents to obedient social performers of required roles or inflate persons into 'free agents' rather than entities that operate 'as if' they were.

But forms of systematization of conduct and social forms of personality *do* differ qualitatively in the capacities and attributes they make possible. Different qualities of conduct between civilizations are often considered absurd, because all too often they have been conceived in an essentialist manner. Culturalist anthropology as represented by Ruth Benedict or Margaret Mead often registers these differences but makes them an emanation of culture pattern as such. 'Cultures' are a form of totality no less dubious than Althusser's 'mode of production'.

Culture unifies a complex of discourses, practices, and institutions as if they expressed a common habitus or spirit. The important point in introducing Althusser's work is to indicate that the forms in which social subjects are constituted have important consequences, consequences which would not arise were his theory no more than a variant of universal determinism. Our civilization has displaced the subject of Christian belief and the mass of social disciplines and practices that accompanied it. Althusser's 'school-family couple' lacks an adequate substitute for this complex. Only in this century have we attached to secular educational institutions the tasks of training and socialization previously conducted under the aegis of religious institutions, and invested education with some of the expectations of a 'better world' previously associated with religion. Most of us no longer believe we will be judged in another world, or accept the need to steward our souls or accept the stewardship of the confessor. This is a double-edged good. For all the benefits of freedom of conduct or freedom from anxiety which stem from a decline in religious practice, subjects are no longer 'interpellated' as obligated to duty and charity. We face problems of motivating people to behave in altruistic and considerate, dignified, and conscientious ways without transcendental goals. This is not a matter of 'ideals' or 'morals' but of a daily practical mechanism of conduct, keyed-in to practices and institutions. No civilization can provide its members with means of conducting themselves that depend entirely for compliance and performance on utilities, pleasures, satisfactions, and reasons. Means to resolve conflicts, cope with failures and suffering, endure everyday dullness are necessary in every social order. Social democrats and libertarians alike predicate the future of social organization on an unproblematic world of satisfactions, the one a managed utopia of material means provided by economic growth, the other a world of conflictless plenty based on popular freedom and an end to exploitation and oppression. Those Marxists who believe that the mode of production determines the conducts appropriate to it will also echo these views. Socialism as an economic and political system will necessarily create corresponding and satisfactory forms of social organization. We beg to doubt this.

   Without a new model of a pattern of conduct and disciplines to accompany it we can expect increasing problems in the management of behaviour. Violence, selfishness, laziness, and indifference are by no means 'innate' in human animals, a pattern of behaviour to which they tend to revert. But a calm, altruistic, diligent, and concerned subject is by no means the natural man within us awaiting to emerge when the evil influences of a corrupting social order are removed. Conducts are *constructed*, they are not mere 'subjective registers' of economic relations — which are somehow more 'real' or 'objective'. Our problem is that for all our wealth, technique, and knowledges, indeed, in part *because* of them, we lack the ideational means to order and justify social actions often possessed by many 'poorer' and more 'ignorant' peoples.

Notes

1   Still the best general introduction to this work is R. Coward and J. Ellis *Language and Materialism* (1977). On Derrida, see Mark Cousins' 'The Logic of Deconstruction' *Oxford Literary Review* (1978) and on Foucault, as his work relates to this issue, Colin Gordon, 'The Birth of the Subject', *Radical Philosophy* (1978).

2   Bernard Edelman in *Ownership of the Image* (1979) discusses the role the concept of the person as a self-possessive 'free agent' plays in the main doctrines which justify or provide the grounds for judgement in the French law of property.

3   For a discussion of the complexities of social organization and the limitations involved in concepts like 'rights' see Hirst, 'Law, Socialism and Rights' (1980).

4   For a discussion of the fantastic nature of Rousseau's conception of the society of the 'social contract' see Hirst 'Political Philosophy and Egalitarianism: Marx and Rousseau' (1976b).

5   Which should lead us to caution in dismissing ideas as absurd or 'unscientific'. Mesmer based his practice of hypnotism on the theory of 'animal magnetism', that the sun, moon, and stars influenced all things by means of a 'subtle fluid'. This occult power pervaded the universe and linked all things together in one universal harmony. We are already back in the world of Paracelsus and the Cabalists. *But* this theory did serve as the means of production of a genuine technique with far-reaching implications.

6   Precursors are always to be found for any 'discovery' — this greatly weakens the value of an otherwise interesting book by Lancelot Whyte *The Unconscious Before Freud* (1962). Whyte quite fails to register Freud's *theoretical* originality because he does not consider the specific effects of psychoanalysis as a *practice*.

7   See Althusser (1971). For a fuller summary and criticism of his position see Hirst *On Law and Ideology* (1979: Chs 2 and 3).

8   Very often this doctrine of the soul as a 'property' to be stewarded is taken to be a 'reflection' of economic relationships, that 'possessive individualism' is the ideological product of a nascent capitalism. The problem with this view is that doctrines of possession or private property are in no sense *specific to capitalism* or even to economic affairs. What is ignored in such a view is the specifically religious form of the doctrine which exceeds or even negates conceptions of capitalist rationality. This view of the soul is by no means confined to Protestants in general or to Calvinists, it cannot be treated as a product of the 'protestant ethic' alone. Cartesianism and Jansenism both treat the subject as an entity self-possessed by consciousness.

8

PSYCHOANALYSIS AND
SOCIAL RELATIONS

Psychoanalysis began as a revolutionary 'discovery' on the frontiers of medico-psychiatric practice, a frontier which involved the clinical treatment of 'hysteria' by means of hypnosis. But Freud's discovery took him outside of the clinical field in his therapeutic methods, and it forced him to create a new theoretical discipline which touches and disturbs all the human sciences. Freud's discovery had four linked components: that hysteria was a complex psychical formation, a neurosis, linked to the sexual history of the individual; that the 'symptom' was no mere physical register of mental disorder but was part of a pattern of significance; that these signs and the pathological formation could only be unravelled and made intelligible by bringing to light repressed unconscious psychic material; and that the means for doing so was the speech of the neurotic in a special relationship with the analyst, 'transference'. The comprehension of the therapeutic efficacy of this method, transference, took longest of all to recognize and work out. Baldly stated it appears compromising and sordid, that the analyst becomes the object of the analysand's libido and the pathological components of this sexual organization are worked out through their projection onto the analytic relationship. This libidinal attachment is crucial to the overcoming of the resistances to the unconscious expression of repressed sexual desires.

It is transference more than anything else which has limited the role of analysis proper in clinical-medical psychiatry. Other methods, developed initially in schism from Freud's own, have proved more adaptable to a hospital context, especially in the USA. Freud never became an 'anti-psychiatrist', never castigated the clinic or medical psychiatry as such. Psychiatry has tended to shun or to marginalize Freud, but not merely for reasons of distaste or fear of ideas like the unconscious, infantile sexuality, and so on. The 'transference neuroses', the primary object of analytic therapy, form a definite and limited class of mental pathologies. Freud tried strenuously to extend analytic *concepts* to cover and explain the psychoses, but psychoanalysis, as a therapeutic *method*, has faced a fundamental problem in dealing with psychosis, the difficulty of establishing a relation of transference. The reason is given by the classic analytic account of psychosis, a pathological and chronic narcissistic fixation of the patient's libido on his own ego and a withdrawal from reality into an internal psychic world or a delusional system.

Freud's discovery remained centred on a therapeutic practice and retained the concept of *pathology*. Neuroses resulted from a failure to successfully repress certain sexual desires, which remained active in the unconscious and found their expression, against conscious censorship, in the form of the symptom. The symptom is not a stable 'abnormal' sexual organization, thwarted and stigmatized by social norms, but an instance of failed repression. The irruption of unconscious wishes generates guilt, and secondary mechanisms of repression and denial which are necessarily ineffective and in turn generate further defence mechanisms. Neurosis is an economy of failed repression; a pattern of developing, transforming and migrating symptoms — often of baffling complexity. Analysis is thus often an equally complex process of uncovering successive diffuse pathological mechanisms and resistances; consequently analysis is often protracted and frequently broken off or terminated too soon. As a therapeutic practice, analysis has no simple measure of its efficacy. The challenges of psychologists like Eysenck, who claim it has a low rate of 'cure' and a high rate of 'relapse' are therefore largely beside the point. Analysis has never been nor claimed to be a therapeutic 'magic bullet', a psychic equivalent of penicillin.

Freud never conceived analysis as a practice of adaptation to accepted social norms, the conversion of neurotics into 'normal' family men or conventional wives and mothers. All too often neurotics are outwardly just this to begin with. It is the acceptance by the neurotic of the highest standards of current sexual morality and social life which poses the problem, for therein lies the source of guilt and self-reproach. Freud did not seek to convert the homosexual, for example, into a conventional paterfamilias, but, rather, to enable him to come to terms with his own, socially condemned, sexuality and to lead the fullest and most creative life, to overcome immobilizing guilt and fear.[1]

However, Freud never assumed, as many psychiatric radicals do, that it was possible to create a social order in which all sexual desires could be met, in which repression, dissatisfaction, and pathology could be overcome. Indeed, he has often been criticized for this, for example, by the Marxist philosopher Herbert Marcuse in *Eros and Civilization* (1955). But Freud retained the concepts of pathology and perversion, not because he wished to enforce the prevailing notions of sexual discipline and normality, but because he argued that *all* human society necessarily repressed and directed sexual desires towards certain ends. Infantile sexuality is polymorphous and perverse. The child, far from being an asexual innocent, begins life as a demanding, narcissistic, and auto-erotic animal who is gradually forced to accept the existence of others, and certain socially sanctioned organizations of its sexual needs.[2] The child is forced to recognize the demands of an extra-psychic 'reality', in the form of the necessities of association with others and the attainment of a pattern of sexual objects and gratification ('genitality') which will make possible the reproduction of new members of the species, themselves in turn subject to social necessities and the needs of the species. Freud retained throughout his work the concepts of a sexual *energy*, which must be directed and harnessed to certain objects ('cathexis'), and an evolutionary-biological notion of men as a species of animals who adapt to their environment through the formation of certain psychic structures which produce the effect of reproduction. Culture, in organizing psychic life, attains the effects served by instinctively patterned behaviour in less complex and developed species.

It is the process of repression, denying and directing sexual desires and drives, which creates the split between conscious and unconscious mental systems. Central to this gradual process, a process of psychic development which does not correspond to an orderly succession of 'stages' based on physical maturation, is the taboo on incest, the forbidding of the mother or the father, brother or sister, to children of the opposite sex. Genital sexuality is established as the end to which psychical development is directed. Were this 'end' the culmination of a simple biological process, then the repressions, disasters, and failures of human sexuality would have no place, no conditions of existence.

Culture has a psychic kernel for Freud, the taboo on incest, and the triadic relationship between the father who imposes the law, who forbids the child the mother as a sexual object with the threat of castration, and who thereby forces the child to seek satisfaction in the foundation of a family of its own.[3] Human children are born with no *psychical* sexual identity; the sexual drives of the infant are bisexual, polymorphous, and perverse. It is through the 'Oedipus complex' and its resolution that sexual differences and sexual identities, men and women with distinct and complementary patterns of object choice, are produced. Sexuality, for Freud, is culturally implanted and enforced. The Oedipus complex is the universal kernel of all human culture. Culture is no given attribute of the species, it is something which is far from inevitable and is painfully attained in the development of man.

It is here that Freud goes beyond the limits of a new therapeutic method. Freud claimed to have discovered in analysis of neurotic patients something which went beyond the domain of pathology and which underlay it. Pathology was no particular defect to be located in the life history or biology of the individual. On the contrary, the neurotic individual was a product of a process which concerned the foundation of all human subjects. The neurotic differed from other men not in possessing repressed sexual wishes, but in the *failure* of this process of repression, not in the desire for his mother, but in the *failure* of its resolution and redirection.

It is here that Freud challenges and comes into conflict with the established human sciences of sociology and anthropology. Where, behind particular social norms and family institutions, Freud supposes a universal psychic kernel, a triadic nuclear relationship, the social sciences recognize only a diversity of family structures, customs, and institutions, and in place of his common human civilization they recognize distinct and radically different patterns of behaviour, ideas, and affect. Bronislaw Malinowski was the first social scientist to clearly draw attention to this dichotomy in the suppositions and concepts of those two bodies of knowledge concerned with human social relations and the attributes which follow from them. His *Sex and Repression in Savage Society* (1937) is an honest attempt to reveal the paradox for psychoanalysis of the existence of distinct family institutions. As he presents them, the familial institutions of the Trobriand Islanders have no place for the 'nuclear complex' which is the kernel of human civilization in Freud's theory. We will consider this debate here, not in order to plead the claims of one discipline against the other, nor to resolve the paradox in some higher synthesis, for such is not to be had, but to show how two theories of human civilization are both necessary, both produce valuable knowledges, and yet contain incompatible suppositions and irresoluble contradictions. As matters stand, the analysis of social relations and human attributes can be reduced to no theoretically consistent order, nor should we expect the 'progress of knowledge' necessarily to lead to some resolution. The idea that knowledges or sciences ultimately form some single rational order corresponding to the unity of 'reality' is a metaphysical proposition. It is one we must learn to lay on one side if we are to exploit all that psychoanalysis and cultural anthropology have to offer.

Before we turn to Malinowski we must consider in greater detail how and why Freud is led to the theory of a universal Oedipus complex.

Sexual instincts and the Oedipal order

Freud's theory of neuroses is concerned with the vicissitudes that befall the organization of human sexual desires in the process of psychical development. It is necessary therefore to consider what Freud means by sexual energy, or 'libido', and sexual 'instincts'.

Freud thinks of sexuality as based on an 'instinct'. His developed concept of *Sexualtriebe* is the product of a cautious and partial differentiation by him between *drives* (*Triebe*) and *instincts* (*Instinkte*). Freud does not simply reproduce contemporary biological conceptions of instinct in his conception of sexuality.[4] The biological concept of instinct refers to organically determined patterned behaviour. It is a response of the organism governed by its nervous system and identified with and triggered by a specific context of sensory information.[5] A *drive*, by contrast, is a more complex somatic/psychological formation: the behaviour of the organism is not patterned by the organic elements which provide its conditions of existence. The context of expression, its objects, and the resultant pattern of behaviour are psychically shaped and determined. Drives, nevertheless, do have a definite somatic foundation and functional effect for the organism: drives are conceived by Freud as a determinate form of somatic *pressure* and as directed toward needs of the organism (self-preservation, release of tension, etc.). Freud never abandoned the *somatic* element in the drives; this element has a conditional and causative role, it has effects on the psychical apparatus (but *through* psychical representation) independent of any conscious choice on the part of the subject. Nor did he abandon the functional equilibrium of the organism (including its equilibrium of internal stimuli and its equilibrium in relation to the environment, its threats and excitations) as a crucial point of reference. Thus Freud remains within the field of the biological theory of instincts, although differentiated from it. Thus 'instincts' (drives) might be considered as a concept substituted for instinct (in the strict biological sense) in the analysis of an animal with higher psychical functions, Homo Sapiens. Freud attempted to retain contact with the evolutionary biology of the nervous system, the growth and enlargement of the cortex and the diminution of the relative role of autonomic nervous reactions in human behaviour.

In his concept of sexual instinct Freud is careful to avoid two other possible theoretical options. The first is *pan-sexualism*, the reduction of behaviour to a single sexual instinct as the foundation and source of all others, to a single determinative principle. Freud is far from 'reducing everything to sex' as ill-informed critics often claim. Pan-sexualism is generally accompanied by the essentialization and biologization of sexuality; it is closer to the conception of 'sexologists' like the Englishman Havelock Ellis than to Freud's view. Freud insists on the multiplicity of instincts. In the first stage of theorization, before 1920, Freud is concerned with two broad groups of instincts, those of self-preservation (corresponding to the 'reality principle' and the demands of the environment, demands mediated by the ego) and those of sexuality (corresponding to the pleasure principle, the economy of excitation and release of tension in the organism, an economy whose demands are mediated by the unconscious). In the second stage of theorization, inaugurated by *Beyond the Pleasure Principle* (1920), the opposition and antagonism is between the 'life instincts' (subsuming the first two groups) and 'death instincts' (instincts which seek release of tension through destruction and which are expressed in aggressiveness, whether directed towards others or the self). The death 'instinct' is not merely a metaphorical concept, it is not a simple biological *drive* but a complex tendency observed in organized matter and psychic life.

Freud thus avoids reducing human behaviour to sexual needs and motives conceived in the narrow sense, of genital and perverse adult sexuality. The sexual instinct is somatic in foundation but it has no given form. In the beginning it is polymorphous and perverse, and need not be expressed in terms of objects or ends commonly regarded as 'sexual'. It is not directed toward the preservation and perpetuation

of the organism, and its demands for satisfaction expressed by the unconscious pay no regard to the reality principle or to socially accepted or
recognized modes of gratification.

The second rejected theoretical option is the multiplication of instincts
or drives, the identification of distinct patterns of behaviour – eating,
sexuality, aggression, etc. – and the ascription of each to a distinct
motivating instinct. Freud thus avoids the forms of circularity to be
found in the explanations of human behaviour by contemporaries like
William Mcdougall.

In his major theoretical work on the theory of sexual instincts and
their organization, *Three Essays on the Theory of Sexuality* (1905),
Freud considers the different combinations of the *object*, *aim*, and *source*
of the drive. Sexuality is in no sense confined to genitality. Freud considers all the various complexities of infantile sexual development and the
possibilities of its partial, or 'arrested', resolution, the aberrant or perverse
forms of adult sexuality. The object, aim, and source of the sexual
instincts are in no sense given, and distinct combinations of these three
components are possible. 'The *object* of an instinct is the thing in regard
to which or through which the instinct is able to achieve its aim.' The *aim*
is a specific form of pressure and release of tension (pressure), psychically
encoded. The *source* is the bodily site or process of excitation. Virtually
any orifice, organ, or function can serve as the source of a sexual aim.
Freud here radically rejects any automatic process of sexual excitation or
any given associated behaviour. He is unable to locate this diverse and
complex somatic pressure in any specific physiological mechanism, in any
gland, secretion, or hormone (but he *would* have done so *had* such biological knowledges been available to him – they are no more available to
us). *But*, the *Three Essays* should not be regarded as a monument to
relativism, as contending that sexual desire is merely conventional and a
matter of personal preference. The notion of somatic basis remains
crucial. Freud constantly gives expression to this in the 'economic'
metaphors of pressure/tension and the necessity of its release through
cathexis on objects. The somatic component of the instinct (or drive) is
necessary to its insistence on the psyche and to the non-voluntary nature
of its pressure and effects.

Sexuality is thus in the first instance a somatically definite but
expressionally diffuse *pressure*. It is a pressure because energy is bound
in it and seeks expression through it. Somatic sexual energy is the basis
of *all* psychic energy, libido serves the 'fuel' of the psychic engine. Libido
serves as the foundation of *all* psychical functions: complex thought,
art, science, and industry are 'sublimated' sexual energy. The objective
of the *Three Essays*, the different organizations of the object, aim, and
source, arises from the fact that sexuality is *psychically constructed*:
libidinal energy is psychically bound into definite forms of excitation
and discharge. This binding takes place through the developmental history
of the individual, through the intersection between an inherited

instinctual 'constitution' (individuals differ in their predispositions and capacities), and the particular circumstances of his or her family, experiences, and so on. The diffuseness of the instinct, its construction through psychical forms, and the consequent 'binding' of energy to particular psychic contents create the space for a wide range of possible combinations of object, aim, and source. The somatic diffuseness of the drive gives rise to psychically patterned difference. It is this crucial intervention of psychic significance in the direction and formation of the drive which distinguishes it from any given sexual 'need' and it is the binding of somatic energy which gives a necessity and consistency to the psychical pattern thus established which goes beyond any matter of conscious choice or any mere attribution of social value or cultural significance.

But sexual energy, however necessary to the economy of the whole somatic-psychial system, is diffuse. The somatic component of the sexual instincts, because the behaviour of the organism is largely determined by the autonomous activity of the higher brain centres, cannot be effective in and as itself. How does what is without direct psychical organization (somatic pressure/energy), and, therefore, without psychical effectiveness, acquire it? The libido becomes effective, becomes organized and, therefore, a psychically effective pressure through what Freud calls the *'psychical representative'* of the drive. Sexuality is constructed in its psychical representations, and these always take the form of a definite organization of the instincts toward certain objects and sources of pleasure. Thus there is no pre-given sexual 'aim', sexuality can invest virtually any object, organ, or activity. The development of a particular personal organization of the instincts proceeds through two linked processes:

i.   Through attachment to the functions of the 'life instincts' – a process Freud called 'anaclisis' or propping. The sexual instincts attach themselves to, or are propped up by, other sources of excitation and spheres of activity. Thus the infant comes to derive pleasure from the necessary activity of sucking at the mother's breast; bodily functions (feeding, thumb-sucking, defecating, etc.) become the school and model for the excitation of sexual instincts. Sexuality is *always* a derived form, there is no original or primal sexuality. Thus the auto-eroticism of the infant is not something it is born with, it is a development subsequent to an anaclitic constitution of the sexual instincts.[6]

ii.   Through phantasy. Propping provides linkages between sexual instinct and the order of excitation and activity. Phantasy is the primary form in which sexual instincts become organized through their 'psychical representatives'. Phantasy is the psychical construction of desire, the construction of imagined sexual objects and means of satisfaction. Infantile and unconscious adult phantasies bear no relation to 'reality' in the sense of sanctioned adult genital sexual activity. The desire constructed in phantasy must be repressed and attached to the sanctioned genital order.

But this order is not easily attained. The child's sexuality must be both directed and yet repressed in the considerable period before it becomes capable of adult sexual activity. At the same time the child must be formed as a social agent or subject, capable of playing its part in social relations. Thus the organization of the instincts cannot be random, the field of object choice must be rigidly structured. The child must identify with his father before he can *be* a father, and he must identify with something more than the particular individual who confronts him. In other words, genitality must take a symbolic form. 'Father' must be a symbolic category with a power and significance greater than the child's immediate and stronger rival for the mother. It is the father-as-symbol who wields the threat of castration, a compulsion which forces the child to relinquish a phantastic (but perfectly real and 'satisfiable' — in displaced forms) sexual aim. It is the father-as-symbol with whom the child can identify long before he can become a real father. Genitality is thus a *psychical end* imposed on the process of the child's development from the beginning, an end he is brought to recognize and adopt as his destiny long before it can be 'attained'. It is imposed on all children long before and irrespective of their biological capacities to become mothers or fathers; the woman who will be sterile, the man who will be impotent are no less subject to this regime.[7]

Thus for Freud this 'end' (genitality) is a symbolic one, part of the child's development as a social subject, and not a given somatic process of maturation. The decisive stage of this process of sexual identification takes place long before puberty. But this does not mean that genitality should be conceived of as a social norm which is imposed upon the child, a 'role' with which he or she identifies and acts out. Freud's theory is as opposed to socially normative conceptions of genitality as it is to biological reductionism. Because the symbolic father exceeds the real father, because he wields a threat (castration) which social rules in the form of law actually proscribe the real father, the child cannot identify in the way he would with a social 'role'. In a sense *no* man can actually occupy the place of the father. Equally, the child does not choose or happen to identify with the sexual norm, or, on the contrary, choose to adopt some 'deviant' pattern. The biological and sociologistic conceptions of genitality fit very well together; for the sociological relativist genital sexuality is a merely given biological capability which may be accepted or rejected by individuals in their adoption of sexual roles. Genitality is, on the contrary, for Freud, a symbolic construct which dominates *all* organizations of the sexual instincts.

Genitality, the law of the father, is the symbolic matrix which governs *all* object choices. The *Three Essays*, as we have said, might appear on a casual reading to offer a relativistic theory of different and parallel object choices. Freud set no great store by social norms or conventions as such. We have seen that he clearly regarded the stigmatization of homosexuals as barbarous and unjust. This is because the law of the father is *not* a social norm; the homosexual's object 'choice' is a vicissitude of his sexual history and not merely an act of 'deviance', it has a psychic necessity which renders notions of 'deviant behaviour' absurd. Freud retains in the *Three Essays* the concept of pathology and perversion. They exist however in another register from concepts of deviation from the average or from social norms. Genitality is not a social norm from which other organizations of the sexual instincts deviate in the form of being *different*, since they are no less subject to its symbolic order. Genitality is the psychical end which dominates the symbolic and the process of development of the child as a social agent. Perversions and neuroses are developments under the sign of genitality, failures to resolve the Oedipus complex and, therefore, as much under the sway of this psychical end and symbolic order as 'normal' instinctual organizations.

The Oedipal structure, what Malinowski calls the 'nuclear complex', is the symbolic system of places (Father-Mother, Brother-Sister) necessary to the constitution of genital sexual difference, to the construction of 'men' and 'women' who can in turn stand in the places of this symbolic system. We have stressed Freud's commitment to a sexual *instinct* with a somatic referent and have shown how, paradoxically, this makes the symbolic order — culture — necessary to the construction of sexual differences and identities. The libido is polymorphous, perverse, and bisexual. Sexual difference is psychically constituted and *physical* differences are both recognized and given significance on this basis. Physical differences in themselves cannot give rise to sexual identity: a biologically fully developed man whose libido is narcissistically fixated on his own ego simply confirms this point. Children's sexual identities are formed before physical sexual maturation. The significance of the male and female sexual organs is recognized before puberty and through the threat of (in the case of the boy) or recognition of (in the case of the girl) castration. Freud contends that both male and female infants believe they possess a *phallus*, the boy identifies it with his as yet tiny penis, the girl lives in expectation that hers will grow. These infantile imaginings are rudely shaken. But it is the symbolic phallus that makes recognition of sexual identity possible — through the threat of castration in the case of the boy it links the penis that is (and the Oedipal desire that must remain a phantasy) with the penis that will be. Sexual identity, far from being an 'obvious' physical matter, is symbolically constructed.

We can now recapitulate the elements of the symbolic-cultural order necessary to the formation of genital sexual identities. Central are a series of terms which give the father primacy: the phallus and the threat of castration, the denial of the mother *and* the sister to the male child. These terms make the incest taboo necessary. It is the proscription of the mother and the sister which installs the father in the primary place in the

Oedipal system. The taboo on incest is the lynch-pin of the whole system. For Freud the taboo on incest, the primacy of the father, and the Oedipus complex are necessarily human features of human culture. Now we have seen that the father is a symbol exceeding the 'real' father, who may be a weakling, absent, or dead, while the threat wielded by this father or spoken in the father's name by the mother, relative, or nurse is an act which, if carried out, would put its perpetrator in goal as a violator of human laws. Freud's all-powerful and savage father, like the god of the Hebrews, might be said to dwell among us in at best a symbolic sense.

Totem and taboo

But for Freud this symbol must be vivid, alive, and effective in the human psyche and the family of the Oedipus complex — Father, Mother, Brother, Sister — must underlie all forms of the human family. It is in *Totem and Taboo* (1913) that Freud tries to explain this psychic presence at the back of all human institutions and culture. In the book Freud tries to explain why all human societies, and savage peoples in particular, evince a horror of incest and also why primitive peoples practise certain rites in respect of totem animals which serve as the symbols for the clan. He denies that the taboo on incest is practised for eugenic reasons; custom prohibits sexual relations between persons where no threat of inbreeding is pertinent. Instead Freud links the taboo on incest with totemism. Incest and totemism form a system: the prohibition of incest is evidence of a repressed wish to commit precisely this act, whilst the ritual consumption of the normally forbidden totem animal in a common meal by members of the clan reveals an ambivalence towards it which shows that it symbolizes far more than a mere emblem of the clan. The key to this system is to be found in what Freud calls '... a hypothesis which may seem fantastic' (*SE* XIII: 141).

Freud links together three elements to form this hypothesis. Two are anthropological theses. Darwin's thesis in *The Descent of Man* is based on deductions from the behaviour of the higher apes, that early man too lived in 'hordes', in which a single dominant male kept all the females to himself and ruthlessly excluded his sons and rivals.[8] W. Robertson Smith's thesis in *Lectures on the Religion of the Semites* is that the ritual killing and communal consumption of the totem animal was an important part of the totemic stage of the development of religion. The third element is based on Freud's contention that it is legitimate to draw a parallel between the results of the analysis of neurotics and the customs of primitive peoples, that the former can be used to illuminate and interpret the latter. Freud takes a case of his own, Little Hans, and one of Sandor Ferenczi's, Little Árpád, to argue that animals are symbols for the father. The totem animal is the symbol of the father, and the totem meal a ritual consumption of the body of the father.

This meal Freud argues is a symbolic memory of a *real* act. Freud proceeds to convert Darwin's hypothesis into a real event, a 'primal horde' dominated by an all-powerful father who kept the women to himself, who drove out or castrated any of his sons who dared to challenge him. The sons were driven to combine to kill and devour their father. But the feelings of the sons to their father were ambivalent — they hated and feared him, and yet they loved and admired him too. This ambivalence was the basis of a sense of guilt which they shared in common. From this guilt and remorse came a 'deferred obedience' to the father. This is an obedience possible *because* of his death, in which he became more formidable than ever he could be alive. The father they symbolized by the totem animal. And they united under the totem to institute the law against incest. This law ended the war of all against all for the women of the horde. Henceforward, a man may not possess a woman of his own clan, that is, a woman of the blood of the father-totem.

Freud was aware that his hypothesis was 'fantastic' and that 'this earliest state of society has never been an object of observation' (*SE* XIII: 141). Even the simplest human societies are already divided into clans and already have a long history behind them (*SE* XIII: 162-63). Freud's hypothesis has been savaged by anthropologists — Freud himself was driven to refer to it as a 'Just-So Story' and a 'scientific myth'.[9] But Freud retained it to his dying day. He also thought the memory of this 'primal event' remained with all of us to this day, that the Oedipus complex operated in its shadow. Freud was well aware that this involved the concept of a 'collective mind', such that the contents of the psyche were not a matter of happenstance, education, and experience in the individual but rather all individuals were connected with one interpenetrating psychic domain. This 'memory' of an event did not necessarily involve an inherited 'racial mind', and, therefore, the inheritance of acquired characteristics. Ontogeny (individual development) did not only recapitulate phylogeny (development of the species) as a biological process, through inheritance, but *within culture*.[10]

Freud argued that this common psychic domain operated at the level of the unconscious and that the 'primary process' was universal in its basic contents and mechanisms:

> 'no generation is able to conceal any of its more important mental processes from its successor. For psycho-analysis has shown us that everyone possesses in his unconscious mental activity an apparatus which enables him to interpret other people's reactions, that is, to undo the distortions which other people have imposed on the expression of their feelings. An unconscious understanding such as this of all the customs, conventions, ceremonies and dogmas left behind by the original relation to the father may have made it possible for later generations to take over their heritage of emotion.'
>
> (Freud *SE* III: 159)

The unconscious is thus only in part 'personal', and men's psyches inter-penetrate in ways which conscious thought and custom cannot control and censor. A Viennese member of the liberal professions and an aborigi-nal denizen of the Australian deserts are linked, under the vast differences of culture and knowledge, by similar mechanisms of unconscious thought and similar desires. It is the universality of the primary process, its mechanisms of entering conscious mental activity, of evading censorship in the complex and displaced forms of symbolization we find in dreams or parapraxes, for example, which explains how it is possible to interpret dreams and other forms of symbolism across differences of culture and personal experience.[11]

Although Freud treats the murder of the primal father as a real event, he is clear that psychoanalysis itself provides the means to challenge this presupposition. Neurotics are tormented by guilt concerning impulses and desires which are 'always *psychical* realities and never *factual* ones' (*SE* XIII: 159). The reports of childhood scenes of seduction, incest, and so on, given by neurotics in analysis generally turn out to be phantasies. For primitive man:

> 'the mere hostile *impulse* against the father, the mere existence of a wishful phantasy of killing and devouring him, would have been enough to produce the moral reaction that created totemism and taboo. In this way we should avoid the necessity for deriving the origin of our cultural legacy, of which we justly feel so proud, from a hideous crime, revolting to all our feelings. No damage would thus be done to the causal chain stretching from the beginning to the present day, for psychical reality would be strong enough to bear the weight of these consequences.'

> (Freud *SE* XIII: 160)

This explanation has the advantage that it does not suppose a single 'event' transmitted in memory to the present day and constantly recreated. But it has the defect that it presupposes the Oedipal-symbolic order *ab initio* — for the symbolic father is never the *real* father and the threat of castration was never *really* carried out. This explanation cannot serve to explain the *origin* of the symbolic system of the Oedipus complex.[12]

Before turning to criticisms of Freud's views, a number of points of clarification need to be made. Firstly, in *Totem and Taboo* Freud is not offering an explanation of the origin of human social life or association as such. Freud is indifferent to sociological considerations, and does not differentiate and characterize social relations as phenomena distinct from the psychic. Freud's concepts of social organization proper are generally hazy — he tends to refer to 'civilization'. Malinowski is, therefore, wrong to suppose that Freud considers the 'primal horde' to be in a pure state of nature.[13] We have seen that sexuality is in no sense 'natural' for Freud — he is not concerned with the transition from nature to culture, from pure instinct to law. Men exist in definite relations of psychic association *before* the institution of totemic clans; in an ambivalent relation to their father, and a bond (with a libidinal-homosexual component) one to another. Freud is explaining the origin of the incest taboo, *not society*, so that whilst the brothers enter into a social contract which institutes the taboo, they already share relations of association and co-operation with one another. This is confirmed by Freud's later remarks on *Totem and Taboo*. In *Group Psychology and the Analysis of the Ego* (1921) Freud treats the primal horde as a 'group' — the brothers are bound in a common affective tie to the dominant father just as the members of a group are to their leader (*SE* XVIII 122-3). In *Civilization and its Discontents* the horde is regarded as a 'family', a stable association, lacking but 'one essential feature of civilization, that is, the arbitrary will of its head, the father, was unrestricted' (*SE* XXI: 99-100).

   Secondly, Freud is not concerned to explain institutions in the way a sociologist or anthropologist would. He derives religion, law, and custom directly from the dynamics of the psyche. He explains institutions as resulting from collective psychic states; thus a 'sense of guilt' (*SE* XIII: 143) leads the brothers to venerate the father in the form of the totem.

   It should be said straight away that the explanatory devices used in *Totem and Taboo* are in no sense peculiar to Freud. *Totem and Taboo* has all the defects of contract theories: an institution is explained as the product of an instituting *event*, men came together and agreed to make it so. Contract theories are no fabulous relic of the pre-history of scientific social thought. The generation of social relations from the 'interaction' of individuals continues to be a theoretical device: Talcott Parsons uses the interaction of an abstract Ego and Alter to explain the development of patterned expectations of conduct in *The Social System* (1951); Peter Berger and Thomas Luckmann in *The Social Construction of Reality* (1967) are forced to invent their own 'Just So Story', the interaction of two isolated individuals, to explain the origin of language. But Freud's totemic contract does echo some of the traditional features of classical contract theory. John Locke in his *Second Treatise of Government* explained the development of *political* society, or government and instituted law, by means of a social contract but this contract is possible because it is made by the members of an already existing human society or association. Freud explains the formation of the Oedipal order but to do so he presupposes elements of the things to be explained or instituted by this order, sexual identities and the place of the Father. Far from explaining the origin of the symbolic, *Totem and Taboo* surreptitiously presupposes it. The consequences of the murder serve in effect to recognize and formalize the already existing patterns of emotion and psychic states. This defect of contract theory has been recognized since Rousseau,[14] but these defective 'Just-So Stories' constantly recur when it is a matter of the explanation of *origins*. We have seen why Freud is driven to explain the Oedipal order in an *event*. It is no immediate out-

PSYCHOANALYSIS AND SOCIAL RELATIONS

growth of biology and yet it underlies all human psychic formations, it is present beneath the differences of custom and institution. The event, shattering and horrible, persists as a memory in the collective unconscious, with all its charges of guilt and ambivalence.

Psychic states give rise directly to institutions – to the incest taboo and the totemic religion. These institutions are fundamental, they underly all the varied forms of kinship organization and all the later developed theologies and Churches. Thus Freud says:

'Totemic religion arose from the filial sense of guilt, in an attempt to allay that feeling and appease the father by deferred obedience to him. All later religions are seen to be attempts at solving the same problem. They vary according to the stage of civilization at which they arise and according to the methods which they adopt; but all have the same end in view and are reactions to the same great event in which civilization began and which, since it occurred, has not allowed mankind a moment's rest.'

(Freud *SE* VIII: 145)

This direct derivation of institutions from psychic states is fraught with problems. Institutions become mere effects of collective psychic states, a mere medium for projecting and resolving psychic conflicts.[15] But Freud in no way shows *how* psychic states give rise to institutions – why does *guilt* lead to the phenomenon of totemism in particular rather than some other institution? Freud in answering such a question would be forced to presuppose a common 'mentality' in which the germinal ideas of the Oedipal family and totemic religion are already present.

Freud's account is clearly unacceptable to any theory which is concerned to demonstrate the specific effects on thought and conduct of different institutional arrangements and the different consequences in conduct of elaborated belief systems and the kinds of entities postulated in them. Yet it is not without its parallels in sociology and anthropology. The famous sociologist Emile Durkheim considered all religion as in essence the veneration of a special class of things, the 'sacred' as distinct from the 'profane'. The 'sacred' transcends commonplace experience and special rites surround it, thereby reinforcing its uniqueness and mystery. In *The Elementary Forms of the Religious Life* – a book published in 1912, shortly before Freud's own – Durkheim too was concerned with the *origin* of religion. He thought its essential features were to be observed in its simplest forms and these were presented to us in the rituals of the Australian aborigines. Durkheim ends up explaining what he claims to be a category of the 'collective consciousness' by means of the *psychic states* of the individual members associated in collective rituals. Individuals form the idea of the transcendent or sacred in a state of exultation through experience of clan rituals in which they are 'taken out of themselves'.[16] Thus Freud's work is no more absurd or bizarre than that of other men of his generation who sought to explain the origins of the family or of religion.

Freud had the misfortune to write just as one form of anthropological theorizing and investigative practice was about to give way to another, to base himself on the work of men like Fraser and Robertson-Smith. The new cultural anthropology based upon systematic field-work methods was about to confront him with materials which could not but be embarrassing. Bronislaw Malinowski's *Sex and Repression in Savage Society* has become an anthropological classic whilst *Totem and Taboo* has become an embarrassment and a scandal. To see why, to have catalogued all the anthropological errors and deficiencies of explanation, one has only to turn to the 1920 review by A.L. Kroeber of the English translation.[17]

Malinowski clearly draws out what is at stake in his challenge to Freud's thesis of the universality of the Oedipus complex: to psychoanalysis

'the Oedipus complex is something absolute, the primordial source ... the *fons et origo* of everything. To me on the other hand, the nuclear family complex is a functional formation dependent upon the structure and upon the culture of a society. It is necessarily determined by the manner in which sexual restrictions are moulded in a community and by the manner in which authority is apportioned.'

(Malinowski 1937: 143)

Malinowski is here asserting that social institutions differ in their specific effects and that cultures mould individuals in terms of the types of entity and patterns of conduct they posit. We appear to have been concerned to assert just this thesis at considerable length earlier in this discussion.

Malinowski points out that in the Trobriand Islands in Melanesia the family structure is radically different from that presupposed in the Oedipus complex. The Trobrianders reckon descent through the female line, the male child inherits property and social status from his maternal uncle, *not* from his father. The maternal uncle is an authority figure for the child, he represents discipline and social sanction. Relations with the uncle are reserved and difficult. The father, on the contrary, acts as a nurse and playmate. Relations with the father are intimate and affectionate. The child does not come into conflict with the uncle as a sexual rival, or with the father as a source of discipline. Infantile sexuality is not denied or repressed as it is in Europe — children and adolescents are allowed to engage in sexual play. Indeed, Malinowski contends that the Trobrianders are ignorant of the role of the father in procreation. They believe that children are conceived by the spirits of dead ancestors, Baloma, entering the mother, whilst she is swimming in the sea, for example. They have no reason to relate the orders of sexuality and paternity. This does not mean that Trobriand sexuality is without its conflicts or forbidden objects. The male child is forbidden the female members of his uncle's clan and, in particular, his sister. This form of incest prohibition is a consequence of the matrilineal system and the form of exogamy it presupposes. Trobriand society thus gives rise to a special and distinct form of 'complex', in which sexual-emotional conflicts can arise; these centre on the relation between brother and sister. The elements of conflict which are superimposed in the Oedipal structure are separated in the Trobriands, since even though the uncle upholds the incest taboo, he is not a direct sexual rival, while the father is not in sexual competition with the child nor does he represent social authority.

> 'In the Trobriands there is no friction between father and son, and all the infantile craving of the child for its mother is allowed gradually to spend itself *in a natural spontaneous manner*. The ambivalent attitude of veneration and dislike is felt between a man and his mother's brother, while the repressed sexual attitude of incestuous temptation can be formed only towards his sister.'
>
> (Malinowski 1937: 80, our emphasis)

Malinowski proposes a theory in which culture moulds and mediates biological needs and instincts. Patterns of sentiment are created within the particular institutions of a culture; impulses and emotions are systematically organized in a particular social context. Culture meets biological needs and impulses but it determines the form in which they are met and socially expressed. Malinowski says: 'Thus the building up of the sentiments, the conflicts which this implies, depend largely upon the sociological mechanism which works in a given society' (1937: 277).

The problem with Malinowski's account arises less from its attempt to assert the specificity of effects of social institutions or doctrines of entity than from its conception of sexuality. Malinowski recognizes *infantile* sexuality but only as a form of playing at genitality. Malinowski is clear that there is no given, biologically determined sexual behaviour − sexuality is organized and regulated by custom, not instinct − but he treats sexuality as *inherently* genital. He fails to consider sexual instincts as polymorphous and perverse. In a sense therefore human sexuality is given and unified at the biological level: sexual instincts are 'needs' which culture must both organize and meet. Sexuality is natural and the infantile attachments of the child for its mother cease 'in a natural spontaneous manner' when other sexual objects become available. Genitality is thus a natural outcome. Freud, as we have seen, is forced to explain the unity of sexuality at the level of its 'psychical representation' − to explain how genitality is attained as a *psychical* end.

Malinowski also refuses Freud's concept of the unconscious. He equates the concept of 'collective unconscious' with the group mind, and considers it a 'metaphysical' conception.[18] Now this objection is an epistemological one: Malinowski here uses positivist criteria of the validity of forms of knowledge to eliminate a concept against which he has no other arguments to marshal. It is metaphysical and occult because it is not observable or an inference from observation. But the collective unconscious is *by definition* not an observable phenomenon, certainly not one which can be derived from the conscious testimony of informants. It is indeed a supra-observational concept but one which attempts to account for and explain definite 'observations' (which are far from being a *brutum factum*, since they are dependent on the practice of analysis, but then, nothing ever is). *All* complex concepts are 'metaphysical'. 'Culture', 'institution', 'rule' etc., concepts necessary to cultural anthropology, are not observables, but means of organizing and analysing statements of native informants. The collective unconscious is a correlate of the notion of an individual unconscious: it follows from the theses of the universality of the primary process and of the interpenetration of the unconscious thoughts of individuals despite conscious censorship. The unconscious cannot simply be bidden by social norms. The unconscious provides an independent dynamic element in subjects' connections with social institutions, one which is subject neither to considerations of physical necessity nor to those of the rules and conventions on which institutions depend. In ignoring this psychic level, Malinowski can treat sentiments as merely the effects of a pattern of culture. Men are united in their physical, biological, needs which cultures must in their different ways recognize and meet. But in respect of sentiments and thoughts they are different, artefacts of culture. Now this thesis has its place and its value in challenging biologistic and psychologistic conception of 'human nature' — of which the various sociobiologies are merely the latest variant. However, Freud's position has no affinity with these reductionisms, while Malinowski's theory of instincts and sentiments has all the defects of the culturalism it tries to avoid. Culture become a series of inexplicable and given differences. Each culture, moreover, imposes itself on its inhabitants as a universe, a totality, in which thought and action are specified in ways which happen to be distinct from elsewhere.

If Freud makes social relations the unmediated results of psychic states, Malinowski makes social relations, in the last instance, patterns of culture. Both positions have different faults. *Totem and Taboo* has a thousand weaknesses, it is neither convincing nor consistent. Yet Freud does in that book and in later works indicate that social relations, kinship structures, law, religion, etc. must mobilize and manage psychic forms that they did not create and on which they depend. In *Group Psychology and the Analysis of the Ego* (1921) and *Civilization and its Discontents* (1930) Freud considers the psychic foundations of complex human associations. Freud argues in the former work that groups are sustained by libidinal ties, that the members' libidinal energies are in part directed at the leader or at one another. This may appear absurd, and, indeed, Freud's account of the Church and the army treats them merely as bodies of individuals tied to a common leader. This would be a fatuous analysis of complex organizations if that was all one could say about them. To *ignore* this element in groups is, however, equally fatuous. Small army units are built on close ties and a sublimated homosexuality; willingness to face danger and ignore privation are based on more than discipline, belief in the purposes of the war, or fear of shame. Love for one's comrades, concentrated by isolation and suffering, leads to commitments on the part of masses of men which exceed duty or prudence. The intense attachments formed by English soldiers in the First World War, the development of paternal feelings on the part of the officers for the men despite differences of education and social class, and the estrangement from people at home are all instances of such libidinal ties, commonly reported in memoirs.[19] Political parties and similar groups can also provide such attachments, as can groups of religious disciples. To ignore the degree to which Nazi ideology and practices fostered this libidiniz-ation would be a serious error, since it clearly played an important part in attracting support and preserving unquestioning adherence to Hitler. Certain ideologies and party practices create favourable conditions for the formation of such ties: bourgeois centre parties are probably least effective in this respect.

In *Civilization and its Discontents* Freud considered another aspect of the question: man's 'unease' in civilization. Freud argues that social relations cannot be measured by the standard of the happiness of the individual:

> 'Here by far the most important thing is the aim of creating a unity out of individual human beings .... It almost seems as if the creation of a great human community would be most successful if no attention were paid to the happiness of the individual.'
>
> (Freud *SE* XXI: 140)

Freud argues 'that necessity alone, the advantages of work in common' (*SE* XXI: 122) will not hold men together. The reason is the Death Instinct. An inherent aggressiveness is the main derivative and mani-festation of this tendency to seek release of tension in the destruction of the organism rather than in pleasure. This aggressivity is 'inherent' in that it is unrelated to circumstances; it reflects neither the functional biological needs of the organism, for territory, for food, self-defence, etc., nor social interests which need to be defended by violence. It is quite unlike what is postulated in modern ethological theories of aggression or territoriality in animals in that it has no adaptive or preservative function. It, like sexuality, exists in the form of psychical representation; it therefore exceeds in its capacity for negativity and destructiveness any biological instinct toward violent behaviour which would be confined to certain motivating stimuli and definite circumstances. Freud introduced this concept at a relatively late stage in his work and with some reluc-tance. It first appears in *Beyond the Pleasure Principle* (1920); he intro-duced it to account for what he called a 'compulsion to repeat' — in which distressing situations are reproduced or relived compulsively. Neither release of tension nor adjustment to reality could explain this phenomenon widely observed in survivors from the First World War.

Social relations depend on the libidinal binding of individuals into groups. In a group the members are united in ties of love which inhibit and deflect aggression one to another. The aggressive instincts are harnessed to the work of civilization as well. Civilization opposes aggressiveness by utilizing it, aggression is introjected, internalized and directed toward the ego. Aggression is linked with morality and governs the psyche in the form of the 'super-ego'. Civilization, because it inhibits the outward expression of the aggressive instincts, must constantly reinforce them in their direction against the individual in the form of a sense of guilt. 'Conscience' is far from being a purely social matter, it is tied to psychical forces which go beyond any particular set of customs and taboos. Morality, far from being merely functional to the social order, imposes too great demands on the ego precisely when it is most civilized and demands the highest standards of conduct. Freud argues both that the Christian commandment, 'Love thy neighbour as thyself', is the strongest defence against aggressiveness and that the civilized super-ego imposes unrealistic demands on the ego, requiring it to have unlimited mastery over the unconscious or id. This is the general paradox of civilization, not merely of Christian ethics, that its means of control of aggression produce both psychic unhappiness and the perpetual revolt of repressed unconscious wishes. Freud is thus far from regarding either custom or sentiments purely as a matter of social relations: social relations, the customs and institutions of particular peoples, intersect with a general psychic domain which is far from neutral.

We see here two quite different forms of theory and investigative practice brought into confrontation, one based on a practice of uncovering the unconscious of civilized European neurotics and the other on recording through intensive field-work studies the manifest reported culture and observable customs of 'primitive' peoples. Malinowski radically misunderstands, as we have seen, Freud's conceptions of sexuality and the unconscious. He is far from being a psychoanalytic ignoramus but he is trapped by his own theses and his own practice. Aware that his attempts to collect and interpret Trobrianders' dreams are doomed to analytic irrelevancy, he is stuck with a paucity of dreams, with a relation to his respondents very different from the analyst's relation of transference and, therefore, stuck with the 'manifest content'.[20] Now the 'manifest content' of dreams is affected by the processes in which the unconscious wishes (the 'latent content') avoid censorship; dreams are like a complex code. The manifest content of *Europeans'* dreams could just as easily be used to 'refute' Freud. Analysts like Ernest Jones (1964) and Géza Róheim (1950) have thus interpreted Trobriand customs and dreams very differently from Malinowski, and both find lurking behind them the structures of the Oedipus complex.[21] Jones, for example, treats matriarchy as a derivative form from the Oedipal structure, a form of repression of its conflicts in the form of social relations. Now not only does this tend to reduce the Oedipal structure from a psychic-symbolic structure to a pattern of manifest institutions overlain by others but, as Malinowski argues, there is no possible evidence, derived from field-work, which can substantiate it. Psychoanalytic anthropological interpretation suffers from a serious defect: where analysis includes a means, the 'transference', for bringing repressed material to light and at the same time a test on its interpretation, this is lacking in work like Róheim's, which — however interesting — is always impossible to assess. We cannot as things stand do what Freud wished to do, bring the materials revealed by the analysis of neurotics to the interpretation of the customs of 'primitive' peoples or, rather, we cannot rigorously and reliably do so.

The problem of relating the two practices does not lie merely on the analytic side. Anthropology has committed itself to a thesis and a method strongly represented in Malinowski's work. The thesis is that sentiments and activities are artefacts of culture. Conduct and belief are primarily determined by the particular institutions and culture of a people, although for Malinowski cultures must meet biological needs. This view is re-echoed against Freud, some decades after Malinowski, by Claude Lévi-Strauss. He argues, correctly, against the derivation of institutions from individual psychic states:

'social constraints, whether positive or negative, cannot be explained, either in their origin or in their persistence, as the effects of impulses or emotions which appear again and again, with the same characteristics and during the course of centuries and millennia, in different individuals.'

(Lévi-Strauss 1964: 69)

He goes on to say:

'We do not know and never shall know, anything about the first origin of beliefs and customs the roots of which plunge into the distant past; but, as far as the present is concerned, it is certain that social behaviour is not produced spontaneously by each individual, under the influence of the emotions of the moment .... Customs are given as external norms before giving rise to internal sentiments, and these non-sentient norms determine the sentiments of individuals as well as the circumstances in which they may, or must, be displayed.'

(Lévi-Strauss 1964: 70)

The authors of the present book are clearly in sympathy with this thesis. It is directed against reductionist theories which seek to explain social relations in terms of biology or psychology — a given human nature. But psychoanalysis, as we have tried to present it, is neither of these. The psychic-symbolic domain interpenetrates with culture and social relations, 'civilization' in Freud's terms, is *more* than particular cultures or societies. Here is Freud's most radical point of contradiction with contemporary cultural anthropology. For anthropology sentiments and activities are particular to a culture, conceived as a limited and exclusive totality of social life. Anthropology in its thesis of cultural determination leaves no space for Freud's psychic-symbolic domain.

We have argued earlier on that doctrines of entity, concepts of person, and repertoires of conduct do have radical effects on belief and conduct.

We argued that social relations affect both forms of mental pathology and the forms of normality in terms of which it is defined and assessed. We are far from retracting our commitment to the specific effectiveness of social relations in psychic life. At the same time we are driven to recognize that social relations do not wholly encapsulate the psychic domain. It too has a specific effectiveness which cannot be reduced to biology or individual psychology. It has a collective and symbolic character. 'Culture', in the anthropological sense, is a totality which encloses and determines the way of life, sentiments, and actions of a people. It tends therefore to deny any place for Freud's form of analysis. We would argue that social relations do not form an inclusive totality in this sense. It should also be said that this psychic domain, postulated by psychoanalysis, is neither fully defined nor explained by it. *Totem and Taboo* represents a signal failure to do so. It has the negative merit of most clearly revealing the problematic nature of the relations between psychoanalysis and cultural anthropology.

Psychoanalysis provides the means to question a central concept of anthropology, the opposition between nature and culture. Lévi-Strauss attempts to use this opposition in his own explanation of the incest taboo,[22] taking the incest taboo to be the foundation of *all* social rules. He argues that the human family is based on institutional rules which deny nature, and it is precisely *because* it is a denial of nature, of a perfectly possible biological relationship, that the taboo on incest is the origin of culture. The rule establishes the first oppositions, between the possible and the instituted, from which follow all other oppositions and cultural differences. But if Freud is right about human sexuality, there is no given 'nature', a biological realm of possible actions, to be denied. It is not merely that 'incest' is a cultural category. *All* organization of the sexual instincts is psychical and symbolic. 'Nature' is a cultural category too. Freud's arguments lead us to recognize that there is no 'nature' *separate* from the psychic and symbolic, which can be opposed and denied. It is this implication of Freud's theory which makes it particularly difficult to put psychoanalysis and anthropology together as complementary human sciences. They are condemned for the foreseeable future to coexist in tension. We should try to make that tension productive rather than sterile. Recognizing mutual incompatibilities and limitations may be one route to doing so.

Notes

1 Freud wrote thus to a woman who sought advice about her son.

> 'Homosexuality is assuredly no advantage, but is nothing to be ashamed of, no vice, no degradation; it cannot be classified as an illness, we consider it to be a variation of the sexual function .... It is a great injustice to persecute homosexuality as a crime − and a cruelty too .... By asking me if I can help you, you mean, I suppose if I can abolish homosexuality and make normal heterosexuality take its place .... What analysis can do for your son runs

in a different line. If he is unhappy, neurotic, torn by conflicts, inhibited in his social life, analysis may bring him harmony, peace of mind, full efficiency, whether he remains homosexual or gets changed.'

(Freud cited by Mitchell, 1975:11)

2   'A cultural community is perfectly justified, psychologically, in starting by proscribing manifestions of sexual life in children, for there would be no prospect of curbing the sexual lusts of adults if the ground had not been prepared for it in childhood' (Freud *SE* XXI: 104).

3   For purposes of economy in exposition we will treat the child as a male. It is often contended that Freud cannot account fully for the development of female sexuality with his concept of the 'Oedipus complex'. Juliet Mitchell in *Psychoanalysis and Feminism* (1975) argues brilliantly and persuasively that this is not the case; we can do no better than refer the reader to her work.

4   Sexual 'instincts' would thus better be rendered as sexual 'drives' but we retain here the usage of the Standard Edition of Freud's works edited by James Strachey, and continue to refer to *Sexualtriebe* as 'sexual instincts'.

5   See, for example, Tinbergen (1951).

6   For a discussion of 'propping' see Jean Laplanche *Life and Death in Psychoanalysis* (1976: 15-18).

7   The French psychoanalyst Jacques Lacan has reaffirmed the signifance of the symbolic order in defining the Oedipus complex, the Father and his 'Law', and therefore genitality. Lacan's work is complex and difficult and it is not lightly recommended as further reading but it does stress important and often misunderstood parts of Freud's theory. For a view of Freud's work broadly based on Lacan and relatively accessible, see Octave Mannoni *Freud, the Theory of the Unconscious* (1971). It should be noted that the concept of the 'symbolic' used here is quite different from White's concept (1949) of the 'symbol' which is discussed in Chapter Three.

8   Darwin's knowledge of the higher primates was limited. As we have seen in Chapter Three whilst baboons do form closed troops with a rigid dominance hierarchy this is not true of apes like chimpanzees or orangutans.

9   See *Group Psychology and the Analysis of the Ego* (*SE* XVIII: 122, 135).

10 In Freud's day the concepts of the inheritance of acquired characteristics and of ontogeny recapitulating phylogeny were far more respectable in orthodox biological science than they are today. Darwin's theory of natural selection was widely criticized in the early 1900s because it did not provide a mechanism for the *transmission* of characteristics. As we have seen in Chapter One this was only provided later in our century by the development of genetic theory. On the lacunae in Darwin's theory see Vorzimmer (1972) and on the state of evolutionary biology in the 1900s Rádl (1909).

11 Géza Róheim, whose anthropological work among the Australian Aborigines was supported by Freud and other analysts, strenuously argues this thesis in *Psychoanalysis and Anthropology* (1950) among other works. He gives interesting examples of virtually identical dream symbolism occuring in cultures as diverse as New York and the Normanby Islands.

12 Freud thus founded the characteristic element of the formation of human sexual identities on an *event*. Freud does not treat the murder of the primal father as pre-given or inevitable. The basic components of the Oedipo-symbolic have been transmitted in memory and myth from that day to this. Freud's explanation is

thus neither evolutionary – involving a necessary succession of 'stages' – nor does it involve a concept of progress. Freud's account differs radically from writers like Morgan and Engels who set up a primitive promiscuity, matriarchy, and patriarchy as successive stages of culture – each more advanced than the preceding one. Matriarchy is not a stage *prior* to patriarchy for Freud – human sexuality is constituted by the law of the father throughout history in *Totem and Taboo*.

13 See Freud's discussion of the emancipation of sexuality from instinct, from direct excitation by olefactory stimili. 'Civilization' is not an event but a gradual process: 'The fateful process of civilization would thus not have set in with man's adoption of an erect posture' (*SE* XXI: 90-100n). The 'horde', thus, is hardly natural or pre-social.

14 In his *Essay on the Origin of Inequality Among Men* (1755).

15 Malinowski observes at this point: 'As we saw, we are asked to believe that the totemic crime produces remorse which is expressed in the sacrament of endo-cannibalistic totemic feast, and in the institution of sexual taboo. This implies the primordial sons had a conscience. But conscience is a most unnatural mental trait imposed on man by culture' (1937: 165). As we shall see above, Freud thought 'conscience' to be a far from unproblematic cultural imposition, that guilt has its own psychic dynamics.

16 The relevant passage is the following:

> 'One can readily conceive how, when arrived at this stage of exaltation, a man does not recognize himself any longer. Feeling himself dominated and carried away by some sort of an external power which makes him think and act differently than in normal times, he naturally has the impression of being himself no longer. It seems that he has become a new being: the decorations he puts on and the masks that cover his face figure materially in this interior transformation, and to a still greater extent, they aid in determining its nature. And as at the same time all his companions feel themselves transformed in the same way and express this sentiment by their cries, their gestures and their general attitude, everything is just as though he really were transported into a special world, entirely different from the one where he ordinarily lives, and into an enviroment filled with exceptionally intense forces that take hold of him and metamorphose him. How could such experiences as these, especially when they are repeated every day for weeks, fail to leave him in the conviction that there really exist two heterogeneous and mutually incomparable worlds? One is that where his daily life drags wearily along; but he cannot penetrate into the other without at once entering into relations with extraordinary powers that excite him to the point of frenzy. The first is the profane world, the second that of sacred things.
>
> So it is in the midst of these effervescent social environments and out of this effervescence itself that the religious idea seems to be born.'
>
> (Durkheim 1915: 218-19)

Claude Lévi-Strauss noted this contradiction, that a 'collective representation' is derived from the affective states and sentiments of individuals, in *Totemism* (1964: 59-61, 70-1).

17 Reprinted in Kroeber *The Nature of Culture* (1952: Ch. 37), see also his later remarks in Ch. 38.

18 Malinowski (1937: 277).

19 Perhaps the clearest examples are to be found in Siegfried Sassoon's *Memoirs of an Infantry Officer* (1965); see also P.J. Campbell *The Ebb and Flow of Battle* (1979) and G. Coppard *With a Machine Gun to Cambrai* (1969).

20 We should stress here that the manifest and latent content of dreams means something quite different from the sociological concept of manifest and latent *functions*. For a discussion of Freud's concept see *Introductory Lectures in Psychoanalysis*, (*SE* XV: Lecture 7). For the distinction between functions see R.K. Merton 'Manifest and Latent Functions' in *Social Theory and Social Structure* (1957). Latent functions are the *unintended* consequences of social institutions and actions, these may be recognized or unrecognized, but they are not subject to censorship nor do they stem from the unconscious in the way the latent content of dreams is and does.

21 See Ernest Jones 'Mother Right and the Sexual Ignorance of Savages', *Essays in Applied Psychoanalysis* (1964); Géza Róheim *Psychoanalysis and Anthropology* (1950) particularly pp. 29-30 and p. 159, also Ch. III and 'Psychoanalysis and Anthropology' in S. Lorand (ed.) *Psychoanalysis Today* (1932).

22 See Lévi-Strauss (1969: xxix and Chs. I and II) and Lévi Strauss (1951).

9

MADNESS AND CIVILIZATION

Michel Foucault's *Madness and Civilization* (1965) is *not* a history of psychiatry. Its path-breaking status and wide-ranging importance are not those of a first attempt to survey the history of that scientific discipline and medical specialism. Such histories abound. What Foucault does is to investigate the *conditions of possibility* of such a discipline and such a practice of therapeutics. In doing this he radically re-orders the time-scale and forms of attention which characterize such histories. A good example of the methods of such histories of psychiatry is Zilboorg and Henry's *History of Medical Psychology* (1941) which traces the beginnings of a 'rational attitude' to phenomena of mental pathology. Zilboorg begins with the Greeks, treating the Hippocratic writings on insanity as the beginnings of a naturalistic and critical account of mental illness. Here, it is claimed, we find the first separation of the phenomena of mental illness from religious doctrines and popular superstitions, an account which finds alongside the Divine sickness — the folly and irrational insight sent by the gods — phenomena which stem not from Divine will but from man's body, from its malfunctionings and its relationship to the environment. This birth of reason is then suppressed in the Dark Ages of Christian religious belief. Psychiatry emerges only when the new critical attitude of the scientific revolution of the sixteenth century can be applied to man himself, when, in the eighteenth and nineteenth centuries, medical reason can displace religious belief and explain mental illness as something other than demoniacal possession.

Foucault dissents from such accounts not because he has a different *timing* of the advent of rationality in mental medicine. It is not that he disagrees with this conception of Hippocratic thought — although works like Dodds' *The Greeks and the Irrational* (1973) would provide the means to challenge the notion of the Greek doctors as the precursors of modern psychiatry — or because he locates 'scientific' psychiatry later, in Kraepelin's clinical breakthrough or in the advent of behavioural methods. Foucault differs from Zilboorg and others like him because he is concerned, not to write the history of a discipline, but to find, outside of it and as a condition of its emergence, the moment when 'madness' became something which *could* become the object of psychiatry.

We anticipate a protest. Surely 'madness' has always been there. Sick

An eighteenth-century image of madness in the form of a political caricature.

Source: reproduced by kind permission of the Fotomas Index.

men and women in need of help, and who were prevented – for reasons of human ignorance and superstition – from receiving it. But the mad are not 'madness'. Madness for Foucault is not some given behavioural or biological fact, it is a category, the product of civilization and its institutions. The very idea that 'madness' is individual pathology, a negative phenomenon, a defect to be remedied, is his object of investigation. This conception of madness is not the achievement of psychiatric rationality. Rather it is a complex and non-intentional social product, which formed the basis for psychiatry. It came into existence not purposively, but as the complex product of many unrelated cultural and social changes that have nothing to do with modern psychiatry itself. For this reason Foucault

calls his enterprise not history but 'archaeology'. This is not some preten-
tious metaphor for the same thing dressed up in an obscure language. It is
a precise and valuable metaphor borrowed from geology. Foucault seeks
to uncover the stratum of categories and institutions *beneath* the language
and practice of psychiatry, which is not to be found in what psychiatry
says but is the basis on which what it says becomes possible.

Conventional histories begin with what modern psychiatry knows and
then look back to find the beginnings of its statements, its language, in
earlier times. They write the history of psychiatry as the development of
a discipline, the growth through its own purposive action of a body of
rational thought, its accumulation through setbacks and victories across
the centuries. Foucault forswears this knowledge because it can only
hide from him the conditions which make it possible:

i.   the transformation of madness from a complex and dispersed set of
     social valuations to a uniform category of pathology, something which
     has no place in normal life, something which has nothing specific or
     valuable to say;
ii. the exclusion of those who are 'mad' from normal social life, their
     isolation in a specialist domain of pathology and its rectification.

Foucault is concerned to argue that psychiatry becomes possible when
madness is conceived negatively in opposition to reason, as unreason,
and when the mad have been isolated and confined as a specific social
category in a specific site. Both the formation of a category of 'reason',
of a normality which admits of only the negative and pathological outside
of itself and in opposition to itself, and the institutional confinement of
the mad *preceded* psychiatry. Psychiatry emerged as a reform of existing
forms of confinement, converting the forms of exclusion into a therapeutic institution, the asylum. It became a specialist means of correction,
a distinct branch of medicine, only through a complex development from
preceding medical systems which recognized no specifically 'mental'
illness, which continued to unite somatic and psychic medicine. The
negative valuation of madness did not give rise straightaway to psychiatry,
but only by a complex and non-cumulative transformation of pre-existing
structures.

Now in saying that his object of analysis is the transformation of 'madness' into a negative and uniform category of 'unreason', Foucault is not
saying that the mad are thereby stigmatized, labelled, and made deviant
for the first time, or that there was no madness or insanity under the
preceding institutional and cultural forms. Madness is not merely a label.
Foucault is aware that what falls under the category of 'madness' could
be as terrifying and incapacitating to its victims in the Middle Ages as it is
to severe psychotics today. Rather, he is concerned to say two things.
First, that the mad were not unified and homogenized into a single,
negative, social category in the Middle Ages. Second, that what the mad

experienced and had to say was not at that time treated as a mere pathology to be rectified; madness was not isolated from normality and human culture in a univocal way. The line between the mad and other men was not drawn so clearly and those other men *listened* to the mad and the madness in themselves. Madness was considered, partially and unevenly, as part of human culture and not in opposition to some unified reason and normality. What is at issue are the forms of categorization and treatment of the insane, the relation of madness to general human culture, and not some process of stigmatization or labelling whereby conducts become defined as mad. Foucault has too much practical psychiatric experience and too much sympathy for the sufferings of the insane to treat madness as a mere label. In this he differs from much of the medical sociology and deviancy theory which has appropriated his work.

The scope of Foucault's work is the period between the end of the Middle Ages and up to and including the reforms of Pinel and Tuke. It *ends* with the 'founding fathers' of modern institutional psychiatry, at the very point where most histories pass from the stage of precursors to the main substance of the story. But Foucault's investigation ends with the creation of a specialist mental medicine concerned with the therapeutic and correctional confinement of the insane in specialist institutions. This structure, created on the basis of theoretical systems radically different from our own, is nonetheless the form of categorial status and social placement of the insane which has persisted until today. All the developments in institutional psychiatric theory and practice have taken place on the basis of this structure of placements and categories which modern psychiatry has inherited, which it did not create, and which form the specific social basis of its theorizing and activity. Psychiatry does not encounter a natural phenomenon, 'insanity'; it deals with a population constituted in specific institutional conditions. Psychiatry did not devise the 'surfaces of emergence' of its phenomena, it came into existence with them, and they were the product of a constellation of specific and unrelated changes and developments which came together at the end of the eighteenth century.

Madness and Civilization is an extremely rich and complex book. The original French edition, of which the English translation is a substantial abridgement, contains far more discussion of literature and cultural phenomena, and is even less like a history of psychiatry. To summarize it fully is impossible, and we have no wish to reduce it to the barest bones, a sequence of simplified changes. It is necessary to be ruthlessly selective, to the point of distorting many of Foucault's emphases. It is also necessary to bear in mind that the book is primarily, if not exclusively concerned with France. Space prevents a full discussion of the growing literature on the birth of the asylum in this country; we must, regretfully, refer the reader to the best specialist works.[1]

The Middle Ages

In the European Middle Ages 'madness' formed no coherent figure. There was no uniform concept of madness or insanity and no uniform treatment of persons and conducts which would, from the standpoint of nineteenth-century psychiatry, be regarded as 'insane'. In the medieval categorizations it was the leper who occupied the place of exclusion; leprosy was a scourge which provoked the forms of fear and unease we tend to feel toward the insane. But the lepers, excluded as they were in the specialist confinements of leprosaria, were not regarded as merely pathological, as the victims of a purely personal, natural defect. Leprosy was God's scourge and the leper was chosen by God's grace to be punished in *this* world for his or her sins. Religious perceptions and practices radically limited the forms of division of conduct which are characteristic of modern societies. Such possibilities as possession and prophecy, the life of hermits, created a range of conducts and conceptions which disturb our divisions of normality and pathology, from Joan of Arc with her 'voices' to the abbot who regarded the fleas which inhabited his robe as little demons sent to disrupt his meditations.

Medieval societies did not refuse the category of madness, however, and they differentiated between fools and madmen in both concept and practice. 'Folly' was not despised as sickness or pathology. The fool was both sacred and blessed and, in certain circumstances, possessed of wisdom. Folly was God's visitation and a testament to his mercy in removing the fool from man's sufferings and trials. The fool, in the world and yet not of it, could recognize and comment on, through his difference, the evil and folly of man. Cities appear to have catered for their own 'insane' poor, lodging them in municipal 'hospitals', places of care rather than custody or therapy, or licensing them to beg. The furious and raving were typically lodged in the available empty secure spaces, the gatehouses and towers of the city walls, within sight and earshot, rather than being hidden away in dungeons. No shame attached to madness as such. Some forms of madness were considered as specific and temporary attacks which might pass, 'melancholy', sudden frenzies, etc. Beds were reserved for these madmen at the Hôtel-Dieu in Paris, but no specific treatments were offered. Other madmen who were vagabonds and strays were entrusted by cities and authorities to sailors and boatmen, dumped out of harm's way (especially in Germany, on the Rhine and its tributaries). Madmen were sent on pilgrimages since certain shrines were thought to be blessed with the power of curing insanity, for example, Gheel in Belgium or Besançon.

We see here no uniform system of social placement, no uniform conception of madness as pathology or individual sickness for which therapies must be sought. There is no uniform exclusion of the mad, except the violent, from social relations or culture. The fool could serve as a source of wisdom, as a popular leader or a prophet. In popular festivals the whole

THE KNIGHT

In a moment shall they die, and the people shall be troubled at midnight, and pass away: and the mighty shall be taken away without hand. *Job xxxiv, 20.*

E'en in a moment shall they die,
At midnight shall men quake with fear,
The mighty shall not be pass'd by,
Nor know who thrusts the fatal spear.

THE LADY

The Lord do so to me, and more also, if aught but death part thee and me. *Ruth i, 17.*

The love by which they are united,
By faith should teach them, ere too late,
That soon such unions may be blighted,
And Death step in to separate.

THE SENATOR

Whoso stoppeth his ears at the cry of the poor, he also shall cry himself, but shall not be heard. *Proverbs xxi, 13.*

Ye rich, who cautious counsel take on gain,
Ye cannot hear the starving poor man sue;
But, at the last, ye too will cry in vain,
And God will turn as deaf an ear to you.

THE MISER

Thou fool, this night thy soul shall be required of thee: then whose shall those things be which thou hast provided? *Luke xii, 20.*

This very night shalt thou know Death!
To-morrow be encoffined fast!
Then tell me, fool! while thou hast breath,
Who'll have the gold thou hast amassed?

Source: Hans Holbein the Younger, *The Dance of Death,* facsimile edition 1971 (New York: Dover Publications).

population entered into folly. Festivals were commonly held under the rubric of a 'feast of fools' in which the established order was mocked and inverted, under the authority of elected kings of fools or lords of misrule.[2]

Madness in the Renaissance

At the end of the Middle Ages madmen, madness, and folly come to occupy a central place in European culture, in popular religious imagination, in literature, and in art. This is connected with the dominance of the themes of the end of the world and the imminence of the Second Coming – a cultural furore connected with the degeneration of the Church and the movements for its reform. Madness

'symbolized a great disquiet, suddenly dawning on the horizon of European culture at the end of the Middle Ages. Madness and the madman became major figures, in their ambiguity: menace and mockery, the dizzying unreason of the world, and the feeble ridicule of men.'

(Foucault 1965: 53)

Until the middle of the fifteenth century it is Death which symbolizes this crisis, which mocks men and serves to remind them of the vanity of earthly existence, which, in other words, serves as an image of negation. Madness comes to supplement it and replace it. The madman serves as a symbol of and a point of commentary on the human condition. The wisdom of the mad is to see and serve as a mirror for the folly of men. *All* men are fools: passion, lust, pride, and greed lead them to foolishness. Literature and the visual arts trace this concern with madness in separate and different ways. The painters conjure a more threatening and profound experience of unreason. In the works of Bosch, Grünewald, and countless other painters, terrors and monstrosities are made visible, threatening, and even dominant, as a glance at the savage landscape and monstrous beings which torment Saint Anthony in Grünewald's *Temptation* will illustrate. In literature a cooler tone prevails: madness is used as a device and as a satire on the follies of men in works like Sebastien Brandt's *Ship of Fools* (1494) or Erasmus' *In Praise of Folly* (1509), in which the follies and foibles of every profession and estate are mocked. Even at the end of the sixteenth century madness and folly serve as a powerful device, dramatic machinery, and place of criticism. Shakespeare's Hamlet and King Lear are mad, yet active in human drama, and the means by which tragedy is furthered, revealed, and resolved. Cervantes' Don Quixote presents through the forms of his delusion an inverted view of the world in which *its* activities and ambiguities are revealed in a device similar to Montesquieu's composed and philosophical Persian strangers or Diderot's wise and assured Tahitians in the *Supplement to the Voyage of Bougainville*.[3] In the sixteenth century madness, far from being a negative value, a pathology at the margins of life, is a central part of and means of presenting the whole human condition. Foucault sums up this point in a later work:[4]

> 'This is not to say that the Renaissance did not treat the mad. On the contrary, the fifteenth century saw the opening, first in Spain (at Sara-gossa), then in Italy, of the first great madhouses. There the mad were subjected to a treatment based very largely no doubt on Arabic medicine. But these are exceptional cases. Generally speaking, madness was allowed free reign; it circulated throughout society, it formed part of the background and language of everyday life, it was for everyone an everyday experience that one sought neither to exalt nor to control. In France, in the early eighteenth century, there were famous madmen who were a great source of entertainment for the public, and the cultivated public at that; some of these, like Bluet d'Arbères, wrote books that were published and read as works of madness. Up to about 1650, Western culture was strongly hospitable to those forms of experience.'

(Foucault 1976: 57)

The Great Confinement

At this point everything changes. Foucault locates this change in the 'economic crisis' of the early and middle seventeenth century and in the new practice of social economy which accompanied the development of the Absolutist state. In France the price revolution of the sixteenth century (an inflation of unprecedented dimensions caused by the influx of gold and silver from the Spanish mines in Mexico and Peru) and the civil wars led to the formation of hordes of vagabonds and dispossessed peasants. This crisis and mass beggary had its echo throughout Europe and it overwhelmed the already senescent institutions of social welfare based on Catholic charitable foundations. As an instance of the scale of the crisis Foucault recounts that when Henri IV laid siege to Paris the city, which had less than 100,000 inhabitants, contained more than 30,000 beggars.

It is less the crisis itself than the response to it which is of significance for Foucault's argument. The response is a new system of 'police', meaning administrative supervision and control. This system worked by bringing all the indigent, poor, and incapable within forms of public order, confining them under supervision in 'houses of correction'. All those unwilling or unable to work were grouped together: the unemployed, the poor, beggars, criminals and vagabonds, libertines and degenerates, and the insane. The 'marginal classes' were to be eliminated through confinement; they are conceived negatively as a threat to social order, an affront to morality, and as a wasted resource. Confinement and forced labour would confer discipline on those capable of reform and, for those not so capable, would 'govern' them in exclusion from the social body. This development of the confinement of the indigent, criminal, and marginal is in no sense peculiar to France. The first such house opened in Hamburg in 1620 — others followed in Germany, Holland, and England in the second half of the century.

In 1656 Louis XIV established the Hôpital Général in Paris; it grouped existing charitable and welfare institutions into a single new administration, a single apparatus of repression:

> 'The year after — Sunday, May 13th 1657 — a high mass in honour of the Holy Ghost was sung at the Church of Saint-Louis de la Pitié, and in the morning of Monday the 14th the militia, which was to become in the mythology of popular terror "the archers of the Hôpital", began to hunt down beggars and herd them into the different buildings of the Hôpital.'
>
> (Foucault 1965: 49)

Four years later the houses in Paris held some 6000 persons, of whom perhaps some 10 per cent were madmen. In 1676 the king decreed the general extension of the system to all of France. The Hôpitaux were institutions expressly created by royal power and outside the scope of the courts, and their directors were given absolute powers to dispose of their inmates as they thought fit. Louis had annexed and re-used many of the old, now functionless, lazar houses, turning their buildings and revenues over to the Hôpital. Madness, poverty, and illness now occupied the places of exclusion previously reserved for lepers, and attained a fearful status which mirrored all that was negative in the leper's condition. The Church followed the initative of the state; its charitable institutions and lazar houses were reformed by St. Vincent de Paul into houses of correction for the poor.[5]

The new system of 'police' depended on three pillars, the Crown, the Church, and the family. A new apparatus provided for the repression of all who could not work or who threatened family honour. Through the system of *lettres de cachet* the King provided the heads of families, in addition to the disciplinary assistance they could call upon from their religious overseers, with a means of detention without trial in houses of correction and places of confinement. As Foucault remarks, it is an 'authoritarian model' in which confinement enforces industry and virtuous conduct, which serves social order, religious conceptions of the virtuous life, and family honour and peace. It *polices* idleness, libertinage, and all that threatens work and morality. Insanity becomes a purely negative and marginal conception: the mad are incapable of work and threaten public decency, and thus become candidates for exclusion.

Colbert, Louis XIV's economic overlord and the architect of the policy of mercantilism, regarded assistance through forced labour in confinement as a remedy for unemployment and as a stimulus to the development of manufactories. Yet it would be too simple to regard this 'authoritarian model' as a response to the demands of a nascent capitalism. The system of houses of confinement, religious foundations, and *lettres de cachet* never served merely or effectively as a solution to the problems of poverty. Forced labour was never economically productive nor did it serve to control unemployment and regulate the labour force. The injunction to labour did not merely serve the interests of economic utility. It had a moral and religious value, as the foundation of a well-ordered state and of true Christian conduct. This is instanced by the words of Colbert himself: 'All the poor who are capable of working must, upon work days, do what is necessary to avoid idleness, which is the mother of all evils, as well as accustom them to honest toil and also to earning some part of their sustenance' (Foucault 1965: 53). Labour in *both* Protestant and Counter-Reformation Catholic doctrine acquires a new religious significance: the body of the faithful is defined by active work as part of an orderly and religious life, labour is a moral necessity, God's compulsion and curse to fallen man, and industry is a sign of a faithful obedience to God's will. It has a moral rather than an economic value; even if labour is unproductive and sterile it has a positive value as the opposite of idleness. Sloth has replaced Pride as the cardinal sin. Just as the leper was excluded from the body of the faithful (but not from God's mercy) by his disease, so the pauper and the madman were excluded from the active and orderly community of the faithful by their unwillingness or inability to work. But, unlike the leper, they could not be left in their own isolation to God's mercy. They had to be 'governed' in their exclusion.

The insane were now institutionalized but *not* for the purposes of a therapy directed at a specific and curable pathology. Even so, it was quickly recognized that they could not be subjected to nor confined within a regime of forced labour. The insane came to occupy a relatively specific and segregated place within the system of confinement, differentiated from the other elements of the confined population. They could not be left mingled with the general population of the houses of confinement both because of the disorder they caused and because they were incapable of work. They were also treated differently from the ungovernable degenerates and libertines who were committed under the *lettres de cachet* in order to their spare their families shame and to prevent a scandal that would threaten public morals. But while these moral degenerates were hidden away to prevent scandal, the mad in confinement were *exhibited*. The mad could be shown in their chains to a visiting public because (once behind bars) they threatened no moral scandal and, unlike the leper, no contagion. This is because of prevailing social and medical ideas as to what condition madness was.

The mad were not *sick*. They were healthy in body but *without reason*. Current medical ideas conceived insanity *in extremis* as a reduction to animality. Insanity is characterized by delusion and unreason. The mad were like animals, without normal human sensations and, therefore, hardier than normal men. The mad could stand extremes of cold and were indifferent to their condition. What the reformers were to recognize as 'ill treatment' was not the product of a deliberate cruelty but a belief that the mad did not suffer and could not benefit from better treatment. Frenzied, raving, and deluded, they needed to be restrained when violent and extravagant, hence the armoury of means of restraint encountered by reformers like Howard during their visits to places of confinement. Paradoxically, the mad were allowed, when they were not raving and dangerous, a certain liberty in confinement. Unlike the libertine, their extavagance posed no moral threat; it was a different liberty — that of the beast.

Medicine and insanity in the Classical era

The chapters in which Foucault reconstitutes the seventeenth- and eighteenth-century medical theories of madness are the most dense and complex in the whole book. For a background in the history of medicine it is perhaps advisable to read them in conjuction with Foucault's study of eighteenth-century medicine and its transformations, *The Birth of the Clinic*. It is this medicine of the 'Classical' period which must be the main victim of the condensation and selection we are forced to practise here. Classical medical systems, whether based on developments of the theory of humours, the concept of animal spirits, or the mechanics of 'fibres' all unite soma and psyche as one interpenetrating complex. Man's body and mind are a unity traversed by multiple interconnections and causalities: diet, climate, mode of life, and physiological processes all interact and can produce complex alterations in the normal workings of body and mind. There is no space here for a purely 'mental' medicine.

The brain and the soul (or mind) form one system. Passion, excess or imbalance in feelings or ideas, is the fundamental source or form of madness. Madness is chacterized by excess, it is 'no more than a derangement of the imagination' (Foucault 1965:93). It consists in attaching certainty and conviction to ideas which go beyond truth, beyond a proper and accurate relation to things. The essence of madness is delusion, an irrational commitment to false beliefs and perceptions. This unreason does not fully suspend the laws of working of the mind, for the madman sees, thinks, and reasons. Rather, the mad are characterized by a rigorous but irrational reason, a syllogism that leads to systematic illusion and irrationality. It is in these disordered elements of reason that there lies the possibility of cure. The madman can be restored to a balanced imagination only by removing the seeds of unreason, by expelling the negative which is delusion and restoring the normal workings of the mind. To the idea of the criminal extravagance of madness, restrained in the regime of confinement, is added the idea of madness as reason off the rails — and thereby a possible therapeutics.

The interaction of the mind and body means that this logic of false connections in the realm of ideas directly extends to pathology and derangement in the internal economy of the body. This reinforces and fixes delusion and error through physiological mechanisms and flows. It follows that two modes of treatment are equally open to medicine confronted with madness. The first is to treat delusion itself, to work on the system of unreasonable ideas and to enforce a new and rational logic of connections between thoughts and perceptions. Foucault gives the example of a treatment of a man who thought he was dead and therefore refused to eat because the dead do not eat. This syllogism was interrupted by a staged counter-delusion: persons dressed as if they were dead entered his room and proceeded to eat, insisting that the dead do eat like the living. The second method is to use physical therapies to restore organic balance or to shock the brain into a normal pattern of working. Numerous forms of therapy were employed: bleeding, purging, inoculating with scabies, various forms of water treatment, sudden shocks, etc.

Eighteenth-century medicine, when it did treat the mad, did not use a distinct 'psychiatric method' — there is in its systems no distinct category of *mental* illness. Indeed, what we would regard as 'psychological' treatments are regarded as part of normal medicine, as treating the whole man, body and mind. We have said that confinement was *not* for the purposes of treatment or therapy but for containment and exclusion from the rest of the population. To the extent that the mad were treated in hospitals, it is not because hospitals were regarded as a specialist site of therapy or correction. To the extent that 'mad doctors', specialists in cases of insanity, did exist, it was not because they were special psychiatrists; they were merely specialists in one part of general medicine concentrating on a particular class of cases, like gerontologists today.

But eighteenth-century medicine did provide a complex and roundabout route to a conception of a class of distinct *mental* illnesses. This lay in the accentuation of the role of passion and mode of life in tracing its action on body and mind, through the concept of 'sensibility' and the notion of the 'hysterias'.

Diseases of the 'nerves' are increasingly conceived as a register of the state of the soul and mode of life. Soft living, moral excitation, too great a liberty in beliefs and emotions, all tend to a weakening of the physical condition, a too ready receptiveness to excitements, shocks, and disappointments. The 'nervous' constitution is a disease of civilization; an over-developed 'sensibility' leads to a magnification of the physical and mental effects of sensation and passion. Gradually the 'mental' component in this complex of elements of madness comes to dominate, over-reach, and subordinate the somatic. It creates the space for a conception of madness as a direct product of moral constitution in which madness becomes 'the psychological effect of a moral fault' (Foucault 1965: 158). Madness becomes equated with *guilt*, with an abnormal regime of life which directly leads to psychological degeneration. The way is open to a therapy which acts directly on the regime of life itself, which seeks to instil a new, ordered regime of conduct. 'Moral methods' of treatment then become possible, in which the physiological register has all but disappeared. Therapy becomes identified with an enforced moral regimen and a controlled regime of conduct. Though the concept of 'nervous disease', of a sensibility acting on the constitution, was produced by somatic medicine, it leads to the exclusion of this very medicine from the treatment of madness. To the extent that physical methods are retained by Pinel, they are not viewed as the techniques of a therapeutics but as a means of *punishment*, a means to enforce conformity to a regime and to submit to moral direction. Confinement becomes not containment but the means to establish an ordered regime of conduct. The hospital becomes a necessity for therapy, not as a specialized site for physical treatment, but as a controlled environment of moral direction. A purely psychological medicine becomes possible.

The birth of the asylum

Possible but not necessary: nothing guaranteed that the places of confinement would become therapeutic institutions for the ordering of conduct. The asylum is not an actualization of medical ideas, an institution purposively designed to carry out a new programme. However, for a number of reasons, the old system of confinement had become an administrative scandal and an object of liberal and radical political opposition. This had several sources in France. First, the system of *lettres de cachet* and preventative detention was identified with Absolutism, and criticism of this system was part of the liberal and radical challenge to the monarchy itself. Second, opposition from economists to confining the poor, as well as the failure of the forced labour system, challenged the very foundations of the original mercantilist conception of the houses of confinement. The Revolution would seek to abolish confinement as the basis of 'welfare'. Poor relief, medical assistance, and so on were to be provided to people in their homes — the old system was identified with the Bastille of Absolutism as a threat to liberty. Third, the attempts to reform the system of criminal punishments proposed by Beccaria and others, instituting certain penalties adjusted to the severity of the crime, did not envisage the prison, i.e. confinement, as a means of punishment. Before and in the early years of the Revolution, we encounter a general challenge to closed institutions.

In the founding myths of institutional psychiatry Pinel is credited with having 'liberated' the insane, not merely from physical restraint but from being mixed pell-mell with criminals and vagabonds. This principle of separation of the different classes of persons was a central common plank of the reformers. Long before Pinel, the notion that the insane should be segregated from the general institutionalized population had become established, not least among the directors of the houses of correction themselves — who realized that where the insane mingled with the general population of the workshops disorder was the inevitable result. Foucault asks:

'Did Esquirol and Reil and the Tukes do anything more than shout at the top of their lungs what had been, for years, commonplaces of asylum practice? The slow emigration of the mad ... from 1720 onwards to the Revolution, was probably no more than the most visible effect of that practice.'

(Foucault 1965: 22-3)

The reason for this gradual separation was partly considerations of efficiency but it also involved a new and distinct perception of madness. The mad should be segregated because it was unjust that the poor and criminal prisoners should suffer the indignities of being lumped together with the insane. The mad took on an additional negativity and specificity — as the lowest and most feared part of the confined population. Initially lumped together as part of the indigent and disorderly, now the mad were separated from others as a debasement and threat. The general critique of confinement in the eighteenth century worked *against* the liberation of the mad: of all the population of the houses of confinement they were the ones who most fittingly belonged there, who *should* be segregated and confined. The Revolution, in dismantling the authoritarian system of social discipline instituted by Louis XIV and its cornerstone, preventative detention, insisting in the Declaration of the Rights of Man that no one should be detained except by law and for a definite crime, was left with the residual problem of the insane. Madmen could not be released nor could they, on grounds of efficiency and in justice to the convicted, remain in the criminal prisons. A legal rubric and a form of confinement appropriate to them had to be devised within the liberal order. The necessity of a distinct legal status of 'insanity' and a special procedure for committal, within the law but differing from an ordinary criminal judgement, is created within the very reforms which bring in the 'liberal' order. What Foucault neatly exposes is the special status of the insane which emerges from the challenge to the arbitrary exclusions and un-checked power of the Absolutist correctional system.

The Revolution in France enables Foucault to draw a neater line between two regimes of confinement than can be found in England. It highlights, in the contrast with Absolutism, the *specific* exclusion of the mad within the social regime of liberalism. This exclusion took place on the level of administrative arrangements in a hurried 'reform' which cleared the insane from the overcrowded prisons of revolutionary Paris, one which separated the insane but did not determine as such the mode of their treatment.

Enter Philippe Pinel. In 1793 Pinel is given charge of Bicêtre. He strikes off the chains of the insane, and mental illness enters the modern age. Foucault examines not only the work of Pinel but of the English-man, Samuel Tuke. In 1792 Tuke founded the Retreat at York, which can lay claim to being the first modern 'mental hospital'. Foucault's contrast of Pinel and Tuke has a strategic value. As we saw earlier in our discussion of mental illness, their theoretical and ideological systems were quite different and, here we may add, so too were the political and institutional circumstances in which they worked. The asylum appears not as the result of a single new medical rationality, a reform springing from a new system of medical or philosophical ideas as such. Tuke had no definite or developed medical theory of insanity. Nor is the asylum the product of some uniform political-institutional reform. Tuke's foundation is a 'private' act, one the British state was long unwilling to follow and did so only tardily. What constitutes the common link between Pinel's practice and Tuke's is something quite different — neither medical-theoretical nor 'political' — a new conception of the role of confinement, a new regime of management of the insane, a new role for the physician.

The Retreat was founded in response to the death of a member of Tuke's religious community, the Quakers, in suspicious circumstances in the existing asylum at York. The Retreat offered a confinement which would not disturb Quakers' religious and moral sensibilities, which had none of the casual violence and indecency of public places of confinement. It employed radical Protestant notions of the systematization of conduct, the internalization of morality in 'conscience', and the philanthropic tending of souls in the new task of the care of the mind. It reconstructed within a closed house the forms of religious discipline and supervision practised by the Quakers and other sects in their communities and congregations. The Retreat is famous for its 'domestic' atmosphere, but it imposed order on the insane *through* domesticity and religious conformity. It created a closed regime of enforced morality in which the slightest difference or deviation was immediately apparent, and checked by a subtle system of threats and punishments. The individual was encouraged to internalize this regime as conscience, to control through his own efforts at self-discipline his own extravagance, to recognize his disorder as deviation and guilt, as a straying from the proper ways to which he must return.

Through an extension of traditional methods of disciplining the flock and self-direction the Retreat introduced a new order of management in which the systematic overseeing of the inmates' behaviour and the direction of their conduct replaced the haphazard methods of previous forms of confinement. The objective of confinement was no longer mere exclusion and physical restraint, it was the reconstruction of souls.

Pinel at Bicêtre and La Salpêtrière enforced a less domestic regime with a less explicitly religious mode. The prevailing anti-clericalism of the Revolution and an Enlightenment recognition of the dangers and pathologies of religious 'enthusiasm', prevented any precise parallel with the moral climate at York. Pinel was a disciple of the French philosopher Condillac whom we mentioned in Chapters Two and Three. Condillac proposed, following the English empiricists, that all human knowledge ultimately derived from sensation. The complexity of the sensory organs, combined with the existence in signs (particularly language) of a means of linking perceptions, provided the foundation of human reasoning.

Re-order sensory experience and it was thereby possible to re-order thought and, with it, man. Yet, for all Pinel's intellectual debt to Condillac, his therapeutic regime is *not* merely a naturalistic re-ordering of experience, for his regime assigns a crucial role to morality and the inculcation of moral self-government. Thus Pinel is closer to Tuke than any strictly historical account of the very different intellectual 'influences' acting upon them would indicate. But the similarities between Citizen Pinel's order of management and that of Tuke are even more striking: in both cases the individual was subjected to continuous surveillance, constantly measured against norms of conduct imposed by the director, and pressed to internalize those norms as the key to self-government and the elimination of madness.

Pinel and Tuke dispensed with chains, cages, and barred cells for the mass of the asylum population. External constraints and mere physical confinement could not attain the ends of the new regime. The insane were to be placed in a regime of systematic control aimed at enforcing conformity with morality and instilling — through a uniform orderly daily round and, when necessary, through fear of punishment — quiet and conforming conduct. These are the outward conditions which make possible the struggle to instil and internalize self-government — moral direction — within each individual. The insane must be forced to recognize their disorder and deficiency and be placed in circumstances where the least deviation could be immediately recognized and checked. This demanded close supervision and the segregation of the different classes of the asylum population — the quiet from the raving, the active from the deteriorated — as well as a staff who themselves acted quietly and morally in conformity with the director's plans to attain his therapeutic ends.

Therapy consisted in creating within the asylum an artificial community, a regime which made up for the deficiency, idleness and extravagance, moral weakness, and lack of direction of the inmates — a deficiency they had acquired in the outside world. Confinement, as exclusion from the distortions *and the liberties* of normal society, is necessary to create this regime. Separation and surveillance are necessary to concentrate undivided or undistracted moral effects on each individual. Hence the new confinement is more rigorous in its controls than the old. In thus challenging the notion of 'liberation' of the insane Foucault is not interested in casting doubt on the motives or humanitarianism of the reformers but in illustrating what it is that is specific to the new confinement. It is not the old containment now 'humanized' (although he does not doubt that an end to random brutality and systematic neglect could not but be a benefit) but a machine of correction governed by new objectives. The insane individual is not merely enclosed in new constraints: silence, isolation, outward conformity. He is transformed as an individual, he becomes the object of a moral discourse and a subject for transformation into a self-governing moral being. Central to constraint is its role as a precondition for the acceptance by the individual that he is sick. Madness must become for itself pathology; this recognition is the key to the 'cure'. The madman must recognize his own madness as a deficiency to be eliminated, as something he must be aided to master and exclude as part of his re-birth as a self-governing moral being. To do so, to govern himself, he must submit to direction. He must accept the asylum director as one possessed of the knowledge of his condition and as possessing in that knowledge his future path to cure. But there is no dialogue between madness and its therapy — cure consists in submission and in the elimination of those abnormal traits which are madness itself. The opposition between reason and unreason, the negativization of madness, is now complete. Madness is now inextricably linked to custody *and* therapy. It remains within the asylum, as what is acted upon there.

The new regime also creates the 'psychiatrist'. The asylum director, defined in his place by the new site of confinement, is a specialist in a strictly 'mental' pathology. The medical personage takes on a new significance and autonomy in relation to insanity, an autonomy which stems from the asylum. Madness now becomes a matter of 'medical' judgement. It is committal to the asylum which defines madness and this exclusion is now based on a new legality which consists in, is delegated to, a 'medical' diagnosis of insanity. Against the arbitrariness of the 'old regime', exclusion for reason of insanity is to be based on a *knowledge* of madness, and it is the judgement of the psychiatrist (who possesses such knowledge) which forms the basis for action in law.

This 'medicine' has nothing specifically somatic about it. The psychiatrist is not the lineal descendant of the 'mad doctor'. The psychiatrist attains a *new* medical authority as the director of the asylum, as a clinical judge of insanity — a clinicity based on his knowledge of the specialist asylum population — and as one who possesses, by reason of the asylum regime, a distinct power over mental pathology.

> 'Within the asylum itself, the doctor takes a preponderant place, insofar as he converts it into a medical space. However, and this is the essential point, the doctor's intervention is not by virtue of a medical skill ... justified by a body of objective knowledge. It is not as a scientist that *homo medicus* has his authority in the asylum, but as a wise man.'
>
> (Foucault 1965: 270)

The new therapy is not as such specifically medical: its conception of a regime of correction and the new practices of management would be applied in non-medical sites — prisons, workhouses, reform schools, etc. — to correct crime, idleness, and delinquency. Thus it is not as administrator of the therapy that the psychiatrist is a doctor; it is because, as a medical man, he takes on a new social and legal status.[6] Through his knowledge of the specifically 'mental' in pathology, he becomes the guarantee of the justice of the committal, and also a person morally fit

to manage the insane. His authority is medicalized and given a new therapeutic mystique. This mystique, the conviction that he possesses a *knowledge* of madness (although lacking in any specific 'scientific' justification),
is the condition for his authority and for the patient's submission to it
which is necessary for and constitutive of the cure.

Foucault remarks: 'The asylum of the age of positivism, which it is
Pinel's glory to have founded, is not a free realm of observation, diagnosis
and therapeutics' (1965: 269). For all that asylum practice comes to
identify itself with the observational methods of clinical medicine, for
all that physical treatments come once again at the end of the nineteenth
century to enjoy an overwhelming prestige in the treatment of the insane,
the asylum remains rooted in the structures created by 'moral methods'.
The regime of management of institutions, the conception of mental
illness as individual pathology — a negative defect in the person to be
eliminated or controlled by therapy — and the position of the psychiatrist
as one who 'knows' about madness and to whose direction the patient
must submit all remain unchanged.

Foucault reaches back beyond modern clinical psychiatry to the Great
Confinement and its transformation into the asylum. He does so because
he is concerned to show something that the 'medical model' of psychiatry
as the technical treatment of the individual sickness does not, that is, that
psychiatry always operates within institutional forms, power relations,
and social demands which go beyond the technical therapeutics of the
'cure'. Normality itself, the object of the cure, is implicated in wider
conceptions of social competence, the current prevailing tolerable limits
of abnormality, and the demands of the state and other institutions for
manpower and order. Psychiatry is part of an apparatus of social discipline
just as certainly as were the houses of correction instituted by Louis XIV.
It is not that psychiatry's clinical entities remain nebulous or that the
action of its methods of treatment (psychotropic drugs, ECT, and psychosurgery) remain largely unknown that is at issue here. If psychiatry *did*
approach in its methods the more scientific portions of somatic medicine
it would still remain, and necessarily so, an institution of social discipline
and normalization. The norms against which madness or mental illness is
measured, the demands for social competence, the requirements of
restraint and control can never be a purely medico-clinical matter, even if
clinicians as social agents take a leading part in formulating those very
demands. Psychiatry cannot escape its social placement, nor is it at
'fault' if it fails to do so. Foucault's work is *not* an anti-psychiatry
precisely because it is a social and cultural placement of psychiatry. It
explains both its conditions of possibility *and* its necessities. Psychiatry
cannot step out of power relations, out of its role as an arbiter and
mediator of legal decisions. It remains part of the 'political order',[7] and
can never be a mere technical practice, the purely rational extension into
a socially neutral practice of an objective knowledge. To ask that it do so
is an act of gross naivety, and to imagine that it could be supplanted

without *other* practices of normalization, discipline, and control taking its place is an act of utopian dishonesty. In this respect, *Madness and Civilization* anticipates Foucault's later work *Discipline and Punish*.

The asylum population formed the basis for subsequent developments in clinical observation, the 'surface of emergence' for all the subsequent categorization and classifications of disease entities in the sphere of mental illness. Asylum populations formed the raw material for experimentation in new techniques and methods of therapy. The asylum came in the nineteenth century to enclose the phenomenon of madness and define the site of psychiatry's knowledge of it. Institutional psychiatry was born in and took its status from the forms of confinement constructed at the end of the eighteenth century. If institutional confinement is no longer so crucial in the practice of psychiatry, if the legal framework of the definition of mental illness has been loosened and liberalized, these developments do not overturn Foucault's analysis. They arise in part from an autonomy and confidence psychiatry drew from its dominion over the asylum, a confidence which gave it the capacity to extend beyond its walls, to enter, in uneasy collaboration with psychoanalysis, the sphere of education, social work, and juvenile correction.[8] These developments modify but do not abolish the structures which constitute the modern definition of madness outlined in *Madness and Civilization*.

Lest it be thought Foucault's work overstates its case for continuity between the birth of the clinic and psychiatric modernity one has only to consider Goffman's influential and popular book, *Asylums* (1961). Goffman's account makes it plain that systematic surveillance, a regime of order, the definition of mental illness as negativity, and the requirement of acceptance of the authority of the doctors and the fact of one's sickness as a condition for 'cure' and release are all continuing features of the mental hospital.

Foucault and Goffman — a contrast

Foucault's work has been accepted in sociology as a contribution to the critique of psychiatry. This has been undertaken mainly by radical American deviancy theorists. It thus appears as a complement to Goffman's work. Such a coupling can lead to serious misunderstandings which we will try to counter here by explaining the radically different nature of the two enterprises.

Goffman's *Asylums* has two components. First, it is a record of his close-quarters observation of a large Federal mental hospital in Washington DC with some 7000 inmates in the late 1950s. Goffman deliberately chose to consider the institution not in terms of psychiatric rationality, its formal objectives and official organizing knowledges and practices, but instead as a specific context of social interaction. He set out to consider how the institution as a form of social organization affected the behaviour and experience of staff and inmates. Second,

Goffman placed this observation in terms of a categorial rubric which stressed what it had in common with other forms of social organization which did not share the rationality and objectives of psychiatry, organizations like warships, prisons, monasteries, and boarding schools. This rubric is provided by the concept 'total institution'.

The concept of 'total institution' is constructed by means of two forms of contrast with 'normal' social life. The first contrast is with what he considers are the normal patterns of participation by individuals in modern society. The predominant contexts of social organization which impinge on individuals are institutions restricted to a specific purpose and whose limited claims on, and limited controls over, their participants are related only to that purpose. Domestic life, work, and leisure are typically segregated in segments of time and in terms of the individuals one interacts with therein. One such context does not necessarily impinge on another. An individual can choose to associate with his work-mates in leisure activities or not. An individual can change jobs without this necessarily impinging on domestic and family arrangements. Individuals are free to restrict the degree to which they participate in such contexts and can 'opt out' of those they find unacceptable, choosing to move jobs, to leave their families, to live alone in a hostel and so on. Secondly, Goffman contrasts the means at the disposal of the individual to 'present' a self-image in normal life and in a total institution. Goffman uses a metaphor from the theatre, 'role-playing', to explain how self-images are forged and presented to others. Such role-playing depends on 'props' and on controlling what is seen, carefully limiting others' access to behaviour to what is chosen as appropriate to the context and consistent with the chosen self-image. Goffman specifies the dominant forms of identity characteristic of individuals in modern society: as autonomous persons, who are what they want to be and control the circumstances of their lives by choice. The individual constructs a self-concept which is independent of any particular context of interaction with others, but which is dependent on his being able to control the devices by which he 'presents' himself to others, having at his disposal a range of 'props' and being able to control the contexts in which he appears. These devices are dependent on the characteristic normal forms of participation since the segregation of spheres of life enables the individual to limit others' perceptions of him, controls over him, and demands on him. Identity depends on autonomy, on the capacity to manage the relationship between spheres of interaction.

It is just this autonomy which the 'total institution' breaks down. In destroying the segregation of spheres of life it undercuts the devices whereby an independent self-image can be constructed for others and thereby reinforced for the self; it also reduces the individual's control over others' perceptions and demands. Such institutions place individuals in one inclusive and continuous context in which activities in any particular situation impinge on and affect the individual's appearance to others in all other aspects of life. But unlike small communities like villages in which this non-segregation is also characteristic, these institutions are formal rather than spontaneous, they are involuntary or custodial to a greater or lesser degree, and directed from above by a specialist administrative staff who control the whole lives of the inmates and possess more or less extensive powers of coercion over them.

In a sense, what Goffman has done is to apply the concept of 'totalitarianism' developed in liberal political theory to a different level, from the polity as a whole to particular social institutions. The distinctive feature of 'totalitarianism' is the absence of a 'private' sphere of individual freedom: all activities are subject to direction by the state and all individuals are mobilized in forms of political participation whether they wish to or not. Pluralism, the presence of a variety of political and social forces which the individual can choose to follow or deny allegiance and involvement, is the precondition for political liberty. This pluralism implies not merely that there is more than one political party but that the state makes limited demands on and has limited controls over the individual; it allows other forms of organization and association, with voluntary membership, to organize important aspects of social life.

Goffman is not concerned with *political* liberty as such. He does not explicitly borrow the concept of 'totalitarianism' or make use of liberal political theory. This is because he is concerned with autonomy in personal identity. 'Total institutions' can exist in formally liberal and pluralistic polities like the United States. What they do to their specific memberships, however, is in the personal sphere equivalent to the forms of compulsory political mobilization characteristic of regimes like Nazi Germany. They deny the autonomy necessary to an independent self-concept and remodel the individual to the demands of the institution.

Personal identity is demolished by the context of social interaction and remodelled according to the objectives and administrative demands of the institution. On entering the institution the individual's 'self', built up by controlling how the individual appears to others by manipulating specific contexts of interaction, is broken down by 'mortification' procedures. The devices of individuation are removed: the name is replaced by a number, clothing is taken away, the head is shaved, etc. The devices of self-presentation are removed and the individual is humiliated, forced to become merely one of an indistinguishable membership of inmates. Individual behaviour is directed to forms prescribed by the institution and the individual is forced to define himself in terms of the rationale of the institution, accepting *its* conception of him as a condition for interaction and performance with other inmates and members of staff.

This procedure of mortification and remodelling takes place in a variety of particular institutions which, despite their differences in formal objectives, have a common need to subject individuals to necessities of mass management. Prisons, concentration camps, POW camps, mental hospitals,

TB sanitoria, boarding schools, military training camps, and monasteries all exhibit a common regime and a common supervision of individual autonomy. Despite their differences they have similar consequences for personal identity.

Goffman's work is thus far from being a pure 'observation'. It is directed by a highly specific concept of personal identity and is primarily concerned to examine institutions in terms of their consequences for this supposed self-concept and its means of construction. *Asylums* has, however, two widely recognized and important points to make. The first concerns the consequences of mental hospitals as administered organizations. He considers the behaviour of inmates of mental hospitals in terms of the effects of institutional contexts rather than specific individual 'sickness':

> 'the student of mental hospitals can discover that the "craziness" or "sick behaviour" claimed for the mental patient is by and large a product of the claimant's social distance from the situation that the patient is in and is not primarily a product of mental illness.'
>
> (Goffman 1961: 130)

The second is that the hospital works through a regime of therapy operated by the staff, such that progress through the institution is defined in terms of psychiatry. Bad behaviours are specified in terms of signs of health or illness, progress and regression. The patient must conform to this context of pathology if he wishes to leave. He must accept that he is 'sick' in order to be 'cured'. Progress is defined in terms of the conducts the staff deem appropriate. Cooperation is a precondition for progress to release, so resistance to staff characterization of behaviour is defined as pathology. The mental hospital as a social context is based on a circular and self-confirming rationality: refusal to 'psychiatrize' oneself, to act 'ill', leads to the language of psychiatry still being talked about one.

Psychiatric and administrative considerations are systematically interconnected. Although psychiatric rationality sets the context of the institutions, most of the staff are not clinicians and are concerned most of the time with non-therapeutic necessities of the management and control of inmates. Attendants and non-medical staff nonetheless control the individual's relationship to the clinical context. Behaviour of patients in relation to the staff is fed up the hierarchy and is interpreted in clinical terms; it forms the main basis of observations, reports, and assessments. It is not possible to behave as if one were an irate 'customer' in the cafeteria and as a cooperative patient in therapy. Overall demeanour is available to the clinical staff through surveillance and reports. Attendants and non-medical staff are in control of the patient's access to resources and progress through the institution. The patient is constrained to act 'sick' and yet seek to be cured, and to be cooperative. Staff can use these circumstances as powers of management, in the interests of administrative convenience. Goffman cites numerous examples of patients being forced to beg for necessities, requests being ignored until such time as it suits staff members to listen, patients being talked to as if they were fools or talked about as if they were not there, being forced to say humiliating and stupid things such as 'pretty please', and so on.

The hospital typically consists in a series of facilities with differential standards of life and prospects of exit. Access to these facilities is largely determined by behaviour and degree of cooperation. The staff use these differential facilities as a system of rewards and punishments whereby they are able to control large numbers of inmates with a minimum of attention and effort. Informal relationships with patients who act as informers and 'trusties' reinforce this system. The chronic sick wards, where facilities are worst, serve both as a dumping ground for the senile, brain-damaged, and hopelessly degenerated and also as a punishment for the uncooperative. Controls and punishments, unlike those in special-purpose 'outside' institutions, have an omnibus character. Powers which stem from a psychiatric rationale are used to facilitate social control in the 'total institution'.

Goffman argues that the logic of the system can be countered by individual 'strategies' which conserve personal autonomy. These vary from 'playing the system' — cynically cooperating but inwardly refusing to accept the legitimacy of imposed roles — to withdrawal — using the fact that minimal demands are placed on the inmates of chronic wards to attain freedom from supervision and conformity.

What Goffman calls the 'underlife of a public institution' clearly does exist. Examples of malpractice and brutality which have recently come to light in NHS mental hospitals indicate that there is no room for complacency. The routine humiliations Goffman catalogues pale beside accounts of brutal beatings and neglect. At the same time there are many examples of well-run hospitals and units, with competent medically trained staff. Higher standards of care and administration, where management and therapy are not so casually intermingled and where patients are offered genuine sympathy and help, can be and are attained. Patients, moreover, need such attention. Mental illness is not all a matter of conformity to prescribed roles or of personal strategies of self-preservation. Goffman doubtless knows this, but his technique of presentation is based on a deliberate decision to ignore mental illness in analysing the mental hospital. He is concerned to seek common features of interaction with non-psychiatric institutions. This is all very well but it tends to make the psychiatric rationality of such institutions appear as an arbitrary and oppressive extraneous factor. Goffman's approach tends to obliterate the fact that many patients in mental hospitals *are* severely deranged, disturbed, or deteriorated and these phenomena are not merely products of interaction in the hospital. Goffman also tends to ignore the legitimacy in psychiatric terms of *not* ignoring tantrums in the canteen as part of a clinical assessment.

Perhaps the central problem with Goffman's account lies in his 'drama-

turgical' concept of self. This treats the individual as ideally an autonomous strategist, managing interaction in pursuit of an explicit self-image.
Goffman is able to set up this 'normal' pattern of individuation by mini-
mizing the degree to which, on the one hand, conducts and personal
statuses are set by social conventions which are obligatory rather than
chosen in work, family responsibilities, and public life, and, on the other,
the degree to which individuals' thoughts and conducts are not a matter
of conscious choice but emerge from unconscious psychic dynamics.
Goffman is very much concerned to assert the self-conscious sovereign
individual we have been concerned in earlier parts of this discussion
to question and challenge as an adequate account of persons' psyches
and conducts. He also ignores the extent to which this autonomous
self-concept *conforms* with psychiatric conceptions of normal mental
functioning. It is precisely in such terms that psychiatrists measure the
inmates of mental hospitals and find them wanting in that they *do*
exhibit disorders of identity, difficulties in managing interactions, and
because in cases of diagnosis of schizophrenia patients report beliefs in
control by alien forces, hearing voices, etc. These phenomena are deteri-
orations of the normal self-directed personality.

Nicos Mouzelis (1971) in a criticism of Goffman's book points out
that 'total institutions' are by no means necessarily considered abnormal
or oppressive by their inmates. The monk is not degraded by having his
head shaven, having to abandon personal possessions, and having to
submit to a regime of monastic self-denial and discipline. Further, he
uses the example of Greek peasant boys in the armed services to point
out that Goffman's notion of personal identity is by no means universal.
For the Greek villager his status as a person is invested in family honour
and in being able to meet prescribed social obligations to kin and members
of his community. Military life does not necessarily threaten or touch on
family honour and can be submitted to without humiliation. This is by
no means a special case applicable only to so-called 'backward' cultures
governed by honour and shame, where individuation is supposedly less
developed. Many reports of military service in industrial countries confirm
that the individuals concerned welcomed being part of a community,
sharing life with others from different social classes, and the certainties of
military discipline.[9] Others, of course, have hated it.

To turn now to Foucault. Goffman groups together institutions on a
classificatory basis, in terms of their 'totality'. Hence he recognizes
similarities in regime between prisons, asylums, schools, etc. Now this may
appear to confirm Foucault's grouping of such institutions as exhibiting
a common regime of 'disciplinarity' in his later work *Discipline and Punish*,
which develops and extends certain of the themes of *Madness and Civilization*. But the similarity is a superficial one. Goffman groups certain
institutions together because in them distinct spheres of life are not segregated and because they exhibit hierarchical direction. Thus prisons and
asylums, monasteries and TB sanatoria are all 'total institutions'. Mouzelis

comments that contemporary institutions like sanitoria and privileged boarding schools display radically different regimes from public mental hospitals and concentration camps. Goffman's classificatory category is trans-historical. Foucault's basis for grouping certain institutions together is quite different. Prisons, asylums, and reform schools are linked because they are products of a common historical formation. This formation is a set of discourses, management practices, and architectural forms which pertain to the *government* of such closed institutions. Prisons, houses of correction, the confinement of the mad all pre-existed the transformations Foucault is concerned with. These new forms of government, these restructurings of the role and the character of confinement appear in a specific conjuncture at the end of the eighteenth century. They exhibit a common regime of *discipline*, characterized by continuous surveillance: 'normatizing individuation', whereby the individual is constantly measured against and systematically directed towards standards of performance set by the directing agency; and by the isolation of individuals under discipline and the attempt to transform them into productive portions of the institutional mechanism. This regime of 'government' is found not only in *closed* institutions like prisons, but also in the management of factories and in day schools, where the participants are free to return to their homes at night. Disciplinarity radiates outward from the closed space of the institution to affect conduct beyond its walls, to relate to the family, its domestic economy and internal management. Aspects of the disciplinary regime are to be found in the models of the domestic education of children, the supervision of the poor in their homes, and so on. The techniques of disciplinary 'government' find their systematic concentration in closed institutions like prisons but they are by no means confined there nor are they manifest in all closed institutions. Monastic discipline may well have served as a *model* for certain of the early institutions. Indeed what was probably the first 'modern' prison, where confinement is the primary means of punishment, was proposed by a priest, Father Mabillon, in 1724 to deal with delinquent clerics who could not be punished by execution. But the monastic regime pre-dates the swarming of disciplinary forms, and its contemplative seclusion depends on an internal systematization of conduct which differs from hierarchical surveillance. Likewise, TB sanatoria isolate but do not seek to remodel individuals, systematic surveillance of conduct is not part of their regime; rather control is limited to a *medical* regime and is operative only insofar as mode of life touches on disease.

The distinct character of the disciplinary regime can be further illustrated by considering Foucault's concept of 'normatizing individuation'. We have seen that Goffman considers that 'total institutions' break down individual identity and reduce the person to an anonymous member of an enclosed collectivity. For Foucault, on the contrary, disciplinarity involves a definite form of 'individuation'. Individuals are actually constituted as such through isolation in discipline, surveillance separates and distinguishes those subjected to it, and the regime of government seeks to constitute forms of individuality, to confer attributes, powers, and capacities. Whereas for Goffman, the administrative regime of the institution is merely negative, forced to depersonalize and humiliate individuals in the interests of the convenient control of large numbers of people, for Foucault discipline is a positive power. It aims not merely to control and contain, but to re-model, to create new capacities through its action. Foucault argues that it is an error to conceive power as merely negative, an external domination and constraint. Power is *productive* in its exercise, it does not merely confine.[10] Thus Foucault treats the *examination* as a form of exercise of disciplinary power. In examinations, in day schools, for example, the individual is subjected to 'normalizing judgement', measured in his performance against standards set by the hierarchy, compelled to *perform* in requisite manner. 'Knowledge', whether psychiatric or concerned with matters of military or educational technique, is not something external to and opposed to power, a disinterested contemplation; it is a means and resource of power. Observation and training, knowledge and the devices created by it, serve to extend and reinforce the action of power in the productive transformation of individuals. Goffman tends to treat psychiatry either as knowledge misapplied in the interests of control, on the model of 'pure' medical science, or as mere normativity, moral definition and stigmatization, masquerading as knowledge. For Foucault 'knowledges' like psychiatry can never be neutral nor separated from power and the institutions of its exercise. Psychiatry is part of a regime of power, its 'surfaces of emergence', its conditions and means of observation depend on institutional forms, controls and the exercise of power over individuals. Entry to the asylum, as we have seen, involves powers of exclusion and a legal-medical exercise of judgement. The asylum does not merely *stigmatize* madness, it defines it, constitutes it and brings definite knowledges to bear on it.

It is in this context that we are employing Foucault's work to question the critique of 'institutionalization', as exemplified by Goffman's work. The classic radical objection to institutionalization, whether for purposes of the correction of delinquency or for psychiatric cure, centres on a supposed discrepancy between the objective and the methods of correctional institutions. It is argued that the objective, the rehabilitation of the individual as a member of the wider society, is undercut by the method, the isolation of individuals from the wider society in an abnormal context to which they are socialized to conform. Goffman argues that mental patients are subjected to forms of depersonalization and institutional conformity which compel them to act 'sick', to conform to patterns of interaction peculiar to the mental hospital. Laing argues that hospitalization is destructively adaptive, that it consists in adjusting individuals to a 'sick' society, eliminating the constructive experience and response we call insanity. Szasz argues that involuntary confinement is an unjustifiable denial of rights, an extra-criminal detention and penal treatment of unconventional behaviour which has violated no criminal law.

There are three main objections involved in the critique of institutionalization:

i.   that it is repressively adaptive, enforcing conformity to the norms of the wider society through confinement in unnatural closed institutions;
ii. that the modes of 'therapy', ECT, drugs, and psychosurgery are used to quieten and control individuals' behaviour rather than to cure specific illnesses;
iii. that it is ineffective, because the individual becomes socialized into and dependent on an institutional life which makes him unfitted to live in and adjust to the wider society.

We will consider these objectives in the course of what follows.

Now we have seen that in our discussion of *Madness and Civilization* that mental hospitals came into existence *before* modern techniques of therapy were developed and a specifically 'medical' apparatus was fully imposed on them. Hospitals were controlled contexts for the reordering of experience and the government of conduct. In addition to Foucault's work, D.J. Rothman's *The Discovery of the Asylum* (1971) ably catalogues the ideologies of the reformers. The reform had a reasoned case by which to justify exclusion as a means of adaptation and transformation.

First, the reformers sought to classify the disorders to be enclosed. Institutions were to deal with separate classes of defective — prisons for criminals, asylums for the insane, schools and reformatories for juvenile delinquents, and workhouses for the able-bodied paupers. Within the institutions, different types of criminal or madmen were to be separated, hardened criminals from first offenders, the raving and the deranged from the quiet and depressed. The reason for this separation was to concentrate an effective regime of control and reform on the individual, to prevent the cross-fertilization of disorders and the disruption of the controlled environment. The ideal of the reformed regime was solitary confinement and the close supervision of the inmates; this would facilitate the management of their experience. This regime was common both to doctrines of reform which saw it operating through concentrated moral influence (Tuke) and to doctrines which involved associationalist or empiricist psychology, where an appropriately ordered regime of sensation would produce reform through the effects of experience. In practice there was no rigid opposition between the two doctrines, as demonstrated by the case of Pinel, the disciple of Condillac and a firm believer in moral influence. For both doctrines isolation was conceived as a method *appropriate* to the objective. The individual had to be placed in an artificial and controlled context to remedy deficiencies in his experience and moral character acquired in the outside world.

Second, the proponents of disciplinary confinement by no means considered the wider society as normal, harmonious, and natural. Adaptation was not to prevailing 'average' patterns of conduct and morality, which were held often to be defective and pathogenic. Disciplinary techniques involved a *critique* of the wider society. Dependence on others and a too excitable sensibility were sources of moral and 'nervous' weakness. Man should be self-possessed and governed by a directive conscience; this involved a definite isolation from others, a systematization of conduct toward higher standards of morality and personal efficiency. The institution should not be regarded as abnormal but as the model for a well-ordered *home*. Disciplinary practices were not, as we have seen, to stop at the walls of the institution. Family government and education should employ these techniques to provide a home environment in which the young acquired habits of order, the means of personal competence, and productive efficiency. The disciplinarians were ancestors of all the modern conceptions and practices of child-rearing and home education. Benjamin Spock and Hugh Jolly are the lineal descendants — adjusted to a changed climate which requires liberal norms of 'healthy development' — of the reformers. In Foucault's analysis it is an error to isolate institutions of confinement from practices widely introduced into education and domestic life. Jacques Donzelot reinforces this argument in *The Policing of Families* (1980), arguing that much of social hygienics, pedagogy, and social welfare is concerned to construct the well-ordered home as a site of medically and psychiatrically informed upbringing. The authoritarian ideologies of the reformers have been displaced in his estimation, by new conceptions of the 'natural' development of children and by norms of family life based on psychoanalysis. But the objectives of family government have modified rather than changed, and the techniques of control and education have developed rather than been replaced.

We see in the ideals of the reformers a coherent authoritarian and moral programme of which the institution of confinement is but one part. In this programme mental illness is conceived as the product of social relations and as being capable of transformation through the creation of particular environments of learning and control — the asylum is one of these but the well-ordered home is another. There is no rigid division between the asylum walls and domestic life. The asylum is merely an institution made necessary by the 'failures' of domestic management, a controlled substitute for the family.

Modern radicals tend to identify the asylum with the hospital and somatic medicine, considering it as a misapplication of medical norms. Szasz (1973) recognizes the moralism and the social programme of the reformers — reserving a special animus for Benjamin Rush — but he considers that conduct and the home should be regarded as part of the private sphere. A firm believer in classical liberalism, he holds that social regulation should operate through criminal law alone, leaving families to their own devices where they do not harm others. We have also seen how important a part the notion of an autonomous private sphere plays in Goffman's work. Disciplinarity is a separate ideological formation from classical liberalism in that it refuses to accept that government and control is part of a strictly limited public, 'political', sphere.[10] Social organization cannot leave families and individuals to their own devices, 'government' is as necessary in the 'private' sphere as elsewhere (although it need not be organized by the state). Disciplinarity appears in the heyday of political liberalism to challenge the ideological division of public and private domains (an ideology never actually realized in the politics of the liberal era). Disciplinarity challenges the deficiencies of liberalism precisely at the points where it is challenged by welfarism and socialism. Disciplinary practices continue and extend under modern 'welfare' regimes.

'Discipline' and the government of 'private' life are conceived by Foucault as something other than a megalomaniac conspiracy, as Szasz regards it, or as an exercise in 'moral entrepreneurship', as sociological radicals might. The new regime of techniques of institutional direction and family management arises from a diverse complex of social necessities — it is not an accident or happenstance. The reformers' programmes and ideals are never 'realized'; equally the institutional constructions they reflect are not displaced. Crime, madness, poverty are not eliminated — to imagine they could be is a necessary excess in the discourse of the reformers. Prisons, mental hospitals, and so on in no way correspond in their workings to the blueprints of the reformers — dreams like Jeremy Bentham's *Panopticon*. Equally, they cannot be displaced, for they answer to a complex of necessities of social production, supervision, and control to which classical liberalism has no answer. Socialist regimes likewise cannot dispense with these artefacts of social organization.[11]

Foucault's analyses are often considered to be 'libertarian' because of his own political practice in supporting the prisoners' rights movement and because of the important place of the concept of 'resistance' in his later writings like *Discipline and Punish*. Foucault *is* a libertarian to the extent that he places himself on the side of resistance to disciplinary power, but he is not a believer in some attainable utopian order of freedom in which disciplinarity can be abolished. He recognizes it as too much a part of the warp and weft of contemporary social organization to be displaced and dispensed with. He offers no comprehensive alternative, no system of social relations which could dispense with constraint and control of 'private' life, or a pure libertarian socialism. Such ideologies of a comprehensive and unproblematic 'political' reform, a pure regime of freedom, have no prospect of realization. They ignore the complex roots of disciplinary power, the necessities which are the sources of its social prevalence. Disciplinary power can be checked and controlled by resistance but not abolished; its 'abuses' can be contained by struggle but never removed.

A *limited* critique of institutional confinement and institutional regimes obviously has its place. Too many people are placed in prisons and mental hospitals simply because adequate hostels, supervised accommodation, and day centres are not available. Prison regimes are often needlessly brutal and confining and offer virtually no training in vocational and social skills, while mental hospitals are all to often badly managed and overcrowded. These limited criticisms and proposals for reform remain within the space of available social policies, and differ from wholesale critiques of all confinement. Foucault's analysis serves as much as a critique of the *ideology* of moderate reformism as of libertarianism, however. The idea that we can ever set such institutions 'to rights' once and for all by the application of more training, more staff, and more money to existing institutions is an illusion. Reform is merely a constant corrective of a tendency toward degeneration, toward being merely places of confinement and control, that such closed institutions exhibit. Asylums and prisons rapidly ceased to bear any relation to the 'ideals' of the founding reformers as they developed and proliferated in the nineteenth century. The panoply of modern 'reform' measures – indeterminate sentencing, behaviour modification, vocational training – for all their claimed novelty, are no more than re-statements and refurbishings of the techniques and objectives of the first reformers.

Foucault's *Madness and Civilization* has often been misunderstood and criticized, for example by Sir Aubrey Lewis or John Wing, because it appears to suggest that, outside of psychiatry, 'madness' is a definite human condition with a real language and truth to which we should listen, that psychiatry silences the authentic voice of madness.[12] Foucault has recognized a certain romanticism in that work, commenting on it in *The Archaeology of Knowledge*. He makes it clear that there is no single and objective condition, 'madness', that exists independently of its 'surfaces of emergence'. There is no given 'language' of the mad to which we *can* listen. But this careful clarification does not overturn *Madness and Civilization*. His point there is that madness comes to be treated as unreason and pathology, that there is no space for considering madness as other than purely negative, of communicating with madness as something even potentially capable of revealing something significant about human life. If Western culture closes its ears to unreason this still does not mean that madness speaks with a single voice, that all the insane are seers and prophets. *Madness and Civilization* says virtually nothing about madness or insanity as such, it is rather concerned with the responses of Western culture and psychiatry to it. There is no implication that madness is *one thing*, that it is positive rather than negative; on the contrary, its existence as a phenomenon is dependent on the forms in which it is apprehended and constructed. Foucault's remarks are a comment on the silence characteristic of psychiatry and not, like Laing's work, a paean of praise to all the truths that madness has to speak.

Notes

1 Undoubtedly the best complements to Foucault's work dealing with the Anglo-Saxon countries are, for America, D.J. Rothman's *The Discovery of the Asylum* (1971) and for England Michael Donnelly's *Perceptions of Lunacy in Early Nine-teenth-Century Britain* (1976) a regrettably still unpublished PhD thesis at Birk-beck College, London University. Containing some valuable information on the early history of the prison and asylum respectively are Michael Ignatieff's *A Just Measure of Pain* (1978) and Andrew Scull's *Museums of Madness*: (1979); the theoretical limitations and methodological weaknesses of these two works are ably demonstrated in a review by Jeffrey Minson (1980). Also still of value on the early history of houses of correction is G. Rusche and O. Kirchheimer's *Punishment and Social Structures* (1939). G. Rosen *Madness in Society* (1968) contains a series of studies of the history of madness which largely complements Foucault's work.

2 For a discussion of the role of festivals, the inversion of the established order and the popular use of the motif of 'folly' see M. Bakhtin, *Rabelais and his World* (1968): see also P. Burke *Popular Culture in Early Modern Europe* (1978).

3 Diderot did not shrink from using madness as a mirror, as *Rameau's Nephew* testifies.

4 This work is the greatly revised second edition of *Maladie Mentale et Psychologie* which contains an excellent short summary of *Madness and Civilization* in Chapter Five.

5 It is interesting to note these developments of institutional confinement and a non-religious conception of insanity as individual illness in precisely those Cath-olic countries that were to serve as the bastions of the Counter-Reformation and as sources of opposition to the scientific revolution. They were also the first places where witchcraft persecutions were abandoned, a point we will return to in discussion of witchcraft.

6 For Foucault the medicalization of madness is present from the birth of the asylum, as is the legal definition and role of its medical competence. Foucault is less concerned in *Madness and Civilization* with the precise details of the develop-ment of psychiatry as part of a single legal-medical conception or with the exact development of the relation between law and psychiatry. He has dealt with these developments in later works, *I, Pierre Rivière ...* (1975) and *Discipline and Punish* (1977). There he chonicles the growing investment of the law by medical psychiatry, the intervention of psychiatric 'knowledge' and judgement into legal decision-making.

In this respect he differs considerably from sociologists' accounts like Andrew Scull's *Museums of Madness* (1979), an account of the asylum and the psychiatric profession in the nineteenth century, particularly in England and America. In this work the growth of psychiatry and its incorporation into the medical profession is dealt with primarily as part of a politics of 'professionalization'. Scull uses the radical sociological conception of the profession, as a politics by a group of practitioners concerned to attain an exclusive social status, the monopoly of definition and control of entry into the practice of a particular activity or skill. Foucault, on the contrary, does not ask *how* doctors become the exclusive de-finers of madness, but how was it *possible* for them to become such a corporation with such a task. He analyses the structure which underlies such a politics of professionalization which makes its outcome something other than the doctors' victory over 'quacks' and a gullible public. The legal status of insanity, and the role of the doctor as having authority in matters of madness are not the products of the doctors' own struggles, they make these struggles and the doctors'. victory possible.

7 Foucault defines 'politics' in *Discipline and Punish* as a far wider sphere than politics and the state properly so-called. Foucault challenges the division of the public and the private sphere, and the restriction of the proper domain of power relations to the former, which characterizes the theory of the liberal state.

8 Developments catalogued by Foucault's collaborator Jacques Donzelot in *The Policing of Families* (1980).

9 See for example P.J. Campbell *The Ebb and Flow of Battle* (1979), N. Gladden *Across the Piave* (1971), G. Coppard *With a Machine Gun to Cambrai* (1969) or K. Douglas *Alamein to Zem Zem* (1979). These examples are taken from both World Wars, and from both officers and privates.

10 For a short account of Foucault's concept of power see his essay 'Power and Norm' reproduced in Morris and Patton (eds) *Power Truth Strategy* (1979).

11 See for discussion of this point and critical comment on Foucault, see Hirst (1980: 89-94).

12 See Lewis (1961) and Wing (1978).

10
PSYCHIATRY AND
ANTI-PSYCHIATRY

In the last two decades psychiatry has become a storm centre of intellectual and political controversy. Indeed, so much so that its legitimacy and the need for its very existence have been questioned by many critics. The critics have not lacked for genuine targets. The political abuse of psychiatric hospitalization and treatments in the USSR, the abuse of psychosurgery and other techniques in United States prisons catalogued by Jessica Mitford in *The American Prison Business* (1977), to cite but two glaring examples, have given ample scope for concern that both the powers of confinement and the means of therapy which are an integral part of modern institutional psychiatry can be all too easily misused.

But, for a vocal and influential body of critics, there can be no *proper* use of such powers and therapeutic means. For critics like Thomas Szasz, whose widely read *The Myth of Mental Illness* was first published in 1961 and represented the opening shot in what has become an anti-psychiatric fusillade, *all* institutional psychiatry involves an abuse of power. Compulsory detention and treatment are applied to those whose conduct is neither criminal nor the product of physical pathology. Such intervention without cause or consent is a fundamental threat to the liberties of the individual and involves the unjustified stigmatization of conducts which the psychiatric establishment and the powers that be merely happen to find unacceptable. Madness is 'manufactured' out of conduct which violates both contemporary norms and prejudices, and this stigmatization is justified and hallowed by the prestige that attaches to medicine. But the framework of medicine has no place here. Szasz argues that there is no such entity as the 'mind' which can be diseased, there is only the person's brain or conduct. If a person suffers from some definite physical ailment then this can be treated by their entering voluntarily into a contractual and non-coercive relationship with a physician. If a person's conduct involves violence to others and infringes their rights then it should properly fall under the sanction of the criminal law. All other conduct is a private matter, of concern only to the individuals involved. If people happen to feel disturbed or unhappy and wish to seek help and advice then they are free to do so, to choose voluntarily and contractually to obtain it from any source they deem appropriate.

R.D. Laing, whose major work, *The Divided Self* (1965) appeared

roughly at the same time as Szasz's, has been a no less trenchant, if intellectually more sophisticated, critic of psychiatric theory and practice.
For Laing mental illness, schizophrenia in particular, is not an organically
based disorder which can or should be treated with physical therapies such
as psychotropic drugs or ECT. Mental 'illness', far from being a disease,
can actually be a constructive process of response, an experience of
healing and re-integration, if the person is aided to pass through it. It is
wrong to adapt people to a society which is itself 'sick' and pathogenic.
Schizophrenia has its own roots in a family situation in which the individual is invalidated, in which he or she is constrained to live for others and
as their construction of what the individual should be, and yet in which
the individual's own self-experience is constantly negated and discon-
firmed. The result is a withdrawal into an empty and negative inner self,
withheld from experience and interaction. Schizophrenia is thus a defens-
ive reaction to a social process. Far from being a pathology in the individual, it is a valid response to a pathological and inauthentic context of
interaction. An acceptable therapy therefore consists in assisting the
individual in a 'voyage' of self-discovery and authentication, living through
the experiences of separation and negation. The very 'madness' of the
schizophrenic, his 'symptoms' of disassociation, persecution, negation,
etc., are a valid experience which must be lived through. Conventional
psychiatry alienates this experience; reducing it to so many phenomena,
meaningless except as signs of pathology. Clinical practice and observation
is inherently alienating and denies the possibility of the dialogue which is
essential if madness is to be a positive experience.[1]

Conventional institutional psychiatry is not the only target of anti-
psychiatric criticism. Psychoanalysis has also been increasingly challenged,
particularly in France, as a practice of adaptation and social adjustment,
a sophisticated means of social control. This is evident in works like
Gilles Deleuze and Felix Guattari's *Anti-Oedipus* (1977) or Robert Castel's
Le psychanalysme: l'ordre psychanalytique et la pouvoir (1976).

Why has anti-psychiatry become such a vocal and widely heeded movement in the 1960s and 1970s? The birth of the asylum and the development of modern clinical psychiatry produced no equivalent reaction in
the nineteenth century. Moreover it could hardly be said that contemporary psychiatry is more constraining and authoritarian than in the period
before the last war. Laing's work appeared after the 'liberalization' of the
legal framework of committal in the 1959 Mental Health Act, and at the
same time as considerable attention was being paid to improving the
environment for the patients within mental hospitals. Szasz's work appeared long after the development of psychotropic drugs which reduced
both the need for constraint within institutions and permitted many
individuals to receive out-patient treatment after a relatively brief stay
in an acute ward. In our remarks at the very beginning of Part Two we
suggested that psychiatry has to a certain extent suffered from the revolution of rising expectations in medicine, and that it too has fallen under

the backlash of frustrated hopes — a medical 'nemesis'. Contemporary psychiatric opinion has reinforced these expectations, overestimating the prospects for cure and non-custodial management. Liberalization in the 1950s and 1960s was an attempt to limit the containment and management of insane populations in asylums and integrate psychiatry as far as possible into general medicine. Anti-psychiatry appeared at a time when medical and social welfare opinion, stimulated by new therapeutic means and by the prospect of a full employment economy in which even those with relatively severe disabilities could nevertheless find a place, turned increasingly against physical restraint and confinement. Anti-psychiatry was thus in part carrying to extremes positions already held by many welfare and medical professionals, a strong prejudice against long-term confinement and, particularly on the part of social workers (although much less so among medically trained psychiatrics), a willingness to consider mental disorder as the product of family situation. But the specific nature of anti-psychiatric critiques cannot be explained merely by some notion of a generalized 'backlash' against medicine. Indeed, it appeared long before works like Ivan Illich's influential *Limits to Medicine* (1977) and the craze for preventative health measures among the well-to-do of the industrialized world.

Anti-psychiatry is characterized by a radical libertarianism, in that it challenges the appropriateness of compulsory powers, formal institutions, and allegedly specialist knowledges as against voluntary consent, spontaneous relationships, and mutual learning. Its implications differ radically from the ideologies of most welfare and medical professionals. Anti-psychiatry is a libertarian response to a deepening and extension of state and professional powers and interventions. Since the Second World War social welfare practices and institutions, and the role of psychiatry within them, have expanded out of all recognition, not only in countries, like Sweden or the UK, politically committed to the development of a welfare state but also in the USA and most other industrialized states. This expansion has been made possible by the post-war economic boom whose effects have been felt in different degrees throughout the industrialized world. This expansion is the result both of rising public expectations as to the levels of competency necessary in the mass of the population (in education, hygiene, work skills, etc.) and to the recognition that, in order to develop such competency and retain it, individuals must be protected against the consequences of unemployment, sickness, and other forms of deficiency. Thus individuals are subjected both to a higher degree of training and inspection, in which more is demanded of them, and are provided with increasing public resources in education, health, and welfare. Psychiatry intervenes, particularly in social work and education, to assess individuals and to attempt to manage failures to meet standards of social competency. This has opened a new field of action for psychoanalysis and dynamic psychologies, as against traditional clinical psychiatry linked to medicine. The conception that pathology or deficiency is the product of social relationships, that it can be managed or remedied by non-medical therapy, counselling or assistance, is widespread among social workers and educationalists. Again we see one of the positions of the anti-psychiatric radicals being apparently shared by welfare professionals.

Anti-psychiatry should be considered against this background of extension of powers of inspection, training, and control which increasingly intervene in and direct more and more of the lives of individuals, and in which psychiatric or psychoanalytic knowledges play a large part. The asylum and clinical psychiatry are merely one facet of a mass of welfare and disciplinary practices and institutions. Anti-psychiatry has been paralleled by later movements of a similar type directed against education ('deschooling') and social work, which developed in the 1970s.

Why are these 'anti'-movements so prevalent and so widely heeded? Because they offer the image of individual and communal fulfilment without institutionalization, discipline, and control. They appeal to healthy, well-fed, well-educated, and successfully employed individuals who, on the basis of the means of welfare and disciplinary interventions, are able to make use of the freedoms available to them and can see only constraint in certain powers of control and inspection in the public domain such as psychiatric confinement, educational testing, and social work supervision. Consider the reaction when higher education in this country became widely available to the middle and lower classes in the 1960s, rather than involving considerable financial sacrifice or highly competitive scholarship examinations, as it was pre-war for all but the relatively wealthy. Once higher education became the natural destination for the average middle-class child, then examinations and testing came to appear as onerous and unreasonable to a substantial minority of students.

The expansion of welfare state institutions since 1945 is only one of a series of bursts of development in institutions of 'social' intervention since the late eighteenth century. Medical, psychiatric, public health, and 'social police' measures were extensively introduced from the mid-1850s onwards to deal with such phenomena as infectious disease, TB and chronic syphilis, alcoholism, neglected children, slums, and pauperism. This burst of therapeutic, supervisory, and welfare institutions and practices produced no equivalent of the 'anti-psychiatry' or 'de-schooling' ideologies of today. Vested interests opposed measures like public sewerage systems, Spencerians and free-marketeers challenged the growth of the public power, and the Labour Movement criticized the workhouses, but none of these oppositions had the same character as modern de-institutionalizing critiques. The very evidence of the evils in question necessitated inspection, supervision and control, the provision of public facilities and the coercion of individuals. The objects of contemporary interventions have been less obvious and unambiguous, particularly in the period of apparently unending full employment and prosperity.

Anti-psychiatry has attracted a mass of criticism from across the political, theoretical, and psychiatric spectrum. Rather than repeating the criticisms we will refer the reader to the best of the relevant literature.[2] What we will consider here are the implications for the social order of the 'anti-psychiatries'. What differentiates anti-psychiatry is not a distinctive theory of the nature of mental illness, its causation or treatment; it is, rather, an approach to social relations. Laing, for example, is by no means unique in considering schizophrenia to be a product of a specific family situation. This is just what Gregory Bateson (1973) proposes in his well-known concept of a 'double-bind'. Schizophrenia is a 'disorder of communication' acquired through a pathogenic context of interaction. The individual is subjected to contradictory messages in an intense but ambivalent relationship with someone (typically the mother). In order to continue the relationship the individual must fail to recognize the ambiguity, fail to learn to differentiate between classes of message. The individual is thus placed in a double-bind or 'no-win' situation, he or she cannot successfully respond to both the incompatible messages nor can the individual escape the consequences of this failure. Schizophrenia is in essence a failure to learn to differentiate between classes of message. Therapy is in essence an attempt to promote learning to differentiate and respond to different classes of message through a specific context of interaction. But Bateson's view of schizophrenia involves no necessary opposition to theories of a genetic component in schizophrenia, triggered by appropriate experiential conditions.[3] Further, several commentators have noted that Laing is in the paradoxical position of denying that schizophrenia is a coherent disease entity while at the same time appearing to offer an alternative theory of its causation in his analysis of family situations.

What differentiates anti-psychiatry is that it implies as a solution to problems of mental illness and its treatment by psychiatry a complete reconstruction of social relations. Szasz is clearest in his conception of this reconstruction and in its implications. Medicine is to be governed by the free-market principle and public interventions are to be limited to essential matters of law and order. Those are the conditions for a contractual, non-coercive system in which conduct is not subjected to moral policing and individuals are free to choose how to behave and whether or not to seek help. Szasz's anti-psychiatry involves a free-market utopia. In a perfectly free market it is assumed that an optimum distribution of resources will remove the problem of how individuals are to pay for services, medical or otherwise. Even if we allow this particular pie its place in the sky, a major problem remains. Szasz has abolished mental illness by decreeing that there is no entity 'mind' in which it can reside. Either there is a physical disorder or there is a voluntary conduct. He has conveniently abolished obsessions, compulsions, confusions, and delusions: human beings are rational actors who will seek therapy if they need it and if they do not seek it they do not need it. If individuals' conduct needs to be controlled there is always the police, courts, and gaols. A charmingly 'liberal' prospect.

What Szasz has done is to abolish the whole space of and rationale for the welfare state as well as compulsory psychiatric medicine. He has done so by assuming that individuals' needs and incomes bear some adequate relation one to another — a joke for the citizen of a country such as the US where, despite insurance, even middle-class people dread a serious illness on the part of the bread-winner. He has done so by assuming the inherent rationality of individuals and their right to an undisturbed 'private' sphere of conduct. But, as we have seen in our discussion of Foucault, social policy even in the heyday of liberal political ideology could not be bound by that fantasy. Take just one example, severely disturbed or unmanageable children who need to be taken into public care: in most cases such children suffer from no physical disorder or identifiable psychiatric syndrome; rather the object of intervention, training, and control are what might be called 'disorders of conduct'. These disorders are neither a simple matter of chosen naughtiness nor the product of physical disease, yet they often involve considerable confusion and distress on the part of the children concerned. For Szasz a care order and a psychiatric assessment place the children as victims of psychiatric imperialism and manufactured madness. Szasz denies the legitimacy of any public control and supervision of conduct outside of the criminal law. Szasz restricts the legitimacy of norms governing conduct to *acts* which directly threaten others; preventative interventions, attempts to remedy deficiencies and instil competencies are regarded as violations of liberty. Compulsory psychiatric care is merely one portion of a mass of interventions on the part of the state and other public bodies whose objects are various — to control, to train, to heal — but which have the common characteristic of imposing public norms of conduct and expectations of competency on individuals. Certain of these interventions *can* be oppressive, but the complex as a whole arises neither from a creeping collectivist ethos nor from a therapeutic-professional will-to-power but from urgent social necessities. To remedy oppressive practices in the public sphere is not to return conduct to some supposedly spontaneous and inalienable realm of individual liberty. Rather it must be to reform and reconstruct the public powers in question.

Szasz's social order is a utopia in which the free market and individuals' choices make it possible to dispense with complex forms of social organization, with control and compulsion. It has no place for psychiatry because the practice of that discipline is concerned with a mass of personal difficulties, from raving madness to paralysing depression, which give the lie to the principle on which Szasz's imaginary social system is founded — the sovereign rationality of individual choice.

Szasz's hostility to public standards of welfare and norms of conduct, for all its right-wing implications, struck a powerful chord in the imaginations of radical sociologists. The legitimacy of public standards is suspended in such radical challenges to institutional intervention by a thoroughgoing sociological relativism. The sociologist paradoxically places himself outside of social relations because he refuses to take evaluative responsibility for them and within them. Because the standards differ between societies and are not universal or objective, many radical sociologists distance themselves from the thorny problems of applying and changing such standards within their own society. The result is a curious kind of negative individualism in opposition to public norms and, in extreme cases, a denial of the reality of the phenomena those norms confront, such as violence or madness. Insanity or brutality become mere varieties of human conduct to which labels happen to be attached.

A good example of such relativism in matters of mental illness is Thomas Scheff's *Being Mentally Ill* (1966). Scheff constructs his theory on the basis of evidence of the degrees to which contingencies enter into committal proceedings for insanity in US courts. The label 'mental illness' is a matter of rough-and-ready judgment. For Scheff mental illness is conceived as role-playing developed as a consequence of the societal response to the individual's deviant behaviour. On the basis of the 'primary deviance' of his conduct, the individual is pressured by public expectations into a stigmatized role as 'insane' or 'mad'. As Jeff Coulter (1973) points out, this involves the assumption that the conduct which constitutes 'primary deviance' is inherently neutral and is merely negatively valued by social preferences.[4] Insanity ascriptions by members of the lay public are mere value judgments. Now we have been concerned to argue that 'mental illness' *is* a social category, relative and socially variable, involving in its assessment of and application to individuals norms of conduct and conceptions of personality. But it is not thereby rendered illegitimate as a practical category. Insanity committals, like a mass of other social activities, from witchcraft accusations to the bestowal of knighthoods, are ridden with contingencies; this does not mean we can necessarily dispense with them. If the category of insanity were nothing more than a judgment of social competency, if it involved no recognition of suffering or the need to offer care, then it would still have a definite social legitimacy: certain conducts and incapacities *are* an unacceptable disability in modern social relations. It is *socially* irrelevant that they might be less so or an advantage in other social relations. Scheff uses the fact that insanity judgments are not purely neutral and objective to bracket-off or suspend their validity. The effect is to socially neutralize the sociologist: either a pure psychiatric science without contingencies in its judgments or an unrestrained realm of individual conduct appear to be the only possible alternatives in Scheff's argument to the compromised processes of public and institutional judgement. Since neither of these alternatives is attainable, the sociological relativist appears as a kind of moral alien, committed to socially absurd and unacceptable postulates. As a result, a great deal of justified criticism of the workings of courts, of psychiatrists' standards of judgement, and so on, is ignored and confined to a marginalized portion of the intelligentsia.

R.D. Laing suffers neither from Szasz's sterile antinomies nor from the moral negativism of ths sociological relativists. Whatever its defects, his work shows a powerful sympathy for and concern to relieve suffering. Laing has no explicit social programme like Szasz; his views have always been vague, but in the 1960s involved some form of libertarian socialism (his post-1968 views will not concern us here). His anti-psychiatry nevertheless involves a particular form of thoroughgoing individualism and a rejection of existing forms of social organization to the extent that they involve the control and supervision of individual conducts.

Laing denies the validity of the application of the framework of mental pathology to individuals: all psychiatry involves the alienation of the individual and the naturalization of the person's valid experience into 'illness'. But his denial of pathology in individuals is coupled with a wholesale denunciation of modern social relations as pathological. The mad are the victims of a 'sick' society, but in their alienation from it are healthier than the conformists who are allegedly sane. Szasz likewise reverses the category of pathology, regarding psychiatrists as sick in their power-mad conspiracy to control others. The problem with this judgement of Laing's is that the putative pathology does not refer to (as in the medical sense) a definite impediment or specific functional disorder, which might be remedied by reform. Rather modern society is 'sick' in essence and must be changed as a whole. Sickness is used in a way that makes it the polar opposite of health. Laing never clearly spells out the concomitants of a 'healthy' social order. This is because the very notion transcends institutional arrangements and forms of social organization. A healthy society is one in which each individual is guaranteed an authentic existence, a non-alienating relation to others. It is a social order without fundamental conflicts, or institutional necessities for the control and direction of individuals. It would have to exist as spontaneous and individual interactions since anything else would involve constraint and the imposition of others' standards and objectives. These institutions would have to produce a collective resultant that was compatible with each authentic individual existence. Just as in Szasz's free-market individualism in which social institutions must exist only as the result of individuals' choices, so in Laing's existentialist utopia society can only be the free interaction of individual selves — anything else involves alienation and inauthentic existence for others. Laing is by no means certain that this can be attained, hence the frequent references to his 'pessimism' on the part of critics. But this 'pessimism' in no sense reconciled him to modern society or psychiatry.

The utopias of Szasz and Laing are thus parallel in theoretical implications if opposed in political ideology. Social relations are aggregates of the free interactions of individuals. These aggregates are possible and involve no problematic clashes between individual wills because of the nature of the individuals involved. For Szasz individuals are inherently capable of choosing the course of action appropriate to their perceived best interests. For Laing every individual has a 'self' which is the core of its being. Now it is this conception of an inherent set of attributes of the individual which we have been concerned to question throughout this book. The notion of an essential nature of the individual is often used as the prop for an idealized set of social relations or outcomes of social interaction. All that is required is a social milieu which permits the human being's inherent nature to become manifest.

Laing is not alone in postulating an inherent 'self' which governs conduct. This postulate is a common feature of theories like Bateson's or Scheff's which treat mental illness as a *strategy*, as a response to a context of interaction. The 'self' enters into mental illness as a form of defence against invalidation in Laing's *The Divided Self*: schizophrenia is a defence by withdrawal, a negative existence which involves the decomposition of personality and a refusal of relations to others. Schizophrenia is considered as an intentional (but not necessarily conscious) response to a situation. The 'self' is seen as a directive centre, the inherent origin of action and the reference-point of experience. We have been concerned to challenge this view, to argue that there is no inherent conscious locus 'behind' conduct and independent of social personality which is their real origin. To regard the 'self' as an inherently present entity, as the origin of action, can lead all too easily to a conception of non-spontaneous, non-intersubjective social relations as alienating, as capable of being dispensed with in a realm of interaction appropriate to selfhood. This is to make a nonsense of the controls, the practices of training, and the norms of conduct which have characterized all hitherto-existing social relations. If there is no inherent individual to be realized once the shackles of existing social organization are thrown off, then human beings' capacities and welfare become a matter of what forms of social organization, what institutions, what practices of training and control can and should exist or be developed. Such a view in no way denies the possibilities of betterment of man's lot or removes the need for evaluations. Indeed, this view reinforces the need for such judgement precisely because it denies that there is an inherent nature which it is man's end to realize. Objectives become relative, a matter of assessment as to their desirability and possibility, but not thereby all of a piece.

Anti-psychiatry involves the metaphysics of individualism in its various forms. It is this notion of the person, and the related conception of what society ideally should be that differentiates anti-psychiatry from the criticisms of compulsory hospitalization often expressed by mental health professionals themselves. It should also be clear why welfarism and disciplinarity, and the widening scope for psychiatric and psychoanalytic practices they involve, should be the cause and the object of libertarian challenge. By their proliferation in response to urgent social necessities, such institutions threaten the very idea of a spontaneous and non-coercive social order consistent with the free will of individuals. They threaten this idea all the more because their effects are not merely repressive, a matter of controlling and holding down individuals, but because they endow individuals with new attributes, capacities, and skills. At the same time it should not be thought that 'anti-psychiatry' is the product of mere illusion and misperception.

Welfarism and psychiatry are not means to put an *end* to social ills, rather they manage and contain 'problems' modern social conditions constantly re-create. A definite measure of 'failure' is inherent in their existence and serves as a perpetual ground for criticism. At the same time mass education, modern medicine, and the division of labour which requires a large managerial, technical, and professional class, create individuals with the culture, physical well-being, and economic circumstances to sustain the ideals of personal autonomy so dear to 'anti-psychiatry'. The very people who read Laing, go to 'alternative' therapy, or merely consult a conventional psychoanalyst, have the least need of institutional psychiatry or the more supervisory bits of the welfare state. They are no less the products of a social system permeated by welfarism and public interventionism (a system no less extensive, although differently organized, in the United States) and are perhaps its main beneficiaries.

Having strongly criticized the social implications of anti-psychiatric arguments it should not be supposed that we adhere blindly to the conceptions of the other 'side' of the argument. Our views on the relativity of mental illness as a social category and on the value of psychoanalytic theory and practice should make it evident that this is not the case. John Wing, a leading English clinical psychiatrist, in *Reasoning about Madness* (1978) strongly challenges anti-psychiatric arguments and attempts to justify a strictly clinical-medical approach to mental illness. Wing is strongly opposed to generalized notions like 'madness' or 'mental illness'; for him the only valid categories are those which specify clinically identifiable disease entities like schizophrenia. The strict application of a medical model to psychiatry would limit judgements of pathology to identifiable syndromes, in contrast to what Wing considers the generalizing tendency of certain forms of psychiatric practice, particularly those influenced by psychoanalysis, to find pathology in all sorts of relationships and phenomena. He is thus far from being a power-mad 'manufacturer of madness'. Wing honestly confronts the evidence of the extreme variability of psychiatric diagnosis presented by sociologists and other critics. He argues that this is not evidence to prove that all psychiatry is mere social stigmatizing, but rather that there are too many careless and badly-trained psychiatrists about. He argues that the answer to this variability is not to abandon but to refine procedures of diagnosis and to develop more uniform standards of their application. Wing cites examples of high degrees of agreement in the identification of schizophrenia attained in different countries using a technique of interviewing patients known as the Present State Examination. Wing also provides a trenchant defence of the role of biological over experiential factors in the causation of schizophrenia and of the efficacy of its treatment by pharmaceutical means.[5]

Now we have no specific disagreement with the thesis that the observational syndrome 'schizophrenia' includes within its scope cases and conditions with a biological cause or concomitant, nor do we challenge the efficacy of drugs in alleviating symptoms (whatever the nature of their causation). Clinical analysis and forms of treatment cannot be dispensed with, nor can institutional confinement of the severely psychotic. Although the evidence advanced in support of the biogenesis of schizophrenia has attracted a good deal of intelligent criticism,[6] it should be remembered that *no other* theoretical account of the causation of psychosis has any more rigorous or less challengeable evidence to offer, and no other therapeutic technique has a better record in cases of acute psychosis than the use of pharmaceutical means. Environmental or experiential theories of the causation of schizophrenia have the status of possible and more or less plausible 'accounts' of an individual's response to a reconstructed 'typical' pathogenic situation of interaction. They do not resemble the main lines of biogenetic investigation — twin studies, genetic studies or chemical analysis — in the forms of evidentialization that can be brought to bear on them. It is difficult to decide between experiential and biogenetic accounts precisely because they tend to involve *different* conceptions of knowledge, causation, and demonstration, and each falls short of the other's explanatory expectations. This situation is likely to continue for the foreseeable future. Psychoanalysis has traditionally suffered from theoretical problems in the explanation of psychosis and it has shown a marked failure to deal with severely psychotic patients, so much so that most analysts refuse them. Radical therapies like Laing's have their own well-advertised success stories but also their horror stories. The continued existence of clinical psychiatry is justified not least by the limitations of the supposed alternatives to it.

What is problematic about Wing's position is not his valuable contribution to the study and treatment of schizophrenia but the implications of his rigidly medical model for psychiatric practice in general. He insists that psychiatry proper should be part of medicine, concerned only with definite disease entities it can identify and treat. It should not be a means of general social control, nor should it be called on to manage a mass of personal difficulties and non-specific depression and disorder. Now there is a valuable point in this insistence on the limited scope of clinical psychiatry, which is to reinforce the view that compulsory hospitalization and physical treatment should be limited to strict and specified medical criteria, and that doctors should not permit themselves to be used as mere agents of social control by bureaucrats and politicians. But it is a naive view of the scope and nature of psychiatric practice for a number of reasons.

First, the syndrome schizophrenia designates a functional *mental* disorder. As we have seen, its specification involves a *norm* of general mental functioning against which disorder is measured. This norm is *not* specifically biological or medical, since it involves concepts of personality, normal thought, and appropriate conduct. It is influenced by prevailing social categories and expectations, by the whole gamut of discourses and institutions concerned with policing and checking abnormality. Wing is stuck with a general concept of 'mental health', however much he may protest to the contrary, and one which limits the degree to which a specifically 'medical' and socially neutral specification of disease entities is available to psychiatry.

Second, to render psychiatric diagnosis more consistent in its application of criteria to cases is not thereby to reveal an underlying real condition hitherto masked by subjective error. On the contrary, it is merely to achieve a *pattern of consistency* in the actions of psychiatrists, in their use of standards which have an inescapable normative component and which relate to the judgemental categorization of persons primarily on the basis of their speech and conduct. Obviously we are not opposed to more consistent and competent use of normative-observational categories in diagnosis. But this consistency is a matter of rationalizing practical psychiatric judgements, and in no sense means that we have isolated the phenomena to which these categories are 'really' applicable. An analogy would be the attainment of greater consistency in rates of conviction and patterns of sentencing in magistrates' courts: this consistency in no way allows us to infer that the courts have come closer to identifying those who are 'really' criminal and in dealing justly with them.

Third, Wing's claim to restrict the objects of psychiatric practice to certain disease entities as if they were independent phenomena rests on a naive separation of medical 'truth' from its 'surfaces of emergence'. It is to separate psychiatry's phenomena from the institutions which govern their existence and condition their observability. Without, we hope, wearying the reader, we must repeat that schizophrenia is the *product* of the asylum. It has been identified by clinical observation from amongst the population of patients confined in mental hospitals. It is the previous operations of these institutions which provide the basis for modern clinical categories, yet these categories tend to be presented by psychiatrists such as Wing as disembodied medical truths about phenomena which simply and neutrally present themselves to observation.

Fourth, Wing's claim to limit the scope of psychiatric practice rests on suppositions about the professional autonomy of doctors and their capacity to resist social demands for normalization and control. It is by no means evident that the unrestricted professional autonomy of doctors is an unquestioned good, it leads to numerous problems in health practice and in the administration of health policy. The sort of autonomy in psychiatric decision-making Wing supposes depends on something like the present position of the medical profession in the UK and the USA. Even then doctors are by no means free to remain in the splendid isolation of scientific neutrality, to make judgements on terms of their own choosing or to resist demands on the part of the public and state agencies for the control of individuals. Psychiatric knowledge plays an important role as a source of assessment for courts and other bodies in decisions as to fitness to plead, criminal responsibility, social competency, and so on. The cases in question and the criteria which have to be brought to bear on such decisions — such as 'does this person properly belong in prison or in a mental hospital?' — are in no sense those proper to 'scientific medicine'. Courts, the police, and social workers constantly refer persons to psychiatrists and hospitals for abnormalities which are not identifiable as those of some specific functional disorder. To attempt to separate the 'really' scientific and medical from other demands placed on institutional psychiatry is to pursue an illusion. It remains a compromised practical activity concerned as much as anything else with supervision and normalization of conduct. This is not a fault but a necessity, galling as it might be to the medical-scientific aspirations of certain professionals.

Lastly, clinical psychiatry is no more than one important part of a complex of institutions of supervision and control, therapy and training. Psychiatric knowledges and practices are widely deployed outside the medical profession. Social workers, educational psychologists, counsellors of various kinds, and devisers of training procedures make use of psychiatric, psychological, and psychoanalytical concepts and techniques. To attempt to limit the role of psychiatric knowledges to medically trained specialists is also impossible, although it is possible to so limit the use of surgery and some kinds of medication. To the extent that Wing's self-denying ordinance worked it would merely shift the institutional site of psychiatric decisions and act to reinforce the use of behavioural and psychoanalytic rather than medical-clinical categories and therapies.

In conclusion we may remark that there is no single theoretical position which can satisfactorily account for the phenomena which fall under the category of 'mental illness' nor is there one generally effective therapeutic method. The various 'psychiatries', medical, psychoanalytic, etc., whatever their mutual antagonisms, continue to exist for good reasons and to cater for different publics and different categories of disorder. *Because* 'mental illness' is a social category, involving expectations as to normal conduct and competence, demands for control and therapy, it can be neither relativized nor medicalized anyway. This is, we feel, a more appropriately *sociological* conclusion, concerning the necessities and problems which arise from social relations, than the sociological relativization of values which has in fact been the primary sociological practice in the analysis of mental illness and the mental hospital.

Notes

1 Foucault's *Madness and Civilization* was published in England in 1965 in a series edited by Laing. One can see its attraction to Laing in its claim that the modern Western conception of madness as unreason, as wholly negative and insignificant, creates a new and radical separation between the sane and other men. But, Foucault is not concerned to judge and has no positive theory of madness; as we said at the end of the last chapter, 'madness' is a category and Foucault is concerned with the response to madness on the part of Western civilization and not with the mad and what they are. Madness is neither authentic nor inauthentic, silent pathology nor full of meaning. His point is not that there is something to hear but that our culture refuses to listen.

2 See Wing (1978), Clare (1980), Coulter (1973: Chs. 2 and 3), and Sedgwick (1972).

3 For Bateson's concepts see *Steps to an Ecology of Mind* (1973: Part II), especially 'Epidemiology of a Schizophrenia' and 'Towards a Theory of Schizophrenia'.

4 Coulter (1973: 63-7).

5 Anthony Clare, *Psychiatry in Dissent* (1980) also provides an excellent account of the state of debate on the aetiology of schizophrenia which corroborates Wing's view.

6 For a review of these criticisms see Coulter (1973: Ch. 1).

III
WITCHCRAFT AND RATIONALITY

Two deny manslaughter of woman in 'exorcism'

A preacher and his friend kicked a mentally unstable woman to death as they tried to rid her of Judas Iscariot's evil spirit, the Old Bailey heard yesterday.

During the 'exorcism' John Sherwood and Anthony Strover punched Miss Beatrix Rutherford, aged 31, until she was unconscious, then kicked and jumped on her stomach, it was said.

Strover was said to have told police Miss Rutherford spoke in a strange voice which claimed to be the spirit of Judas. Sherwood said that he must have been possessed by the devil.

Sherwood, aged 30, a preacher, of no fixed address, and Strover, aged 25, unemployed, of Wood Lane, Shepherd's Bush, London, deny the manslaughter of Miss Rutherford in March.

Mr David Tudor Price, prosecuting, said it was not claimed that they intended to kill her. 'But it was the sad result of their misguided and unlawful act that brought about her death.'

Mr Price said that Miss Rutherford became mentally unstable after the end of a lesbian relationship with Mrs Valerie Bott.

Mrs Bott told the court that she went to Miss Rutherford's flat in Edmonton, North London, on the day she died. Her hair was filthy, her head was bound, and she was huddled on the edge of the bed, mumbling.

Sherwood and Stover were sitting in front of her and 'I got the impression of an interrogation,' said Mrs Bott.

Mr Tudor Price said that the next day the two men went to Edmonton police station and Sherwood said: 'I think I have killed a woman trying to get devils out of her'.

In a statement, Strover said that the 'exorcism' started with Sherwood hitting Miss Rutherford. 'I told him to hold her legs and started hitting her in the stomach and then I seemed to go beserk.'

When they realized that she was dead 'we prayed that God would bring her back to life'.

The trial continues today.

The Guardian 4 September 1980

11

INTRODUCTION

To the modern consciousness, the very idea of witchcraft is preposterous. To believe in the capacity of persons to exploit occult powers or spirits, whether for good or bad purposes, is absurd. Self-professed 'witches' continue to exist in contemporary Britain but they are fodder for the *News of the World*, venal characters, cranks, or deluded seekers after significance in life who could easily have joined another 'fringe' religion. Indeed, the very 'absurdity' of witchcraft beliefs has constituted a serious problem for modern social theories: witchcraft is a major stumbling block for Western rationalist accounts of human mentality.

Many African peoples continue to be governed in their lives by the decisions of diviners and oracles, and spend a great deal of their energies in the avoidance of the maleficent consequences of witchcraft or magic. Anthropology since the nineteenth century has taken a hostile and cynical attitude to the claims and performances of 'primitive' shamans and diviners: witchcraft, shamanism, and divination are empirically false beliefs, a sign of and a cause of backwardness. Non-western peoples' practice of witchcraft and magic has formed an important basis for claims that 'primitives' are irrational or exhibit a distinct 'pre-logical' mentality (as Lucien Lévy-Bruhl argued).[1] Against this some anthropologists tend to argue that, in using magic or defending themselves against witches, 'primitives' are using rational conceptions of cause and effect, but employing technologies unfortunately directed toward non-existent entities. Many modern anthropologists are willing to understand witchcraft beliefs sympathetically but practically none are willing to give credence to them. The predominant response is Evans-Pritchard's: when on fieldwork in Zandeland do as the Zande do, but not in your study afterwards.[2]

Like anthropology, the history of ideas has been perpetually uneasy with the European 'witch craze' of the sixteenth and seventeenth centuries — an explosion of witch persecutions and demonological beliefs coincident with the Renaissance and Reformation. Until recently, historical writing could shelter in the illusions of the Enlightenment, and characterize witch beliefs as a hangover from the Dark Ages. For the noted nineteenth-century historian Jules Michelet, witchcraft was the product of a brutal and life-denying feudal Christianity which drove sexuality, under the scourge of celibacy, into suspicion and pathological fantasy, which persecuted the women healers who were the only solace of the sick poor; which denied and persecuted the old native religions; and which drove the starving poor to rebellion in the sabbats. But the witch stereo-type and the legal machinery for the persecutions were no relics of medieval Christian darkness. They were in essence products of the fif-teenth century elaborated in the sixteenth.[3]

Luther lived in dread of witches. Pico della Mirandola wrote what is now regarded as a classic of rational humanism, *On the Dignity of Man*, in the service of a Neo-Platonic philosophy according to which man's power reaches its climax in the *magical* manipulation of the spirits of the world. Jean Bodin, one of the founders of the modern conception of the state, himself a secret heretic, argued for the relentless legal persecution of witches.[4] The astronomer Johannes Kepler, a leading force in the revol-ution which established the new heliocentric astronomy, remained committed to astrology and drew horoscopes.[5] Only by means of extensive and judicious 'editing' can the leading intellectual figures of the Renaissance and Reformation be made to serve as exponents of modern humanism, rationalism, and empiricism.

From the comforts of the Enlightenment conception of progress, we have turned to the melancholy wisdom of our own times to explain away this spectre of the witch craze. Norman Cohn, in a brilliant work, *Europe's Inner Demons* (1976), treats the witch craze as a pathological persecution on a par with Hitler's camps or Stalin's purges. But this explanation covers only the witches' persecutors who must be conceived as either deluded or cynical. The *problem* of witchcraft beliefs among the educated and ruling classes in Renaissance Europe vanishes into the slogan 'collective psychopathology'. The problem is that witchcraft was an inescapable component of a context of religious and scientific ideas, a context in which there was no place for an opposing 'normality'. The pertinent analogy would be to imagine we were all Nazis deeply committed to concepts of race and racial purity; then the camps would not appear pathological to educated 'reasonable' men — and the pyres of the witches did not seem so to the reasonable men of the Renaissance.

The intellectual and political movements which are termed the Renaissance and Reformation in fact *intensified* witch beliefs and notions of spiritual magic. Innovations in civil legal procedure which introduced judicial torture as a means of proof — innovations identified by their authors with rationality — made the persecutions a self-multiplying machine for the manufacture of guilt. The 'scepticism' about witchcraft of men like Montaigne, Reginald Scot, and Johann Weyer failed to provide an adequate critique, collapsing into a cynical 'worldly-wise' attitude or affirming the categories it denied; nor could it provide a religious, legal, and political substitute for the categories and practices it obliquely challenged.

Explaining away witchcraft beliefs and the metaphysical suppositions they entail brings us face to face with our own very different metaphysical premises. The problem is to accept that these premises of ours *are* meta-physical, for they claim to establish a view of the world bounded by empirical validity and instrumental rationality. Materialism and a belief in the virtues of ordered observation and critical testing of experience are the metaphysical foundations of the ideology which claims to be contemporary 'common sense'. This ideology is threatened by witch-craft beliefs because *they too* appeal to and are confirmed by experience on the basis of premises. The suppositions of materialism, just like beliefs in the existence of spirits, can be neither proven nor disproven: it is a precondition for certain kinds of explanations, presupposed but not proven by them. Observation and the 'testing' of experience are always relative to premises as to the nature of phenomena which *can* exist and cannot be independent means for the assay of beliefs because they are implicated in them. Within the context of a spiritualist ontology, ample confirmation of possession and maleficent action can be found by obser-vation and testimony.

Quesalid, the Kwakiutl shaman whose case is cited by Lévi-Strauss,[6] began his career as a sceptic, joining a group of shamans in order to uncover their practices. In spite of himself he succeeded in healing magic, humiliating other practitioners in the process, and he became to everyone's satisfaction a leading and powerful shaman. He doubted his own powers but could not deny their effectiveness and ended sceptically convinced that 'real' shamans do exist although he had uncovered many frauds. Never was Pascal's aphorism more amply confirmed: enter the church, kneel, pray, and you will believe.

The metaphysics of contemporary 'common sense' which identifies itself with the 'scientific attitude' is threatened by observations it cannot accept and phenomena it cannot test. Parapsychology was, and largely remains, an intellectual scandal. Sir William Crookes damaged his repu-tation as a scientist in a century of confident materialism by championing the 'evidence of his eyes': empiricism and materialism can be brought into contradiction, just as the beliefs of the Zande form a contradictory unity. He failed to evince the attitude exemplified by Hugo Muenster-berg's comment to the medium Edgar Cayce, 'I have come here to expose you' (cited in Inglis 1977: 948). An attitude which has more in common with witch hunters like Heinrich Kramer or Matthew Hopkins than it would care to admit. Muensterberg could not 'expose' Cayce and left threatening to return. Yet the activities of Cayce and those of the most spectacular medium of all, D.D. Home (who also remained free of the charge of imposture), were witnessed by scientists, and this is what threatens the reliability of observation and public testimony of scien-tifically competent men which is so central to the mythology of empiri-cism. If they can 'see' and attest to *that* they can see anything! Hence the charges of fraud and imposture levelled against the mediums.

The unconscious is no less of a mystery to those orthodox experimental psychologists who have made the metaphysics of scientific 'common sense' almost into a religion. 'Refutations' of Freud can be counted in the hundreds, experimental falsifications based on experience. They proliferate alongside the knowledges and therapeutic practices of psycho-analysis, forever inadequate because they start from a refusal to recognize the entities of psychoanalysis or the mechanisms of their production. Analytic 'experience' and observation are *ipso facto* discounted as means of demonstration in these forms of 'test'. 'Tests' of this kind can thus only serve to confirm the methodological doctrines and ontological suppositions of those who employ them. Yet those doctrines and suppo-sitions are in no way privileged over those of psychoanalysis.

The point which will be made here in Part Three is that what is at stake in the question of witchcraft is our *beliefs about witchcraft*. What is revealed is the existence of certain fundamental assumptions about the nature of things no less on our part than on the part of those who believe in witches. This discussion will consider *responses to* witch beliefs, attempts to explain how men, apparently 'rational' and able to conduct their lives to their own satisfaction, could believe in witchcraft. Those men are not merely members of a 'primitive' tribe but Luther or Bodin. It is *our* concept of 'rationality' and rational conduct which is threatened by witchcraft, not the very different categories of Luther nor those of the Azande.

In our discussion we will concentrate on explanations of the European 'witch-craze' of the sixteenth and seventeenth centuries, rather than the analysis of witchcraft beliefs and practices in contemporary non-Western 'primitive' societies, favoured by social science textbooks. The anthropo-logical analysis of witchcraft is not to be slighted by this preference, rather the objective is to bring the 'problem' of witchcraft closer to home. The Zande or other peoples can all too easily be regarded as cultural curiosities. It is rather more difficult to take this attitude to the official 'founding fathers' of our modern religious, scientific, and humanistic beliefs. First, in Chapter Twelve we will examine Gregory Zilboorg's account of contempor-ary medical conceptions of witchcraft and insanity in his book *The Medical Man and the Witch During the Renaissance* (1935). We will challenge his view that the objective foundation of witchcraft beliefs was insanity and his claim that in the works of Johann Weyer the beginnings of a 'modern' attitude towards the witch craze are to be found. Zilboorg is interesting because he attempts to demonstrate both the accuracy of contemporary fifteenth- and sixteenth-century observation and the reality of the phenomenon observed, contending rather that the explanation and treatment of that phenomenon involved a disastrous category mistake. The problem of the 'rationality' of our ancestors thereby disappears: they acted reasonably on the basis of observation but were led into error by religious dogmas which had not yet been overcome.

Second, in Chapter Thirteen we will consider views which regard the 'witch craze' as a persecution mania, a stereotyping of innocent victims in the service of fabricated dogmas. This view is presented subtly by Norman Cohn (1976) and in a much more simplistic form, as a persecutory conspiracy, by Thomas Szasz in *The Manufacture of Madness* (1973).

Third, in Chapter Fourteen we will consider the literature on the 'decline' of witchcraft, magic, and astrology in the seventeenth century. The rapid collapse of support for witchcraft accusations and the rapid abandonment of witch beliefs by the educated and ruling classes has often been explained as an acceptance of the modern scientific attitude, coincident with the success of the scientific revolution, and of a new-found security of life. We will argue that the 'scientific revolution' in astronomy and mechanics substituted one religious world-view of the universe for another. In doing so we will concentrate on the paradoxes of Sir Isaac Newton. In seeking an alternative account of the decline of witch persecution, we will also argue that enforced religious conformity, the tightening of religious practice and supervision resulting from Calvinism and the Counter-Reformation, paradoxically weakened the scope for heresy-hunting and opposition. This increased religious supervision and uniformity was coupled with a centralization of state power and an increased power of apparatuses of law which, on the one hand, could not survive without eliminating the competing persecutory authorities so central in sustaining the persecutions and, on the other hand, diminished the need for torture in judicial procedure. By contrast, scientific materialism, increased material security, and religious 'tolerance' played only a minor part in the decline. The major part was played by the conformity of opposed and stable religious 'blocs', the displacement of spiritualist by providentialist 'scientific' metaphysics, and the rationalization of legal apparatuses and procedures.

Finally, in Chapter Fifteen we will consider the role of witchcraft in 'primitive' societies. Here we will concentrate on the classic work of anthropological analysis of witchcraft, Evans-Pritchard's *Witchcraft, Oracles and Magic Among the Azande* (original edition 1956, abridged 1976). The focus of attention will be Evans-Pritchard's own dilemma in his approach to Zande witchcraft. Following on from this, we will consider the debate about the concept of 'rationality' largely provoked by the book, focusing on the exchange between Peter Winch (1963) and Alasdair MacIntyre (1972). It will be argued, largely in sympathy with Winch, that there is no concept of 'rationality' in general whereby beliefs and actions may be assessed. Nor are these problems confined to explaining the beliefs and actions of declining and marginal 'primitive' peoples. Religious beliefs no less challenging than those of Zande witchcraft to Western 'common sense' conceptions of rationality are growing rather than declining in influence. The recrudescence of militant Islam and the mass suicide of the followers of James Jones in Guyana bear witness to this.

Notes

1 Lévy-Bruhl was by no means consistent or unambiguous in his formulations of the concept of 'primitive mentality', but he never intended this idea of a distinct 'pre-logical' mentality to imply that primitives were either irrational *tout court* or in some way inherently inferior to modern Western man. For his classic statement, see *Primitive Mentality* (1966).
2 See 'Some Remarks on Fieldwork', Appendix 4 to *Witchcraft, Oracles and Magic among the Azande* (1976).
3 Norman Cohn in *Europe's Inner Demons* (1976) effectively demolishes the evidence for a long pre-history of systematic witch hunts before the fourteenth century, showing important sources for such earlier medieval trials to have been faked. See also Kieckhefer (1976) for a corroboration of the same point. On witch trials generally see also Peters (1978). For examples of local studies and ones of general significance for the explanation of the witch trials see Macfarlane (1971) for Essex, Midelfort (1972) for southwest Germany and Monter (1976) for the Swiss borderlands.
4 Jean Bodin (c. 1530-96) was a leading jurist and author of *Six livres de la république*, a pioneering work of systematic political analysis and a contribution to establishing the concept of sovereignty on a modern basis. Bodin enjoyed wider fame in his time as a man of encyclopaedic knowledge. For a brief sketch of his career see Mandrou (1978: 145). For his political theory, see J. W. Allen *A History of Political Thought in the Sixteenth Century* (1928). Bodin, for all his support for the extirpation of witchcraft was hardly, in private, an adherent of religious orthodoxy: 'By the end of his life Bodin had ceased to be a Christian, and believed in a kind of simplified archaic judaism' (Walker 1958: 171).
5 Johannes Kepler (1571-1630). For Kepler's interest in astrology, see L. Thorndike, *History of Magic and Experimental Science* (1923-58: Vol. 7).
6 C. Lévi-Strauss, 'The Sorcerer and his Magic', Chapter IX of *Structural Anthropology* (1968).

12
WITCHCRAFT AS INSANITY

In writing a history of psychiatry, Gregory Zilboorg is forced to confront the 'problem' of witchcraft. His *History of Medical Psychology* (1941) conceives that history as the progress of a science, a tenacious process of uncovering truth in the face of illusion and error. In this 'triumphalist' account, modern psychiatry is considered to be by and large theoretically sound and empirically correct. The writing of its history thus consists in reading backwards, aided by our modern knowledge and attitudes, and discovering how this state was arrived at. Decisive in this context is the formation of the scientific 'attitude', the precondition for the rational analysis of any body of phenomena. This attitude consists in a refusal to accept traditional authorities without reference to experience and in a sceptical and critical testing of the phenomena of experience themselves. It therefore involves a break from religious dogmas, tradition, and super-stition.

In both *The History of Medical Psychology* and *The Medical Man and the Witch during the Renaissance*, Zilboorg identifies the sixteenth and seventeenth centuries as the decisive period of the break with dogma and superstition in science and medicine — except, that is, in the sphere of mental phenomena and mental pathology. Only in the nineteenth century does the scientific attitude finally triumph in the sphere of mental life.

'In one regard, however, the sixteenth century ... continued to lag behind, and it did so for at least another three centuries, apparently unable to cast off the fetter of tradition — it was as yet unprepared even to begin to develop a sound medical psychology.'

(Zilboorg 1935: 71)

Zilboorg conceives the Renaissance as the beginning of the scientific revolution, the key to intellectual progress. But it coincides with the height of the witch persecutions. To this paradox he responds by con-tending:

i.   that the religious and secular authorities, although in general rational and pragmatic in outlook, were still at the mercy of religious super-stitions in the sphere of human conduct;

ii. that the authorities observed but misrecognized manifestations of mental illness as phenomena of witchcraft.

The persecution is represented as a hangover from a previous era, a lagging behind of scientific rationality. It can be explained by the baleful influence of religious dogma which leads honest, well-meaning, and observant men to make a category mistake. Thus he refers to Heinrich Kramer and Johannes Sprenger, the authors of the classical textbook of forensic demonology, *Malleus Maleficarum*[1] (1486), and men frequently considered by other authorities to be brutal or pathological, as 'two honest dominicans'. *Malleus* rather can be regarded as a record of the real condition of the mentally ill in this period:

> 'The illustrative examples cited in the *Malleus Maleficarum* bear witness to this ... the millions of witches, sorcerers, possessed and obsessed, were an enormous mass of severe neurotics, psychotics, and considerably deteriorated organic deliria .... At times one is almost loath to admit to one's self the indisputable fact that for many years the world looked like a veritable insane asylum without a proper mental hospital.'
>
> (Zilboorg 1935: 73)

But the Devil is a bigger obstacle than can be removed by the pen. *Malleus Maleficarum* is a work of forensic demonology, its categories *and* its observations are conditional on Christian theology and the object of subjecting witches to judicial process. It is not a collection of misunderstood observations. Sprenger and Kramer themselves give the best answer to this reading:

> 'those err who say that there is no such thing as witchcraft, but that it is purely imaginary, even though they do not believe that devils exist except in the imagination of the ignorant and vulgar, and the natural accidents which happen to a man he wrongly attributes to some supposed devil. For the imagination of some men is so vivid that they think they see actual figures and appearances which are but the reflection of their thought and then these are believed to be the apparitions of evil spirits or even the spectres of witches. But this is contrary to true faith, which teaches us that certain angels fell from heaven and are now devils, and we are bound to acknowledge that by their very nature they can do many wonderful things which we cannot do. And those who try to induce others to perform such evil wonders are called witches.'
>
> (1971: 35)

Zilboorg expostulates, 'How can one raise objections to the assertion, "but this is contrary to true faith"? The fusion of insanity, witchcraft and heresy into one concept and the exclusion of even the suspicion that *the problem is a medical one* are now complete' (1941: 155, our emphasis).

But what 'problem' is it that is the medical one? Zilboorg assumes a constant realm of behaviour and conduct which can be classed as normal or pathological according to modern symptomatologies. Zilboorg assumes that religious and legal categories are simply inapplicable, empirically out of court. People who believed they were witches or possessed are cases of mental illness who garbed their pathologies in the ideological trappings of their era. But Sprenger and Kramer have an unerring logic on their side. The entities postulated in Christian religious categories cannot be placed empirically out of court, declared non-existent by reference to 'experience', because they transcend experience and its proofs. Knowledge of God and His works is possible only by faith and revelation. Devils and witches are a theological matter, and man's conduct in respect of them a matter for ecclesiastical law. God, Christ, the Devil, and witches are not, because they happen to transcend Zilboorg's conception of 'experience', merely matters of superstition, merely ideological illusions in which men clothe their conduct. They organize and are productive of discourse and conduct: men live in fear of the Devil, starve, and wander in penance and pilgrimage. Zilboorg cannot tell us what they are 'really' afraid of or doing; he must reduce their conduct to the consequences of illusion. One may as well declare Luther and St Teresa as mad as those poor devils who confessed to being, and believed themselves to be, witches. One must either reject God, recognizing that one is making a non-empirical judgement in the process, or accept the rigours of some theological system.

Within their own premises, Sprenger and Kramer's argument is rigorous and logical, and they carefully marshall 'evidence' to support it. Given the premises of God and the Fall, they draw out the ontological consequences; what can exist is here determined by theological argument. Given this ontology, then its *legal* concomitants — in terms of the procedure for the examination of persons to determine whether they are witches — are rigorously derived. Sprenger and Kramer are not ignorant of theological and other objections to demonology, and they set out to counter them by argument and evidence.

Indeed, the opponents of forensic demonology were consistently defeated in open argument and failed to carry the day during the period of the persecutions. Only afterwards were they rediscovered and assigned the status of precursors of the modern 'rational' attitude. Zilboorg's *Medical Man* is primarily such an exercise of pleading on behalf of Johann Weyer, a sixteenth-century physician. Weyer's *De praestigiis daemonorum* (1563) is conceived by Zilboorg as an attempt to plead the case of the mentally sick, to deny them the status of witches, to release them from the hands of the lawyers into the hands of the doctors. It is certainly an attempt to challenge witch persecutions, but Zilboorg's mode of reading it is to draw his conclusions from it *without reference to the mode of argument*. Weyer is concerned to assert the prestidigitatory nature of the Devil — that, like a magician, he produces illusions in men's minds. 'Witches' do not actually accomplish the things they believe and report, they *imagine* them. The Devil cannot do anything contrary to nature and nor can witches. Witches are victims of evil illusions and deserve our sympathy.

It can quickly be seen that the argument depends centrally on the category of the Devil. Zilboorg's comment that 'Weyer uses the word *devil* in a rather free manner and somewhat as we use the colloquial expression crazy' (1935: 138) is both absurd and inconsequential. Zilboorg doubts 'whether Weyer believed in the existence of the Devil at all'; whether he did or not, he was still forced to use the *category*. This leaves him open to and helpless before three obvious replies to his argument. First, that if the Devil can affect men's *imaginations*. why should he be denied other capacities for action? He is a fallen angel and enjoys some superhuman powers. To deny the Devil supernatural powers and his capacity to aid evil men by means of them is to threaten God's own powers and aid, to deny miracles. Second, even if men merely *imagine* evil, they still *think* it, and the thought is no less evil than the act. They ought, therefore, to be punished. Third, the Devil can only overcome a person whose fortitude and faith in God is weakened, only sinners are the devil's victims.

Weyer was not alone in his objections. Reginald Scot's *The Discoverie of Witchcraft* (1584), follows a similar line of argument in characterizing witches as poor deluded folk. It was challenged by James VI in his *Daemonologie* (1597) and when he became King of England, he had Scot's work burnt. It should not be assumed that those who supported or practised the persecutions were uncritical and took no note of circumstances or other explanations. Nor should it be imagined that there were no available categories of mental pathology — categories such as melancholy and mania existed and were employed. They differed in their symptomatologies and conditions of application from the categories of 'possession' and 'witchcraft'. 'Possession', further, was conceived as something different from the conscious conspiracy with the Devil which was involved in witchcraft. In cases of possession a weak or troubled soul was invaded by evil spirits. The 'possessed' required spiritual counsel rather than either medical attention or the stake. Ambroise Paré, a radical innovator in surgical techniques and surgeon to the King of France, strongly supported the persecution of witches, but this did not make him unwilling to use clinical judgement in establishing whether or not a case was a genuine possession or some other form of pathology. In the case of demoniacal possession of a young nobleman he remarked, 'Any well-advised physician would have said that we were dealing with a case of genuine epilepsy, were it not for the fact that the senses and mind of the patient remained unaffected throughout the attacks' (Zilboorg 1935: 84-5). In like fashion the Spanish Inquisition after 1610 refused to prosecute or execute 'witches', and openly regarded 'witchcraft' as a delusion and those who confessed to it as insane.[2] The Papal Inquisitors released a magician arrested for dealings with evil spirits when he showed them the tricks whereby he attained his effects.[3] Demoniacal possession

was a specific category identified by reference to definite conducts and
generally countered by religious means. It was particularly important in
France. Witchcraft was something else again and was a legal rather than a
medical or pastoral matter. Thus the important place of doctrines of
witches in theological discourses, the differentiation of categories of
witchcraft and possession, the existence of categories of pathology – all
these make Zilboorg's category mistake hypothesis untenable. Further,
witchcraft was an object of specifiable legal proceedings which can be
regarded as neither mere instruments of prejudice nor at odds with the
'emergent rationality'.

Properly conducted, the inquisitorial procedure for the detection of
witchcraft was designed to extract an explicit confession. It required that
the accused be conscious and coherent. Testimony was subjected to
critical questioning, to proofs and tests. If, however, the accused with-
stood torture and refused to confess, then they should by law be released,
conviction and execution requiring the confession of the accused. Cohn
estimates in *Europe's Inner Demons* (1976) that even at the height of the
witch hunt, one in ten were thus set free.[4] Inquisitorial procedure was a
form of trial, bound by rules, and not merely the application of a closed
set of prejudices to the stigmatization of victims. As a procedure it was
not beyond criticism and was regarded by contemporary enlightened
jurists as capable of reform. Johann Godelman in his *Tractatus de Magis*
(1591) argued that witch trials should be conducted according to normal
civil procedure rather than the extraordinary procedure which weakened
the rights of the accused.[5] The accusation should require two witnesses
to the same act, and criminals, excommunicants, etc. should be banned
from giving evidence, just as they were in other trials. The accused should
be allowed counsel, and confessions to impossible acts should not be
upheld. The confession must be made seriously and also be confirmed
by two witnesses.

Zilboorg would regard Godelman as a spokesman of the emerging
'rational' attitude. The problem with such a judgement is that the normal
civil procedure Godelman pleads for is also inquisitorial, systematically
employs torture, and requires the confession of the accused for a full
proof. The inquisitorial process was a relatively recent innovation in
judicial procedure and brought with it the use of torture to obtain a
confession. Torture as a means of producing evidence was thus no relic
of the Dark Ages but rather emerged as the inquisitorial procedure replaced trial by ordeal. The arbitrariness of trial by ordeal could not
satisfy the growing royal, episcopal, and municipal jurisdictions, since the
imposition of the forms of order possible within the limits of feudal
state power depended on a reasonable certainty of conviction. At the
same time, because of those very limits of state power, the decision of the
judge alone could not command sufficient respect, an unshakeable conviction was needed to silence the accused's kin, feudal allies, or the mob.
That certainty lay in confession. Since confession would seldom be

given voluntarily, it depended on coercion, but coercion within pre-scribed boundaries. In civil procedure torture could only be applied when there were strong 'partial proofs' of guilt (one witness, circumstantial evidence, and so on — the evidence necessary to justify torture was more than might be needed to hang a man in our era).[6] Torture can be regarded as part of a process of juridical rationalization. Though we shudder at the idea of torture, we accept standards of proof in respect of serious crimes which would horrify a Renaissance lawyer. John Langbein in *Torture and the Law of Proof* (1977) and *Prosecuting Crime in the Renaissance* (1974) demonstrates why systematic torture was introduced as part of a process of procedural reform, an evolution which duly shocks Enlightment conceptions of progress.

In witchcraft trials, however, the safeguards in the normal criminal procedure were largely discarded. This is due to two factors. First, the nature of the offence itself, which on the Continent consisted in the beliefs and occult actions of the accused, rather than definite acts of malice as in England. The result was to weaken the requirements of evidence on the part of witnesses, so that accusation could take the form of denunciation. Secondly, the conception of witchcraft as a 'clear and present danger', an epidemic of demonology almost beyond control. Henri Boguet, a judge in Burgundy in the reign of Henri IV, is a good example of the attitude of the authorities: 'I believe that the sorcerers could form an army equal to that of Xerxes . . . . As to myself, I have no doubts, since a mere glance at our neighbours will convince us that the land is infested with this unfortunate and detestable vermin' (cited in Zilboorg 1935: 74).[7] We know from our own times that procedural safe-guards are almost valueless in such a climate. The US Courts and Consti-tution hardly served to protect the victims of the Smith Act, HUAC and Joe MacCarthy in a more recent period of 'clear and present danger'. Jurists were a field force struggling against the multiplying hosts of Satan.

In this context, the worldly-wise scepticism of men like Montaigne or, later on, Cyrano de Bergerac could be dismissed with contempt. It has nothing to offer except the comfortable, tolerantly cynical wisdom of the well-placed *bon viveur*. States cannot be conducted nor the faithful consoled with such a philosophy. It could also be dismissed as ignorant, for it did not want to *hear* what came from the mouths of the accused. It is widely believed that the accused confessed to everything suggested to them in order to avoid further torture. But in England, where torture was not applied as part of the legal procedure, 'witches' confessed nonetheless. On the Continent the confessions of many accused witches contain a wealth of detail and a subjective conviction which suggests they were not merely repeating under duress the stereotypes of their judges. Nor should we think such confessions a thing of the past. Cohn cites the trial of a Shona woman in Rhodesia in the 1950s accused of being a cannibal-istic night witch; she confessed in elaborate detail to riding hyenas at night and to cannibalism.[8] She confessed this to European-trained police who used no torture and she maintained her confession in the face of sceptical white magistrates and judges. She was not judged to be insane. What proportion of confessions in the period of the 'witch craze' stemmed from genuine participation in witchcraft practices is impossible to determine. The confessions served, however, to confirm a set of definite beliefs held by the persecutors about the organization and practice of the witch cult. Judges lived in a nightmare of confirmation of their worst fears. Torture, as an instrumental part of the rationalization of judicial procedure, served to make possible a multiplication of denunciations and convictions beyond anything possible with the older accusatory procedure and trial by ordeal.[9] For even if witches believed in their confessions, they had little reason to make them without compulsion or to denounce others without being forced to do so.

We have been arguing that, far from being a hangover from the Dark Ages, witchcraft and magic attained a new centrality in European culture as a result of the intellectual developments of the Reformation and the Renaissance. Before the late fourteenth century, most of the higher clergy and educated laymen regarded popular beliefs and fears about night witches and their *maleficium* as mere superstition. They did so largely because they sought to differentiate Christianity from folk religion and in order to influence the often semi-literate and credulous rural priests. As Cohn argues, these very popular beliefs and fears were taken into service as part of the intellectual machinery of heresy-hunting. Inquisitorial procedure was introduced not to hunt witches as such but to try heretics. Witch beliefs became more important in European culture and institutions – not less so.

The reason for this is to be found in the 'Reformation'. In order to understand this process, we must begin by recognizing that the tendencies within Christianity summed up in this concept did not begin on the day Luther pinned his theses to the door of the University church in Wittenburg in 1517.[10] 'Reform' had a long pre-history in the medieval Church. A series of movements of religious reform had challenged Papal orthodoxy from the twelfth century onwards in England, France, Italy, and elsewhere. Some like the Franciscans were incorporated by orthodoxy. Others like the Fraticelli, the Lollards, the Waldensians were persecuted as heretics. A number of common themes ran through these reform movements:

i.   a criticism of the Church hierarchy for its addiction to worldly wealth and corruption, much criticism centred on practices such as raising funds by selling indulgences granting a certain period of remission from Purgatory.
ii. a conviction that religious knowledge should be placed directly in the hands of the people, that they should be encouraged to interpret and act on the message of the Gospels. In contrast, the hierarchy conceived salvation in terms of attendance at formal services, confession and receipt of the sacraments, and knowledge of set forms of prayer: the priests and the hierarchy mediated

with God through set forms of worship and penance. The reformers stressed the practice of preaching to the masses and explaining to them the meaning of the Gospels in direct terms and in their
native language. Further, they supported the translation of the Bible
into the vernacular and encouraged educated laymen to study and
pray. The effect of these practices was to promote a more directly
personal relation to God on the part of laymen and to encourage
discourses of informal prayer, thereby encouraging among the people
practices hitherto confined to monastic mystics.

iii. Consequent on the criticism of the venality of the hierarchy and the
challenge to its function as the sole channel of mediation to God was
a challenge to the powers of the institution as such. This had two
aspects, first, more or less radical proposals to limit the institutional
powers of the Papacy and the episcopate, and second, a challenge to
the spiritual powers of the institution, denying the efficacy of sacraments, the capacity of charms, symbols, and mechanical prayer to
ward off evil, and denying the infallibility of the Pope.

What made Luther's Reformation different from these other, often
more radical, movements of reform was no special innovation in doctrine.
Rather it was the fact that it coincided with the political struggle of the
Papacy and its episcopal and secular allies in Germany with the German
Princes. It was the support of state power which led to a different outcome in the case of these 'heretics', and conversely it was their very
'moderation', the fact that Luther allied himself with established authority rather than attempting to create a popular mass movement to
threaten existing relations of wealth and power, which made them effective religious revolutionaries.

The 'Reformation' had a number of pronounced effects on the beliefs
about witchcraft and on the institutions of its discovery. First, Protestant
Christianity greatly increased the threat of occult *maleficium* to ordinary
people by dismantling the spiritual defences offered by Catholic practice.
Witchcraft had been a matter of popular belief and concern among the
peasants throughout Europe in the centuries before the Reformation, and
what they feared were specific acts of magically induced harm on the
part of neighbours with some reason to bear malice towards them. Although
the higher clergy set little store by these beliefs and fears, the Church in
practice offered ample defences against them. *Maleficium* could be directly countered by charms and talismans (the cross, a relic of a saint), by
repeating formal prayers (*Ave Maria*, etc.), by blessings or exorcisms on
the part of the priests. Keith Thomas in *Religion and the Decline of Magic*
(1973) points out that in 'rationalizing' belief and practice, Protestantism
disarmed the people against spiritual malice. Protestants outlawed charms,
relics, and so on, and they denied the priest the role of spiritual agent
sharing in the spiritual power of the Church transmitted by God through
the Pope. He became instead a religious functionary whose role was to

impart religious knowledge, to offer counsel, and to lead prayer. Only prayer and its solicitation of the action of God could have any effectivity. God could not be counted on to respond automatically to prayer. The peasant was thus very much on his own, without immediate spiritual defences, and dependent on God's uncertain will. As a result peasants and other victims of 'witchcraft' sought an institutional rather than a spiritual or magical solution: they were forced by the absence of other recourse to denounce the witch or sorcerer to the authorities. As we have seen, the obstacles to doing so had been greatly reduced by the substitution of the inquisitorial for the accusatory procedure. The Catholic Church had employed inquisitorial methods to eliminate the reformers and heretics who were the precursors of the Protestant reformation. Protestants cleared away the mass of charms, saints, shrines, and so on, denying them spiritual power because they were a presumptuous annexation of God's power and because they acted irrespective of the quality of faith or conduct. In demolishing these beliefs and practices they simultaneously reinforced those relating to witchcraft.

Second, at the very moment they did so, the figure of Satan, the master of witches, had grown to awesome dimensions. The Devil grew in proportion to the personalization of belief and the development of a more direct relation to God. In the early Church, the Devil and demons had stood in a marginal position in opposition to the Church as a sacral community. Membership of the institution invested the believer with a spiritual defence and guaranteed redemption; redemption was for the community of the faithful as a whole. With the growing personalization of belief, it was the faith and conduct of the individual which increasingly determined his redemption. Temptation thus grows in importance, as God and Satan compete for the allegiance of the individual soul. This personalization developed within the monasteries and was carried beyond them by the reform movements and by the Church's attempts to incorporate and contain these movements by promoting preaching orders. By the fifteenth century, Satan and his demons had become a vivid and powerful presence in the popular imagination, a development visible in the proliferation and elaboration of the iconography of Satan, devils, Hell and its torments. Scenes like the mural of the Triumph of Death in the Campo Santo in Pisa contrast torment and the rewards of the blessed by showing demons torturing the damned in the confines of Hell; later the paintings and woodcuts of Bösch, Dürer, and Grünewald show angels and devils everywhere competing in wild combat for human souls, in which men are surrounded by fiends and monsters luring them to destruction. Accompanying this development is a growing apocalypticism, the belief that the world will soon end in a cosmic battle between the forces of good and evil, to be followed by the Last Judgement. Added fears attached to temptation and the influence of witches as a result. The Reformation popularized Hell and Satan, in popular preaching, in woodcuts in printed books, and so on. In Germany in particular there was a large literate population, particularly of

St Michael fighting the dragon

Source: W. Karth (ed.) (1963) *The Complete Woodcuts of Albrecht Dürer* (New York: Dover Publications), Plate 116.

urban citizens. Bibles, religious tracts and cheap woodcut picture books were printed in numbers that would be impressive even today – in hundreds of thousands. The discursive and visual basis of witch beliefs and fear of Satan were powerfully and immediately available in a way they had never been before. The new media promoted the new terrors.

Third, the religious struggles of the Reformation intensified heresy-hunting. Cohn argues in *Europe's Inner Demons* that the struggle of the Church hierarchy against the heterodox movements of reform, particularly the Waldensians, led to the equation of heresy and witchcraft. Both Protestants and Catholics, in their struggles with one another and with other forms of religious deviation, used the procedures the Church and the civil authorities had elaborated to deal with earlier heresies. What made the inquisitorial procedure capable of sustaining mass persecutions was the equation of heresy with allegiance to Satan and identifying the forms that allegiance took with traditional popular beliefs about night witches. Formal conformity in doctrine and practice ceased to be a defence against accusation, as eminently respectable clerics, nobles, and lawyers were denounced by tortured witches as secret agents of Satan. The adoption by the hierarchy of popular beliefs about witches flying to do evil and meet together, and the combination of those beliefs with the theological stereotype of organized worship of Satan as Anti-Christ thereby generated a means for producing mass denunciations and accusations. Accused witches could name people *because* they had seen them at sabbats, and the belief in the capacity of witches to fly at night undetected served to extend the conspiracy beyond local bounds and beyond accusations based on open acts of hostility.

Traditional popular beliefs on their own could not have produced the 'witch craze'. Definite antagonisms between neighbours could and did regularly lead to charges of *maleficium*, but they required acts of malice, sudden sickness or misfortune, for example, as a pretext. Further, accusations would be limited by the prevailing relations of antagonism, and could not be extended beyond narrow limits without destroying networks of neighbourliness and kinship. The victims of local accusations relating to specific acts of malice did indeed tend to be the old, single or widowed and poor women we identify as the typical victims of trials. In England witch trials largely depended on popular antagonisms, on local complaints filtering up through the legal machinery. Because the English courts did not use the inquisitorial procedure and its identification of heresy with witchcraft, judges and magistrates demanded proof of *maleficium*. Accusations flowed from popular discontents and fears centring on particular persons, and remained limited in scope by the particular and situational nature of those very fears until the Commonwealth and Matthew Hopkins' activities in Essex and East Anglia as a kind of bastard Inquisitor General.

On the Continent, matters were different:

'Left to themselves, peasants would never have created mass witch-hunts — these occured only where and when the authorities had become convinced of the reality of the sabbat and of nocturnal flights to the sabbat. And this conviction depended on, and in turn was sustained by, the inquisitorial type of procedure, including the use of torture. When suspected witches could be compelled, by torture, to name those whom they had seen at the sabbat, all things became possible: the mayor and town councillors and their wives were just as likely to be accused as were peasant women.'

(Cohn 1976: 252-53)

Witchcraft had become a matter of high ecclesiastical and civil politics. Protestants and Catholics fought in their respective territories to establish orthodoxy by means of a procedure which not only stemmed from a failure to recognize the possibility of legitimate religious differences (grouping all such differences together as 'heresy') but also from an identification of deviation with Satanism. Calvinists used the same stereotype of the witch-cult, and the same legal procedures, as the Catholics. The victims of inquisitorial process were turned into 'witches' wherever they stood and *whatever they stood for.* Protestant and Catholic domains were by no means internally homogeneous or stably differentiated. In Germany and France in particular the battle lines of faith and political conflict were complex and shifting. E.W. Monter (1976) points out that Calvin's Geneva was relatively 'lenient', with a high rate of acquittal. This is evidence of stable religious authority rather than any 'enlightenment' in Calvinist theology.

The Calvinists were no more minded to suffer a witch-heretic to live in Switzerland than the Inquisitors who scoured the French mountain valleys. Religious and political differences, persecution, and religio-political struggle cannot be separated. The Reformation began as the fusion of religious dissent with high politics, in the schism of the German princes. States were threatened by religious schisms, by the enemy within. They fought the various non-conformities with arms when they showed themselves in the field as did the Huguenots or the Czech Protestants, and with religious terror, a blunt and indiscriminate instrument whose main weapon was the witch trial. The Reformation, in intensifying religious schisms and immeasurably increasing the political issues at stake, intensified the scope of and the need for heresy-hunting. By then, for both sides in the battle, to hunt heretics was at one with hunting witches. The hunting of witches cannot be identified with a superstitious and popish Catholicism as against a rational and humane Protestanism, as a battle of opposing ideas.

The other intellectual movement which began at about the same time as the first stirrings of what was to become the Protestant Reformation, that 'revival' of the texts and knowledges of Greek and Roman antiquity we now call the Renaissance, in no way served as a basis from which to challenge witchcraft beliefs. This may seem strange when we reflect on the modern popular myths of the Renaissance as an awakening of rationality and the critical spirit. However, the ancient learning revived by this movement was saturated with spiritualistic and demonic beliefs, and one of the main 'arts' revived was the magical conjuring of spirits. If we begin with a conventional turning point in this process of recovery of learning in the mid-fifteenth century, we find that the particular sought-after knowledges of antiquity were invested with religious and political interests. The texts were brought into Italy from the libraries of orthodox monasteries as a consequence of two developments: one was the process of commercial and political penetration of the decaying Byzantine Empire by the Italian city states, and the other was the destruction of that empire by the Ottoman Turks, culminating in the capture of Constantinople in 1453. An important interest which motivated the recovery of the ancient knowledges was religious reform. Among the intellectuals who formed the staffs of the princes and republics there was strong support for a reform of the Church and also a movement for union with the Eastern church. Ancient wisdom, hidden in the Greek manuscripts, was thought to provide the foundation for such a reform. Another such interest was the struggle of the rulers of the Italian states for means of power and prestige. That Cosimo di Medici, the *de facto* ruler of Florence, actively sought after manuscripts, has much to do with his role of patron of the arts and learning. After all, such patronage paid off handsomely in the ideological struggle between leading families and between states. But there were straightforward considerations of political advantage at work in this search through Greek manuscripts.

In 1462 Cosimo ordered his client, intellectual Marsilio Ficino (who had been taught Greek by John Argyropolos, a native of Constantinople), to translate into Latin, as a first priority, and in precedence to Plato, a manuscript which contained what subsequently became known as the *Corpus Hermeticum*.[11] The only modern equivalent for such an interest on the part of a ruler would be the formula for the atomic bomb. What the *Corpus* promised, apart from the solace of wisdom to an old and dying man, was the knowledge and techniques necessary to command demons and manipulate through spirits and sympathies the phenomena and powers of the universe. The Renaissance began as a dream of the power locked in ancient knowledge on the part of the princes, and continued as a search for power, for means to manipulate nature, on the part of philosophers.

The search for the occult powers promised in late Antique learning occupied the major portion of the intellectual energies of Renaissance philosophers. In the fifteenth, sixteenth, and for most of the seventeenth centuries alchemy, astrology, and natural magic were accepted as central areas of study and as one of the main forms of contemporary rationality by the vast majority of the European scientific intelligentsia. Those who opposed astrology, magic, or the new Neo-Platonic philosophers of nature did so primarily on theological grounds — Calvinists objecting that they removed powers from the domain of God's will, and Catholic traditionalists defending the Thomist synthesis based on Aristotle.

The proponents of occult philosophy and natural magic did not always pretend to religious conformity, for example Pico della Mirandola and

Cornelius Agrippa both envisaged the ancient Egyptian wisdom of the *Corpus* as the basis for a new syncretism, a reform of Christianity through religious union. Even so, they were forced to denounce witchcraft and sorcery as *evil* magic. The conjuring of demons and other magical techniques smacked of witchcraft to all but a circle of intellectual initiates and powerful patrons. The noted Elizabethan polymath and exponent of occult philosophy, John Dee, was commonly thought of as a sorcerer but was probably saved by his connections at court. Less circumpect and well-connected exponents of natural magic fell foul of orthodoxy. Giordano Bruno was burnt for heresy (his status as a 'scientific martyr' in ortho-dox materialist Marxism is curious, given that his world-system was permeated by spirits and occult powers). Thomaso Campanella spent many years in prison.[12] Weyer (a devout Protestant) who argued for a relaxation of the witch persecutions was violently opposed to sorcery and natural magic, as was Bodin (a nominal Catholic), who favoured the utmost severity in the persecutions. The theology of the witch cult and the philosophy of natural magic were capable of generating a complex terrain of debate, in which they could be brought into harmony or opposition, but in neither case could the occult philosophy of the Renaissance serve as a basis for a criticism and displacement of beliefs in spirits, magic, and the capacity to conjure hidden powers.

Lucien Febvre (1973) considered the witch beliefs of the sixteenth and seventeenth centuries to be part of another mental universe from our own. This universe entails different forms of reasoning, grounds for belief and conduct which have quite different premises from ours, which posit quite distinct entities and which specify what are from our standpoint quite bizarre forms of practice. This universe would remain unintelligible to us to the degree that it was thought absurd, inferior, or irrational in terms of our own beliefs. In *Le problème de l'incroyance au 16e siècle* (1962) he argued that scepticism could only operate within the limits of the entities which could be legitimately affirmed or denied. Renaissance thought was weakly 'exclusionist', it permitted occult entities, remote relationships of correspondence and sympathy between phenomena and things, and it sought to synthesize authorities and phenomena.[13] It could not serve to produce those forms of 'demystification' the inhabitants of modern forms of mentality identify with rationality, experience, and common sense.[14] Febvre shows that the philosophies and intellectual practices of the Renaissance contradict those very forms of Western humanist rationalism which tend to trace their origin to them. This does not mean that Renaissance thought was inferior to our own, still 'medieval'. It used categories of experience, observation, and experiment but it did so within rather different premises and toward different objects. Its knowledges had concerns, spiritual and cultural, that ours do not. Its knowledges and sciences are not mere prototypes of modern thought, led astray by mistaken superstitions. To make such a judgement is to conceal a difference in concerns, a disvaluation of the religious and spiritual as central to science and intellectual culture.

Notes

1 *Malleus Maleficarum* — literally 'hammer or the *female* evil doers'. There can be no doubt that witches are female in the learned demonological literature (but not necessarily so in popular tradition). This has led to the view that the witch persecutions were a form of clerical misogyny. Jeffrey Russell, a leading historian of witchcraft beliefs, goes a long way to endorse this view in his recent popular history (1980: 113-18). Our whole analysis contradicts this view, see our discussion of Cohn's 'Speculative Postscript' in Chapter Thirteen. Anti-female stereotypes do abound in demonological treatises and the majority of victims were poor women, but the persecutions are inexplicable *merely* in those terms, not least because they involved large numbers of men as victims too.

Alan Macfarlane in *Witchcraft in Tudor and Stuart England* examined witchcraft beliefs, accusations and trials in Essex; in England neither the Continental legal procedures which permitted denunciation nor (generally) the learned stereotypes were operative. Women still greatly outnumber men in these accusations. He sensibly remarks, however, 'There is no evidence that hostility between the sexes lay behind the persecutions' (1971: 160). He argues that in England, where the legal procedure demanded some definite hurt to a victim, accusations reveal points of tension in social relationships between neighbours. Macfarlane says that women acted as witnesses 'as often as men against other women' (1971: 160). As we shall see below, Macfarlane contends that women predominated as the targets of accusations because of the positions they occupied in a changing village social structure.

Other systems of beliefs in witchcraft and the forensic practices associated with them give predominance to *men*, for example, those of the Azande discussed below. Those beliefs, and the whole topic of witchcraft, cannot be considered in terms of a misogynist crusade.

For a caricature view of the persecutions as an attack on women healers see B. Ehrenreich and D. English, *Witches, Midwives and Nurses* (1974). Where they offer anything more than an account of a jealous, male medical profession eliminating its (effective) female rivals it merely repeats Michelet's (1975) view of witch persecutions as the product of feudal oppressions and a life-denying Christianity. We discuss the limitations of this view in Chapter Fourteen. Unlike Szasz (1973) Ehrenreich and English argue that there *was* a definite real object in the persecutions, but like him they reduce the witch craze to a 'frame up', a cover for instrumental motives. The point we will make below is that while diverse social forms and 'interests' of various kinds are indeed at stake in the trials, these forces and interests do not explain them or witchcraft beliefs. The whole set of beliefs and practices cannot be 'accounted for' by being reduced to some particular group's interests or to easily comprehensible psychological motives. As we shall show, witchcraft beliefs are part of the complex of developments in European society and culture as a whole signalled by the labels of the Renaissance and the Reformation. It is the ensemble of beliefs and practices which enables us to understand the character and import of the 'craze'. We learn more from treating witchcraft beliefs, and the forensic practices aimed at eliminating them, *sui generis* than we do from starting with the assumption of their irrationality and, therefore, seeking to explain them in terms of an origin in categories of motives or interests *we* find more rational or compelling as grounds for action. To suppose that the persecutions reveal a conspiracy by greedy doctors and misogynist monks is a view little less fantastic than the beliefs of demonologists themeselves. As a conspiracy theory, it lacks the excuse and intellectual support the believers in the conspiracy of witches had, the dogma of Christian belief in the fall of Satan.

2   See Kamen (1976: 273) and Szasz (1973: 146).

3   See Zilboorg (1935: 148).

4   Cohn (1976: 225).

5   See Shumaker (1972: 65-7).

6   See J. Langbein, *Torture and the Law of Proof* (1977) for this point.

7   See also Shumaker (1972: 61).

8   Cohn (1976: 221-22).

9   As Cohn's *Europe's Inner Demons* (1976: 23, 160-63) points out, under the accusatory procedure the initiative in bringing charges lay with a private individual, whereas under the inquisitional procedure it lay with the authorities. The accusatory procedure was thus largely confined to trying complaints against specific acts of *maleficium* rather than serving as an instrument for a general heresy hunt. The procedure also involved definite perils for the accuser who was forced to conduct his own case and, should he fail to prove it, the judge could award a penalty equivalent to what the accused would have suffered. This penalty was called the *talion*. Under trial by ordeal the accuser could be challenged to a combat which would decide the issue of the trial.

10 In the following discussion of the Reformation we have relied extensively on Keith Thomas *Religion and the Decline of Magic* (1973), particularly for the movements preceding the Reformation and for the consequences for popular practices of Protestant beliefs. K.B. McFarlane gives a brilliant critical sketch of an important 'precursor' of the Reformation in *Wycliffe and English Non-Conformity* (1972). For general accounts of the Reformation which stress its social and cultural aspects, see A.G. Dickens *Reformation and Society in Sixteenth-Century Europe* (1966) and *The German Nation and Martin Luther* (1976); and for further discussion of the social basis of Luther's theology and the religious issues at stake, see J. Atkinson *Martin Luther and the Birth of Protestantism* (1968). R. Mandrou *From Humanism to Science 1480-1700* (1978) provides a general intellectual background which stresses religious controversies and which is slanted toward France.

11 The *Corpus* was considered to be the work of Hermes Tresmegistus — 'thrice great Hermes', savant, ruler, and God — who was supposed to have been an Egyptian ruler-sage identified with the God Thoth. The Renaissance, which privileged 'ancient' wisdom, considered this to be the most ancient of all and the most powerful. For the most accessible account of Hermeticism and Renaissance magic see Shumaker *The Occult Sciences in the Renaissance* (1972: Chs 3 and 5). For a more thorough account see F.A. Yates *Giordano Bruno and the Hermetic Tradition* (1979a) and D.P. Walker *Spiritual and Demonic Magic from Ficino to Camapanella* (1958).

12 For Bruno, see Yates (1979a) and for Campanella, see Walker (1958). As Yates has recently remarked:

'Surely it is significant that the *Démonomanie* of Jean Bodin, one of the writers most influential in fomenting the witch craze, opens with an attack on Pico and Agrippa for what Bodin held to be the wicked use of Cabala for magic. That the Renaissance occultism of Pico and his successors was directed towards religious reform laid it open to frantic propaganda against heresy, with which sorcery was so often associated in the minds of the orthodox. Under these pressures of alarmed public opinion, the Renaissance magus turned to ever greater secrecy, while his image turned into the Faust image. Giordano Bruno, who abandoned all caution and openly preached a religious reformation based on the magical religion of the Egyptians, as described in the terrible *Asclepius*, very naturally ended his career at the stake.'

(Yates 1979b: 38)

13 An excellent picture of this type of outlook is Alexander Koyré's (1971) essay on Paracelsus. Michel Foucault also typifies this form of thought in *The Order of Things* (1970 Ch. 2).

14 Febvre's notion of 'mentalities' clearly owed a great deal to Lévy-Bruhl. The dangers and weaknesses of Lévy-Bruhl's views have been constantly emphasized by commentators, but at the expense of converting 'primitives' into Westerners who have not yet got things right. Febvre is right to stress Lévy-Bruhl's strong point, the otherness of forms of thought and the fallacy of supposing a basic 'human' set of perceptions, significances, and motives. Febvre's position is also relatively free of that old (and actually far more common than is supposed) fallacy in the history of ideas, the positing of a *Zeitgeist* − a single and coherent 'outlook' corresponding to a period. Febvre's work makes clear that the Renaissance was riven with conflicts and fundamental theoretical differences. Neo-platonism and its spiritual analogues did not rule unchallenged. But what they were challenged by − established scholastic philosophy and later, in the sixteenth century, a new non-Thomist Aristotelianism which stressed 'experience' − could not remove the fundamental Christian theses or the authority of the Bible which gave the belief in witches such powerful support.

13
WITCHCRAFT AS
PERSECUTION MANIA

Zilboorg (1935) regards the 'witch' persecutions as a category mistake on the part of 'reasonable men' who mistook the phenomena of mental illness for possession by or conspiracy with Satan. Others regard the persecutors rather than the victims as pathological. Thomas Szasz, in *The Manufacture of Madness* (1973) regards the witch craze as the stigmatization and persecution of innocent victims by an organized apparatus of repression.[1] Szasz, as we have seen, denies the validity of the category of 'mental illness', arguing instead that there can be no limits to conduct other than *legal* ones, and that those limits should be based on real acts of harm to others. For Szasz the categories of 'mental illness' and 'witchcraft' serve identical functions: they create a generalized licence for intervention in and restriction of the conduct of others. These categories legitimate and sustain the working of institutions of exclusion, the Inquisition and the pyres, psychiatrists, mental health experts, and the insane asylum. Paradoxically, he also views Inquisitors and psychiatrists as the agents of a pathological will-to-power (a paradox given his denial of the legitimacy of the category of 'mental pathology' or 'sick conduct).

Szasz'z view of the 'innocence' of the victims is not an idiosyncratic or cranky one. Cohn in *Europe's Inner Demons* (1976) regards the persecutions as a symptom of 'the urge to purify the world through the annihilation of some category of human beings imagined as agents of corruption and incarnations of evil' (1976: xiv). 'Witches' suffered from the consequences of the very same urge as did the Jews in the camps. Cohn regards the persecutions, like the chiliastic phantasies of the poor and excluded,[2] as manifestations of 'collective psychopathology'. Cohn separates the two main explanatory themes in Michelet's *Satanism and Witchcraft*: that sorcery is the response of the poor to times of despair, and that the ideas surrounding witchcraft, of possession by Satan and the carnal indulgences of the sabbat are the products of sexual repression and self-denial. Popular beliefs and practices did not change markedly in the fifteenth century. What did change was official attitudes and practices. For Cohn the persecutions cannot be explained by any real increase in sorcery. In a 'Speculative Postscript' Cohn elaborates in terms of psychoanalysis the other theme Michelet treated with such sympathy and imaginative reconstruction. Christianity stresses the conscious control of instinct and sexual appetite in the service of spiritual fulfilment and purification. Satan and the sabbat are the forms in which repressed sexuality emerges, collective myths in which unconscious resentment is expressed in fantastic and destructive forms. The tension between conscious beliefs and unconscious desires,

> 'operating in a whole stratum of society ... end by conjuring up an imaginary outgroup as a symbol of apostasy and of licentiousness — which is practically what witches became in many parts of Europe. In that case the tens of thousands of victims who perished would not be primarily victims of village tensions but victims of an unconscious revolt against a religion which, consciously, was still accepted without question.'

> (Cohn 1976: 262)

We must stress again that we are very far from being opposed to the use of psychoanalytic concepts and explanations. But Cohn's explanation is not without its problems. Firstly, it reads like a pastiche of Freud's *Civilization and its Discontents*, until we remember the very generality of the thesis in the latter work. The return of the repressed in destructive and negative forms has no specific connection with witchcraft or Christianity. It is the paradox of *civilization* itself. Indeed, the kind of civilized, non-violent, and liberal world Cohn would (sensibly) prefer would pose just as severe problems of repression by denying an outlet for aggressive instincts and phantasies. The unconscious for Freud does not merely consist in 'normal' sexual wishes which, if gratified, will go away and cease to trouble us. Aggressive and perverse sexual phantasies are a pervasive element in psychic life and are not merely a symptom of personal or cultural pathology. Freud's concept of the Death Instinct postulates a desire which goes beyond satisfaction, and to which 'normal' sexual satisfaction offers no antidote: a will to non-existence. Psychoanalysis has a 'surplus' philosophical and conceptual content which threatens the specificity of its application to explain particular instances of social or cultural 'pathology'. Freud's very concept of culture is of a world of intellect, morals, and conduct perpetually threatened by the conditions of its own making.

Secondly, the dangers of employing psychoanalysis on historical documents and literary texts *as if a subject were being analysed* are all too real. The discourse is treated as a presentation of the psyche of its author. The notion of 'presence' underlying this type of critical practice leaves the text-subject very much at the mercy of the interpreter. The interpreter is here in a very different situation from the analyst. In analysis the analyst's own interpretations are limited and controlled by the responses and repetitions of the analysand, by the relationship of transference, by the working through and representation of the pathological material. The 'results' of analysis are often provisional in the extreme. They certainly do not amount to the analyst imparting to the subject a knowledge of who or what he or she 'is'. The analytical 'cure' involves reformulation and displacement of the pathological material in *the relation-ship with the analyst* ('transference'). In interpretation, however, where the dynamics of the relationship of transference and the process of working through are absent, the only controls on the interpretation are plausibility and the presence of certain features in the text. Those features are taken as expressions of the psychic state of the author. Writing be-comes 'expression' rather than an activity governed by conventions as to genre, material and topics, stylistics, etc. The discourse is displaced as the product of a particular supra-subjective mechanism of writing and its thematics are equated with the characteristics of its author as a subject. Writing becomes a creative form of expression of the 'self' in the Romantic sense. Analysis becomes a kind of characterology, in which themes or tropes are the univocal signs of certain personal attributes.

Freud himself is especially guilty of treating discursive materials as 'documents' in which a subject is psychically present. *Leonardo* is an outrageous example of this practice. It is an interpretation even the author knows to be wild and speculative. A better example for our purposes is Freud's analysis of the seventeenth-century German painter Christoph Haizmann's encounter with the Devil, 'A Seventeenth Century Demon-ological Neurosis'.[3] Freud simply regards Haizmann's memoir and paint-ings as 'symptoms' of pathology. Haizmann evidently did suffer from some form of breakdown, but we cannot treat every reported experience of Satan, or of God for that matter, as evidence of neurosis or psychosis of its author. Haizmann's Devil[4] is no more 'pathological' *as an image* than any of Dürer's or Grünewald's satanic and monstrous figures. No-body seriously presents Dürer as a psychotic or disabled by neurosis, although Wittkower and Wittkower (1969) suggest[5] he suffered from melancholy. Of Grünewald we know too little to speculate.

In Cohn's case he does not even have a particular 'text' to read in which the psyche of its author-subject can be conceived to be present. Rather, if his avowedly speculative explanation is taken seriously, a mass of discourses, reports of practices, and images are underlain by a single and comprehensive unconscious phantasy. It can be argued that Renaissance discourses on witchcraft do have a thematic and conceptual unity. We have argued that they are concerned with a certain range of problems which they formulate by means of certain categories; both the categories and the problems can be legitimately demonstrated by textual analysis. But this is not equivalent to nor does it imply either a *psychic* unity or that these discourses are the product of similar subjective dynamics. It is easy, from the pages of the *Malleus*, to portray Sprenger and Kramer as frustrated monkish mysogynists. It is less easy to so place Johann Weyer who, by the words written, is just as committed to the category of Satan and the power of his action on his victims, or Reginald Scot, whose opinion of the deluded old woman he thinks falsely persecuted is scarcely better or more flattering.

It is naive to suppose that a comprehensive religious system like Christianity has a singularity of doctrine and practice which consistently leads to the denial of sexual gratification. Stern Calvinists and pious afficionados of Saint Teresa alike feared witches and Satan. The cult of the Virgin and the monastic practice of mystical union with God offer their particular sublimations or fetishes. Sexual expression and gratification can, as we have contended, take complex forms and lead in those forms to stable economies of repression. It is also naive to suppose that 'a whole stratum of society' — clerics, lawyers, and notables — alike experienced the same frustrations of 'normal' genital sexual activity. Instances of either free open sexual indulgence of an entirely different, but no more repressed, climate of sensibility from our own could just as easily be found in the documents and art left to us from the period between the fifteenth and late seventeenth centuries. With respect to art, the relation between the prevailing iconographical code and any 'explanations' we might wish to add in order to explain the components and conventions of the code, is problematic since there can be no direct reading of psychological states. What can be done is to consider the types of image considered appropriate to the qualities and attributes in the prevailing code. For example, Grünewald's Saint Lucy or Bernini's Saint Teresa hardly demonstrate a suppression of sensuality. What *we* would read as sexuality or sexual ecstasy is used as the very image of perfect faith or sublime religious experience. It is interesting to add that the worldly also read such images in our way at the time. Charles de Brosses wrote of Bernini's statue, 'If this is divine love, I know it well' (cited in Wittkower and Wittkower 1969: 180). To turn from images to practices, the army that marched under the Duke of Alva to crush the revolt of the Netherlands in the interests of Spanish rule and Catholic orthodoxy was accompanied by its own organized battalion of prostitutes as well as by its other and equally normal auxiliary complement of confessors and monks. The sensuality of women was alternately reviled and applauded in different contexts. Sexual pleasure was denied and also publicly celebrated in the bawdy of the carnivals and feasts of fools. [6] Equally the witch persecutions were not confined to stern Calvinists or fanatical monks. If 'men of the world' like Montaigne scoffed at witchcraft, other worldly men like Bodin believed in it.

Neither 'collective psychopathology' nor a pathological will-to-power explain the prevalence of beliefs in witchcraft and the legal search for witches. If many of those tried and burnt were not guilty of witchcraft as charged, neither were they 'innocent', innocent, that is, in the sense of being random, unmotivated, victims. 'Witchcraft', or rather practices which could be identified with the official categories of forensic demonology, had a definite social existence. Among the powerful and learned we have noted a search for the magical manipulation of the world through the conjuring of spirits: philosophers *did* try to conjure demons. Among the popular classes 'wise women' and 'cunning men' were a regular recourse for medicine, counter-magic, divination, the discovery of stolen goods, etc. The *uniformity* of the categories and institutions of the 'witch hunt' does not mean that the whole affair was a colossal 'frame-up', Stalin's purges and the persecution of the Jews notwithstanding. The victims of witch hunts were given the same uniform status as agents of Satan, a status applied to many different circumstances, but they were by no means all 'innocent'. 'Innocent' victims would presuppose a *pure* persecution. Behind the uniformity of categories and procedures, cultural, legal, and political battles were taking place in which the victims, if not guilty as charged, were not the 'innocent' but the 'motivated' victims of repression. Many people did fall by happenstance into the net, but others were demonized for very definite reasons. Szasz, in his conception of a pure persecution, ignores the social struggles at stake and fails in consequence to do the losers the honour of taking them seriously.

Let us begin by clearing the ground and considering a once-popular interpretation which attracted a good deal of hostile criticism from modern scholars (notably Cohn, Trevor-Roper and Thomas). Margaret Murray's *The Witch-Cult in Western Europe* was first published in 1921.[7] A folklorist, she applied the insights and methods of 'modern' anthropology — principally Sir James Frazer's *The Golden Bough* — to the analysis of witch-beliefs. Murray attempts to read beyond the 'demonization' of the persecutions to the beliefs and practices of the victims. She uses folklore and literature to supplement and assist in the interpretation of the records of the trials and her book abounds in strange correspondences and interesting insights. Her thesis is that there really were 'witches', that witchcraft was the form taken in the Christian era by the old folk religions of Europe. Driven underground by the Church, the fertility religion and its gods defined themselves in opposition to Christianity and accepted the Christian equation of their traditional worship with diabolism. Sabbats were real, if secret, meetings at which members feasted and plotted evil against their opponents, and the 'devil' was the leader of the cult dressed up in ritual garb.

Murray culls elements from European folklore to make a society of witches appear possible but she then *presumes* the existence of an organized degenerate folk religion as the basis of her explanation. Many popular beliefs and practices continue to this day in many parts of Europe, but there is no reason to suppose that they ever formed part of a single organized cult. The most powerful argument against Murray is that if the cult existed as a real threat to Christianity throughout the Middle Ages, why did the mass witch persecutions not take place at that time rather than beginning in the fifteenth century? Popular beliefs about witches and practices of magic were an important source of vital components of the demonological stereotype (particularly flying) but they do not imply a European-wide organized cult.[8]

The forces and issues underlying the persecutions are diverse. They were no simple inversion of the demonological stereotype. It is the predominant method of modern anthropology in the analysis of witchcraft

The devil seducing a woman.

Witches transfigured into animals.

A witches' feast.

Witches making hailstorms and thunder.

Source: Ulricus Molitor (c. 1488-93) *De lamiis et phitonicis mulieribus* (Strasburg: J. Prüss), cited in Shumaker 1972.

beliefs and practices to consider witchcraft accusations and confessions as 'motivated', as stemming from definite tensions in social relationships.[9] Alan Macfarlane (1971) has applied this 'anthropological' method to the records of trials for witchcraft in sixteenth- and seventeenth-century Essex. Witchcraft is seen as the product of definite tensions between neighbours. Like Keith Thomas in *Religion and the Decline of Magic* (1973), he explains the level of accusations and trials as a product of the religious and social changes wrought by the Reformation. We have already seen that after the reform the common people were more 'exposed' to evil. Not only were charms and spiritual defences taken away from them but misfortune and sickness were ascribed to God's will and to fault in the victim. At the same time in England the apparatus of Catholic charity and alms-giving was dismantled. After 1600 relief of the poor was institutionalized in the Poor Law regulations for parish relief. Charity was replaced by state action and taxation. Relationships and obligations of mutual help and neighbourly assistance were thereby severed.

From these religious and social changes Macfarlane and Thomas derive a 'typical' situation of accusation. Need and poverty were regulated by the Poor Law but not eliminated. The poor and the old, particularly women and widows, still found the need to beg and seek assistance. Their wealthier and better-placed neighbours might well refuse them, particularly if the poor persons in question were persistent in their demands, quarrelsome, or unprepossessing. Indeed, old and marginal women might well beg through threats (as certain 'gypsies' still do today), and refusal could result in an altercation and a threat on the part of those refused. Macfarlane argues that the refusal might well provoke feelings of guilt on the part of the refuser, a guilt which derived from a violation of the old Catholic ideals of charity so recently discarded. This guilt surfaced in a displaced form, in an attribution of a malicious and evil intent to the person refused charity. In a situation of sudden and inexplicable illness or misfortune the victim or their kin would seek a reason or explanation. As among many African peoples they would examine their social relationships, seeking sources of this misfortune in a malicious human agency. Guilt and tension would point to the refusal and the threat which followed it. An accusation might well follow.

Thomas documents a mass of magical practices, both innocent and maleficent, concerned with healing, the welfare of animals and fertility, sexual attraction, and so on. 'Cunning folk' were to be found within easy reach of most villages. Specialist astrologers or diviners would be consulted about future actions or the recovery of stolen goods. The possibility of malice through magical or spiritual means was remote neither from people's experience nor the practices they themselves engaged in. Accusations based on fear of *maleficium* on the part of ordinary people stemmed primarily from these traditional beliefs and practices, but what enabled the English authorities from the mid-sixteenth century onwards to take witchcraft accusations more seriously, and to punish witchcraft with execution, was the importation of the Continental demonological stereotype with its associations of heresy and Satanism.[10] This importation resulted from the struggle between Catholics and Protestants in England. Popular beliefs and the charges which flowed from them came to be given greater credence by the educated and ruling classes. The accusations did indeed have a specific 'motivation', but one very different from those attributed in the categories of forensic demonology.

Despite the improbability of Murray's thesis of a generalized witch cult, there are other social sources of 'motivation' of witchcraft accusations and convictions than the tensions between neighbours outlined above. It is possible that some movements of popular resistance to established religious and political authority took the form of secret societies. Such secretly organized resistance, whatever its ideology, would be equated by the authorities with heresy and such conspiracy with witchcraft. Emmanuel Le Roy Ladurie in *The Peasants of Languedoc* (1974)[11] argues that witchcraft in the mountains of southern France was a form of popular resistance, taking its ideology from the inversion of Christian rituals. Norman Cohn discounts this.[12] Arguing against Murray he says, 'Stories which have manifestly impossible features are not to be trusted in any particular, as evidence of what physically happened' (1976: 115). Perhaps not, but then we are faced with the problem that all first-hand accounts of witchcraft practices will almost inevitably include some features we find 'impossible'. Anthropologists could hardly collect and work by means of 'texts' from native informants if they abided by Cohn's rule. And if we accept it we can hardly credit a report of the behaviour of the priest, Jean Souhardibels, cited by Ladurie: 'At this Mass, Souhardibels performed the elevation with a black Host, while raised off the ground, his feet up and his head inverted facing the Devil' (1974: 208). Ladurie uses such reports to demonstrate the *symbolism* of inversion and its connection with popular revolt. It is evidence of a discourse characteristic of challenge to authority. Whether Souhardibels did or did not levitate upside down is a question we cannot answer, but in and of itself the inclusion of an account of levitation by no means invalidates a testimony of revolt in the symbols of Anti-Christ. Cohn's rule would obliterate almost all study of *Christianity* if taken seriously. Saint Teresa was reported to have levitated. This does not lead us to doubt that she existed or that she went to mass.

In cases of underground and repressed resistance the documentation available to us will almost always be scanty and will frequently violate Cohn's rule.[13] Ladurie uses the reports of Satanism in company with other reports of resistance in the forms of inversion. A notable example is his account of the carnival at Romans in 1580. This bizarre incident was part of a struggle of the popular party, composed of peasants and citizens, directed toward the radical if vague objective of overthrowing the established order. Popular revolutionary Protestant and Anabaptist ideas played a considerable part in this agitation. Carnivals and festivals were

frequent events and an officially tolerated inversion of established
authority and morality, a period of licence under the reign of Folly.[14] The
carnival of 1580, however, transcended the festival atmosphere and
became a struggle between nobles and poor on the plane of symbols. The
popular party turned the carnival into a dance of death, in which they
menaced the rich with suggestions of cannibalism and the appropriation
of their wealth, wives, and daughters.

> 'This popular ballet expresses better than words the latent motivations
> of the rebels. Certain dancers with Swiss drums and bells on their feet
> brandished naked swords; others flourished rakes, brooms, threshing
> flails and death shrouds .... And so these flail bearers cried at the top
> of their voices that "before three days are out Christian flesh will be
> selling at six *deniers* the pound".'
>
> (Ladurie 1974: 194)

The rich and nobles interpreted this symbolism for us: the symbolic
struggle was settled by a bloody massacre in which Jean Serve, the popular
leader, was murdered and his followers hunted down in three days of
bloodletting within the barred walls of the town.[15]

It is possible that secret societies using sorcery and other symbolic
and actual means of terror existed in Renaissance Europe. Secret societies
for the practice of witchcraft and magic are a commonplace in the anthropological literature. It is also well-known that they are difficult to study.
A good example is the *Mani* association among the Zande which Evans-
Pritchard joined but about which he was unable to obtain more than
superficial information. Such societies have often been a means of resistance to established colonial authority. Secret societies practising magic
and claiming to take the form of animals to seek out and mutilate their
victims are regularly reported from various parts of Africa into modern
times. An example would be the 'Human Leopards' of Sierra Leone,
eliminated by the British Colonial government at the turn of the century.
Other cases have been reported since.[16] An analogy with activities of these
kinds would make sense of some of the witch trials in which the accused
do seem to have been associated and not merely dragged into court.

But one has to be cautious. Lycanthropy, or werewolfism, the nearest
analogue in Europe to the 'Leopard Men' or the witch beliefs among
the Shona mentioned earlier, seems to have remained a peasant belief
confined to backward rural areas like the Jura. This is despite the fact
that witches could take on the appearance of animals in both intellectual
demonology and popular tradition. Witches and werewolves never completely fused. Lycanthropy could be regarded as a crime distinct from
witchcraft and werewolves were tried as such. Thus a Gilles Garnier was
executed in 1574 at Dôle for allegedly eating a young girl. Even so courts
and clerics were less likely to take peasant fears about werewolves
seriously. Although intellectual demonologists adopted popular beliefs
about night witches they were in general sceptical of the reality of were-

wolves. The authors of *Malleus Maleficarum* ignore the question, for example. Renaissance Europe and modern Africa cannot automatically be equated. Witchcraft beliefs and practices vary considerably *between* different African tribal societies. To transpose patterns of belief and practice from one institutional and cultural context to another threatens to turn witchcraft and sorcery into a kind of anthropological constant. Although *methods* of analysis developed by anthropologists have proved valuable in the analysis of European witchcraft accusations, as the work of Macfarlane (1971) shows, it by no means follows that substantive propositions about witchcraft in other cultures can be applied too.

A final source of 'motivation' for the prosecutions lies in the legal institutions themselves. The trials are partly the product of conflicts of interest between the different ecclesiastical and legal authorities. In Catholic countries (notably France) ecclesiastical and civil jurisdictions were locked in battle. The crime of witchcraft and the inquisitorial procedure provided the ecclesiastical authorities with a powerful means of general intervention in social and political affairs. Vice versa, the *Parlements* and other courts began to bring witchcraft charges. Authorities jostled to establish their competence and primacy. Trials were thus motivated by bureaucratic politics. Divisions *within the church*, rivalries between the various monastic orders and between them and the regular priests, led to accusations and trials. Michelet (1975) gives an extended account of how such conflicts and jealousies played an important part in certain of the notorious French trials concerning nuns and their confessors.

A simpler and more mercenary motivation might be noticed at work in the law.[17] Under certain of the Continental procedures the convicted witch's property was forfeited to the court or its prosecuting officials. Although most of those accused as witches were poor, the legal apparatus apparently had a good deal to gain from the trials, for notables and merchants were also accused and convicted. The wealthy and well-to do could also be made to pay bribes to drop or modify the charges.

It would be absurd to reduce the persecutions to a venal motive or even to argue that it was an important one. What is interesting is that it was not thought improper for the Inquisition or secular officials to benefit in this way. We should remember that state offices were commonly sold as a short-term source of revenue, and that in the unreformed Church, money-making was not automatically considered alien to a religious vocation. Lucien Febvre's paper 'Excommunication for Debt in Franche-Comté' (1973) throws an interesting light on such attitudes. Ecclesiastical courts used the denial of communicant status, with all that implies in religious terms, as the sanction in a procedure for recovery of debts. These suits were brought by private individuals who used the courts like ordinary civil ones to enforce their rights, and excommunication was just like a writ or an injunction today. The apparent incongruity stems from *our* conceptions of the role of religious institutions and what is proper for them to do. For most of us churches are specialized institutions concerned with the worship and ethics of their own members, with matters pertaining to religious belief in a narrow sense. The medieval Church was a pervasive institution rather than a specialized one because religious belief and practice were far more important in people's conduct. As an institution it sought to organize and make claims on 'secular' activity, challenging the conduct of individuals and states. To be excommunicated was to be placed outside the receipt of the sacraments, but also outside a place where business was done, where the priest made commercial announcements and where contacts could be met after services. Hence the mundane side of a 'sacred' institution did not appear incongruous or unnecessary. Luther and Calvin challenged the 'corruption' of the church but not its claims to intervene in secular life. Indeed, the more extreme Calvinists and Puritans sought to fuse the community of the faithful and political society, to abolish the state as such and absorb its functions in a religious community. It would not have seemed odd or important that law officers or the religious community might make money out of sending people to the stake.

Notes

1   Szasz scathingly attacks Zilboorg in this book.
2   These 'phantasies' are documented by Cohn in *The Pursuit of the Millenium* (1957).
3   Freud (*SE* XIX: 69-105).
4   Freud (*SE* XIX: 69).
5   Wittkower and Wittkower (1969: 104).
6   See above Chapter Nine Note 2.
7   See Cohn (1976: 6), Thomas (1973: 614-17, 627) and Trevor-Roper (1978: 41n).
8   These points are ably made by Cohn in *Europe's Inner Demons* (1976: Ch. 6).
9   See, for example, M. Douglas (1970b), also Marwick (1970), and Middleton (1967).
10 Thomas (1973: Ch. 14).
11 Le Roy Ladurie (1974: Part Two Chapter Five).
12 Cohn (1976: 107).
13 It is only fair to point out that Cohn has extensively studied such struggles and the forms of inversion of the social order they seek to bring about.
14 See above Chapter Nine Note 2.
15 Ladurie has now produced a full study of these events: *Carnival* (1979).
16 See Webster *Primitive Secret Societies* (1968: 127n4). Such activities are also the subject of colonialist *canards*, witness the Mau Mau hysteria. On lycanthropy see the entry in the Encyclopedia Britannica 1911 edition; see also Monter (1976: 145-51): he points out that Calvinist demonologists denied the reality of werewolves — claiming that they were illusions created by the Devil.
17 Russell (1980: 83) argues that confiscation of goods was not an important motive. We agree, but the *attitude* toward the appropriation of goods is an interesting phenomenon in itself. See Midelfort (1972) for a discussion of the subject of confiscation in southwest Germany.

14
THE DECLINE OF
WITCHCRAFT PROSECUTIONS

Witch prosecutions declined dramatically in Western Europe after the middle of the seventeenth century. Outbreaks of witch-hunting occurred later on particularly, for example, on the Protestant periphery in Mecklenburg after 1690 and in America, in New England, in 1692.[1] Laws against witchcraft and sorcery remained on the statute books in many countries well into the eighteenth century: in England the Witchcraft Act was repealed in 1736, in France the last execution for witchcraft was in 1745, and in Poland in 1793. Witch beliefs and magical practices continued unabated among the masses, lynchings of witches continued into the nineteenth century. So when we talk of a decline of witchcraft beliefs, we mean a withdrawal of support on the part of the educated classes for the demonological stereotype and a refusal on the part of the ruling powers to take notice of popular charges of *maleficium*. The inquisitorial procedure ceased to be used to examine witches. We return to something like the *status quo ante* of late medieval practice.

How are we to explain this rapid decline? Modern historians commonly attribute it to something like a 'mental revolution' of the kind Febvre (1973) referred to. Henry Kamen gives an excellent thumb-nail sketch of this revolution:

> 'In the 1540s we are in the world of Copernicus and Paracelsus; the one a hesitant, tradition bound, secretive ecclesiastic whose "revolutionary" Heliocentric theory was little more than a re-discovery of the ancients; the other a fantastical medical practitioner with unorthodox cures and a profound belief in "natural philosophy" and magic. By 1660, with the foundation of the Royal Society of London we are in the empirical, experimental world of Boyle and Newton, a world in which God was an external maintenance engineer rather than an immanent spirit.'
>
> (Kamen 1976: 474)

It is true that the new physics and astronomy enjoyed wide diffusion, and this is partly because they impinged on practices of great importance to men of affairs, navigation, gunnery, and astrology. Scientific discoveries were undoubtedly better appreciated by a significant proportion of the educated and middle classes than they are today, when the very proliferation of knowledges and the forms of mathematization exclude not only laymen but scientists of other specialisms.[2] Many astrologers supported the new astronomy in the hope that it would make their calculations more effective and they diffused knowledge about the new world systems in their almanacs.[3] But even if we accept this view of the new science separating itself from medieval and Renaissance confusion and magical beliefs, we face a problem. To the degree that this knowledge was purely 'empirical' and inscribed in a mathematical calculation of the movement of bodies and the measurement of forces, its impact upon theological and metaphysical world views would have been indeterminate and capable of marginalization. As a realm of specific technical operations and measurements it could have no impact on the central issues of witch belief. Its propositions could be accepted as a set of 'hypotheses' necessary to certain operations, which reserved ultimate explanations about the world to religious knowledge through revelation, faith, and reason. This division between 'hypothesis' which accounted for 'appearances' and the truth of religion was a sophisticated epistemology supported by the Papal intelligentsia which allowed the scientists the freedom to research while it kept them in a theological ghetto. Had Galileo accepted this epistemological doctrine, he would have remained untroubled and unhumiliated.[4]

The point is that the new science could not be a realm of pure empiricity and technique. It required metaphysical foundations in order to create certain domains of investigation and to justify certain methods.[5] Those metaphysical foundations did not arise from 'experience' and 'experiment'. We should be careful in crediting the Royal Society or the notion of an 'advancement of learning' with a conception of scientificity which *can* be opposed to the magic of Paracelsus. Bacon's conception of a new organization of knowledge for the benefit of humanity remained saturated with Renaissance occultism: knowledge was to be restored to its state before the Fall and one of the sciences to be reformed was astrology. The Royal Society included as active members not only Boyle but men like John Aubrey, the antiquary, and Elias Ashmole — both strong supporters of astrology.[6] Indeed, the 'mechanical philosophy' championed by Boyle never became wholly acceptable because of its threat to religious faith. Newton rejected it despite being a part of Boyle's intellectual milieu. Conversely the language of empiricist declamation was also used by Paracelsians in the service of alchemy and iatro-chemistry:

'that youth may not be idly trained up in notions, speculative and verbal disputes, but may learn to inure their hands to labour, and put their fingers to the furnaces, that the mysteries discovered by Pyrotechny, and the wonders brought to light by Chymistry, may be rendered unto them: that they may not grow proud with the brood of their own brains, but truly taught by manual operation, and experiment . . .'

(cited in Rattansi 1963: 27)[7]

'Empiricism' was always utilized in the service of definite theories. Far from being a pure neutral observation of phenomena it promised to reveal nature's *hidden secrets*. Hermeticist and Cabbalistic conceptions of knowledge presented themselves as practical reason, as promising a realm of truth to be uncovered by the senses. In the field of discourse of the mid-seventeenth century 'empiricism' had no single critical value, it was dispersed across a field of theories postulating quite different entities to be revealed by 'experience'.

Moreover, the rejection of 'authority', apparently so important to the new rationality, was hardly complete and consistent. Alchemists and astrologers were often the ones who strongly supported the rejection of the heritage of accumulated opinion and the authorities of Antiquity. Bacon and others believed knowledge had declined since the Fall of Adam and needed to be completely restored, an opposition to the book-learning of Antiquity but one entirely governed by a higher authority, the Bible, and its revelation of a higher state of enlightenment before the Fall. Newton, on the other hand, sought the support of the authorities of Antiquity for his theory of gravity. He believed God had vouchsafed to the Ancients a knowledge of the action of gravity as a universal cosmic force, that this knowledge had become obscured and was handed on from Egypt to the Greeks and retained in a partial form.[8] Newton regarded this search through Antique astronomical writings not as an optional extra, to convince traditionalists, but as a *proof* of the propositions of the *Principia*.

Newton, inductivist and empiricist that he was, conceived mathematical natural philosophy as possible only on the basis of a general ontological doctrine which explained *how* observation and calculation could penetrate beyond appearances to the essence of things. Galileo had defended mathematical analysis in terms of the doctrine of the 'Book of Nature' (a doctrine he shared with the Hermeticists and Paracelsians). Nature was rational and intelligible, it is to be conceived as a 'book' whose secrets and truths are 'written in mathematical characters'. Mathematical measurement is thus no mere technique, a means of accounting for appearances, rather it is appropriate to, part of, nature itself.[9] The discoveries of science are not 'hypotheses' but truths, knowledge of reality itself. Newton's epistemological doctrine has definite similarities: induction is a possible method because God's universe is a rational whole governed by God's constant action, so that the connections between observed phenomena are therefore not random but necessary and certain and they can be calculated because God is consistent. God is 'omnipresent, not *virtually* but *substantially*; for virtue cannot exist without substance. In Him are all things contained and moved' (cited in McGuire and Rattansi 1966: 122). Movement, gravitational force, is God's action: gravity is not merely the relative action of particular bodies but a universal all-pervasive force. Natural philosophy and theology stand together and support each other.

The metaphysics of the new science was not confined to doctrines of method. It postulated an *infinite* universe. It replaced the previous finite cosmos, a world in which the spheres composing the heavens centred on the earth or the solar system. Both the old and the new universes were a plenitude of completed being, a whole complete in itself and governed by stable laws.[10] This infinite universe was fully consistent with religious beliefs, and fully compatible with an omnipotent God for it denied that there were any *limits* to his creation. What it did challenge were the doctrines of the interconnection and harmony of the microcosm and the macrocosm, the world of man and the heavens, on which astrology and Renaissance magic had been based. But it did not necessarily convert God into a 'maintenance engineer'. Newton would have recoiled before the very idea, and for his rival, Leibniz, the very excellence of the design meant that maintenance was unnecessary. These metaphysical doctrines transcended any means of proof the new sciences could offer, indeed they were the grounds for accepting those proofs' claims to establish validity. Physical science did not challenge religion, it offered it support but also reform. Where the scepticism of Montaigne could not challenge the religious basis of witch beliefs, the earnest religious beliefs and metaphysics of men like Newton did so, because they offered an effective substitute belief which displaced *Satan*. Trevor-Roper puts the point very well:

> 'No mere scepticism, no mere "rationalism", could have driven out the old cosmology. A rival faith was needed ... the final victory which liberated Nature from the biblical fundamentalism ... was that of the English deists and the German Pietists, the heirs of the Protestant heretics of the seventeenth century, the parents of that eighteenth-century Enlightenment in which the duel in nature between a Hebrew God and a medieval Devil was replaced by the benevolent despotism of a modern scientific "Deity".'
>
> (Trevor-Roper 1978: 110-11)

An 'infinite spirit' which 'pervades all space *into infinity* and contains and vivifies the entire world' squeezes out all lesser spirits (Newton, cited by McGuire and Rattansi 1966: 120). It excludes the individual purposive spirits or daemons of natural magic and it renders the possibility of the Devil's action problematic on pain of Manicheism. But this God, however much the scientists may be his champions, is neither the creation nor the special preserve of the new astronomy. Indeed, Newton could entertain Him only to the extent that He had already become *theologically possible*. The new universe is no special preserve of mathematical natural science. To the degree that it is not, it can be acceptable to laymen and, to the degree that the new sciences are founded upon these theological beliefs, they can be acceptable to and a support to lay belief. The 'mental revolution' Febvre referred to is no displacement of metaphysics by 'experience' and 'experiment' — it is a *revolution in metaphysics*.

Still that revolution was hardly complete or accepted among the intelligentsia at the time when the witch-hunts stimulated by authority came to a stop. Many of the books of the new sciences joined the books of the sceptics like Weyer and Scot on the *Index Librorum Prohibitorum* in Catholic countries. Puritans were no less hostile to seeing the God whose will governed every personal circumstance displaced by a constant and rational Divine Artificer. 'Toleration' alone, and as a religious attitude rather than a calculating and reversible state policy, cannot explain the decline in witchcraft persecution. In 1672 Louis XIV's minister, Colbert, abolished the charge of *sorcellerie sabbatique*[11] but in 1685, as part of a process of repression, the regime revoked the Edict of Nantes, and the Huguenots were persecuted and forced to flee abroad.

This is not to say the radical change in belief was not a condition for a *lasting* decline in witch persecutions. The new metaphysics effectively diminished the figure of the Devil, a figure whose growth in the later Middle Ages had strengthened the credibility of the power of witches. Many historians have attempted to find other reasons for the decline and for the parallel decline in the practice of astrology. Keith Thomas (1973) cites for England the increased security and stability of life, instanced and partly brought about by the growth of insurance. It might also be argued that a willingness to accept misfortune in terms of 'chance', rather than in personalized terms of malevolence or punishment for sin, stemmed from a growth in urban living and commerce. This would be paralleled by explanations of changes in urban Africans' attitudes to misfortune which follow from the severing of the ties of traditional village life and the implication in commercial relationships.[12] The market, it might be argued, offers a model of an impersonal process affecting individuals' lives and, in impersonal competition, a new kind of relationship between men on which to blame failure. But the classic notion of a transition from 'tradition' to 'modernity', centred on the growth of the market, can be wheeled in to explain anything. There is no reason to posit some late seventeenth-century watershed in commercial activity leading to those attitudinal consequences: such a watershed could just as easily, and arbitrarily, be set a century earlier or a century later. Alan Macfarlane in *The Origins of English Individualism* (1979) points to attitudes and practices associated with competitive 'individualism' and important elements of a money and wage-labour economy long before the sixteenth century. The diary of Ralph Josselin (1617-83), an Essex clergyman, indicates that he could comfortably combine commercial-capitalist calculation with a belief in witchcraft.[13] Insurance could indeed protect people of modest means and those involved in speculative ventures from the worst consequences of misfortune; although the fact that loss of ships at sea or houses by fire had seldom been ascribed to witchcraft in any case perhaps explains why people were willing to take economic and institutional precautions against those losses rather than counter them by persecuting individuals for *maleficium*. Insurance could not, however, protect ordinary countryfolk from sickness or losses among their animals and the landed gentry could survive well enough without it. Between them it was these two classes which produced the accusations and tried them in the courts. So whatever changes there may have been in urban centres, this does not explain the decline in witchcraft prosecutions.

The latter half of the seventeenth century marks no real improvement in the living conditions or security of the mass of people in Western Europe, no 'objective' foundation for a decline in fears and misfortune. In Languedoc, for example, whose agrarian relations have been examined in depth by Le Roy Ladurie (1974), we find that the latter half of the seventeenth century is a period of economic crisis. The wars and heavy taxation of Louis XIV's reign placed a heavy burden on the French peasantry as a whole. Medical therapeutics can hardly be said to have been revolutionized in this period.[14]

The explanation of the 'decline' of witch persecutions will remain problematic. But there is more than mere chance connecting the events of the years 1672 and 1685. The abolition of the charge of witchcraft and the persecution of the Huguenots only appear contradictory from the standpoint of an abstract 'tolerance'. A confirmation of this is the lack of interest shown from early in the seventeenth century by the Italian and Spanish Inquisitors in 'witches'. Tolerance and deistic metaphysics cannot be at work here. *The suppression of religious dissent and organized heresy is a condition for the decline of witch hunting. Indeed, paradoxically, the persecutions of heretics and witches are part of the very process by which witch hunting is finally eliminated.* Geneva, often considered to be 'totalitarian' offers, as we have seen, an example of relative 'leniency' in its witch trials. Italy and Spain are the two powerhouses of the Counter-Reformation, the sites of its earliest and most complete victories.[15] A number of elements are involved in this paradox.

i.   The formation of stable religious 'territories' and a stable relation between religious authority and state power: the struggle between Protestantism and Catholicism in Germany and France, and the struggles between the different Protestant sects, created storm centres of unstable religious authority, competing orthodoxies and heresies. In such conditions relations of religious authority were radically threatened. No one could be sure if whole communities or apparently orthodox notables were not secret heretics and allies of Satan. Witchcraft trials were the symptom of heresy beyond the limits of normal police mechanisms. The attitude of Henri Boguet cited above (p.224) exemplifies the authorities' recognition of this in the forms of demonology. Heresy in Italy and Spain came to be confined to definite, identifiable, and marginalizable groups. The Inquisition was thereby limited to a definite and measured disciplinary role. After the Thirty Years War (1618-48) a relatively stable 'territorialization' of the different religious powers is established. Louis XIV's persecution and exclusion of the Huguenots is an attempt to bring this process to completion within the borders of a restored France.

ii. This 'territorialization' makes possible the restoration and extension of religious 'disciplines' which reduce deviation in belief and conduct to individual weaknesses to be policed. The Counter-Reformation had already transformed the institutions and practices of the Church, creating an effective inspectorate and educational force in the Society of Jesus, curing abuses in administration and ecclesiastical conduct, and imposing higher standards of religious observance and supervision of the flock. Attendance at mass and confession were subjected to new norms and an attempt was made to impose them on the mass of the laity; Catholic countries created the means for exclusion of the Devil by policing the faithful and motivating them to conformity. The educational and pastoral work of Protestant congregations had a similar effect. Monter (1976) suggests that the educational work in the rural communes of Geneva played a large part in eliminating peasant superstitions and, therefore, one source of witchcraft accusations.

Protestant congregations closely policed their own flocks but they were threatened by continual doctrinal schism. The solution to this problem of proliferating heresy was 'toleration'. This should not be confused with an attitude of 'tolerance'. It was a matter of policy and operated within strict limits. In England the restored monarchy of Charles II continued the policy of suppressing the most radical sects' activities practised by the Common-wealth. 'Toleration' meant freedom to worship, at the price of civil and political disabilities, for *containable* non-conformists. At the same time an ideological battle against 'enthusiasm' was waged by the official Church. In Holland and Geneva, stabilized state power based on the urban patriarchate brought the more radical clergy to order and imposed a form of toleration based upon firm *political* supervision by the state.

iii. The formation of religious 'Territories' is coupled with an increase in and transformation of the capacities of state power signalled somewhat inad-equately by the word 'Absolutism'. Republican Holland enjoyed certain of these capacities just as surely as the regime of Louis XIV. This increase in state power entailed the supervision or curtailment of local aristocratic and municipal fiscal and military powers. National taxes, standing armies, and a network of fortresses and garrisons created a new form of central-ized state power and represented new means of political control. New objectives and practices of state power accompany the new means. The rationalization of the state's territory, the control of foreign trade, the promotion of production, and the elimination of idleness, all serve to promote the national wealth which is the basis of the state's power.

But it must be stressed that the new apparatuses of state tended to *parallel* rather than wholly eliminate previous institutions. Administration in France, for example, became *more* complex as a result of the develop-ment. The patchwork of competing judicial authorities was but little simplified (certainly in France where a thorough reform of the structure of courts had to wait until the revolution of 1789). It remained very much *ad hoc*.

What did change was the capacity of local powers to sustain themselves against the centre, a crucial factor in eliminating local and regional centres of heresy. What also changed were expectations on the part of the managers of the new state apparatuses, and their religious and commercial allies, as to the levels of internal peace and order that were possible. Witchcraft trials are a part of conditions of *disorderly legality*. They are desperate measures and by their very form they undermine the possibility of creating a stable, useful, and pacified population. Although conducted by authority, and serving as a means to enforce religious conformity, they threaten both political order and religious conformity. For if the courts of authority provide the theatre, popular accusations and the confessions of the accused determine the cast, and those accusations are not limited by considerations of social standing or outward belief. Beggar women can denounce merchants and councillors. Midelfort (1972) suggests that this was a major check on the persecutions in southwestern Germany. This disorderly legality must become unacceptable when there are means to displace it. Witch trials, like the disorder of festivals and organized licensed begging, threaten to give rise to an institutionalized anarchy in which popular forces rather than state agencies set the norms of conduct. 'Absolutism' is threatened more directly by this disorderly legality than the older more fragmented state powers because the means of its new power specify new demands for order.

iv. The middle decades of the seventeenth century are the crucial period of formation and consolidation of 'Absolutism' particularly in France. Indeed, the Reformation and the civil strife it brought in train *retarded* the centralization and development of the French state. Two somewhat longer-term processes are associated with the development of the state's capacities. They follow from a strengthening of the state's apparatuses and the new demands for order coincident in the new means to enforce it. The first is the reduction in the use of torture in normal civil procedure. Langbein (1977) points out that confession as a proof of guilt, and the torture made necessary by it, was a function of the institutional weakness of the courts and the insecure status of judicial decision.[16] With the radical weakening of feudal and communal powers, the centralization of the judiciary and a strengthening of the position of the judge as agent of a more formidable state power, a process well-established in the sixteenth century, judicial decisions had less need to be legitimated by confession and could rely to a greater extent on other evidence. The Ordonnance of 1670, which Michel Foucault cites in *Discipline and Punish* (1977) to demonstrate the bloody nature of French Absolutist justice, was already on the way to being displaced, in respect to the practice of torture in trials. The quite different ritual of torture prior to execution, however, remained as a means of spectacular *punishment* for those whose crimes ideologically challenged the royal power, at the same time as judicial torture ceased to be the principle means of *proof*. The law was gradually moving towards a condition which would make the procedural necessity of judicial torture superfluous. Torture had long since ceased to be important in normal procedure before it was abolished towards the end of the eighteenth century in most European countries. This shift marked out even more the anomalous nature of the procedure in trials for witchcraft. The judiciary acquired more rigorous means of assessment of evidence, against which the charges and materials offered in the witch trials could hardly have stood up. It is probably because of their higher standards of competence and immunity from popular pressure or threat that the Papal and Spanish Inquisitions were willing to assess and discard witchcraft charges as they thought fit. In France and Germany in the first half of the seventeenth century, many judges lacked the insulation from popular pressure and the confidence in their judgement to act with equal discretion. The judiciary probably moved closer to the position of men like Godelmann not because of 'humanitarianism' but because of new practices of assessing evidence and reaching decisions. Resistance to witch charges probably increased among the corps of jurists because of changes in the practice of proof, rather than any new infusion of 'experiment' or 'rationality'. Judicial procedure remained *inquisitorial* and brought by the authorities, but torture became less central to it.

The other longer-term process associated with 'Absolutism' is the transformation of the regulation of poverty, indigence, and idleness. The effect of these measures was to lessen the possibility of the 'typical' situation of accusation outlined above. As Macfarlane (1971) argues, this situation was to some extent transitional,[17] dependent on the guilt generated by the relatively recently discarded ideals of Christian duty in charitable relief. The institutionalization of relief gradually removed the source of conflict. Witch beliefs and misfortunes continued but the situations of tension which focused accusations in certain strained social relationships were lessened. Whatever the effect on accusations, most states adopted new practices of regulating and confining the poor, vagabonds, and the socially incompetent generally. It will be recalled that in 1656 Louis XIV ordered the founding of the *Hôpital Général* of Paris and in 1676 the system was generalized to the whole country.[18] This intervention of the state was coupled with a rationalization of the institutions of Catholic charity. They worked in association with the state and in terms of a similar ideology to regulate and control the poor. The institutional confinement and state supervision of the poor struck at the basis of witchcraft accusations in another and more radical way than Macfarlane suggests. It created a new mechanism of control with new interests in orderly conduct, reform, and discipline. Witchcraft prosecutions, set alongside these practices of confinement and coercion in the interests of socially useful conduct, could only appear as an excess. The poor were to be transformed. They ceased to be numbered among the legions of the Devil but became part of a problem of 'order' made possible by new means of regulation. Rather than extending the 'Kingdom of Darkness' they were now conceived as 'diminishing the wealth of the King-

A seventeenth-century image of poverty.

Etching entitled *Woman and Child Before a River Landscape*, by Gerrit van Schagen, after Adriaen Brouwer. Reproduced by kind permission of Atlas van Stolk, Rotterdam.

dom'[19] — executing them could in no way make them help to increase it. In the Amsterdam *Rasphius* or in the galleys of the French King they served the state. At the *auto da fé*, just as on the scaffold, they did nothing but threaten it.[20] The new institutions in no sense eliminated the poverty, crime, or vagrancy. These problems remained and multiplied. What they produced was a new *response* on the part of the authorities to questions of order and the regulation of the common people.

Notes

1 See Trevor-Roper (1978: 95).
2 For the popularization of mathematics and the sciences for practical purposes in England see Hill (1972).
3 See Capp (1979).
4 For accounts of the orthodox Catholic epistemology of 'hypotheses' which account for experience, see P. Duhem *To Save the Phenomena* (1969). For, Galileo, see A. Koyré *Metaphysics and Measurement* (1968) and *Galileo Studies* (1978). For a challenging anti-empiricist discussion of the issues at stake in the 'case' of Galileo see P. Feyerabend *Against Method* (1975).
5 For a discussion of the role of metaphysical concepts in the creation of the conditions for modern forms of scientific theory, see E.A. Burtt *Metaphysical Foundations of Modern Science* (1932).
6 On Bacon's links with the Hermetic-Cabalist tradition, see F.A. Yates *The Rosicrucian Enlightenment* (1972: Ch. 9). For Aubrey and Ashmole, see Capp (1979: 188).
7 J. Webster, surgeon in the Parliamentary Army. Paracelsus' concept of 'experience', which Webster is using, would make modern empiricists' hair stand on end.
8 For this point and for our discussion of Newton generally see J.E. McGuire and P.M. Rattansi 'Newton and the Pipes of Pan' (1966).
9 For Galileo's epistemology, see Koyré *Metaphysics and Measurement* (1968) and for Newton's see Koyré *Newtonian Studies* (1965).
10 For this change in world-views and the complex metaphysical debates accompanying it, see A. Koyré *From the Closed World to the Infinite Universe* (1968).
11 For the abolition of *sorcellerie sabbatique*, see Trevor-Roper (1978: 95).
12 See J.C. Mitchell 'The Meaning of Misfortune for Urban Africans' (1965).
13 See Macfarlane (1970).
14 See Ladurie *The Peasants of Languedoc* (1974) and Goubert *The Ancien Regime* (1973) for a brief account of the popular classes in France and their conditions.
15 For the Counter-Reformation, its educational practices and religious disciplines, see Pierre Janelle *The Catholic Reformation* (1971). For a general account see A.G. Dickens *The Counter-Reformation* (1968). For the 'totalitarianism' of Geneva see 'Totalitarian Elements in Pre-Industrial Societies' in J. Barrington Moore (1962).
16 See J. Langbein *Torture and the Law of Proof* (1977).
17 Macfarlane (1971: 206).
18 The discussion of Foucault's *Madness and Civilization* in Part Two Chapter Nine above, will be of relevance here.
19 This is how the poor are classed and tabulated in Gregory King's *Natural and Political Observations and Conclusions upon the State and Condition of England* (1696). King's work was one of the first attempts to measure and statistically tabulate the sources of production of wealth and the national income. The tables taken from this work are reprinted in C.B. Macpherson *The Political Theory of Possessive Individualism* (1962).
20 See Michel Foucault *Discipline and Punish* (1977).

15

WITCHCRAFT, RATIONALITY,
AND OTHER CULTURES

One of the more interesting and intense debates in contemporary philosophy and social science has concerned the concept of 'rationality'. This debate has primarily dealt with two questions: first, whether there is a general set of criteria for assessing the rationality of human conduct, and secondly, whether human beings are in general constrained to attempt to act 'rationally'. This debate has not surprisingly centred on the assessment of witchcraft beliefs and practices in 'primitive' societies. Are men attempting to act rationally in warding off witchcraft or practising magic, but simply using inappropriate technologies? Do witchcraft beliefs evidence a failure of that critical, empirical, assessment of beliefs and circumstances which is essential to rational conduct? Are there objective limits to illusion and irrational conduct, constraints imposed by the very nature of our world and our adaptation to it? Mary Douglas has pointed out that witchcraft beliefs commonly do not rely on occult spiritual beings but on the occult powers of humans, and that such concepts belong to the realm of the prosaic:

> 'The belief is on the same footing as belief in the conspiracy theory of history, in the baleful effects of fluoridation or the curative value of psychoanalysis – or any belief presented in an unverifiable form. The question then becomes one about rationality.'
>
> (Douglas 1970: xvi)

That is, the question becomes one about *why* such beliefs cannot be subjected to empirical validation and *why*, given their falsity, they continue to persist.

E.E. Evans-Pritchard's *Witchcraft, Oracles and Magic among the Azande* (original date 1937, abridged edition 1976) is the point of departure for this debate.[1] It is *the* classic modern anthropological study of witchcraft beliefs, rituals, and practices. Its pre-eminence is explained by the fact that it offered a paradigm of a method of analysis: beliefs were to be examined in the context of the social practices they articulated or accompanied, by means of detailed fieldwork observation and the collection of 'texts' from native informants. In analysing witchcraft beliefs the central issue was the determination of the social relationships in which they were implicated and which motivated them. Witchcraft accusations

thus indicate particular sources of tension in relations between neighbours, and provide the society in question with a mechanism for the
exposure and resolution of these tensions. As Evans-Pritchard presents it,
witchcraft is a central feature of Azande society, an ever-present force
and source of concern. It cannot be dismissed as a marginal or residual
belief of little relevance to daily activity.

A characteristic feature of the book, the problem around which it is
structured, is a fundamental ambiguity of attitude towards witchcraft on
Evans-Pritchard's part. This ambiguity is no external inference as to his
thoughts and motives. It is a central thematic component of his text and
part of the way in which the book is written. The two poles of the ambiguity are a consequence of two quite distinct belief systems being brought
together; the assumptions of the ideologies surrounding Western 'scientific'
practices, and the participation by a sympathetic observer in native
beliefs. First, Azande beliefs are founded on error: 'Witches, as the Azande
conceive them, clearly exist' (1976:18). Witchcraft beliefs therefore
need *accounting for*. The entities posited by witchcraft beliefs cannot
exist because of what is claimed about them. The issue is then to explain
why people *capable of rationality* persist in practices deriving from
mystical beliefs about non-existent entities. They do so, on the one hand,
because the structure of their thought does not permit them to discover
their error and, on the other, because their beliefs are implicated in social
relationships which they cannot dispense with. Thus, even though a man
may doubt the claim that he is a witch, he is forced to act, and therefore
to believe, in certain ways to preserve his relationships with others:

> 'We must remember that since witchcraft has no real existence a man
> does not know that he has bewitched another, even if he is aware that
> he bears him no ill-will. But, at the same time, he believes firmly in
> the existence of witchcraft and in the accuracy of the poison oracle
> so that when the oracle says he is killing a man by his witchcraft, he is
> probably thankful for having been warned in time.'
>
> (Evans-Pritchard 1976:44)

Secondly, Evans-Pritchard was a sympathetic observer who participated
as fully as he could in native life and belief. He draws his own, uncomfortable conclusion from this immersion:

> 'In no department of their life was I more successful in "thinking
> black" ... than in the sphere of witchcraft. I, too, used to react to
> misfortunes in the idiom of witchcraft, and it was often an effort to
> check this lapse into unreason.'
>
> (1976:45)

Apart from its threat to his 'reason' this lapse presented him with no real
difficulties. The life of a Zande was viable and had its own adequate means
of organization. Thus Evans-Pritchard found the poison-oracle, despite its
foundation in 'unreason', an adequate means of conducting affairs:

'I always kept a supply of poison for the use of my household and neighbours and we regulated our affairs in accordance with the oracle's decisions. I may remark that I found this as satisfactory a way of running my home and affairs as any other I know of.'

(1976: 126)

Native practices, futhermore, stand up in the face of the tests of illness and pain: 'When you have lived for some time in Zandeland you will have ample evidence of the therapeutic value of the kind of treatment which witch-doctors employ' (1976: 108).

Evans-Pritchard tries to resolve this contradiction by explaining, on the one hand, why the Zande do not uncover the falsity at the heart of their beliefs and, on the other, why in spite of this falsity those beliefs can serve as a viable medium of conduct. He lists twenty-two reasons 'why Azande do not perceive the futility of their magic' (1976: 201). Here we will group them into five main explanatory themes, and then comment on his explanations.

1. Social structural obstacles to the generalization of beliefs and the collation of information

Social situations and mores determine the concept to be applied in a given case. The doctrine of witchcraft does not explain *any* misfortune, only a class of sudden and inexplicable deaths, illnesses, and failures. No one will take an inexperienced potter seriously if he blames witchcraft for the breaking of a pot in finishing. A man who kills another with a spear will be dealt with as a murderer. Beliefs are 'functions of situations' (1976:221). They articulate specific contexts of action and conduct. Beliefs are thus fragmented across a series of situations and are never present at the same time. This means that contradictions *between* context-specific beliefs do not emerge. The structure of accusations is also serial, so that the implications of the pattern of accusations for the claims made in beliefs remains hidden. If this pattern were examined, given Zande beliefs about the hereditability of 'witchcraft substance', then virtually everybody would be a witch. This occlusion of the contradictions implicit in the pattern of accusations was reinforced by the weakening of central political authority by the British. Witchcraft ceased to be a crime punishable, and therefore examinable, by the royal courts.

2. 'Categorical' reasons

The Azande make no distinction between 'natural' and 'supernatural' phenomena in the way that the ideologies of contemporary Western 'common sense' or the 'scientific attitude' do. They therefore lack the categorical conditions for the exclusion of phenomena as beyond the realm of demonstrable causality. This does not mean that the Azande ignore what we would count as 'natural' causality, nor do they deny it a place in the events surrounding witchcraft. They employ what would be in our terms a plural or multiple scheme of causation. They are aware, for example, that a man died by being crushed by a falling house. That is *how* he died. But they go on to ask *why* was it that it collapsed at the precise moment the man happened to be sitting beneath it. Witchcraft explains the conjunction of elements in the event. This latter question permits explanations of an order we would not permit. The conjunction of elements is for us a matter of coincidence or chance.

3.   Limits in the mode of experimentation practised by the Azande

The Azande both incorporate the results of 'experience' into their conduct and are often sceptical of the reliability of oracles, the power of witch doctors, etc. But this reference to 'experience' and this scepticism alike operate to *confirm* the basic structure of belief, for they can account for experiences of failure in divination and healing. This is exemplified by the practices surrounding the poison oracle, the most important and reliable of the oracles the Zande use and only brought into operation to confirm a lesser oracle. It consists in administering a poison called *benge* to fowls. The oracle is questioned in a complex form, a sequence of questions using more than one fowl which includes a cross check on erroneous answers due to the failure of bad poison or the intervention of witchcraft. *Benge* is an *intelligent substance* which should 'understand' the questions put to it. It is discriminating, killing some fowls or letting others live in response to questions. If all the fowls die or all live, then it is a sign that the poison is bad, i.e. indiscriminate. The use of the oracle makes no sense if it works as a natural 'poison' in our meaning of the term. It is the *question* put to the oracle, not the chemical composition of the poison, which should decide the result.

The Azande thus use procedures of testing and checks as to the efficacy of practices. But they do not experiment *systematically* to test whether their beliefs as such are true or not. Failures of the poison oracle cannot therefore serve to disconfirm the structure of their beliefs surrounding it. Experiment takes place within a framework of 'mystical notions'. The failure of the oracle, therefore, is 'explained' by reference to the intervention of entities or forces which depend on other or the very same mystical notions: *benge* has lost its virtue or a witch is distracting it.

4.   The absence of the technology of reason

The Azande lack means of the rationalization of existence, of memory, of movement, and calculation of forces such that they could make an objective assessment of states of affairs. Having no clocks, they are unable to measure and therefore to recognize that the ritual of placing a stone in a tree in no way retards the arrival of sunset.[2]

5.   Thought as a 'mental structure'

Evans-Pritchard was troubled by the implications of Lévy-Bruhl's notion
of 'mentalities', but he treats the Zande as people capable of and often
using 'common sense' who are nonetheless trapped within a self-reinforcing
structure of 'mystical notions'. Witchcraft, oracles, and magic form a
coherent and self-reinforcing system, each element of which explains away
the contradictions and problems raised by others. Zande reasoning is
trapped within the 'web' of their own thought, and they cannot think
outside a mesh of 'mystical notions':

> 'And yet the Azande do not see that their oracles tell them nothing!
> Their blindness is not due to stupidity: they reason excellently in the
> idiom of their beliefs but they cannot reason outside, or against,
> their beliefs because they have no other idiom in which to express
> their thoughts.'

(1976: 59)

Given this dominance of entities specified by mystical notions, it is
difficult to see how many of their activities could 'fail'. Magic is employed
against mystical powers, and as these powers transcend experience they
can hardly be contradicted by it.

Evans-Pritchard's explanations are wholly dependent on his asking a particular question: why the *Azande* cannot recognize the 'problem' in their own
system of thought, that it is founded on error. Yet the error is *attributed
to it*. Similar questions could be asked, from other metaphysical premises,
of the beliefs surrounding Western natural scientific activities. The question
'are there witches?' cannot be answered except within a definite system of
thought to which attach unprovable metaphysical postulates and theoretical criteria of what is to count as an explanation. Evans-Pritchard
is always uncomfortably close to recognizing this. Much of his account
could be taken simply as a map of the differences in the assumptions and
procedures implicated in Zande beliefs and those of what is called Western
'common sense'. Each of his explanatory themes can either be applied to
Western belief systems or shown not to be a problem *within the context*
of Zande thought. Let us consider them in turn.
i.   Evans-Pritchard recognizes that there are analogous plural causalities
in Western thought, and that the type of explanation offered depends on a
social situation. We insist upon naturalistic explanations of disease and
insanity, reducing statements and behaviour produced in a fever or
delirium to consequences of pathology. But in matters of 'normal'
conduct we insist on a voluntaristic account of statements and behaviour;
we refuse to treat crime as a pathological behaviour at par with those
produced by certain diseases. Evans-Pritchard says, 'We accept scientific
explanations of the causes of disease, and even of the causes of insanity,
but we deny them in crime and sin because they militate against laws and

morals which are axiomatic' (1976: 27). We may use doctors to certify disease and insanity, but they do so in relation to *conventional categories of classes of action*. Crime is not a scientific concept, but a class of acts dependent on convention. Notions surrounding the category of 'crime' treat human beings as autonomous agents capable of self-reflection and volition. The person as a *subject*, as the author of its actions, is, for all its pervasiveness in our culture, a category which orders experience and one with implications as metaphysical as those of 'witch'. When a judge refuses to consider poverty, a dreadful upbringing, or a man's criminal ancestors as adequate explanations of his behaviour, he is asking the question *why* in a way analogous to our Zande informant in the case of the house.

ii. If the Azande suffer problems from the lack of a distinction between the natural and supernatural, that distinction itself brings problems in its train. The category 'supernatural' is a means of limiting the classes of phenomena capable of explanation. It rests on a metaphysical limitation of the entities which *can* exist, and it limits phenomena to those ascertainable by certain means. Certain forms of 'experience' are denied. Whereas Zande thought lacks means of exclusion of entities as 'impossible', our means of exclusion are probably too powerful. A whole range of entities from regularly attested 'paranormal' phenomena like pre-cognition and telepathy, to the manifestations of the unconscious or various 'psychosomatic' interactions have been strongly condemned as contrary to common sense and scientific reason. Now it is precisely in this region, and in the sphere of herbal medicine, that claims for the effectiveness of divination and magical therapy tend to be advanced. Most anthropologists place the question of the efficacy of magical and shamanistic practices to one side. Discounting the truth of witchcraft beliefs, they tend to explain their persistence in terms of their foundation in, and consequences for, social relations. Hardly anyone wants to get the reputation of a 'crank', by considering efficacy seriously, which may mean doing so in terms of concepts analogous to those of native informants. Further, in many cases the prospect of such an assessment is long past — native relations of authority, confidence in their own beliefs, and knowledge and skills have often been destroyed or reduced to a shadow of their former selves. Arseniev's informant Darsu did not merely believe that one could talk to tigers.[3] He claimed to have survived 'conversations' with them. His beliefs and the skills associated with them perished with or were disarticulated by Westernization.

iii. The Zande experiment with *benge* in the context of beliefs that it is an intelligent substance. Western natural scientists engage in many different practices of experiment, but in doing so they do not set out to contradict their basic concepts of causality, or the basic forms of entity specified by them. Indeed, they *could* not do so for it is these very concepts which make possible particular practices of experimental questioning of relationships between phenomena. Thus the famous nineteenth-century experimental physiologist, Claude Bernard, wrote in his methodological textbook, *An Introduction to the Study of Experimental Medicine*, that 'there never are any unsuccessful experiments' (1957: 117). If an expected phenomenon is not produced in an experiment as it should be according to the schema of causation adopted and in contradiction to previous results, the causes of this divergence must be sought in conditions outside those predicted for and controlled. This explaining of the phenomena which intervened to change the result leads to a progressive specification and control of the conditions of experimentation.[4] Clearly, the Zande attributing the failure of *benge* to a variety of intervening factors and causes is not engaged in the same practice as Bernard's experimental physiologist. But the physiologist, like the Zande, is not questioning the basic structure of his theory or mode of thinking, and he cannot do so if experimental procedures are to be productive. The scientist must use categories of determinism and of consistency of causal action in order to engage in experimentation. The results, although generally consistent with those categories, are predicated on them and do not independently confirm them. The scientist is no less a prisoner of his premises than the Zande engaged in divination.

iv. The Zande may lack means of the 'rationalization' of existence, such as clocks, but the primary objective of their procedures could not be furthered by clocks and calculation based on them. Thus the Zande ritual with the stone displaces worry about the fall of night, something a glance at one's watch could only reinforce. The dangers of calculating journeys in terms of time and distance are repeatedly confirmed by many travellers in Africa.[5] Again with oracles, the procedure may seem to be an absurd way to decide when to make a journey or where to build a new house. But, like astrology, the objective is to produce *decisions*, means of ordering action. The non-manipulable oracle delivers such a decision. As Evans-Pritchard admitted,[6] it was as good a way of conducting life as any other. This is particularly true where the elements in a decision are not subject to calculation. It should not be assumed that the conduct of activities in terms of clocks and other forms of measurement promotes 'rationality' or makes decisions more calculable. Modern war is a good example. It is governed by clocks, calculations of distance and times of movement, the scale of resources required, etc. But these activities of staff officers coexist with forms of thought and decision on the part of the mass of soldiers that would make a Zande with his poison oracle appear a veritable technician. For ordinary participants, war is a mass of incidents and incalculables, which cannot be reduced to order. Yet decisions *have* to be taken and the conduct appropriate for survival depends on morale. Soldiers' lives are riddled with the equivalent of the Zande's stone in a tree: whether to stay in a shell hole or leave it; whether one will die today or not. These are questions of vital importance, questions whose resolution is in no way aided by the possession of a watch, a ruler, or the latest casualty statistics. Soldiers develop positively 'mystical notions': in the value of talismans, that one will anticipate one's death, that a particu-

lar shell is destined to meet a certain soldier, and so on.[7] And for soldiers, one can read miners, farmers, and so on. Self-advancing pit props and the substances of Messrs Fisons have not yet killed the Zande in us. Technology — clocks, computers, and cannons — create conditions just as haphazard and undecideable as the possible rogue elephant on one's journey through the bush, conditions which still require us to decide and to order our conduct. Oracles and rituals order conduct and make decisions where other forms of calculation cannot, and where a full recognition of the haphazard nature of the situation would paralyse any action.
v. Zande beliefs form a 'mental structure', a self-reinforcing set of mutually confirmatory notions which govern the interpretations placed on experience. Interestingly enough that is almost exactly how the philosopher Thomas Kuhn (1970) conceives the basic theoretical structures in the natural sciences, which he calls 'paradigms'. At any given moment there is one dominant paradigm in a particular scientific field. This includes a set of assumptions and concepts which structure perception, which govern the kinds of questions that can be asked and the types of answers given. In a period of 'normal science', scientific work consists in 'puzzle-solving', answering questions set by the paradigm according to its rules of adequacy. In a period of scientific revolution when a paradigm tends to accumulate problems and anomalies it cannot answer, change takes place only when another paradigm which is capable of 'covering' the problems unanswerable in the first comes into being. Paradigms are never 'refuted'. They are abandoned for other 'incommensurable' schemes with different basic assumptions. Scientific change is change in the ruling 'mental structures' which govern the scientific community's perception of reality. Kuhn's *The Structure of Scientific Revolutions* (1970) is a controversial work. What particularly exercised critics is the radical relativism implied in the notion of paradigms as 'incommensurable' schemes for ordering our perception of the world, schemes which cannot in themselves be subjected to verification. But Kuhn's position is not an aberration. A number of modern philosophers challenge the verificationist account of the sciences and problematize the very idea that scientific theories are or can be 'refuted' by reference to 'reality'.[8]

Evans-Pritchard's attempt to differentiate Zande thought by pointing to its closed and irrefutable nature only works if there is a form of thought to counterpose to it which is open to empirical criticism. This is just what writers like Kuhn are challenging. Evans-Pritchard is committed to the view of the natural sciences as bodies of propositions which are verified by independent reference to the pertinent facts in their domain. Kuhn challenges this notion of a realm of neutral and independently accessible facts by means of which we can assess theories. Scientific analysis can only take place on the basis of a structure of unverifiable beliefs and concepts which determine what phenomena we *can* see and how we can explain them.

This is not to say that we accept Kuhn's view or consider it unproblematic. Kuhn's conception shares the weakness of Lévy-Bruhl's notion of a distinct pre-logical 'primitive mentality' — a tendency to convert theories and forms of thought into wholly incommensurable mental universes. As a result the contradictions *within* conceptual schemes tend to be obliterated, and the possible co-presence of a number of different or alternative belief systems or theoretical schemes is denied. If 'paradigms' were completely incommensurable or the 'primitive mentality' wholly illogical, then it would be impossible to move from one paradigm or thought system to another. The main strength of positions such as Kuhn's is that they challenge the tendency to privilege of one form of thought over another, and the assertion that Western rationality is closer to 'reality'. Thus, when Evans-Pritchard points to the unresolved contradictions and 'mystical notions' which are part of the web of Zande thought and which prevent them from recognizing error, it can be pointed out that unresolved contradictions abound in the modern natural sciences. Modern theoretical physics consists in a number of competing and incompatible accounts of sub-atomic structure and the structure of the universe. Evans-Pritchard defines 'mystical notions' as 'patterns of thought which attribute to phenomena supra-sensible qualities which . . . are not derived from observation, or cannot be logically inferred from it, and which they do not possess' (1956: 12). Sub-atomic physics is entirely concerned with 'supra-sensible' entities, such as neutrons. If 'sensible' means the ordinary human capacities of sight, touch, etc., then these entities are outside 'common sense', for they can be neither directly observed nor inferred from observation. What qualities these supra-sensible phenomena 'possess' can only be determined by scientific instruments constructed by means of theories and where the results of the employment of these instruments are matters for interpretation by theory. As to the existence of these entities we are wholly dependent on the scientists' theoretical account of them. Evans-Pritchard's criterion for differentiating mystical and non-mystical thought depends on the notion of a direct and independent sensory access to 'reality'. As we shall see in discussing Peter Winch's contribution to the debate on rationality it is just this notion which is problematic.

One final point ought to be made before turning to that contribution. Kuhn and Evans-Pritchard have one tendency in common and that is to refer to forms of mentality such as 'science' or 'common sense' *grosso modo*.[9] Yet a mass of distinct discourses and practices is to be encountered in that domain we signal by the concept 'the natural sciences', for example. Epistemological doctrines purport to unify this complex. Similarly the notion of 'common sense' attempts to unify all human 'practical' thought, as the basic human outlook consistent with sense experience and a rational adjustment to the facts of the sensible world. In our discussion of witchcraft beliefs we have consistently spoken not of 'common sense', as if it were a real and present human attitude, but of the 'ideology' of contemporary common sense, and likewise, we have spoken of the epistemological 'doctrines' associated with the modern natural sciences. These ideologies or doctrines purport to govern the discourses and practices they refer to, but the relationship is one of claim rather than undisputed dominion. Definite discursive structures (for example, Neo-Platonism and its philosophical alternatives in the Renaissance) and conditions of practice do constrain what can be said and done, what can be argued or constructed. But these structures and conditions are not 'mentalities' — that is, a collective mode of 'thought' which is prior to and which governs its expressions. Such a concept of 'mentality' merely restores the worst defects and excesses of Durkheim's 'collective consciousness' or para-Hegelian notions of *Zeitgeist*. However, discursive structures and conditions of practice are effective and operative only through the mode in which a discourse is written and continued, through the process of a trial or an experiment. The notion of forms of 'mentality' has its value, particularly in challenging universalist notions of human nature, but it also has its limits. To enter fully into these limits would entail writing a different, far more theoretical, and even less accessible book.

Peter Winch in his paper 'Understanding a Primitive Society' (1979) poses clearly the problem of the 'rationality' of witchcraft beliefs tormenting Evans-Pritchard. The practice of falsification of Zande beliefs would involve reference to *another thought system*. We, guided by 'rationality' and 'common sense', can see the error at the heart of Zande beliefs. Evans-Pritchard clearly believes he is doing more than use the alternative criteria of his own belief system to assess what phenomena can or cannot exist. To do that would be simply to presume the validity of one's own system and would in no way demonstrate it. The central question, therefore, is the putative *independence* of the tests and criticisms of beliefs proposed in Western 'rationality' from the beliefs from which those tests derive. That is, the refutation of beliefs is based on their independent reference to reality itself. In other words, the claim is that Western rationality or science is able to avoid the trap of its own beliefs and assumptions because those very beliefs give it access to an independently existing and intelligible reality.

> 'Evans-Pritchard is in fact thereby put into the same metaphysical camp as Pareto: for both of them the conception of "reality" must be regarded as intelligible and applicable *outside* the context of scientific reasoning itself, since it is that to which scientific notions do, and unscientific notions do not, have a relation.'

(Winch 1979: 81)

Winch contends that Western science is not the only system of thought to conceive the real as independent of the knower and intelligible in itself. Many religious beliefs do just this on the grounds that the world was made by God and bears witness to His intelligent action. Winch argues that Evans-Pritchard is trying to work with a concept of 'reality' which is not determined by its form of use in the conventions of a language:

'What Evans-Pritchard wants to be able to say is that the criteria applied
in scientific experimentation constitute a true link between our ideas
and an independent reality, whereas those characteristic of other
systems of thought — in particular, magical methods of thought — do
not. It is evident that the expressions "true link" and "independent
reality" in the previous sentence cannot themselves be explained by
reference to the scientific universe of discourse, as this would beg the
question. We have then to ask how, by reference to what established
universe of discourse, the use of those expressions is to be explained;
and it is clear that Evans-Pritchard has not answered this question.'

(Winch 1979: 82-3)

Winch is contending that all statements about 'reality' are interpretative
and that they stem from definite 'universes of discourse' which are not
'reality' itself. He is denying that reality is intelligible *independent of
discourse*. Such an idea of independence has two basic ways of formulation. One is the positivist philosopher's notion of an independent
observation language against which theoretical languages are measured,
and the other is of a directly meaningful 'experience' of nature or God,
a poetic or religious revelation.[10] In both cases language is inscribed
within the real, a neutral *language* of observation, the voice of nature or
of God which speaks directly to the soul of the poet or mystic. This
notion of reality itself serving to signify the 'true link', to confirm or
disconfirm our ideas, rests on assumptions which transcend observation:
that the world of appearances is coherent and intelligible, that is does
not consist in a mass of sense impressions dispersed apart from the forms
of order we impose on them. In order to make the *claim* for a neutral
observation language it is necessary to present an argument which depends
on non-observational terms.

Winch makes his argument in terms of the Austrian philosopher Ludwig
Wittgenstein's later theory of meaning.[11] It is not necessary to elaborate
or to agree with this theory to agree with the point Winch makes. Briefly,
however, Wittgenstein denies his own earlier view that meaningful statements consist in propositions which model states of affairs and argues
that the meaning of statements is dependent on their context of use and
the rules specifying usage. Language is not a model of reality, and there
are no necessary limits to meaning other than those imposed by systems
of language rules and the 'forms of life' to which they relate. Different
conceptions or uses of words like 'reality', 'existence', or 'entity' are,
therefore, possible. The positivist philosopher and the mystic will make
use of these words in different ways. Both work in terms of a discursive
doctrine of possible entities and both have concepts of what types of
tests of adequacy are to count. Both may utilize a concept of experience.
The positivist has to choose by convention not to count the mystic's
world. Both have doctrines of the entities which are possible and these
doctrines transcend and limit observation and experience. The question

of which entities are to count can only be settled *within* a form of discourse by the rules it proposes, and not *between* discourses. Evans-Pritchard can deal with the Azande in the terms of Western thought or in terms of their own belief systems. He cannot, despite the claims of certain Western doctrines of scientific method, use the one to *independently* or objectively refute the other by reference to 'reality'.

Winch points to the inescapable relativity of distinct theoretical schemes and belief systems. That one can assess phenomena only within a system or scheme, and that the tests one uses depend on but do not validate that system or scheme. Alasdair MacIntyre (1979) is strongly critical of Winch precisely because of this relativism. MacIntyre argues that it *is* possible to settle whether or not Zande beliefs can be assessed as rational or irrational. That assessment *must* be relative to Western scientific knowledge. Societies are *not* equivalent. Social development provides new means and standards for explaining the world and controlling it. Relativism can only be sustained by setting that process of development to one side:

> 'It seems to me that one could only hold the belief of the Azande rationally *in the absence of* any practice of science and technology in which criteria of effectiveness, ineffectiveness and kindred notions had been built up. But to say this is to recognize the appropriateness of scientific criteria of judgement from our standpoint .... It is only *post eventum* in the light of later and more sophisticated understanding that their belief and concepts can be evaluated at all.'
>
> (MacIntyre 1979a: 67)

We cannot dispense with our own criteria because, relative to other beliefs, they *are* rational. To ask for a meta-proof of these criteria is to seek a philosophical realm outside the actual dialectical process of development of rationality. That dialectic is one of a pluralism and conflict of views: it means that in society undergoing development there will be alternative views in contest. It is these transitions from one system of belief to another that make it possible to choose between alternative views:

> 'In seventeenth century Scotland, for example, the question could not be raised, "But are there witches?" If Winch asks, from within what way of life, under what system of belief was this question asked, the only answer is that it was asked by men who confronted alternative systems and were able to draw out of what confronted them independent criteria of judgement. Many Africans today are in the same situation.'
>
> (MacIntyre 1979b: 129)

The problem with this account is the notion of 'independent criteria of judgement'. Independent of what? We have seen all too clearly that the critics of the legal persecution of witches did *not* have criteria independent of Christian religious beliefs. To have had such criteria would have led them to the stake or at least to utter marginality. Lacking independent criteria and dependent on the premises of their opponents, their criticisms were effectively discounted as incompatible with both received religion and experience. Further, the field of debate was primarily *forensic*. The question 'But are there witches?' was actually posed as 'Should people who *believe themselves to be* or are accused as witches be tried and punished?' That question could be answered by denying certain of the claims following from witch beliefs and yet insisting that 'witches' be tried for *what they thought*, which was sin enough. The question 'But are there witches?' could not be satisfactorily answered within the terms of debate or the 'alternative' means of discourse available; nor did a negative answer lead to an end to the legal process. Africans' transitions are all too typically between their tribal pagan beliefs and some variant of Christianity, a step to social promotion and, if possible, a comfortable urban existence. How one measures the relative merits in terms of 'rationality' of traditional paganism and, say, Methodism or Pentacostalism, is a question MacIntyre does not try to answer. But this is the typical pattern of such 'transitions' from one set of beliefs and practices with undemonstrable metaphysical premises to another.

And not all transitions are so cosy. The mass of native peoples never encountered Western beliefs and practices as a higher, more ordered, and rational world. To the Aztecs dying *en masse* of Old World diseases and subject to the Spanish fury, to the South Sea Islanders dying of the same diseases and drink, to the American Indians or the Eskimos, Western civilization came as a calamity.[12] It shattered their confidence in their own beliefs and practices. It left them as the slaves or ethnographical museum pieces of their Western conquerors. It brought them next to nothing. It dealt them blows whose only Western standard of measure is the scale of the Lisbon earthquake or Hiroshima.

In thus shattering viable and often prosperous ways of life, developed cultures and civilizations, Western penetration did not bring 'progress'.[13] It brought new, and often more problematic and ecologically less viable, conditions of living for reduced and servile populations. On the other hand, it would be dubious to use population growth as a measure of progress.[14] The populations of areas of Western imperial conquest, India, China, Latin America, have grown rapidly in this century. This owes something to economic intervention and to public health measures — benefits of Western 'rationality'. But it would be unwise to over-emphasize the role technology or medicine has played in population growth or to ignore the problems that growth has brought in train. China's population, for example, grew throughout epidemics, famines, a declining standard of living, conditions of administrative incompetence, and collapse of public order directly connected with and even fostered by imperialist intervention. Most Chinese, until 1949, were born, lived, and died without the benefits of Western medicine and public health, and with all the evils imperialism can visit on a country.

'Post eventum', growing numbers of Westerners are less than happy with the 'criteria of effectiveness' of Western science and technology. To judge our civilization 'superior' by its own standards of technique is to ignore the objectives those techniques are required to serve, and the unintended consequences they bring in train. Those objectives and consequences raise moral and practical problems which cannot be solved by waving the wand of 'rationality'. It would be possible to reply to MacIntyre thus: in a world busily consuming its non-renewable forms of stored energy, probably dependent for the continued maintenance of its current scientific and technical order on the hazards of nuclear power, and possessing the means to create conditions of life in which the survivors would envy the Azande, we raise the question of the relative 'rationality' of forms of belief at our peril. Is a nuclear bomber pilot trained to unhesitatingly obey an order to destroy a city containing millions of people superior to or more rational than a public prosecutor or Inquisitor sending perhaps hundreds to the stake as a consequence of witch trials? Is a man dying of some incurable disease alone in an American hospital crammed with techniques and at a cost which ruins his family better served in his last hours than is a 'primitive' with the ministrations of the shaman and the attention of his relatives?[15]

There are no 'independent criteria of judgement' to answer these questions. Indeed, if we are honest it is hard to answer them at all. Few of us would leave for the bush. 'Alternative' views are riddled with contradictions and are part of what they oppose. We have seen Weyer and Godelmann in such an unenviable position. The ecologists who place 'nuclear power no thanks' stickers on their petrol-consuming cars are in another. It would be too facile to attribute the role of an emergent rationality to the critics of the excesses of Western technology and economic growth. It is difficult to see any props on which MacIntyre's 'dialectic' can fix itself. Things look a good deal less comfortable than they did twenty years ago, and we cannot feel so confident about the place from where *we* speak.

Our discussion has taken the case of the Azande because their thought − presented to us through anthropological reconstruction − poses the question of 'rationality' in its starkest form, and not because we believe primitive societies are in some way 'better' than our own. The celebration of primitivism is no less problematic than the complacent acceptance of Western science and technology. It is as deep-seated a Western response as the belief in 'progress' and the 'rationality' of modern Western standards and techniques.[16] Primitive societies had and have their savageries and suffering. They often pale in comparison with the savageries and suffering our civilization inflicts upon itself and others. We might leave those others with the dignity of being, if not better, then at least different and no worse.

This may seem a strange point at which to end a sociology book. We think it an appropriate one. Sociology can offer some clarifications, if not

answers, to intractable moral and practical questions. To recognize the
otherness and the nagging possibility of the moral and epistemological
equivalence of values and beliefs we do not share, and perhaps only half
understand, is not necessarily to enter some relativistic limbo. On the
other hand, we cannot find in that otherness 'independent criteria of
judgement'; that is too much to hope for. What we can find is some
answers to *why* we are stuck with certain of the values and beliefs we
do have; to see how those beliefs and values serve as media of conduct and
conditions of social organization. At the same time we can see the limits
to some of the metaphysical and ontological *claims* made by the doctrines
which accompany and support those beliefs and values. Claims that
'progress' and 'rationality', 'liberty' or 'justice' are human actualities
or realizable states of affairs cannot be swallowed whole. But neither
can the categories which sustain such claims be simply rejected outright.
We would be infinitely worse off if there were no appeals to liberty and
justice. To reject them would be the equivalent of a Zande confronted
with 'evidence' of his witchcraft quoting Evans-Pritchard and MacIntyre
– supposing he were able to do so. Not only would this be no defence,
it could resolve none of the dilemmas of conduct which confront the
man nor the problems of organization which confront his social relations.
Conduct and organization cannot be separated from categories of morality
and metaphysics, equally those categories are not merely matters of
personal choice or intellectual conviction – they are part of social
relations.

Notes

1   For purposes of quotation the recently published abridged edition will be used
    when possible as it is currently in print. References to the full 1956 edition will
    be signalled.
2   Evans-Pritchard (1976: 203).
3   See S.M. Shirokogoroff 'Talking to Tigers not to Bears' (1954).
4   See P.Q. Hirst *Durkheim, Bernard and Epistemology* (1975: Ch. 1).
5   See, for example, Graham Greene's remarks on this point in *Journey without
    Maps*.
6   Evans-Pritchard (1976: 126).
7   For an account of war as a situation of conduct for the ordinary soldier, see
    J. Keegan *The Face of the Battle* (1976); for instances of such rituals and super-
    stitious beliefs in World War One see D. Winter *Death's Men* (1979) and Paul
    Fussell *The Great War and Modern Memory* (1975).
8   A notable Anglo-Saxon example is Paul Feyerabend's *Against Method* (1975); the
    French philosopher Gaston Bachelard strongly challenged the idea that scientific
    knowledge proceeded by refutation or falsification; for a clear exposition of his
    views see D. Lecourt *Marxism and Epistemology* (1975).
9   This is particularly true of the paper by Robin Horton, 'African Thought and
    Western Science', reprinted in B. Wilson (ed.) *Rationality* (1979) – in which not
    only traditional thought but also Western 'science', in the singular, is treated as a
    single 'mentality', with an essentially common outlook, method, and procedure.

Such a 'science' exists only in the imaginations of certain positivist philosophers.

10 This distinction between theoretical language and a neutral observation language is made by the philosopher, Rudolf Carnap (1956).

11 Presented in his work, *Philosophical Investigations* (1963); his earlier theory of language is to be found in his *Tractatus Logico-Philosophicus* (1961). For an introduction to his later theory see Pole (1958).

12 For an assessment of the demographic disaster produced by the Spaniards see S.F. Cook and W. Borah (1971-73). For a graphic account of the consequences of Western penetration see Alan Moorehead *The Fatal Impact* (1966).

13 For a positive revaluation of the living standards possible in hunting and gathering societies, which are all too often considered to be — by their very nature — at the margins of subsistence, see M. Sahlins 'The Original Affluent Society' in *Stone Age Economics* (1974).

14 Such a view often goes along with an evolutionary-adaptational perspective. The well-known Marxist anthropologist V. Gordon Childe used population growth as a measure of the success of technical developments in the productive forces in *Man Makes Himself* (1956). For a sobering view of the role of medicine in population growth, see McNeill *Plagues and Peoples* (1979) — a book we referred to in Part Two in a similar context.

15 This is a strictly evaluative question and the point where anti-medical writers like Ivan Illich find themselves on strong ground. Modern medicine certainly has failed to manage death and incurable illness, its very commitment to curative techniques based on modern science has led it to neglect social and bodily techniques for coping with pain, discomfort, and death. This does *not* mean that we think modern medicine is a sham or that *we* would prefer to be treated by a shaman.

16 We have already referred to 'primitivism' in our discussion of 'wolf children' in Chapter Two.

BIBLIOGRAPHY

Alexander, F. (1931) Buddhistic Training as an Artificial Catatonia. *Psychoanalytic Review* **XVII**.

Allen, J.W. (1928) *A History of Political Thought in the Sixteenth Century*. London: Methuen.

Althusser, L. (1971) Ideology and Ideological State Apparatuses. In *Lenin and Philosophy and Other Essays*. London: New Left Books.

Ardrey, R. (1961) *African Genesis*. London: Collins.

—— (1971) *The Territorial Imperative*. New York: Dell.

Ariès, P. (1974) *Western Attitudes Towards Death*. Baltimore: Johns Hopkins University Press.

—— (1979) *L'homme devant la mort*. Paris: Seuil.

Atkinson, J. (1968) *Martin Luther and the Birth of Protestantism*. Harmondsworth: Penguin.

Ayer, A.J. (1948) *Language, Truth and Logic*. London: Gollancz.

Bakhtin, M. (1968) *Rabelais and His World*. Cambridge, Mass.: Massachusetts Institute of Technology Press.

Balibar, R. and Laporte, D. (1974) *Le Français national*. Paris: Hachette.

Bateson, G. (1973) *Steps to an Ecology of Mind*. St Albans: Paladin.

Beach, F.A. (1947) Evolutionary Changes in the Physiological Control of Mating Behaviour in Mammals. *The Psychological Review* **54** 6: November.

Benedict, R. (1961) *Patterns of Culture*. London: Routledge and Kegan Paul.

Benveniste, É. (1971) *Problems in General Linguistics*. Florida: University of Miami Press.

Berger, P. and Luckmann, T. (1967) *The Social Construction of Reality*. London: Allen Lane.

Bernard, C. (1957) *Introduction to the Study of Experimental Medicine* [1865]. New York: Dover Books.

Bernheimer, R. (1952) *Wild Men in the Middle Ages*. Cambridge, Mass.: Harvard University Press.

Bettelheim, B. (1959) Feral Children and Autistic Children. *American Journal of Sociology* **LXIV** 5: March.

—— (1967) *The Empty Fortress*. London: Collier Macmillan.

Blowers, A. and Thompson, G. (eds) (1976) *Inequalities, Conflict and Change*. Milton Keynes: Open University Press.

Boas, G. (1948) *Essays on Primitivism and Related Ideas in the Middle Ages*. Baltimore: Johns Hopkins University Press.

Boas, G. and Lovejoy, A.O. (1935) *Primitivism and Related Ideas in Antiquity*. Baltimore: Johns Hopkins University Press.

Boyers, R. and Orill, R. (eds) (1972) *Laing and Anti-Psychiatry*. Harmondsworth: Penguin.

Brill, A.A. (1913) Piblokto or Hysteria among Perry's Eskimos. *Journal of Nervous and Mental Illness* **40**.

Burke, P. (1978) *Popular Culture in Early Modern Europe*. London: Temple Smith.

Burtt, E.A. (1932) *The Metaphysical Foundations of Modern Science*. Revised edition. London: Routledge and Kegan Paul.

Campbell, B. (1974) *Human Evolution*. 2nd edition. Chicago: Aldine.

Campbell, P.J. (1979) *The Ebb and Flow of Battle*. London: Oxford University Press.

Cannon, W.B. (1942) 'Voodoo Death'. *American Anthropologist* **44** 2: April-June.

Capp, B. (1979) *Astrology and the Popular Press*. London: Faber.

Carlen, P. and Collison, M. (eds) (1980) *Radical Issues in Criminology*. Oxford: Martin Robertson.

Carnap, R. (1956) The Methodological Character of Theoretical Concepts. *Minnesota Studies in the Philosophy of Science* **I**.

Castel, R. (1976) *Le psychanalysme: l'ordre psychanalytique et la pouvoir*. Paris: UGE Collection 10/18.

Chaytor, H.J. (1945) *From Script to Print*. Cambridge: Cambridge University Press.

Childe, V.G. (1956) *Man Makes Himself*. London: Watts.

Chomsky, N. (1959) Review of B.F. Skinner's *Verbal Behaviour*. *Language* **35** 1.

—— (1966) *Cartesian Linguistics*. New York: Harper and Row.

—— (1968) *Language and Mind*. New York: Harcourt Brace.

Cipolla, C.M. (1965) *The Economic History of World Population*. Harmondsworth: Penguin.

—— (1969) *Literacy and Economic Development in the West*. Harmondsworth: Penguin.

Clare, A. (1980) *Psychiatry in Dissent*. 2nd edition. London: Tavistock.

Cohen, S. and Taylor, L. (1972) *Psychological Survival*. Harmondsworth: Penguin.

Cohn, N. (1957) *The Pursuit of the Millenium*. London: Secker and Warburg.

—— (1976) *Europe's Inner Demons*. St Albans: Paladin.

Condillac, É. de (1746) *Essai sur l'origine des conaissances humaines*. Translation *Essay on the Origin of Human Knowledge* reprinted by Nugent.

Coppard, G. (1969) *With a Machine Gun to Cambrai*. London: HMSO.

Cook, S.F. and Borah, W. (1971-3) *Essays in Population History: Mexico and the Caribbean*. Berkeley: California University Press.

Coser, L. and Rosenburg, B. (eds) (1957) *Sociological Theory*. New York: Macmillan.

Coulter, J. (1973) *Approaches to Insanity*. Oxford: Martin Robertson.

Cousins, M. (1978) The Logic of Deconstruction. *Oxford Literary Review* 3 2.

Coward, R. and Ellis, J. (1977) *Language and Materialism*. London: Routledge and Kegan Paul.

Crombie, A.C. (1961) *Augustine to Galileo*. 2nd edition. London: Heinemann.

Darwin, C. (1970) *The Origin of Species* [1859]. Harmondsworth: Penguin.

—— (n.d.) *The Descent of Man* [1871]. New York: Modern Library.

Davis, K. (1961) *Human Society*. New York: Macmillan.

Deleuze, G. and Guattari, F. (1977) *Anti-Oedipus*. New York: Viking.

Derrida, J. (1976) *Of Grammatology*. Baltimore: Johns Hopkins University Press.

Devereux, G. (1956) Normal and Abnormal. In J.B. Casagrande and T. Gladwin (eds) *Some Uses of Anthropology*. Washington, DC: Anthropological Society of Washington.

—— (1958) Cultural Thought Models and Modern Psychiatric Theories. *Psychiatry* **21**.

de Vore, I. (ed.) (1965) *Primate Behaviour*. New York: Holt, Rinehart and Winston.

—— (1965) The Evolution of Social Life. In Sol Tax (ed.) *Horizons of Anthropology*. London: Allen and Unwin.

Dickens, A.G. (1966) *Reformation and Society in Sixteenth Century Europe*. London: Thames and Hudson.

—— (1968) *The Counter Reformation*. London: Thames and Hudson.

—— (1976) *The German Nation and Martin Luther*. London: Fontana.

Dobzhansky, T. (1955) *Evolution, Genetics and Man*. London: Wiley.

Dodds, E. A. (1973) *The Greeks and the Irrational*. Berkeley: University of California Press.

Donnelly, M. (1976) *Perceptions of Lunacy in Early Nineteenth-Century Britain*. Unpublished PhD thesis, University of London.

Donzelot, J. (1980) *The Policing of Families*. London: Hutchinson.

Douglas, M. (1970a) *Natural Symbols*. London: Barrie and Rockcliff.

—— (ed.) (1970b) *Witchcraft Confessions and Accusations*. ASA Monograph **9**. London: Tavistock.

Douglas, K. (1979) *Alamein to Zem Zem*. London: Oxford University Press.

Dudley, E. and Novak, M.E. (eds) (1972) *The Wild Man Within*. Pittsburgh: University of Pittsburgh Press.

Duhem, P. (1969) *To Save the Phenomena*. Chicago: Chicago University Press.

Durant, J.R. (1980) The Myth of Human Evolution. Paper given at

British Association Annual Meeting.

Durkheim, É. (1915) *The Elementary Forms of the Religious Life*. London: Allen and Unwin.

—— (1951) *Suicide*. New York: Free Press.

—— (1966) *The Rules of Sociological Method*. New York: Free Press.

Edelman, B. (1979) *Ownership of the Image*. London: Routledge and Kegan Paul.

Ehrenreich, B. and English, D. (1974) *Witches, Midwives and Nurses*. London: Compendium.

Eisenstein, E.L. (1979) *The Printing Press as an Agent of Change*. Cambridge: Cambridge University Press.

Elias, N. (1978) *The Civilizing Process*. Oxford: Basil Blackwell.

Engels, F. (1972) *The Origin of the Family, Private Property and the State*. London: Lawrence and Wishart.

Evans-Pritchard, E. (1976) *Witchcraft, Oracles and Magic Among the Azande* [1937]. Oxford: Clarendon Press.

—— (1965) *Theories of Primitive Religion*. Oxford: Clarendon Press.

Febvre, L. (1962) *Le Problème de l'incroyance au XVIème siècle: la religion de Rabelais*. Revised edition. Paris: Albin Michel.

—— (1973a) Witchcraft, Nonsense or a Mental Revolution? In P. Burke (ed.) *A New Kind of History*. London: Routledge and Kegan Paul.

—— (1973b) Excommunication for Debt in Franche-Comté. In P. Burke (ed.) *A New Kind of History*. London: Routledge and Kegan Paul.

—— and Martin, H.J. (1976) *The Coming of the Book*. London: New Left Books.

Feyerabend, P. (1975) *Against Method*. London: New Left Books.

Fortes, M. and Dieterlen, G. (eds) (1965) *African Systems of Thought*. London: Oxford University Press.

Foucault, M. (1965) *Madness and Civilization*. London: Tavistock.

—— (1970) *The Order of Things*. London: Tavistock.

—— (1972) *The Archaeology of Knowledge*. London: Tavistock.

—— (1973) *The Birth of the Clinic*. London: Tavistock.

—— (1975) *I, Pierre Rivière ...* . New York: Pantheon.

—— (1976) *Mental Illness and Psychology*. New York: Harper and Row.

—— (1977) *Discipline and Punish*. London: Allen Lane.

—— (1978) *History of Sexuality*. I: *The Will to Truth*. New York: Pantheon.

—— (1979) Power and Norm. In M. Morris and P. Patton (eds) *Power Truth Strategy*. Sydney: Feral.

Frazer, J.G. (1957) *The Golden Bough*. London: Macmillan.

Freud, S. *The Standard Edition of the Complete Psychological Works* (*SE*), ed. J. Strachey. London: Hogarth.

—— [1900] *The Interpretation of Dreams*. SE **IV** and **V**.

—— [1905] *Three Essays on the Theory of Sexuality*. SE **VII**.

—— [1905] Fragment of an Analysis of a Case of Hysteria. SE **VII**.

—— [1913] *Totem and Taboo*. SE **VIII**.
—— [1916-17] *Introductory Lectures on Psychoanalysis*. SE **XV**.
—— [1920] *Beyond the Pleasure Principle*. SE **XVIII**.
—— [1921] *Group Psychology and the Analysis of the Ego*. SE **XVIII**.
—— [1922] A Seventeenth Century Demonological Neurosis. *SE* **XIX**.
—— [1930] *Civilisation and Its Discontents*. SE **XXI**.
Fussell, P. (1975) *The Great War and Modern Memory*. London: Oxford University Press.
Gardiner, M. (1980) Monkey Business. *New York Review of Books* **XXVII** 4: 20 March.
Gardner, R.A. and Gardner, B.T. (1969) Teaching Sign-Language to a Chimpanzee. *Science* **165**: 15 August.
Gelb, I.J. (1963) *A Study of Writing*. Chicago: Chicago University Press.
Gillispie, C.C. (1959) *Genesis and Geology*. New York: Harper and Row.
Gladden, N. (1971) *Across the Piave*. London: HMSO.
Glass, B., Temkin, O. and Strauss, W.L. (eds) (1968) *Forerunners of Darwin*. Baltimore: Johns Hopkins University Press.
Goffman, E. (1961) *Asylums*. New York: Doubleday.
Goodall, J. (1965) Chimpanzees of the Gombe Stream Reserve. In I. de Vore (ed.) *Primate Behaviour*. New York: Holt, Rinehart and Winston.
Goody, J. (1977) *The Domestication of the Savage Mind*. Cambridge: Cambridge University Press.
—— and Watt, I. (1963) The Consequences of Literacy. *Comparative Studies in Society and History* **5**.
Gordon, C. (1978) The Birth of the Subject. *Radical Philosophy* **17**.
Goubert, P. (1973) *The Ancien Regime*. London: Weidenfeld and Nicolson.
Green, G. (1971) *Journey Without Maps*. Harmondsworth: Penguin.
Gussow, Z. (1960) Pibloktoq among the Polar Eskimo. In W. Muensterberger (ed.) *The Psychoanalytic Study of Society*. New York.
Hacking, I. (1975) *Why Does Language Matter to Philosophy?*. Cambridge: Cambridge University Press.
Hagen, V.W. von (1973) *The Ancient Sun Kingdoms of the Americas*. St Albans: Paladin.
Hegel, G.W.F. (1971) *The Philosophy of Mind*. Oxford: Clarendon Press.
—— (1956) *The Philosophy of History*. New York: Dover.
Hertz, R. (1960) *Death and the Right Hand* (introduction R. Needham). London: Cohen and West.
Hewes, G.W. (1973) Primate Communication and the Gestural Origin of Language. *Current Anthropology* **14** 1-2: February-April.
Hill, C. (1972) *Intellectual Origins of the English Revolution*. London: Panther.
Hirst, P.Q. (1975) *Durkheim, Bernard and Epistemology*. London: Routledge and Kegan Paul.
—— (1976a) *Social Evolution and Sociological Categories*. London: Allen and Unwin.

—— (1976b) Political Philosophy and Egalitarianism: Marx and Rousseau. In A. Blowers and G. Thompson (eds) *Inequalities, Conflict and Change*. Milton Keynes: Open University Press.

—— (1979) *On Law and Ideology*. London: Macmillan.

—— (1980) Law, Socialism and Rights. In P. Carlen and M. Collinson (eds) *Radical Issues in Criminology*. Oxford: Martin Robertson.

—— (1981) The Genesis of the Social. *Politics and Power* 3.

Hollingshead, A.B. and Redlich, F.C. (1958) *Social Class and Mental Illness*. New York: Wiley.

Horton, R. (1979) African Thought and Western Science. In B. Wilson (ed.) *Rationality*. Oxford: Basil Blackwell.

Hsu, F. (ed.) (1972) *Psychological Anthropology*. Cambridge, Mass.: Schenkman.

Ignatieff, M. (1978) *A Just Measure of Pain*. London: Macmillan.

Illich, I. (1977) *Limits to Medicine*. Harmondsworth: Penguin.

Inglis, B. (1977) *Natural and Supernatural*. London: Hodder and Stoughton.

Janelle, P. (1971) *The Catholic Reformation*. London: Collier Macmillan.

Jones, E. (1964) Mother Right and the Sexual Ignorance of Savages. In E. Jones *Essays in Applied Psychoanalysis* 2. New York: International Universities Press. Reprinted 1974 as *Psycho-Myth, Psycho-History*. New York: Hillstone.

Kamen, H. (1976) *The Iron Century*. London: Cardinal.

Keegan, J. (1976) *The Face of Battle*. London: Cape.

Kieckhefer, R. (1976) *European Witch Trials*. London: Routledge and Kegan Paul.

Kiev, A. (1972) *Transcultural Psychiatry*. Harmondsworth: Penguin.

King, J.C. (1980) The Genetics of Sociobiology. In A. Montagu (ed.) *Sociobiology Examined*. London: Oxford University Press.

Koyré, A. (1965) *Newtonian Studies*. London: Chapman and Hall.

—— (1968a) *Metaphysics and Measurement*. London: Chapman and Hall.

—— (1968b) *From the Closed World to the Infinite Universe*. Baltimore: Johns Hopkins University Press.

—— (1968c) *Galileo Studies*. Hassocks: Harvester.

Kramer, H. and Sprenger, J. (1971) *Malleus Maleficarum* [1486]. London: Arrow.

Kroeber, A.L. (1952) *The Nature of Culture*. Chicago: Chicago University Press.

—— (1957) The Superorganic. In L. Coser and B. Rosenburg (eds) *Sociological Theory*. New York: Macmillan.

—— and Parsons, T. (1958) The Concepts of Culture and Social System. *American Sociological Review* 23 5: October.

Kroeber, T. (1961) *Ishi in Two Worlds*. Berkeley: University of California Press.

Kuhn, T.S. (1970) *The Structure of Scientific Revolutions*. Revised edition. Chicago: Chicago University Press.

Laing, R.D. (1965) *The Divided Self*. Harmondsworth: Penguin.

Lancaster, J.B. (1968) Primate Communication Systems and the Emergence of Human Language. In P.C. Jay (ed.), *Primates*. New York: Holt, Rinehart and Winston.

Lane, H. (1977) *The Wild Boy of Aveyron*. London: Allen and Unwin.

—— and Pillard, R. (1978) *The Wild Boy of Burundi*. New York: Random House.

Langbein, J.H. (1974) *Prosecuting Crime in the Renaissance*. Cambridge, Mass.: Harvard University Press.

—— (1977) *Torture and the Law of Proof*. Chicago: Chicago University Press.

Laplanche, J. (1976) *Life and Death in Psychoanalysis*. Baltimore: Johns Hopkins University Press.

Leakey, R. and Lewin, R. (1979) *People of the Lake*. London: Collins.

Lecourt, D. (1975) *Marxism and Epistemology*. London: New Left Books.

Le Gros Clark, W.E. (1970) *History of the Primates*. London: British Museum (Natural History).

—— (1978) *The Fossil Evidence for Human Evolution*, ed. B. Campbell. 3rd edition. Chicago: Chicago University Press.

Lerner, L.M. (1968) *Heredity, Evolution and Society*. New York: Freeman.

Le Roy Ladurie, E. (1974) *The Peasants of Languedoc*. Urbana: University of Illinois Press.

—— (1979) *Carnival*. New York: Georges Brazillier.

Lévi-Strauss, C. (1964) *Totemism*. London: Merlin.

—— (1968) *Structural Anthropology* I. London: Allen Lane.

—— (1969) *The Elementary Structures of Kinship*. London: Eyre and Spottiswoode.

—— (1971) The Family. In H.L. Shapiro (ed.) *Man, Culture and Society*. London: Oxford University Press.

Lévy-Bruhl, L. (1966) *Primitive Mentality*. Boston: Beacon.

Lewis, A. (1961) The Story of Unreason. *The Times Literary Supplement*: 6 October.

Lewis, I.M. (1971) *Ecstatic Religion*. Harmondsworth: Penguin.

Linden, E. (1976) *Apes, Men and Language*. Harmondsworth: Penguin.

Livingstone, F.B. (1969) Genetics, Ecology and the Origins of Incest and Exogamy. *Current Anthropology* **10** (1): February.

Locke, J. (1965) *Second Treatise of Government*, ed. Laslett. New York: New English Library.

Lopez, B.H. (1978) *Of Wolves and Men*. New York: Charles.

Lorand, S. (ed.) (1932) *Psychoanalysis Today*. London: Allen and Unwin.

Lord, A. (1960) *A Singer of Tales*. Cambridge, Mass.: Harvard University Press.

Lorenz, K. (1966) *On Aggression*. London: Methuen.

Luria, A.R. (1975) *The Mind of a Mnemonist*. Harmondsworth: Penguin.

Macfarlane, A. (ed.) (1970) *The Family Life of Ralph Josselin*. Cambridge: Cambridge University Press.

—— (1970) *Witchcraft in Tudor and Stuart England*. London: Routledge and Kegan Paul.

—— (1979) *The Origins of English Individualism*. Oxford: Basil Blackwell.

McFarlane, K.B. (1972) *Wycliffe and English Non-Conformity*. Harmondsworth: Penguin.

McGuire, J.E. and Rattansi, P.M. (1966) Newton and the Pipes of Pan. *Notes and Records of the Royal Society of London* **XXI**.

MacIntyre, A. (1979a) Is Understanding Religion Compatible with Believing? In B. Wilson (ed.) *Rationality*. Oxford: Basil Blackwell.

—— (1979b) The Idea of a Social Science. In B. Wilson (ed.) *Rationality*. Oxford: Basil Blackwell.

Maclean, C. (1979) *The Wolf Children*. Harmondsworth: Penguin.

McLuhan, M. (1962) *The Gutenburg Galaxy*. London: Routledge and Kegan Paul.

—— (1964) *Understanding Media*. London: Routledge and Kegan Paul.

McNeill, W.M. (1979) *Plagues and Peoples*. Harmondsworth: Penguin.

Macpherson, C.B. (1962) *The Political Theory of Possessive Individualism*. Oxford: Clarendon Press.

Mair, L. (1969) *Witchcraft*. London: Weidenfeld and Nicolson.

Malinowski, B. (1937) *Sex and Repression in Savage Society*. London: Routledge and Kegan Paul.

Malson, L. and Itard, J. (1972) *Wolf Children and the Wild Boy of Aveyron* London: New Left Books.

Malthus, T.R. (1970) *An Essay on the Principle of Population* [1798]. Harmondsworth: Penguin.

Mandrou, R. (1978) *From Humanism to Science 1480-1700*. Harmondsworth: Penguin.

Mannoni, O. (1971) *Freud — The Theory of the Unconscious*. London: New Left Books.

Marcus, S. (1967) *The Other Victorians*. New York: Bantam.

Marcuse, H. (1955) *Eros and Civilisation*. New York: Vintage.

Martin, R.D. (1979) Review of R. Leakey and R. Lewin *People of the Lake*. *New Society*: 11 October.

Martinet, A. (1964) *Elements of General Linguistics*. London: Faber.

Marwick, M. (ed.) (1970) *Witchcraft*. Harmondsworth: Penguin.

Mauss, M. (1979) *Sociology and Psychology*. London: Routledge and Kegan Paul.

Mayr, E. (1978) Evolution. *Scientific American* **239**: September.

Mead, M. and Calas, A. (eds) (1954) *Primitive Heritage*. London: Gollancz.

Merton, R.K. (1957) *Social Theory and Social Structure*. New York: Free Press.

Michelet, J. (1975) *Satanism and Witchcraft*. Secaucus, NJ: Citadel Press.

Middleton, J. (ed.) (1967) *Magic, Witchcraft and Curing*. Garden City, NY: Natural History Press.

Midelfort, H.E. (1972) *Witch Hunting in Southwestern Germany 1562-1684*. Stanford: Stanford University Press.

Midgley, M. (1979) *Beast and Man*. Brighton: Harvester.

—— (1980) Gene-Juggling and Rival Fatalisms. In A. Montagu (ed.) *Sociobiology Examined*. London: Oxford University Press.

Minson, J. (1980) Review of Ignatieff and Scull. *Sociological Review* **XXVIII** 1: February.

Mirandola, P. della (1965) *On the Dignity of Man*. Indianapolis: Bobbs-Merrill.

Mitchell, J. (1975) *Psychoanalysis and Feminism*. Harmondsworth: Penguin.

Mitchell, J.C. (1965) The Meaning of Misfortune for Modern Africans. In M. Fortes and G. Dieterlen (eds) *African Systems of Thought*. London: Oxford University Press.

Mitford, J. (1977) *The American Prison Business*. Harmondsworth: Penguin.

Montagu, A. (ed.) (1980) *Sociobiology Examined*. London: Oxford University Press.

Monter, E.W. (1976) *Witchcraft in France and Switzerland*. Ithaca: Cornell University Press.

Moore, J.M.B. (1962) *Social Science and Political Theory*. New York: Harper and Row.

Moorehead, A. (1966) *The Fatal Impact*. London: Hamish Hamilton.

Morris, M. and Patton, P. (eds) (1979) *Power, Truth Strategy*. Sydney: Feral.

Mouzelis, N. (1971) A Critical Note on Total Institutions. *Sociology* **5** 1: January.

Muensterberger, W. (ed.) (1960) *The Psychoanalytic Study of Society* **I**. New York.

Murray, M.A. (1921) *The Witch Cult in Western Europe*. Oxford: Clarendon Press.

Napier, J. (1962) The Evolution of the Hand. *Scientific American*: December.

Needham, R. (ed.) (1973) *Right and Left*. Chicago: Chicago University Press.

Ogburn, W.F. (1959) The Wolf Boy of Agra. *American Journal of Sociology* **LXIV** 5: March.

—— and Bose, N.K. (1959) On the Trail of the Wolf Children. *Genetic Psychology Monographs* **60**.

Ozment, S.E. (ed.) (1971) *The Reformation in Medieval Perspective*. Chicago: Quadrangle.

Parker, S. (1960) The Wiitiko Psychosis in the Context of Ojibwa Personality and Culture. *American Anthropologist* **62**.

Parsons, T. (1951) *The Social System*. London: Routledge and Kegan Paul.

Pavlov, I.P. (1979) *Lectures on Conditioned Reflexes*. London: Friedman.

Peters, E. (1978) *The Magician, the Witch and the Law*. Hassocks: Harvester.

Polanyi, K. (1966) *Dahomey and the Slave Trade*. Seattle: Washington University Press.

Pole, D. (1958) *The Later Philosophy of Wittgenstein*. London: Athlone Press.

Polhemus, T. (ed.) (1978) *Social Aspects of the Human Body*. Harmondsworth: Penguin.

Premack, D. (1971) Language in Chimpanzee? *Science* **172**: 21 May.

Prescott, W. (1959) *History of the Conquest of Peru*. London: Allen and Unwin.

Rádl, E. (1930) *The History of Biological Theories*. London: Oxford University Press.

Rattansi, P.M. (1963) Paracelsus and the Puritan Revolution. *Ambix* **XI**.

Reynolds, V. (1976) and (1980) *The Biology of Human Action*. 1st and 2nd editions. Oxford: W.H. Freeman.

Róheim, G. (1950) *Psychoanalysis and Anthropology*. New York: International Universities Press.

Rosen, G. (1968) *Madness in Society*. Chicago: Chicago University Press.

Rosenhan, D.L. (1973) On Being Sane in Insane Places. *Science* **179**: 19 January.

Rothman, D.J. (1971) *The Discovery of the Asylum*. Boston: Little, Brown.

Rousseau, J.-J. (1913) *Discourse on the Origin of Inequality Among Men* [1755] and *The Social Contract* [1762], both in Cole (ed.) *Social Contract and Discourses*. London: Dent.

Runciman, S. (1978) *A History of the Crusades* **I**. Harmondsworth: Penguin.

Rusche, G. and Kirchheimer, O. (1967) *Punishment and Social Structure* [1939]. New York: Russell and Russell.

Russell, J. (1980) *A History of Witchcraft*. London: Thames and Hudson.

Sade, D.S. (1968) Inhibition of Son-Mother Mating Among Free-Ranging Rhesus Monkeys. *Science and Psychoanalysis* **12**.

Sahlins, M. (1959) The Social Life of Monkeys, Apes and Primitive Man. *Human Biology* **31**.

—— (1960) The Origin of Society. *Scientific American*: September.

—— (1974) *Stone Age Economics*. London: Tavistock.

—— (1976) *Culture and Practical Reason*. Chicago: Chicago University Press.

—— (1977) *The Use and Abuse of Biology*. London: Tavistock.

Sargant, W. (1976) *The Mind Possessed*. London: Pan.

Sassoon, S. (1965) *Memoirs of an Infantry Officer*. London: Faber.

Saussure, F. de (1966) *Course in General Linguistics* [1915]. New York: McGraw-Hill.

Scheff, T.J. (1966) *Being Mentally Ill*. Chicago: Aldine.

Schrier, A. (ed.) (1971) *Behaviour of Nonhuman Primates*. New York: Academic Press.

Scull, A. (1979) *Museums of Madness*. London: Allen Lane.

Sedgwick, P. (1972) R.D. Laing: Self, Symptom and Society. In R. Boyers and R. Orill (eds) *Laing and Anti-Psychiatry*. Harmondsworth: Penguin.

Segal, H. (1978) *Introduction to the Work of Melanie Klein*. London: Hogarth.

Service, E.R. (1966) *The Hunters*. New Jersey: Prentice-Hall.

Shapiro, H.L. (ed.) (1971) *Man, Culture and Society*. London: Oxford University Press.

Shattuck, R. (1980) *The Forbidden Experiment*. New York: Farrar, Straus and Giroux.

Shirokogoroff, S.M. (1954) Talking to Tigers Not to Bears. In M. Mead and N. Calas (eds) *Primitive Heritage*. London: Gollancz.

Shumaker, W.C. (1972) *The Occult Sciences in the Renaissance*. Berkeley: University of California Press.

Simpson, G. (1968) The Biological Nature of Man. In S.L. Washburn and P.C. Jay (eds) *Perspectives in Human Evolution*. New York: Holt, Rinehart and Winston.

Singh, J.A.L. and Zingg, R.M. (1942) *Wolf Children and Feral Man*. New York: Harper and Row.

Snell, B. (1953) *The Discovery of Mind*. Oxford: Basil Blackwell.

Stam, J.H. (1976) *Inquiries into the Origin of Language*. New York: Harper and Row.

Szasz, T.S. (1972) *The Myth of Mental Illness* [1961]. St Albans: Paladin.
—— (1973) *The Manufacture of Madness*. St Albans: Paladin.

Thom, A. (1967) *Megalithic Sites in Britain*. Oxford: Clarendon Press.

Thomas, K. (1973) *Religion and the Decline of Magic*. Harmondsworth: Penguin.

Thompson, E.P. (1978) *The Poverty of Theory*. London: Merlin.

Thorndike, L. (1923-58) *A History of Magic and Experimental Science* **I-VIII**. New York: Columbia University Press.

Tinbergen, N. (1951) *Instinct*. Oxford: Clarendon Press.

Trevor-Roper, H.R. (1978) *The European Witch Craze*. Harmondsworth: Penguin.

Van der Post, L. (1963) *The Lost World of the Kalahari*. Harmondsworth: Penguin.

Van Loon, F.H.G. (1927) Amok and Lattah. *Journal of Abnormal and Social Psychology* **21**.

Vorzimmer, P.J. (1972) *Charles Darwin, the Years of Controversy*. London: University of London Press.

Walker, D.P. (1975) *Spiritual and Demonic Magic from Ficino to Campanella* [1958]. Notre Dame: University of Notre Dame Press.

Wallace, A.F.C. (1972) Mental Illness, Biology and Culture. In F. Hsu (ed.) *Psychological Anthropology*. Cambridge, Mass.: Schenkman.

Washburn, S.L. (1960) Tools and Human Evolution. *Scientific American*: September.
—— (1978) The Evolution of Man. *Scientific American*: September.

—— (1980) Human and Animal Behaviour. In A. Montagu (ed.) *Sociobiology Examined*. London: Oxford University Press.

—— and de Vore, I. (1961) The Social Life of Baboons. *Scientific American*: June.

—— and Hamburg, D.A. (1965) The Implications of Primate Research. In I. de Vore (ed.) *Primate Behaviour*. New York: Holt, Rinehart and Winston.

—— Jay, P.C. and Lancaster, J.B. (1965) Field Studies of Old World Monkeys and Apes. *Science* **150**: 17 December.

—— and Lancaster, C.S. (1968) The Evolution of Hunting. In S.L. Washburn and P.C. Jay (eds) *Perspectives on Human Evolution*. New York: Holt, Rinehart and Winston.

Webster, H. (1968) *Primitive Secret Societies*. New York: Octagon.

Weber, M. (1949) *The Methodology of the Social Sciences*. Chicago: Free Press.

Wendt, H. (1970) *Before the Deluge*. St Albans: Paladin.

White, H. (1972) The Forms of Wildness: Archaeology of an Idea. In E. Dudley and M.E. Novak (eds) *The Wild Man Within*. Pittsburgh: University of Pittsburgh Press.

White, L. (1957) The Symbol. In *The Science of Culture* [1949] and reprinted in L. Coser and B. Rosenburg (eds) *Sociological Theory*. New York: Macmillan.

Whyte, L. (1962) *The Unconscious Before Freud*, London: Tavistock.

Wilson, B. (ed.) (1979) *Rationality*. Oxford: Basil Blackwell.

Wilson, E.O. (1975) *Sociobiology*. Cambridge, Mass.: Harvard University Press.

—— (1978) *On Human Nature*. Cambridge, Mass.: Harvard University Press.

Winch, P. (1963) *The Idea of a Social Science*. London: Routledge and Kegan Paul.

—— (1979) Understanding a Primitive Society. In B. Wilson (ed.) *Rationality*. Oxford: Basil Blackwell.

Wing, J.K. (1978) *Reasoning About Madness*. London: Oxford University Press.

Winter, D. (1979) *Death's Men*. Harmondsworth: Penguin.

Wittgenstein, L. (1961) *Tractatus Logico-Philosophicus*. London: Routledge and Kegan Paul.

—— (1963) *Philosophical Investigations*. Oxford: Basil Blackwell.

Wittkower, R. (1977) Marvels of the East: A Study in the History of Monsters. In *Allegory and the Migration of Symbols*. London: Thames and Hudson.

Wittkower, R. and M. (1969) *Born Under Saturn*. London: W.W. Norton.

Yap, P.M. (1951) Mental Diseases Peculiar to Certain Cultures. *Journal of Mental Science* **97**.

Yates, F.A. (1969a) *The Art of Memory*. Harmondsworth: Penguin.

—— (1969b) *Giordano Bruno and the Hermetic Tradition*. New York: Vintage Books.

—— (1975) *The Rosicrucian Enlightenment*. St Albans: Paladin.

—— (1979) Article in *New York Review of Books*: 22 November.

Young, J.Z. (1971) *An Introduction to the Study of Man*. Oxford: Clarendon Press.

Zilboorg, G. (1969) *The Medical Man and the Witch During the Renaissance* [1935]. New York: Cooper Square.

—— and Henry, G.W. (1941) *A History of Medical Psychology*. New York.

Zingg, R.M. (1940) Feral Man and Extreme Cases of Isolation. *American Journal of Psychology* **LIII** 4: October.

Zuckerman, S. (1932) *The Social Life of Monkeys and Apes*. London: Routledge and Kegan Paul.

NAME INDEX

SUBJECT INDEX